Bonhoeffer and King

Bonhoeffer and King

— Their Legacies and Import for Christian Social Thought —

Edited by Willis Jenkins
and Jennifer M. McBride

Fortress Press
Minneapolis

BONHOEFFER AND KING
Their Legacies and Import for Christian Social Thought

Cover image: Brad Norr
Cover design: Brad Norr Design
Book design: PerfecType, Nashville, TN
Illustrations: Dietrich Bonhoeffer, Lewis Williams SFO © 2003. Martin Luther King of Georgia, Br. Robert Lentz, OFM © 1984. Images courtesy of Trinity Stores (800.699.4482) www.trinitystores.com

Library of Congress Cataloging-in-Publication Data
Bonhoeffer and King / their legacies and import for Christian social thought / edited by Willis Jenkins and Jennifer M. McBride.
    p. cm.
  Includes bibliographical references and index.
  ISBN 978-0-8006-6333-9 (alk. paper)
  1. Christian sociology. 2. Bonhoeffer, Dietrich, 1906-1945. 3. King, Martin Luther, Jr., 1929-1968. 4. Christian ethics. 5. Church and social problems. 6. Social ethics. I. Jenkins, Willis. II. McBride, Jennifer M., 1977-
  BT738.B618 2010
  261'.10922—dc22

                                2010013484

Manufactured in the U.S.A.

14 13 12 11 10 1 2 3 4 5 6 7 8 9 10

Contents

Preface

Dietrich Bonhoeffer and Martin Luther King Jr. exercise a peculiar hold on the Christian social imagination. They stand as compelling figures for Christian thought on justice and love. They are touchstones for reflection on social witness, political hope, and personal courage. We turn to them when considering how religious faith makes a political difference, what social form Christian confession should take, and how justice should confront violence. We consider their responses to the big questions of ethics and evil, religion and politics, theology and self-commitment, not only because their words offer vivid guides but because their lives enact brilliant, troubling dramas that place us anew before those questions.

The legacy of each leader, however, is also ambiguous, claimed by a wildly diverse range of interpreters—political conservatives and radicals, theological traditionalists and revisionists, Christians and humanists, debunkers and hagiographers. Books are constantly published from left and right that purport to recover the real King, and simply cataloguing the schools of claims on Bonhoeffer's legacy has occupied academic volumes. While the two men were undoubtedly different from one another, as essays in this book show, their legacies are similar in that they are both so contested and so resonant. In ways rare for pastors of the last century, they are publicly remembered: both appear routinely in top ten lists of the most influential Christians, and statues of each stand in Westminster Abbey. Perhaps they figure so vividly in Christian memories precisely because the reception of their legacies remains so uncertain and controversial.

The idea for this book began from our participation in the Project on Lived Theology, which we first encountered as graduate students at the University of Virginia. In conversations with that community of scholars, pastors, and activists, we noticed how many Christian social thinkers—whether "organic" or academic—shaped their thought in ongoing encounter with King or Bonhoeffer or both. In the years since, we have wondered how other conversations in the fields of theology and ethics have been shaped by these legacies. In 2008 we convened a panel at the American Academy of Religion dedicated to that question, which met as a joint session of the Martin Luther King Jr. Consultation and the Bonhoeffer: Theology and Social Analysis Group.

Those conversations helped frame this book. We invited leading Christian social thinkers to consider King and Bonhoeffer together in order to help us interpret their ambiguous legacies and the influence their memories have had on the central questions of Christian social thought. Each essay approaches a major issue in Christian ethics, with scholars who have written and taught both figures, sometimes together, presenting a single topic in light of the influence of both men. What does a mutual reading mean for our views of peacemaking and violence, racism and poverty, the institutional church, contemporary martyrdom, politics and responsibility, justice and reconciliation, the public pastorate?

These essays therefore not only interpret Bonhoeffer and King; more importantly, they engage the issues that construct their enduring theological and American importance. By receiving their legacies together, this book considers how the two figures help make sense of one another, where their respective thought contests one another, and what dangers to theology and memory lie in receiving them together. We think that this book will enliven classroom discussions, inform readers of both lives, and, we hope, help start new conversations in social ethics and Christian theology.

We wish to thank each of the contributors willing to offer an interpretation of two daunting legacies. We are grateful to Charles Marsh for inviting us into the work of the Project on Lived Theology and to all those engaged in the conversations of that community who have encouraged the development of this book. We have since moved into other academic communities. Willis acknowledges his indebtedness to students at Yale Divinity School who helped reshape his views of Bonhoeffer and King, and to colleagues who have entered conversation with him about the project, especially Emilie Townes and Andre Willis. He also thanks his research assistant Kathryn Salisbury, who did the index. Jennifer is grateful for a Postdoctoral Fellowship in Religious Practices and Practical Theology at Candler School of Theology, Emory University, which not only granted her time to work on this project but also stimulated the work in unforeseen ways, as the fellowship led her to a city bursting with contested legacies. She wishes to acknowledge colleagues at Emory that engaged the project, particularly Timothy P. Jackson, John Snarey, Andrea White, and Letitia Campbell. She is also thankful for the collegiality and friendship of Raphael G. Warnock at Ebenezer Baptist Church and for the ongoing conversations about Bonhoeffer and King at the Open Door Community.

Passion Week 2010

Contributors

Michael Battle is Provost and Canon Theologian of the Cathedral Center of St. Paul in the Episcopal Diocese of Los Angeles. He lived in residence with Archbishop Desmond Tutu in South Africa for two years, 1993–1994, was ordained a priest in South Africa by Tutu in 1993, and has written a number of books out of his studies and friendship with the archbishop, including *Reconciliation: The Ubuntu Theology of Desmond Tutu* (1997) and *Blessed Are the Peacemakers: A Christian Spirituality of Nonviolence* (2004). His most recent book is *The Black Church in America: African American Christian Spirituality* (2006).

M. Shawn Copeland is Associate Professor of Theology at Boston College. She has taught at Marquette University, Yale University Divinity School, and serves as an adjunct associate professor of systematic theology at the Institute for Black Catholic Studies, Xavier University of Louisiana, New Orleans. She has lectured extensively in the United States as well as in Australia, Belgium, Canada, and Nigeria. A prolific author, she has written more than seventy articles and book chapters, is editor of *Uncommon Faithfulness: The Black Catholic Experience* (2009), and author of *Enfleshing Freedom: Body, Race, and Being* (2010).

Jean Bethke Elshtain is the Laura Spelman Rockefeller Professor of Social and Political Ethics at the University of Chicago Divinity School, with appointments in political science and the Committee on International Relations. Often regarded as one of America's foremost public intellectuals, she writes frequently for journals of civic opinion on themes of democracy, ethical dilemmas, religion and politics, and international relations. Her books include *Augustine and the Limits of Politics* (1995); *Who Are We? Critical Reflections, Hopeful Possibilities* (2000); *Just War Against Terror: The Burden of American Power in a Violent World* (2003); and the publication of her Gifford Lectures, *Sovereignty: God, State, and Self* (2008).

Stephen R. Haynes is Professor of Religious Studies at Rhodes College in Memphis. He serves on the regional advisory board for Facing History and Ourselves and on the Church Relations Committee of the United States Holocaust Memorial Museum. Haynes has edited and written books on religion and racism, Jewish-Christian relations, and religion and higher education in addition to *The Bonhoeffer Phenomenon: Portraits of a Protestant Saint* (2004); *The Bonhoeffer Legacy: Post-Holocaust Perspectives* (2006); and, with Lori Brandt Hale, *Bonhoeffer for Armchair Theologians* (2008).

Timothy P. Jackson is Professor of Christian Ethics at Candler School of Theology, Emory University, in Atlanta, and a Senior Fellow at the Center for the Study of Law and Religion at Emory. He is the author of *Love Disconsoled: Meditations on Christian Charity* (1999) and *The Priority of Love: Christian Charity and Social Justice* (2003). He is also the editor of and a contributor to *The Morality of Adoption* (2005) and *The Best Love of the Child* (forthcoming). His present book project is entitled *Political Agape: Prophetic Christianity and Liberal Democracy*.

Geffrey B. Kelly is Professor of Systematic Theology at La Salle University in Philadelphia, and has served as the president of the International Bonhoeffer Society, English Language Section. In addition to the coedited volume *A Testament to Freedom: The Essential Writings of Dietrich Bonhoeffer* (1995), he and F. Burton Nelson are coauthors of *The Cost of Moral Leadership: The Spirituality of Dietrich Bonhoeffer* (2003). Kelly is coeditor with John D. Godsey of Bonhoeffer's *Life Together and Prayer Book of the Bible* (DBWE 5, 1996) and *Discipleship* (DBWE 4, 2001). He is author of *Liberating Faith: Bonhoeffer's Message for Today* (2002) and *Reading Bonhoeffer: A Guide to His Spiritual Classics and Selected Writings on Peace* (2008).

Charles Marsh is Professor of Religious Studies and Director of the Project on Lived Theology at the University of Virginia, Charlottesville. He is author of *Reclaiming Dietrich Bonhoeffer: The Promise of His Theology* (1994) and is currently writing a new biography of Bonhoeffer, for which he has been awarded a Guggenheim Fellowship. Marsh has written numerous books on religion, race, and civil rights, including *God's Long Summer: Stories of Faith and Civil Rights* (1997), which won the 1998 Grawemeyer Award in Religion, and *The Beloved Community: How Faith Shapes Social Justice from the Civil Rights Movement to Today* (2005).

Rachel Muers is Senior Lecturer in Christian Studies at the University of Leeds in the United Kingdom. She has edited anthologies and written numerous journal articles and book chapters on a broad range of topics, many of which revolve around the relationships between feminist thought, modern Christian doctrine, and ethics. She is also involved in joint Jewish-Christian-Muslim theological work through the Society for Scriptural Reasoning. Muers is author of *Keeping God's Silence: Towards a Theological Ethics of Communication* (2004), a Quaker theology of communication in dialogue with feminist thought and the theology and ethics of Bonhoeffer, and *Living for the Future: Theological Ethics for Coming Generations* (2008).

Larry L. Rasmussen is the Reinhold Niebuhr Professor Emeritus of Social Ethics at Union Theological Seminary in New York and a lay theologian of the Evangelical Lutheran Church in America. He has published more than a dozen books on theology, ecology, and social ethics, including *Earth Community, Earth Ethics* (1996), which won the 1997 Grawemeyer Award in Religion, and *Reinhold Niebuhr: Theologian of Public Life* (1991). He is author of *Dietrich Bonhoeffer: Reality and Resistance* (1972), *Dietrich Bonhoeffer: His Significance for North Americans* (1990), and is editor of *Berlin, 1932–1933* (DBWE 12, 2009). He now resides in Santa Fe, New Mexico.

Stephen G. Ray Jr. is the Neal F. and Ila A. Fisher Professor of Theology at Garrett-Evangelical Theological Seminary in Evanston, Illinois, and an ordained minister of the United Church of Christ. Ray has served as associate professor of African American studies and director of the Urban Theological Institute at Lutheran Theological Seminary at Philadelphia, associate professor of theology and philosophy at Louisville Presbyterian Theological Seminary, and lecturer at Yale Divinity School and Hartford Seminary. He is the author of the 1996 exhibition, "A Struggle from the Start: The Black Community of Hartford, 1639–1960," a product of the Hartford Black History Project (1996); *Do No Harm: Social Sin and Christian Responsibility* (2002); and coauthor of *Black Church Studies: An Introduction* (2007).

Gary M. Simpson is Professor of Systematic Theology and Director of the Center for Missional Leadership at Luther Seminary in St. Paul, and is an ordained pastor of the Evangelical Lutheran Church in America. He serves on the editorial board of *Dialog: A Journal of Theology* and has been the chair of the editorial board of *Word & World: Theology for Christian Ministry*. He is author of *Critical Social Theory: Prophetic Reason, Civil Society, and Christian Imagination* (2001); *War, Peace and God: Rethinking the Just-War Tradition* (2007); and editor of *The Missional Church and Global Civil Society* (forthcoming). His most recent book project, with New Testament scholar David Fredrickson, is entitled *Future of the Body: Christology, Trinity, and Ecclesial Leadership.*

Craig J. Slane is Frances P. Owen Distinguished Professor of Systematic Theology at Simpson University in Redding, California. He serves on the board of directors for the International Bonhoeffer Society, English Language Section, and is author of *Bonhoeffer as Martyr: Social Responsibility and Modern Christian Commitment* (2004).

Glen H. Stassen is the Lewis B. Smedes Professor of Christian Ethics at Fuller Theological Seminary in Pasadena, California. He is author and editor of numerous books on peacemaking, including *Just Peacemaking: The New Paradigm for Ethics of Peace and War* (2008); *Kingdom Ethics: Following Jesus in Contemporary Context* (2003), which received *Christianity Today*'s Award for Best Book of 2004 in Theology or Ethics; *Living the Sermon on the Mount: A Practical Hope for Grace and Deliverance* (2006); and, with D. M. Yeager and John Howard Yoder, *Authentic Transformation: A New Vision of Christ and Culture* (1996). He is also the editor of the English edition of *Authentic Faith: Bonhoeffer's Ethics in Context* (2007).

Emilie M. Townes is the Andrew W. Mellon Professor of African American Religion and Theology at Yale Divinity School and past president of the American Academy of Religion. Prior to her appointment at Yale, Townes served as the Carolyn Beaird Professor of Christian Ethics at Union Theological Seminary in New York. Among her many publications are *Womanist Justice, Womanist Hope* (1993); *In a Blaze of Glory: Womanist Spirituality as Social Witness* (1995); *Breaking the Fine Rain of Death: African American Health Issues and a Womanist Ethic of Care* (1998); and *Womanist Ethics and the Cultural Production of Evil* (2006). She is an ordained American Baptist clergywoman.

Raphael Gamaliel Warnock is Senior Pastor of Ebenezer Baptist Church in Atlanta, a center for the King legacy. Among other churches, he has served as youth pastor and assistant pastor of Harlem's historic Abyssinian Baptist Church while studying for his M.Div., M. Phil., and Ph.D. at Union Theological Seminary. As an activist-pastor he has defended voting rights, advocated for prisoners and death-row inmates, and worked on public policy through The National Black Leadership Commission on AIDS.

Andre C. Willis is Assistant Professor of the Philosophy of Religion at Yale Divinity School. He has taught at Wellesley College, Boston College, Fairfield University, College of the Holy Cross, Wesleyan University, Quinnipiac University, San Jose State University, and San Jose City College. His main intellectual focus is modern liberal philosophy of religion and theological thought, and he is currently completing a work on David Hume's philosophy of religion. Willis has published articles on American pragmatism and religion, religion and democracy, African American thought and history, and jazz music. He is a regular contributor to the website theroot.com and is editor of *Faith of Our Fathers: African-American Men Reflect on Fatherhood* (1996).

Richard W. Wills Sr. is Assistant Professor of Ethics and Theology at the Proctor School of Theology, Virginia Union University, Richmond, and is currently serving as pastor of the First Baptist Church, Hampton, Virginia. Prior to joining the faculty at Virginia Union he taught at Hampton University and Virginia Commonwealth University. During his tenure as pastor of Dexter Avenue Baptist Church, Montgomery, Alabama, he coauthored a work entitled *Reflections on Our Pastor: Dr. Martin Luther King, Jr., 1954–1960* (1998). He most recently is author of *Martin Luther King, Jr. and the Image of God* (2009) and is currently engaged in his next publication entitled *The Pastor King* (2011).

Josiah U. Young III is Professor of Systematic Theology at Wesley Theological Seminary in Washington, D.C. A prolific writer, Young's books include *Dogged Strength within the Veil: Africana Spirituality and the Mysterious Love of God* (2003); *No Difference in the Fare: Dietrich Bonhoeffer and the Problem of Racism* (1998); and *A Pan-African Theology: Providence and the Legacies of the Ancestors* (1992).

Editors

Willis Jenkins is Margaret Farley Assistant Professor of Social Ethics at Yale Divinity School. He is author of *Ecologies of Grace: Environmental Ethics and Christian Theology* (2008), which won a 2009 Templeton Award for Theological Promise, and editor of *The Spirit of Sustainability* (2009).

Jennifer M. McBride is the Atlanta Theological Association's Director of the Certificate in Theological Studies at Metro State Prison for Women and a visiting lecturer at Candler School of Theology, Emory University. She was a 2008/2009 Postdoctoral Fellow in Religious Practices and Practical Theology at Emory and is presently a Virginia Seminar Writing Fellow for the Project on Lived Theology at the University of Virginia. McBride serves on the board of directors of the International Bonhoeffer Society, English Language Section, and is author of *The Church for the World: A Theology of Public Witness* (forthcoming).

Communal Receptions and Constructive Readings for the Twenty-First Century

Jennifer M. McBride

I n the city of Atlanta, a mile and a half down Freedom Parkway from the Martin Luther King Jr. National Historic Site, the Open Door Community gathers in their dining-hall worship space every Sunday evening for song, scripture, prayer, and celebration around the Eucharist table. This ecumenical, intentionally interracial, residential community shares "life together" in a fragile expression of "beloved community," to combine key phrases of Bonhoeffer and King. They are ordained ministers, former inmates, retirees, scholars-turned-activists, persons formerly homeless, seminarians, and seasonal volunteers. Together they enact a "costly discipleship" comprised of voluntary poverty, works of mercy and hospitality on behalf of the homeless, and struggles for justice—particularly with and for their friends on the streets and in prison. They gather for worship and dinner in preparation for a week of soup kitchens, showers, and clothing exchange, foot care at their free clinic, fellowship in the front yard and on the streets, prison visits, peace vigils, anti-death-penalty protests, and, when necessary, civil disobedience.

All of these practices serve as acts of resistance to forces of death and dehumanization. They reflect the Open Door's conviction that, in the words of Bonhoeffer, "God . . . waits for and answers sincere prayers and responsible actions."[1] So with their friends (those living on the streets, nonresident volunteers, partners in prison work, and various visitors drawn to their witness), they pray as their Savior Jesus taught them,

Our Beloved Friend
Outside the Domination System
May your Holy Name be honored
    By the way we live our lives.

Your Beloved Community come.
    Guide us to:
    Walk your Walk
    Talk your Talk
    Sit your Silence
Inside the courtroom, on the streets, in the jailhouses
As they are on the margins of resistance.

Give us this day everything we need.
Forgive us our wrongs
    As we forgive those who have wronged us.
Do not bring us to hard testing,
    But keep us safe from the Evil One.

For Thine is:
    The Beloved Community,
        the power and
        the glory
            forever and ever. Amen.

Friends like me, who commute from privileged places such as the academy, park our cars in the gravel lot behind the Open Door and enter the two-story brick building from the rear. The first image that greets those who arrive through the back entrance is Dietrich Bonhoeffer's, and appropriately so. For, under the framed picture of the German theologian are his now-famous words from "After Ten Years," summarized in the prophetic call of Open Door cofounders, Ed Loring and Murphy Davis, to "reduce the distance" between those whom society privileges and those whom society oppresses.[2] It reads, "We have for once learnt to see the great events of world history from below, from the perspective of the outcast, the suspects, the maltreated, the powerless, the oppressed, the reviled—in short, from the perspective of those who suffer."[3] Turning an immediate corner, one approaches a mural with Dorothy Day's face sketched at one end and Martin Luther King Jr.'s at the other. Between them are the faces of Daniel Berrigan, Fannie Lou Hamer, César Chávez, and Jeff Dietrich and Catherine Morris of the Los Angeles Catholic Worker. Another quick turn places one in an extensive hallway lined with poster art depicting slave religion and the black freedom struggle; guest rooms named "Ella Baker," "Gandhi," and "Septima Clark"; flyers announcing peace and justice rallies around the world; and most importantly, under the words, "No, no, no, they are not numbers, they are names!," the one hundred-plus pictures of the Community's homeless friends, whom Ed Loring refers to as his "central teachers."

As this visual cloud of witnesses attests, the Open Door's theological influences are many. In addition to those who show up on the walls, they include friend and fellow Georgian Clarence Jordan, with his original vision of Koinonia Farm, as well as the liberation theologies and action-reflection hermeneutic arising from the base communities of Central and South America. Among this great cloud, Ed Loring and Murphy Davis consider the lives, writings, and witnesses of King and Bonhoeffer to be crucial. Each man's interconnected life and thought were foundational to the start of the Open Door and to the ecclesial work preceding it in the late 1970s, and their witnesses remain central to the Community's theological praxis: Bonhoeffer's call to "costly discipleship" undergirds the work as a whole and King's influence guides the Community's methods of social analysis and strategies of nonviolence. The pervasive influence of King is symbolically expressed not only in the mural by the back door but also in an eight-foot Martin Luther King Day banner hanging in the front entrance way. His is the first face seen by friends who enter directly off the streets.[4]

The Open Door as Communal Reception of Bonhoeffer and King

I offer this snapshot of the Open Door Community for two reasons. First, to articulate what may be obvious to this book's primary audience and all those whose interest in religion and public life emerges from social and political struggle: The legacies of Bonhoeffer and King demand action. This anthology receives their legacies for Christian social thought, aware that "thought" for Bonhoeffer and King remained incomplete without courageous, constructive, redemptive social engagement.

Second, the cloud of witnesses depicted in the hallway of the Open Door raises an important question: Why devote a book only to Bonhoeffer and King? Why not include Dorothy Day and Fannie Lou Hamer? Although Bonhoeffer and King are foundational to the Open Door, Loring says he "can't have King without Dorothy Day or someone like that who lived out her life in a community of hospitality informed by a particular set of daily practices."[5] Indeed, why focus on individuals at all when making sense of legacies constructed by movements and communities?

The conversation in this book forms in *response* to the many scholars, students, practitioners, and pastors who have begun to consider these two men's lives and writings together when deliberating over basic questions in Christian social thought. Across and because of the significant differences in their historic, sociopolitical contexts, Bonhoeffer and King have become touchstones for many Christian conversations about peace and violence, love and justice, church and world, and faith and public life. This anthology offers a resource to those discussions by presenting careful, informed, and focused reflections from contemporary social thinkers who have wrestled with their legacies— sometimes in quite different ways.

The contributors to this volume share my concern that Christian social thought work in the service of transformative action, and readers will be challenged in these pages not to curtail the difficult and necessary task of social analysis by simplistic or static appeals to Bonhoeffer and King as theological authorities. As Emilie Townes argues in the opening chapter, we appropriate the insights of King or Bonhoeffer respectfully when we reciprocate with our own labor—when we construct, as Steve Haynes's essay urges, not "monuments" that enshrine these figures and their thought, but a "better world." The Open Door exemplifies how the legacies of Bonhoeffer and King may inhabit contemporary communities seeking to do just that.[6] As we receive the legacies of these two men for Christian social thought, the work and witness of the Open Door awakens our moral imaginations to what is possible, to the kind of concrete engagement that may result from such deliberate reception.

Among the insights the Open Door appropriates are the methods driving King's and Bonhoeffer's social and theological analyses. From Bonhoeffer, the Open Door learns to stay vigilant to the trajectories of state or public actions that masquerade under the guise of reason or respectability yet actually reflect what Bonhoeffer calls "contempt for humanity." The city of Atlanta expressed contempt for "the real human being"[7] whom God loves—indeed, for Bonhoeffer, who God became—when it spent hundreds of thousands of dollars jailing (and thus banishing from sight) homeless people caught in the humiliating act of public urination or defecation but refused, until recently, to spend a fraction of that amount on public toilets in its municipal parks. The city now has installed a few public toilets in some of its parks,[8] yet it continues to express contempt for the real human being in its refusal to make decent and affordable housing a priority. That which causes the Open Door concern, be it in the form of public policies or city planning initiatives, the Community announces in shouts of protest. From King, the Open Door has learned the centrality of the streets in these protests and that "the beloved community is not formed apart from the streets because," says Loring, "the streets are a primary place to meet the stranger and love the enemy."[9] They also learn from King to develop their social analysis around the theological question, What are the obstacles barring beloved community from being realized today in this place?

The Open Door answers this question by participating in the civil rights movement's unfinished agenda of racial and economic justice. Still, the Community knows firsthand that persevering in this work does not necessarily entail steady movement forward. Our cities have yet to achieve justice in the form of decent and accessible housing for all, and contemporary society's basic answer to this civil rights demand has been blatant consent to a subculture of homelessness. Murphy Davis says, "American citizens essentially have said, 'You want to talk about housing? Okay, how about this: No housing.' Well, no one had even thought of that in the '60s.'" The Open Door's attempts to dismantle obstacles barring the achievement of beloved community also lead to protests against the "criminal control system." Research on southern prisons and decades of ministry in them have taught Davis and the Open Door that there is historical continuity between chattel and penal slavery, a link constitutionally sanctioned by the thirteenth amendment, which did not abolish slavery completely but, rather, allows it as "punishment for crime." A trajectory of racial domination runs from antebellum plantations to the post-Reconstruction convict lease system and Jim Crow segregation to the staggering growth of the prison industry over the last forty years. "We think we defeat forms of oppression," Davis says, "but they just kind of go underground. You've got to watch for where they're going to come up again."[10]

The Open Door illustrates that there is not only continuity but also discontinuity in resistance work and in the forces of oppression we identify. Previous conceptions of the powers fueling oppression prove to be incomplete, and so the Open Door focuses in ways that Bonhoeffer and King did not on the web of destructive forces that entangles racism and classism with heterosexism and sexism, an issue explored in this volume in Rachel Muers's feminist rereading of Bonhoeffer and King. Nevertheless, as these two men write and speak out of their particular times and contexts, they "strike a chord of universality," says Davis, which enables "their writings to become living texts in the same way that Scripture becomes a living text." Living texts invite conversation and the mutual indwelling of worlds. Most North American Christians, however, are not able to relate to the sociohistorical world of Jesus, and Davis argues that this is not primarily a matter of "now being different from then" but a matter

of "the world of the privileged being different from the world of the poor."
She says that "the Gospels cannot have the meaning of the time unless you see
decaying flesh or hear the cries of the victims of domination. . . . When you
engage human history in ways that are similar to how King engaged history
and how Bonhoeffer engaged history, then the gospel is alive, and so are their
texts. . . . then the discipleship movement and the beloved community reach
back in time. We become companions of Martin King and Dietrich Bonhoeffer
and of all the resistors, and they become companions of ours."[11]

With Bonhoeffer and King as our companions, the chapters that follow
seek to broaden and sharpen our theological imaginations for the struggles for
justice and peace that claim us, in the words of King, in "the fierce urgency of
now."[12] "What are we waiting for?" Bonhoeffer asks in a 1934 international,
ecumenical speech, "The time is late."[13]

Entering the Conversation

This anthology examines Dietrich Bonhoeffer and Martin Luther King Jr. in
relation to basic questions in Christian social thought and, by doing so, asks
what place their theologically resonant, politically contested legacies have
come to occupy in the twenty-first century. How might reading and teaching
them together facilitate our understandings of each and influence the ways
various communities appropriate their legacies? How might such a reading
assist communities in the larger project of constructing theologies that meet
the demands of the social and political realities they face? What distortions
and projections have their legacies absorbed, and what new distortions and
conflations are made inadvertently by treating them together? In what directions do their distinct and often ambiguous ideas propel us when interpreted
in light of specific social issues? What emphases come into focus again and
again? What insights are conveyed that we might have neglected had we not
heard the polyphony of their voices?

The chapters in this volume address a range of topics and may be read
independently of one another. Each essay reaches beyond itself, though, serving as an entry point to the subject matter rather than a comprehensive and
conclusive reading. In this way, the chapters mirror the fragmentary, unfinished, and open character of Bonhoeffer and King's own writings. With some
exceptions, the Dietrich Bonhoeffer's Works and *The Papers of Martin Luther
King, Jr.* are filled with unsystematic material such as sermons, letters, and
other occasional pieces, which reflect that, for these men, theology did not—
and perhaps could not—speak the dynamic word of God as a tidy system.

The fragmentary form creates space for God's living word to speak concretely into the contemporary moment and facilitates the continual unfolding of fresh theological insight.[14] As with the writings of Bonhoeffer and King, the chapters in this text invite readers to extend the lines of thinking begun here, and many of the authors suggest avenues for doing so.

The essays reach beyond themselves in another sense as well, in that they hold conversation with one another. Themes embedded in the thought of these two men (such as community, peace, Jesus Christ) are interwoven throughout these essays. Readers will discover, for example, important insights into Bonhoeffer's and King's Christologies not only in Gary Simpson's chapter on Jesus and social ethics but also in Shawn Copeland's chapter on Catholic social thought and Josiah Young's on race. Likewise, the reader will find substantial discussions on peace and the nature of violence not only in part 4, "Practices of Peace," but also in Larry Rasmussen's essay on the social ecologies of Bonhoeffer and King and in Craig Slane's essay on martyrs. Readers are invited to delve into the interpretive work themselves, noting points where themes converge, where contributors agree or disagree, and where the legacies seem to point in other directions. The sections of this anthology suggest one path through the volume, as they are organized around lessons learned from collectively reading Bonhoeffer and King together in the twenty-first century.

Part 1, on gaining "Critical Distance," equips readers for the interpretive task. Emilie Townes's essay on appropriation and reciprocity and Stephen Haynes's essay on the use and misuse of contested legacies draw our attention to methods of appropriation and patterns of thinking that inevitably distort the lives and thought of inspiring figures yet remain a constant temptation for their admirers. We can easily place Bonhoeffer and King beyond criticism, commodify their stories to bolster a contemporary argument or agenda, and depend on their witness instead of our own to speak prophetically and act justly. When we do so, we presume a false immediacy between them and us.[15] Rachel Muers's essay, "Bonhoeffer, King, and Feminism: Problems and Possibilities," models the kind of critical and constructive engagement that avoids such temptations. She neither "exonerate[s]" nor "condemn[s]" these figures on account of their being "complicit in the evil of sexism." Rather, Muers's appraisal leads her to deepen these men's insights about community and to raise broader questions about the ecclesiologies that shape the study of Christian social movements. Finally, while examining "Political Order, Political Violence, and Ethical Limits," Jean Bethke Elshtain alerts readers to substantial differences in the sociopolitical contexts in which Bonhoeffer and King lived. She highlights the distance between the two figures by examining how these contexts influenced both the questions each man asked and the manner in which they each understood political possibility.

The topics in part 2—social ecology (Rasmussen), racism (Young), Catholic social thought (Copeland), church/world relations and political agape (Jackson), and martyrdom (Slane)—demonstrate from a number of different angles the first lesson learned from reading Bonhoeffer and King together: receiving their legacies compels Christians to attend to the interconnection of all of humanity in creation, sin, and redemption and thus to consider human mutuality and partnership across difference as intrinsic to biblical faith and essential for Christian social thought and action. Part 2, "Shared Humanity," illuminates Bonhoeffer's and King's theological grounding for solidarity, resistance work, and human rights, as well as their rejection of what Timothy Jackson describes as any social or metaphysical privileging of "us" over "them." Larry Rasmussen's chapter on social ecology sets the stage by arguing that, after Bonhoeffer and King, solidarity, resistance, and rights may no longer be relegated to the margins but belong at the center of Christian concern. The theological basis for human interconnection is perhaps most evident in King's *imago Dei* anthropology and in Bonhoeffer's Christology, yet collectively the essays in this section suggest the need for further reflection on the correlation between anthropology and Christology within and between each thinker. Whether their thinking is based on a view of God as Creator, God as Reconciler, or some combination thereof, Bonhoeffer and King each affirm human and cosmic mutuality, what King calls "the inescapable network of mutuality" and "the interrelated structure of reality" and Bonhoeffer, "Christ reality."[16] While the essays of Rasmussen, Young, Copeland, and Jackson regard a profound commitment to our shared humanity as definitive for Christian faith and practice, Craig Slane's essay, "The Cross and Its Victims," further demonstrates the theological foundation and promise of such a conviction by constructing a theology of the cross based on Bonhoeffer's and King's cruciform lives. Slane argues that these men each model human mutuality through a "decision against distance, a decision for a new hermeneutic" that emerges "in proximity to violence and its victims" in order to resist forces of evil, identify with victims, and love enemy-oppressors.

If a Christian commitment to our shared humanity leads to a "decision against distance," a decision for solidarity and human rights—if it leads, in the words of the Open Door Community, to a decision to "reduce the distance" between society's beneficiaries and victims—then this *movement toward* places of violence and dehumanization simultaneously will prepare the way for peace and justice by carving out new spaces that invite redemption. Part 3, "Spaces of Redemption," expresses the second lesson learned from reading Bonhoeffer and King together: Preparing the way for peace and justice requires creating, cultivating, and legitimating nontraditional vocational and communal spaces. Charles Marsh's "Bonhoeffer on the Road to King: 'Turning from the Phraseological to the Real,'" Richard Wills's "Interpreting Pastors as Activists," and Raphael Warnock's "The Ministry of Preaching and Prophetic Witness" examine how Bonhoeffer and King lived out their vocations as theologians and pastors. These essays argue that receiving their legacies disrupts familiar, static notions of the academic theologian, parish pastor, and preacher, respectively. Together the lives of Bonhoeffer and King announce a dynamic vocational reconfiguration that weaves together elements of all three roles. Thus, their lives and thought raise vital questions for us about institutional structures in the academy and in churches that impede sustained and concrete connection between theological reflection, pastoral ministry, and social activism.

Stephen Ray's essay, "Embodying Redemption: Martin Luther King Jr. and the Engagement of Social Sin," focuses on the need to cultivate new communal spaces for redemption at that same intersection of theology, ministry, and activism. Ray argues that King responded to structural and social sin through practical ministry that envisioned the beloved community as the "creation of . . . new publics" whose purpose was to redeem American society. Although Ray's essay focuses on King, he argues that Bonhoeffer and King "understood communal vocation in the face of social evil in the same way" as "cruciform communalism." Both men thought that the requisite response to social evil was the formation of communities of resistance that embodied Christ. Andre Willis's essay, "Culture in Bonhoeffer and King: Deweyan Naturalism in Action," argues that both men cultivated communal space for redemption, understood in a different sense, through their savvy use of culture. Their cultural work included the aesthetic appeal of their writings, speeches, and sermons, which, to varying degrees, destabilized and reoriented traditional modes of thought dominating society.

The new communal spaces that Ray refers to as cruciform communities invite and empower redemption specifically through intentional practices of peace. Part 4, "Practices of Peace," is organized around the third and final lesson learned from collectively reading Bonhoeffer and King together: receiving their legacies occasions serious attention to the Sermon on the Mount in the sociopolitical realm. Glen Stassen's essay on peacemaking, Geffrey Kelly's on spirituality, and Gary Simpson's on images of Jesus each argue that Bonhoeffer and King understood the Sermon on the Mount as a gospel mandate—a nonnegotiable command to *make* peace amidst hatred and violence. Whereas dominant traditions in Christian social thought have deemed the Sermon on the Mount politically unrealistic or even irresponsible, Bonhoeffer and King disclose the Sermon's deep, abiding realism as each man "views reality anew," says Kelly, "from the perspective of Jesus' teachings." Viewing political reality and social responsibility from the perspective of the Sermon on the Mount requires proactive courage and creativity, strategy, and discipline. For, it is not immediately apparent how forgiveness, love of enemy, forbearance, and reconciliation can overcome entrenched hatred and violence. Furthermore, Jesus' peace ethic—as shown through Bonhoeffer's and King's distinct and divergent lives—requires commitment to peace as a way of life, obedient submission to the "commanding Christ," as Simpson says, and, as Kelly argues, conformation to Christ's life, death, and resurrection. Stassen's essay demonstrates how this ethic may be understood in the twenty-first century through the emerging paradigm of "just peacemaking," which he argues is "christologically grounded," "empirically effective," and characteristic of the kind of peace ethic Bonhoeffer and King each sought.

Finally, Michael Battle's essay on reconciliation connects the practice of peace to communal worship. Battle argues that by undervaluing communal spirituality, Western Christians have neglected to see that true worship unfurls in struggles for justice and peace that transform society. Through an analysis of Desmond Tutu's reception of Bonhoeffer and King in South Africa, Battle demonstrates how the legacies of these two men may simultaneously reinforce, critique, and complicate one another.

The anthology as a whole demonstrates the complementing and complicating dynamic at play when considering Bonhoeffer and King together in the twenty-first century. Inheriting their legacies is a critical undertaking requiring that, like the Open Door Community, those who identify intentionally with their work and witness must continually assess how contemporary realities problematize their appropriation. Just as the Open Door awakens our imaginations to the possibilities of a constructive reception of these legacies, the studies that follow intend to challenge, prod, disrupt, and deepen previous understandings of Bonhoeffer and King for students, scholars, practitioners, and communities who must live within the tensions and ambiguities of our own historical moments.

Part One

Critical Distance

CHAPTER 1

Notes on Appropriation and Reciprocity

— Prompts from Bonhoeffer and King's Communitarian Ethic —

Emilie M. Townes

G reat men often beget excessive sycophancy. When coupled with issues of appropriation and reciprocity, a rather large moral conundrum sets in. Dealing with such towering figures as Dietrich Bonhoeffer and Martin Luther King Jr. is akin to being a prized turkey caught on a barbed-wire fence on the first day of hunting season[1]— entrapped by someone else's ideal of security and exposed to all manner of predators and sympathetic passersby. My concern in this situation is that neither Bonhoeffer nor King is seen in the full expanse of his respective thought. Rather, the general tendency is to appropriate excerpted thought from both men in order to underscore a contemporary argument. What remains wanting are explorations into the deeper ways in which the contradictions and challenges in their respective thought do not easily fit into postmodern moral discourses and the ways in which they differ from each other theologically.[2] This becomes even more so when contemplating Bonhoeffer and King in conversation or in tandem.

The essays in this volume attempt, in large measure, to heed the cautions and challenges in dealing with figures we often see as moral giants and martyred activists. However, there remains for me a more general concern about the ways in which contemporary Christian social ethics deals with the overarching issues of appropriation of the culture and insights of culturally marginalized groups in contemporary U.S. life and the global implications and manifestations of this and the particular contribution black women in the United States can make in troubling these waters so that there emerges a thick description of our moral lives and living. With Bonhoeffer and King as stout moral sentinels, this essay explores some of the key features I believe are important to be mindful of regarding our attempts at thoughtful appropriation and respectful reciprocity as we search for ethical pillars to rest our contemporary analysis on in facing the incredible challenges of early twenty-first-century global realities.

I

For decades, there was silence about or, more appropriately, few listened to structurally marginalized voices. Whole worlds were left outside of dominant discourse and analysis, except as the occasional other who served the needs of oppression and dehumanization. It has only been since the late 1960s with the beginning of black studies programs in secondary and higher education that black realities were studied by black folks in large numbers. Before, the bulk of studies that focused on black Americans were done by white researchers who had varying degrees of awareness of the biases they brought to their studies.[3] Cultural and social differences were funneled into deadly dualisms that carried with them difference, objectification, and, ultimately, domination. W. E. B. Du Bois and others named the experience often felt by the Other as double consciousness—seeing one's self through the eyes of the other rather than through the framework of one's experience and knowledge.[4]

As clarity emerged about the nature of the blight—which entailed processes of objectification and subordination used to define whole peoples, categorized patterns of thought and behavior, and (re)presented chimera as concrete history while counterfeit history became reality—African American women found that the words they had shouted to the winds, the lives they had lived *regardless*, found a place, albeit a small place, in normative discourse and inquiry. Early works by Delores S. Williams, Katie Geneva Cannon, and Jacquelyn Grant from the 1980s has now been joined by the more recent work of Melanie Harris, Eboni Marshall, and Dianne Stewart.[5]

Although several years old at this point, the modernism-postmodernism debate continues. Within this debate, various groups that have been traditionally marginalized, such as darker-skinned women, the poor, and sexual minorities, are insisting on being heard as their lives and cultures are usually the grist for hegemonic moves of appropriation that do not recognize or value the need for reciprocity. However, we stand within a context that is volcanic as modernity radically alters the nature of everyday social lives. Within the modernist frame, there is a high value placed on universal rationality, attempts to establish objective, value-free established knowledge and ontologies. Modernity focuses on the individual who then creates communities rather than being birthed/formed by community. It seeks to institutionalize radical doubt, and it insists that all knowledge is really hypothesis.

On the other hand, postmodernism focuses on a radical historicity in which plurality, particularity, locality, context, the social location of thought, and a serious questioning of universal knowledge are key features. It is this molten-hot sand that provides the backdrop for considering the ways we use and misuse the lives and works of Bonhoeffer and King by often bypassing rigorous considerations about the nature of the other and how each of us shifts in and out of this posture: for at times, we are the subjects who objectify.

The promise of postmodern ethics is that it provides a way for many of us to think our way into concrete knowledge of and contact with African American realities as well as the realities of other structurally marginalized groups; for example, those formed by other racial, ethnic, sexuality, class, or age groups. When postmodern discourse only represents abstract thinking, however, it can commit the same vexing errors found in the modernist assumptions of universal rationality, objectivity, value-free established knowledge, individuals who create communities rather than being birthed/formed by community, institutionalized radical doubt, and knowledge as hypothesis. The challenge for postmodern ethics is to push for theoretical reformulations that embrace the great diversity found within humanity and creation *and* practice a concrete concern for the lives of people and implications of the theologies we espouse.

II

Considering the ways in which Bonhoeffer and King disrupted the status quo of their time in their reliance on a strong communitarian ethic that continues to prod us today, there are two key lessons that can inform postmodern moral discourses so that we do not fall victim to relativizing our actions and theories. This ethic, which insists that we belong to the same moral universe and must be treated with dignity and respect as children of God, reminds us that we must acknowledge that the notion that we are aware of another person's feelings and experiences only on the basis of empathic inferences from our own veers into solipsism. Self-consciousness and awareness of others are not natural or inevitable dance partners. Understanding the other is not predicated on how the individual (or the group) makes the shift from the certainty of her, his, or its inner experiences to the unknowable person. When we make this kind of tenuous shift the outcome generally falls into two categories: *romanticization* (because we are all women, we understand poor women) or *trivialization* (why can't we all get along?). What we must be about as we approach one another's work and lives is care-filled listening, observation, and engagement. This takes time, energy, resources, fortitude, and a stout will to comprehend others. We are not to be theoethical tourists in the lives of others, but are to attempt the hard work of being pilgrims on the journey with others.

Second, it is important to remember that this is not a disembodied voice we seek to hear and understand, but one in which rich traditions and histories have shaped it as it continues to be renewed and transformed. It is a voice from a particular culture whose integrity and worth must be respected. If we rush in too quickly with our tools of correct analysis and solidarity, the voice we will hear is our own echo—a distortion of the original but Dolby in sound. Inept appropriations of cultures that are not our own not only signal a lack of reciprocity in which we share some of who we are as well, it is also stealing. That which is taken becomes a shadow of that culture rather than a rich appreciation of the history, tradition, and current manifestations of it. For example, the mass cultural appropriation of hip-hop has dulled the initial clipped, piercing social criticism that was the heart of the early work of groups from the 1960s like the Last Poets, individual artists such as Gil Scott-Heron, or, arguably, the later work of Marvin Gaye, Curtis Mayfield, and Arrested Development.[6] Today's mass cultural hip-hop does not chronicle social inequities such as poor housing and education; it is a mass of "booty shots" and misogyny wrapped in a glorification of violence as manly and necessary.[7] How far this has come from the West African *griots* who are the wandering poets and praise singers that are the forerunners of U.S.-based hip-hop. They are the repositories of the oral tradition of their societies—they must tell the truth rather than be driven by marketing and stereotypes that reify a fantastic hegemonic imagination that calls us out of our name and warps all of us into gross stereotypes of who we actually are.[8]

III

Naming is a powerful theoethical act. For example, black women and black folk in general in the United States are making a political choice when deciding between "womanist" and "feminist," "colored" and "black," "black" and "African American." There is a history and culture of struggle, dialogue, arguments, and peeling away imposed language to ponder and then utilize an articulate, indigenous witness to the absolute necessity that no one can speak for us but ourselves. This remains true regardless of who is the current resident in the White House and of the policies he or she espouses.

There is power in the ability to take away a name—being called girl or boy when you are in your sixties, seventies, and eighties by hegemonic culture; women being asked to speak, but not preach in black churches. There is deadly power in taking away the ability to name as well. In the important dynamic of appropriation and reciprocity, it is important to recognize that there must be spaces for the structurally marginalized to name their reality, which they may still be in the process of discovering. The point is not perfection, but the important *search* for precision in naming the joys and pain, re-membering the body of race, culture, ethnicity, gender, and more in a dominating culture. It is vital to recognize that in many instances, it remains sadly true that some marginalized groups are only just beginning to name the issues and points of tension that they must deal with internally when considering their work from a position outside of our society or on its fringes. This may mean that these groups will speak in cultural codes and shorthand and that they may be coming from cultures that value oral tradition or visual representation. This may mean that those of us who are not well versed in learning and understanding aurally (words and sound) or with images and pictures or who are not part of these groups must respect that not everything gets put into print in these cultures so we must learn new skills of listening, learning, and understanding.

The structurally marginalized want to tell their stories and be heard. Within a communitarian ethical framework, can we take this in and consider how we have or have not been a part of these stories? If we take up this challenge, it will be important to keep in mind that rather than assume that our attempts at respectful appropriation will mean assimilation into a larger culture which is inequitable at its very foundation for those who have been structurally marginalized, we must recognize that listening to others and hearing what they have to say and understanding the implications of their lives in relation to ours must be in *contrast* to our own traditions and cultures so that we begin to understand and consider how our lives and history are a part of the fabric of creation *with* the structurally marginalized. This means guarding against setting the realities of the lives of the structurally marginalized in our script, having them illuminate points we must or should make on our own (e.g., what it feels like to live in a homophobic and heterosexist society) through the integrity of our witness, analysis, and ability to critique and analyze from the perspectives of our lives as well as from the structures we both create and challenge that support inequitable relationships.

Hence, each of us must begin with our own cognitive dissonance. We cannot appropriate each other's dissonance and have a truly articulate and pithy analysis. We have much to learn from one another as we appropriate and reciprocate but we must not use each other up or down in doing so. Situations in which we are aware that we are experiencing cognitive dissonance and from which we are willing to learn are signs that we may be in unfamiliar terrain where we will learn more about the societies we inhabit; or more importantly, become aware that what we are most familiar with is not all that is occurring in the world. This encourages us to move beyond the notion that a solitary, autonomous individual who is only responsible for her or his own actions is a healthy model for humanity or a faithful moral agent. We are individuals who are socially constructed, and genuine reciprocation means that as we learn and grow from others, we share that knowledge and also share who we are and our perspectives and insights about how to shape a more just and equitable society.

IV

Considering the ways in which the communitarian ethic of Bonhoeffer and King can inform Christian social thought in postmodern worlds means that we are responding to the themes of difference, disruption, marginality, otherness, and transgression as we weigh each other's analysis and work. Whatever we think about postmodernism itself, it can teach us an important lesson. Until recently, and still not to the degree that it should not be, postmodernism has been largely (and narrowly) focused on the West. This is ironic given that it arises from the end of the Age of Europe, the emergence of the United States as a world power, the decolonization of so-called Third World countries, and the rise of China as a major cultural and economic force on the global stage. There continues to be scant mention of the black experience or particularly the writings of black women in postmodernist theory broadly drawn or post-modern ethics.[9] Yet the categories of otherness and difference stand central to its task of critical reflection. For all its promise of providing a different and more useful way forward, postmodern ethics is caught in a paradox that must be acknowledged and challenged as we seek to appropriate with care and reciprocate with respect.

The key lesson to be learned from postmodern conversations is that we must avoid collapsing "otherness" into a universal category much like we have done (and learned not to do) with "women" and "minorities" or some of us will end up writing the second edition of "all the women were white, all the blacks are men, but some of us are brave."[10] The rhetoric and conceptualization of otherness mean that we must engage those peoples and cultures who have a long history without our societies but have not been considered part of the "mainstream" or are often treated as supplementary on course reading lists. To truly engage otherness is to take seriously that there remains much for each of us to know about the rich diversity in our midst and then see this as opportunity rather than threat. It also means that we see this as a means to deepen our scholarship and analysis methodologically. It helps us be more expansive religious communities as we take seriously the ways in which God's revelation is ongoing and may not be bound by our provincial notions of chosenness or faithfulness.

The experience and critical analysis done by structurally marginalized groups have much to offer social moral thought. This is enhanced when the challenges of the communitarian ethic of Bonhoeffer and King, with its emphasis on our being part of the same moral and social universe, are included. We all deserve to be treated with dignity and respect as children of God. The voices of feminists, womanists, mujeristas, liberation theology, Minjung theologies, Asian liberation theologies, queer theologies, and more have much to offer all of us as we stand in the clearing of our respective societies as early twenty-first-century peoples and try to decide where we must go. But I am also aware that other voices have not yet joined the conversation and there are those who are just pulling up to our kitchen table of public moral discourse. The power to name and speak of Native American and indigenous peoples has yet to gain full voice, though it is growing, and there are others. . . .

Our challenge is that as more folk join what has largely (and ill-fittingly) been a black-white dialogue, we accept the invitation, which comes from genuine appropriation and respectful reciprocity, to grow our worldviews and sensitivities to heart with communitarian zeal. In doing so, we must not interrupt these new old voices as they speak. We listen from a profound place and deepen our scholarship, our emotions, our histories when we respond to them with our voices and not an imitation of theirs or a megaphone of our own.

CHAPTER 2

King and Bonhoeffer as Protestant Saints

— The Use and Misuse of Contested Legacies —

Stephen R. Haynes

The word *saint* has many contemporary meanings. For Protestants, it refers rather democratically to all believers. For Catholics, it is a designation for those who, through a carefully prescribed ecclesiastical process, are judged to possess heroic sanctity. But there is a popular notion of sainthood that transcends these institutional definitions. As with Catholic sainthood, its focus is men and women distinguished by their piety and heroism; as with the Protestant conception, sainthood is determined by one's relationship to God, not one's standing with the church. Unlike both, however, popular sainthood is sanctioned by a *vox populi* that answers to no religious authority.

What these unofficial saints have in common, Lawrence S. Cunningham argues, is their paradigmatic lives and their ability to demonstrate new ways of incarnating the Christian message. Thus, they recall something more basic to the faith than the institutionalization of sainthood in the Catholic Church or the reaction to this process in the leveling instincts of the Reformers—to wit, the affinity we feel for men and women who are called by God and remain faithful to that call even in death. "A saint is a person so grasped by a religious vision," Cunningham writes, "that it becomes central to his or her life in a way that radically changes the person and leads others to glimpse the value of that vision."[1] In this sense of the word, Dietrich Bonhoeffer and Martin Luther King Jr. must be numbered among the most prominent and influential Christian saints of the twentieth century.

The Bonhoeffer Phenomenon

In my 2004 book *The Bonhoeffer Phenomenon: Portraits of a Protestant Saint*, I sought to marshal evidence of Bonhoeffer's popular sainthood, in part through a comprehensive examination of the material culture that has grown up around the German theologian's memory. I discussed various editions of Bonhoeffer's own writings (ranging from critical editions of his collected works to volumes packaged and marketed for devotional use), biographies (scholarly tomes as well as texts designed for Christian edification), and fictionalized accounts of Bonhoeffer's life, including dramas and films. Since the publication of *The Bonhoeffer Phenomenon*, evidence of his "sainthood" has continued to come to my attention—including paintings and sculptures, biographies and works of historical fiction, poems and sonnets, films and film scripts, a variety of musical tributes, portraits in stained glass, monuments to Bonhoeffer the martyr in London and Rome, Bonhoeffer "gift books," and devotional texts containing daily readings.

Frankly, keeping track of this material has become overwhelming, particularly since I requested that Google send me an e-mail "alert" every time the name "Bonhoeffer" appears in cyberspace. On an average day, I receive at least a dozen such alerts. As they arrive, I watch allusions to and adaptations of Bonhoeffer's legacy expand by the hour. Since adding "Martin Luther King" to my list of Google alerts in early 2008, I have witnessed a similar phenomenon. From the dozens of alerts I receive daily, I have learned that King's image appears on commemorative plates, posters, statues, monuments, icons, murals, and garbage bags,[2] and that his words fill children's books, plays, "rock operettas," sound recordings, and YouTube videos. This is not the place for a full review of the King cult, but the sheer volume of music, film, literature, and art celebrating his legacy would indicate that admiration for the slain civil rights leader is virtually universal, extending across racial, political, and national boundaries. What is more, perhaps more than any other twentieth-century American, King is likely to be found in the pantheons of private citizens. Jerry Manuel, manager of the New York Mets, no doubt speaks for many when he admits, "If I had three people to fit at my dinner table, it would be Jesus, Gandhi and Martin Luther King."[3] Select company indeed.

Paradoxically, though, during 2008, a year that witnessed the fortieth anniversary of King's assassination and the realization of his "dream" in the election of Barack Obama, there has been an increase in complaints that King's legacy has been diluted, sanitized, revised, and repackaged to the point of becoming "a watered down caricature of resistance that can be embraced by the former

Fig. 2.1 Portraits of King and Bonhoeffer as Saints

oppressor in order to mollify the masses."[4] It is surely ironic that at the height of his popularity the real Martin Luther King Jr. may be harder than ever to identify. As with Bonhoeffer, it would seem, the King phenomenon is a mixed blessing for scholars.

The Perils of Popular Sainthood

Sanctification

When someone is mentioned in the same sentence with Jesus and Gandhi, exploring their flaws seems somehow blasphemous. Thus, one peril of popular sainthood is the tendency to place saints beyond criticism. Contributing to this general reluctance to reproach these popular saints is the striking integrity revealed in Bonhoeffer and King between their thought and behavior, between their visions and their sacrificial willingness to pursue them. This integrity, we are quick to recognize, is rarely to be found around us or even within us. Saints like King and Bonhoeffer also sustain our hope that the religious traditions we care about, though tainted by many failures, are not completely bankrupt.

When popular saints are asked to shoulder the moral credibility of the Christian tradition, revelation of their flaws is naturally followed by disappointment and defensiveness. In the case of Bonhoeffer, it is research on his relationship to the "Jewish question" that leaves his advocates demoralized and defiant. I have addressed this matter in *The Bonhoeffer Legacy: Post-Holocaust Perspectives* and I can say with confidence that exploring the anti-Jewish elements in the thought of a Christian "Holocaust hero" is not a recipe for gaining appreciation from Bonhoeffer's supporters, whether lay or academic. Yet it is important for scholar-advocates to be involved in this work, in part so that our portraits of these men retain credibility.

For King, the alleged failures of integrity concern private behavior. The charges of marital infidelity are perhaps best known, but these charges are discredited to some extent by the means used to obtain the information on which they are based. The matter of King's alleged plagiarism is different, it seems to me. In the case of his dissertation in particular, the offense is demonstrable and amounts to a moral failure that scholars cannot easily dismiss. I have thought a great deal about my own position on this issue because one of my graduate school advisors was Jack Boozer, the man whose Boston University thesis became the source of much of King's own. After Jack's untimely death soon after his retirement, I learned that he had known many years before it became public that King had "borrowed" much of his dissertation. Jack kept the matter quiet, it was said, because he knew that King's opponents would use it to discredit him and his message. It was a silence that bespoke deep integrity, as well as keen judgment, because King's opponents have indeed used the plagiarism charges to attack him and the civil rights movement more generally.

As a Christian and a white advocate of civil rights, Jack's decision to place his intellectual rights behind King's reputation was the right decision. But what about as a scholar, a citizen of the academic world, and an alumnus of the program at Boston University that granted King's degree? Did Jack have an obligation to bring the plagiarized dissertation to the attention of the institution whose academic integrity it had besmirched? I suspect our answers to these questions will differ depending on whether we know that the accused party is one of the most celebrated religious figures in American history. At Rhodes College, our honor code obligates students not only to refrain from cheating but to report any cheating they may witness. Professors have a responsibility to turn over suspected violators to their classmates on the honor council. If I suspected that one of my students had committed plagiarism, but I knew she was deeply engaged as an activist in causes I support, would it be morally defensible for me to overlook the violation or keep it from the honor council?

As men and women committed to mending the world, we may struggle to balance critical honesty with advocacy of the sublime ideas for which Bonhoeffer and King gave their lives. But an unflinching exploration of the ways these men failed to demonstrate integrity between their ideals and behavior will protect our credibility as interpreters. Just as we cannot credibly condemn Christian anti-Judaism while deflecting all criticism of Bonhoeffer's stand on the "Jewish question," we cannot endorse the values of justice and impartiality if we exculpate King for behavior that in other instances we would condemn without hesitation. In unflinchingly facing our heroes' foibles, we help to clarify the human traits that are so easily obscured by the lens of sainthood.

Domestication

Popular images of Bonhoeffer and King are undoubtedly shaped by perceptions that they resisted evil powers "unto death," laying down their lives in the eternal struggle for justice.[5] They are considered "martyrs," perhaps not in the traditional sense of choosing death rather than recanting the faith, but inasmuch as they were killed for steadfastly clinging to their convictions.[6] Given this, it is often tempting to transport these clear-sighted men into the fog of the contested societal issues we care about. If Bonhoeffer is the quintessential anti-Nazi, then invoking his name in a discussion of some controversial question not only harnesses his moral authority but casts the other side as vaguely fascist. If King is the antiracist par excellence, then whatever can be portrayed as out of step with his legacy is by implication racist. When the Bonhoeffer and King cards are played, the symbolic payoff can be great. But ultimately we risk drawing false parallels that distort both sides of the equation.

In Bonhoeffer's case, the problem is most evident in his use by American foes of abortion. The historical basis for making Bonhoeffer an opponent of *Roe v. Wade* is the oft-cited statement in his *Ethics* that "to kill the fruit in the mother's womb is to injure the right to life that God has bestowed on the developing life. . . . And this is nothing but murder."[7] These words seem clear enough, and since they belong to Bonhoeffer the anti-Nazi crusader, they help to fashion a symbolic link between America and Hitler's Germany. Extending the comparison, legal abortion becomes a "silent holocaust" analogous to the "Final Solution" Bonhoeffer risked his life to stop. James Dobson is the most prominent prolife spokesperson to forge a connection between Bonhoeffer, abortion, and the Christian duty to resist an evil government. "What if today were 1943," he asks,

> and you were in Nazi Germany and knew that Hitler and his henchmen were killing Jews and Poles and Gypsies and homosexuals and the mentally handicapped, among other "undesirables"? You knew these helpless people were being gassed, and that little children were standing all

day, on one occasion in a freezing rain, for their turn to die in the gas chambers.

"I thank God," Dobson concludes, "that Dietrich Bonhoeffer did not shrink in timidity when he saw unmitigated wickedness being perpetrated by the Nazis. He spoke out boldly, even though he had to know it would cost him his life."[8]

To the right of Dobson are the radical prolifers for whom clinics are "abortion chambers" and "death camps," and information on abortion providers is collected in "Nuremberg files."[9] Before he was executed in September, 2003, for murdering a physician and his security escort outside a Pensacola, Florida, abortion clinic, Paul Hill reflected on criticism of his actions from the Christian community:

> Before World War II the church in Germany also shrank from resisting the evils of an unjust, oppressive government. Dietrich Bonhoeffer is an example of a church leader who, as an individual, sought to protect innocent life by plotting the death of Hitler. He is now considered a hero and his *Ethics* is used as a college text. A holocaust was going on and no civil leaders arose (they are hard to find under totalitarian rule).[10]

Hill's supporters fervently embrace the Bonhoeffer analogy, which was only strengthened when he himself became the victim of a purportedly unjust government.[11] A website titled "Men of Courage: Paul Hill and Dietrich Bonhoeffer" features photographs of these "martyrs for Christ" and juxtaposes a picture of corpses stacked at Dachau with a photo of aborted fetuses in a waste receptacle.[12]

Whatever our position on the moral status of abortion, I think we can agree that these appropriations of Bonhoeffer lie along a spectrum of increasing falsification. How do we know when we have moved from the realm of illuminating parallels to the realm of distorting equalizations? Perhaps the line is crossed when we care more passionately about the issue under consideration than about Bonhoeffer himself. Most of us can recognize falsifications when we see them. But it is easy to forget that although it may be a great distance between the recognition that Bonhoeffer took a strong stand against abortion in 1940 to claiming him as a role model for assassins of American abortion providers, the compulsion to harness Bonhoeffer's rare moral authority makes the distance between these points a rather slippery slope.

If distortion results when Bonhoeffer's legacy is sharpened for use as a wedge in service of a particular social agenda, there is no less distortion when it is flattened out in order to appear universally relevant. When the compulsion to make Bonhoeffer a nonsectarian hero issues in descriptions of a courageous moral leader guided by "a set of core beliefs,"[13] something significant has been lost. Robert Coles has been a particularly zealous advocate for this universally relevant Bonhoeffer. Coles depicts him as an "idealist," "a compelling moral and spiritual leader" who expressed an "unyielding opposition to evil." The heart of Bonhoeffer's spiritual legacy, Coles writes, "is not to be found in his words, his books, but in the way he spent his time on this earth. . . ."[14]

Such appraisals are not so much inaccurate as incomplete. They ignore the theological specificity of Bonhoeffer's worldview, according to which the values extolled by Coles find their reality in Christ. Thus, they reveal the price of maximizing Bonhoeffer's appeal by marketing his legacy in the currency of "moral leadership." Relying on the generic language of values and convictions, Coles presents a lowest-common-denominator Bonhoeffer who is less than the man himself. Such universalized portraits of Bonhoeffer obscure the particularity of his theological and social commitments in a way that should make us wary.

I suspect King scholars will have intimate experience with the domesticating impulse I have described here. A recent case in point is the use of King's image and words in drawing parallels between the American Family Association's boycott of McDonald's for its purported advocacy of same-sex marriage and the boycotts and sit-ins of the civil rights movement.[15] For a more subtle example of distortion through domestication, let me relate an experience I had in a course on "executive leadership" offered through my college's Center for Lifelong Learning. When I was asked to participate in the course by leading a two-hour session on King's "Letter from Birmingham Jail," I accepted the assignment with confidence since I had discussed the document with undergraduates many times. My approach had been to use King's letter to identify the theological sources of his vision—from Aquinas and Luther to Niebuhr and Tillich—and to argue that these figures were invoked because the white clergymen to whom King was writing would regard them as authorities.

But the curriculum supplied by the session's organizers took a quite different approach. In an effort to make the letter pertinent to the experiences of young executives, King's struggle with entrenched racism in Birmingham was compared with the challenges faced by corporate women. "What does King have to say to women whose advancement is limited by a 'glass ceiling' in their companies?" was the sort of reflection question offered by the study guide. I took the opportunity to argue that King probably had very little to say to such women, and that, in any case, attempting to understand the letter and King's vision in these terms was to distort it to the point of losing both its theological and social significance. (Need I say that I have not been asked back to lead the session on "Letter from Birmingham Jail"?)

In the recent presidential election campaign, Bonhoeffer and King were subjected to domestication by all sides. Support for Barack Obama that associated him with King's legacy—through similarities in vision, rhetorical style, or skin hue—was ubiquitous. The adage "Rosa sat so Martin could walk, Martin walked so Obama could run, Obama ran so our children can fly!" was repeated in many variations. King was even used to defend Jeremiah Wright when he became a problem for Obama. "They wanted King to shut up too," wrote one editorialist, while a blogger posted King's speech "America Too Is Going to Hell"[16] in order to remind us that the men were not so different after all.

Meanwhile, there were many attempts to loosen the Obama camp's grip on King's memory. The National Black Republican Association launched a campaign to convince us that "Martin Luther King was a Republican." King's daughter Bernice was outspoken in her prolife stance, bloggers opined that Obama's position on abortion would have kept King from voting for him, and Randall Terry crashed DNC events while invoking King's "Letter from Birmingham Jail" and suggesting that those who condemn the tactics of Operation Rescue "might forgo celebrating Martin Luther King day."[17] Many bloggers observed that if Obama's blackness was a factor in his supporters' decision to vote for him, then this was hardly compatible with King's dream of a society where people are judged by the content of their character rather than the color of their skin. King was rolling over in his grave, they claimed, because his legacy was being claimed by racists.

Meanwhile, Bonhoeffer, too, was being appealed to on behalf of both candidates. The day after the election a pro-gay-rights blogger explained the success of antigay propositions in several states by noting that in Nazi Germany, too, many had failed to resist evil until it threatened them personally. He cited the well-known "First they came for the communists . . ." statement, which he misattributed to Bonhoeffer. But the left could not claim exclusive right to Bonhoeffer's legacy. An article in the conservative magazine *National Review* declared that Bonhoeffer reminds us "not to expect government to solve all our problems, but rather to encourage or protect those who can."[18] Not surprisingly, Bonhoeffer's comments on abortion in *Ethics* were occasionally thrown behind prolife candidates. By the time election day arrived, Bonhoeffer had also been mentioned in connection with Jeremiah Wright, William Ayers, and Sarah Palin. Without doubt the election campaign demonstrated that figures like Bonhoeffer and King are extremely susceptible to this sort of (mis)use for immediate, partisan, and rhetorical purposes.

Projection

Let me briefly mention a species of distortion to which scholars are perhaps more susceptible than others. Projection occurs when we who know these figures well allow our assumptions to fill out what we don't know. Recently, while I was moderating a session at an international Bonhoeffer conference, one of the speakers described a discussion with another scholar with whom he had coedited a published collection of Bonhoeffer's writings. The speaker related that when he suggested the inclusion of a particular Bonhoeffer essay in their anthology, the other objected on the grounds that "it doesn't sound like Bonhoeffer."

Here, in a nutshell, I thought, is what happens when a religious figure also becomes a saint. That person's legacy is fashioned in a particular way, largely based on how his or her thought and deeds align with contemporary needs and aspirations. That legacy then becomes the implicit standard by which authenticity is judged. The collective ear has been tuned to hear a particular voice, and any words out of phase with this voice stand a good chance of being ignored. And if they are not ignored, these words (or deeds) must bè spun in a way that is protective of the received legacy. The fact that this statement was uttered and left unchallenged in a room full of scholars only reminds us that academics have much at stake in sustaining our images of these saints, since often they represent so much of what we have come to believe or hope about the world.

Conclusion

It should not surprise us that the legacies of these popular saints are mingled in general and scholarly discourse alike. This book is testimony to how many teachers and scholars see the life and thought of King and Bonhoeffer as helpfully informing one another. So it did not surprise me when, on the day I was finishing this article, a "Google alert" brought to my e-mail inbox notification that in celebration of the King holiday the California-based Common Ground Theatre would be presenting a play called "Awaiting Judgment" at Redlands University. According to a press release, the play

> depicts 20th Century theological giants, Martin Luther King, Jr. and Dietrich Bonhoeffer, in adjoining cells (at an undisclosed location and in

an out-of-sync time period) discussing their faith journeys and the challenges that they had encountered. The two examine one another's actions
and explore the decisions that led to their martyrdom. The exchange provides a prophetic, relevant and inspirational message that has resonated
with audiences around the country.[19]

It seems natural to bring the men together on stage, just as many teachers
bring them together in the classroom. But when does the mingling of kin-
dred spirits become entanglement? King is supposed to have said, "If your
enemy has a conscience, then follow Gandhi; but if your enemy does not have
a conscience, like Hitler, then follow Bonhoeffer." It "sounds like" King (and
Bonhoeffer—in fact, the statement appears in the Bonhoeffer movie *Agent of
Grace*). But no one has been able to document that King ever said these words
or to find their source in his writings. Thus, it appears that the statement has
been either misattributed or fabricated. Certainly nothing we know or believe
about either man hangs on the question of the statement's validity. But its
enduring popularity stands as a warning to scholars about the demands of
our scholarly work even, perhaps particularly, when our subjects inspire us as
much as these men do.

A similar fudging of the facts in the service of legend has become evident recently in descriptions of Bonhoeffer's death. Eberhard Bethge's official
biography of Bonhoeffer notes that he was hanged on April 9, 1945, on the
gallows at Flossenbürg concentration camp. But recently bloggers have begun
to embellish this story with the claim that Bonhoeffer "was hanged naked
by piano wire in particularly brutal fashion." Another adds that he was hung
"with piano wire from a meat hook."[20] I'm not sure when this gruesome detail
attached itself to the story of Bonhoeffer's demise, but it appears to have its
source in a conflation of his fate with that of other resisters, many of whom
were hanged from meathooks at Plötzensee Prison. It's a minor error, harmless
perhaps. But it indicates the way that legend can cling to history when we are
dealing with "saints."

Like the other authors in this book, I have immense respect for Dietrich
Bonhoeffer and Martin Luther King Jr., a respect that only grows with time.
I hope they are the first two people I meet in heaven; and if they are I will
stand in awe and in silence. But I believe that those of us who are dedicated
to remembering, respecting, and revering these men must recognize when
our pressing and often frustrated quest for heroes tempts us to preserve pris-
tine versions of their lives at the cost of acknowledging their flawed humanity. We do well to remember the words of Carl Wendell Hines, whose poem

"Now That He Is Safely Dead" is a tribute to Martin Luther King and a warning to us:

> Now that he is safely dead
> Let us praise him
> build monuments to his glory
> sing hosannas to his name.
> Dead men make
> such convenient heroes: They
> cannot rise
> to challenge the images
> we would fashion from their lives.
> And besides,
> it is easier to build monuments
> than to make a better world.[21]

CHAPTER 3

Bonhoeffer, King, and Feminism
— Problems and Possibilities —
Rachel Muers

Both Dietrich Bonhoeffer and Martin Luther King Jr. have embarrassed their successors and admirers in one major respect. These advocates and practitioners of costly Christian responsibility in the face of great social evil both appear to have been ignorant of, and hence in numerous ways complicit in, the evil of sexism. It has been found necessary, in assessing and appropriating their legacies, to pay attention to this fact. In this chapter I shall not rehearse the feminist "cases against" Bonhoeffer and King in detail; rather, I shall look more closely at how sexism can be linked to aspects of their thought that are not immediately concerned with gender relations. The aim is to see how the legacies of Bonhoeffer and King can be appropriated critically and fruitfully by feminist thinkers, without distorting or concealing the complexities of these legacies.

The Sexism of Heroes

When feminist critics look at Bonhoeffer, their attention tends to focus on his writings. Perhaps most notorious is the wedding sermon written from Tegel prison for Eberhard Bethge and Renate Schleicher, but there are examples elsewhere. In the wedding sermon, Bonhoeffer instructed the newlyweds thus: "You may order your home as you like, except in one thing: the wife is to be subject to her husband, and the husband is to love his wife. . . . The wife's honour is to serve the husband."[1] In the notes he made for his *Ethics*, he suggested that the Bible addresses the community of men (Ger.: *Män-ner*, "males"; Gk.: *adelphoi, uioi theou*, "brothers, sons of God"], and that "the equality of husband and wife [*Mann und Frau*] is modern and unbiblical . . . (1 Cor. 11:9)."[2]

By contrast, when we look at King, the obvious focus for feminist critique is less on his writings than on his practice—not only his much-discussed adultery, but his expectation that Coretta Scott King would fulfill the traditional role of a pastor's wife, and perhaps most importantly his failures to recognize and promote the leadership of women within the civil rights movement.[3] Bonhoeffer's practice could, in fact, be placed under similar scrutiny—in particular his expectations in regard to his own marriage (which, of course, never took place)[4]—although it is on record that he readily accepted the leadership roles women assumed in the early years of the Confessing Church.[5]

Looking at feminist criticism of either Bonhoeffer or King, it is easy to respond that the man in question was a "man of his time"—and then to face the uncomfortable fact that both Bonhoeffer and King are looked back on today as men who saw *beyond* their times and who for that very reason were able to have the influence they did.[6] Furthermore, it can be argued, most obviously in relation to King but plausibly in relation to Bonhoeffer, that sexism is incoherent with, or in tension with, some of their major theological insights. Feminist and womanist theologians have drawn on Bonhoeffer and King as sources for their constructive projects and for the practice of feminist criticism.

King adopted a personalist theology and philosophy that placed enormous emphasis on the incomparable worth of *each* human being by virtue of his or her relation to God, and a corresponding emphasis on the nonnegotiable call to love, justice, and respect within human relationships, as befits persons loved by God. Sexism, like any other form of discrimination, injustice, or denial of full human dignity, should have no place within this theological picture. Particularly in his speeches and writings in the early years of the civil rights struggle, King made frequent calls for the promise of America—the promise of freedom and equality—to be extended to all. At least some of the power of his appeals came from the universalizing dynamic of his theology and philosophy: what had been unjustly restricted to some must now be offered to all.

In this context, Rufus Burrow's claim that King would, had he lived longer, have "broadened his liberation project to include women's rights in the public sphere," becoming "a staunch advocate, and a recovering sexist," is understandable.[7] Surely King would eventually have seen and lived out the implications of his basic beliefs in human dignity and mutuality—so Burrow argues, and others such as Katie G. Cannon and Noel Erskine imply.[8] In any case, feminism or antisexism is a logical and unproblematic extension of his thought.

In fact, King has been a major and positive influence in womanist theology, and Cannon and other womanist thinkers who appropriate his work have generally not felt the need either to explain away his sexism or to conceal it. Here we must recall the work of Coretta Scott King herself, whose notable activism for women's rights (alongside numerous other concerns for social justice) arose from her commitment to maintain and develop Martin Luther King's legacy. King's thought does appear, in its subsequent effects, to have outrun his practice—even though, as I shall go on to suggest, this does not render redundant the more critical feminist reading of his life and work.

In my experience, when Bonhoeffer's attitude to gender relations is raised as an issue among Bonhoeffer scholars, comparable claims are often made: if he had survived the war, if he had had the chance to live longer and reflect in less extreme circumstances, he would have changed his views on relationships between the sexes. Here, however, the issue is more complex. Bonhoeffer, unlike King, did specifically articulate a belief in sexual *in*equality, at least within marriage. He believed it to be commanded by God as part of the right ordering of life within the world preserved after the fall.[9] Hierarchical relationships as such were not, for him, problematic—and were particularly unlikely to be so within the context of Nazi *Gleichschaltung*, the "leveling out" of all social distinctions in order to make everyone equally subordinate to the totalitarian state. Indeed, Bonhoeffer's paradigms for "responsible" (*stellvertretend*) relationships, which were for him the basic constituents of human life shaped by the responsible action of Christ, are all socially determined as asymmetrical (parent and child, teacher and pupil, "statesman" and member of the public).[10] Bonhoeffer accepts such asymmetries of power and responsibility within ordered relationships, not straightforwardly as "natural" and unavoidable, but certainly as divinely mandated. His own personalism—his profound emphasis on the "Who?" question as opposed to the objectifying and classifying "How?" question—did not as such imply a commitment to equality, although it did (as his later writings make particularly clear) imply love rather than contempt for the fellow human being in all circumstances.[11] In contrast to the universalizing dynamic of King's thought, Bonhoeffer's "personalism" tends to call for closer attention to the particular demands implied in one's relationship to a specific person. Perhaps ironically, this desire to recognize difference—and to resist the form of "equality" that totalitarianism demanded—made it easier for Bonhoeffer to accept or even celebrate relationships of subordination. This in turn makes it harder for a contemporary reader responsibly to claim that he would, in due course, have accepted feminist arguments.

In the end, however, it is of limited use to argue about whether Bonhoeffer or King, in different circumstances and given more time, would have taken on feminist ideas. Such claims, relying as they do on historical counterfactuals, are impossible to prove wrong. From a feminist critic's point of view, in any case, the attempt to excuse sexism by appeals to historical counterfactuals leaves much to be desired. When this happens, women are, retrospectively, being asked to wait—to wait until the important business of overthrowing Nazism or racial segregation has been completed, before their concerns can be taken seriously. One is tempted to follow King's lead and explain once again "Why We Can't Wait." King, in his essay of that name, uncovered the contradictions between American self-understanding and American political practice, and found in these contradictions the mandate for immediate social analysis and social action. For King, the gulf between promise—a society's own promise and explicit self-commitment—and lived reality prompted the call for immediate repentance and action. In the same way, feminists can reasonably examine and critique the contradictions between theology and practice in the lives of the thinkers they study, especially if this helps a wider feminist cause.

That said, instead of exonerating or condemning Dietrich Bonhoeffer and Martin Luther King Jr., I want now to consider what feminists can learn if we reflect on these men as Christian thinkers who were responding to great social evils and who were also sexist. Remembering their sexism can help us understand and develop key themes in their thought and also shape Christian social activism for their heirs.

What Is Community?

Both Bonhoeffer and King are known for the important role "community" played in their thought. For King, the eschatological promise of God to humanity, prefigured in the lives and actions of Christ's followers now, was existence in the "beloved community," the community in which the love of God for each is reflected in mutual love and service. Successive commentators on King's work have drawn attention to the deep roots of this vision in the life of the black church and in the African cultures that helped shape it. The beloved community is "not yet" while injustice and hatred exists; but there *are* forms of life, even now, that reflect aspects of its reality.[12]

In Bonhoeffer's work, the church is, famously, "Christ existing as community"; the church-community is where Christ is present in and to the world.[13]

Community is where love is made real—where it becomes something other than a distant ideal or a fine feeling. Life in community confronts the Christian believer with the objective and unassimilable reality of the "brother for whom Christ died," the other person who is called and loved by God. Community is also the place where the word of God is heard from another person, as a word I cannot speak to myself. These reflections on community arise from the church struggle and from the Nazi suppression of church activities—that is, from a context in which the historical life of church-communities was really at stake. Bonhoeffer's work in forming the Finkenwalde seminary, shaped by his deliberate study of numerous experiments in Christian community, was an attempt to bring about a real manifestation of church-community in a context of community breakdown.

So both Bonhoeffer and King are interested in the givenness of community and the particular practices that help to realize it in the midst of injustice and broken community. They do not idealize it, and in different ways their understandings of community are rooted in lived experiments—for Bonhoeffer in Finkenwalde and the Confessing Church, for King in the civil rights movement. It is this aspect of King's thought, in particular, that has attracted praise from womanist ethicists. Thus, Cannon describes how King's pragmatism is allied with his vision of human solidarity, and discusses the role of black women as members of the beloved community in particular situations of oppression.[14]

The very givenness of the communities with which Bonhoeffer and King sought to work, however, raises some questions for feminist readers. Their ways of thinking about and practicing community were responsive to what seemed to them, not without reason, to be the most pressing issues. As a result, for both of them women's work to sustain community, and the structuring of community such that certain forms of work (the home-maintainer, the pastor's wife) fell to women, could be—in effect—taken for granted. When the focus is on how the community relates to the world outside it, differences *within* the community are of (relatively) secondary concern. By contrast, differences within the community, in terms of how the community is experienced or how power within it is exercised, are of central concern to feminist thinkers.

For King, the urgent issue for much of his life was that of inclusion within community, the basic recognition of cohumanity. The denial of civil rights to black people forced him to ask: Who is affirmed as a human being? Who is allowed to be part of the networks of solidarity by which we claim that human life is constituted? Who, for example, is allowed to count as "American"? The further question then arises—which King did not ask specifically, although many of his successors have asked it—about the structuring of relationships within any given community (America, or the black church, or the global human community). The beloved community is not only inclusive in regard to its membership, but just and loving in regard to its internal structures.

Bonhoeffer is, as I have suggested, interested in asymmetrical relationships of responsibility and power—particularly in his later work where the focus of his attention is more on the renewal of a wider social order. By contrast, in his best-known community-focused work, *Life Together*, the particular characteristics and social location of the "brother"—that which might give rise to asymmetrical relationships or the possibility of domination—are played down in favor of the brother's objective givenness, as the individual in and through whom I encounter Christ. On the face of it, this sounds as if it should be promising from a feminist point of view. If the foundation of the community is the encounter with the particular other, mediated by Christ and not merely by a set of preconceived ideas about "proper" social relations, the Christian community might be able to become a space of social transformation, in gender relations as in other areas. But Bonhoeffer himself was, we must recognize, not going to realize this possibility. He saw a given set of relationships of subordination not as impediments to Christian community but as part of the reality of the world within which the Christian community has to operate. His thought about community requires further development and a more extended contextual analysis and critique in order to make good on its transformative, as well as its conservative, possibilities.

An instance of how Bonhoeffer's thought can be extended through reflection on relationships to the particular (not the generalized) "other" can be found in recent work on his *Ethics*. Feminist thinkers have drawn attention to the problematic aspects of Bonhoeffer's emphasis on existence "for others" as the form of life conformed to Christ's own life—developed particularly in his discussions, in the *Ethics*, of *Stellvertretung*, vicarious representative responsibility. As Lisa Dahill points out, existing *too much* for and through others can be, particularly for women, the form not of redeemed life but of entrapment in sin. If we look at actually-existing relationships of power—including the abuse of power—we cannot accept some of Bonhoeffer's general claims about the form of an *individual's* existence conformed to Christ. We may, however, be able to use his work as the starting point for thinking about how the *community* conformed to Christ can move beyond the abuse of power.[15]

For both King and Bonhoeffer, then, *church*-community is particularly important for revealing the nature of human community as such; church-community is the place in which beloved community and the presence of

Christ is practiced. Any given church-community is, however, among other things, a place of gendered power relations. One asymmetrical relationship, in particular, may be significant in thinking through the attitudes and practice of King and Bonhoeffer within the movements of resistance to which they contributed—namely, the relationship between the preacher or pastor on the one hand, and the member of a congregation on the other.

View from the Pulpit—or View from Below?

Both Bonhoeffer and King were preachers and pastors. More than this, both were preachers and pastors who had a high view of these roles. King says in his early letter to the elders of his church in Montgomery, "Leadership never ascends from the pew to the pulpit, but . . . descends from the pulpit to the pew."[16] For Bonhoeffer, a clear hierarchy is enacted in the central event of worship, the sermon: "Above there is the office of proclamation and below there is the listening congregation."[17] The metaphorical extension, by both men, of the significance of the pulpit's height is striking. Preaching and pastoral responsibility, within the traditions in which both of these men were deeply steeped, involved a hierarchical relationship that appears to have had for them a certain unquestionable rightness. Both, in different ways, did seek to explain and qualify this hierarchical relationship. With the example of Hitler's appeal to the *Führerprinzip* (the idea of a single charismatic leader) before his eyes, Bonhoeffer was anxious at every stage to relate the preacher's authority to his divinely appointed *office*, never to his personal qualities or charisma—and hence to place strict limits on the proper range of that authority. He noted, for example, the danger of an "arrogant clerical presumption to instruct the masses."[18] Nonetheless, he did extend the preacher's position "above" the congregation beyond the act of preaching, into (for example) the practice of pastoral care.[19]

As Richard Lischer writes, King was clear in his understanding of the role of the preacher in a black church, a role from which political and community leadership, as well as religious leadership, naturally followed. "Like the ministers of no other tradition, the African-American preacher harnessed political necessities to religious power."[20] King's role as a pastor—and hence incidentally also, Lischer observes, as someone who was not dependent in any way on a white employer—was key to his role as a leader in the civil rights movement, in terms both of his self-perception and of the way he was perceived by others. As a preacher he understood himself as personally called to lead in the struggles of the black community, and as a preacher he was likely to be looked to as a leader.

It need hardly be said that both Bonhoeffer and King worked in contexts in which the office of preacher was largely restricted to men. In Bonhoeffer's time, this was increasingly a live issue, given the growing role of the *Theologinnen* (theologically trained women) within the German evangelical church.[21] Within the black church, as recent studies have shown, despite a long history of black women's preaching, the pulpit has often been understood as a male preserve.[22] Bonhoeffer's and King's assumptions and explicit claims about the centrality of preaching, and about the hierarchical subordination of congregation to preacher, are clearly gendered. It is not that either would have prevented women from preaching—but both had a model of leadership that gave priority to an activity that in their context was seen as "man's work."

Furthermore, as Aprele Elliott has explored in relation to King, the model of church authority focused on the preacher and the office of preaching will tend to produce an individualized model of leadership and authority both within churches and within other social and political groupings. Elliott discusses, by way of contrast, the "group-based" paradigm of authority represented and practiced by such civil rights leaders as Ella Baker—a pattern of participatory democracy in which adult education is key, the involvement of all in decision making is a significant goal at all levels, and hierarchy is kept to a minimum.[23] This *modus operandi* was important and influential within the civil rights movement and was particularly furthered and advocated by women activists—but it is one that ran in many ways counter to King's instincts about how leadership functions, instincts shaped by his particular ecclesial context and position.

Some interesting comparisons could be made with the role of women in resistance to Nazism, and in particular within the Confessing Church. As Theodore Thomas discusses, theologically trained women debarred from official pastorates adopted increasing levels of responsibility within both the pro-Nazi *Reichskirche* and the anti-Nazi Confessing Church. Within the Confessing Church, they were especially important in developing congregational Bible study groups. It would be pushing it too far—and questionable on many feminist grounds—to see in their work, or for that matter the work of Ella Baker and others, a distinctively "female" mode of leadership and social activism. Nonetheless, attention to women's leadership alongside that of Bonhoeffer and King forces us to recognize the tendency to focus on the power of the pulpit and to ignore the movements for change that arise from the pew. Both Bonhoeffer and King were profoundly inspirational leaders and thinkers; but we should not assume that their thoughts, their words, or even their exemplary actions were effective without the active participation of those who heard them, organized for them, and provided the social and ecclesial contexts within which they could work.[24]

When we think about appropriating the legacies of Bonhoeffer and King from a feminist perspective, then, wider questions are raised about the implicit ecclesiologies with which we work when we study Christian movements for social change. Do we tend to assume that the church is primarily formed "downwards" from the pulpit, and does this mean that the work, including the theological work, of women is disproportionately forgotten or sidelined? If so, we tend to reproduce the sexist assumptions that colored Bonhoeffer's and King's work. It is, unquestionably, much easier to study the legacies of pastors, preachers, and academic theologians—through their writings and their recorded sermons—than it is to study the "legacies" of the people who heard them preach. However, if we do not at least acknowledge the latter, we risk reinforcing the assumption that these hearers (of whom many are female) are the passive recipients of theologies and political standpoints from the preachers (of whom most are male). In Bonhoeffer's words, there is a need even in ecclesiological contexts to recognize the "view from below."[25] Both King and Bonhoeffer worked within communities and churches that had been forced to take the "view from below"—but both men, as an essential part of their vocation, were also positioned "above" their communities as preachers and political decision makers. Perhaps the challenge for a feminist appropriation of their legacies is further research into the lives and theologies of the people who were "below" them—not in importance (both Bonhoeffer and King would have hastened to add) but in terms of ecclesial and communal authority.

Looking beyond the Heroes

What are the wider theological and political implications of this discussion? Questions about the implicit dimensions of ecclesiology lead naturally to questions about pneumatology. Theologically, feminist readers of both Bonhoeffer and King need to ask whether a focus on the single (male) hero-figure may rely on, or reinforce, assumptions about a God whose power only "descends" through recognizable and hierarchically structured channels. What can be said about the transformative work of God in the groups and movements that prepare for, hear, and enact the word of God? A theological appropriation of Bonhoeffer and King would consider how the same Spirit that forms the "beloved community," the church that is "Christ existing as community," also transforms that community internally—with the same unpredictability, the same manifestation of divine love for every person, and the same passion to overcome injustice. There are hints of this in Bonhoeffer's accounts of trans-formative communal practice in *Life Together*, for example in his discussion of confession of sin, shared work, and worship.

Important lessons can be learned here for the study of figures such as Bon-hoeffer and King. A feminist theologian cannot really look at the ideas of great thinkers and ignore their lived realities—that would be to collude in a dualism of mind and body that is itself deeply gendered. Feminist thought needs to look not only at *what* is said but *how* it is said, by whom and to what effect. But nor, I have suggested, is it particularly fruitful simply to pick out what was wrong with how Bonhoeffer and King lived as individuals. This would focus attention inappropriately on the character of the single "hero" or "vil-lain" viewed in isolation from his context, and would detract from the analysis of sexism itself as a social and political problem—as structural sin. Rather, in studying Bonhoeffer and King as inspirers and proclaimers of transformative social practices, feminist thought should attend closely to the complex and conflictual relationships between their proclamation and the lived realities of the communities to and from which they speak. Feminist thinkers are particu-larly well placed to adopt a "view from below"—from below the pedestal and below the pulpit, from outside unthematized male privilege—and to question any explicit or implicit claim that authority and power for change comes only from "above."

CHAPTER 4

Political Order, Political Violence, and Ethical Limits

Jean Bethke Elshtain

A t first blush, Dietrich Bonhoeffer and Martin Luther King seem compatriots: each confronted a deformation of political power and each called the system he confronted "evil." Indeed, Bonhoeffer's language was even stronger, the Nazi Führer was the anti-Christ; each paid dearly for his involvement in resistance. Theologically, culturally, and sociologically, however, Bonhoeffer and King differ strikingly. Do the differences drive these two exemplary figures apart or link them at deeper levels of theological engagement? I explore the question via direct comparison of the two along a number of vectors.

I begin with a consideration of the sort of thinker each was. How do we characterize them within the frameworks of their respective times and cultures without forcing an analysis that favors by its definition the stance of one over the other? The categories of *vita contemplativa* and *vita activa* help us to take our interpretive bearings. As students of the history of philosophy well know, the conundrum of thought as a higher good than action or action trumping thought haunted the Greeks. What was the better life? What aimed at a higher good and loftier truths? This answer varies, of course, depending on the thinker and tradition of thought. Thinkers since the Greeks have worked these categories; one might note Hannah Arendt's discussion of the *vita contemplativa* and *vita activa* in her monumental work, *The Human Condition*.[1] For Arendt, the *vita activa* names the life of the citizen, a life lived before others within a shared public realm. The life of the philosophers is solitary, contemplative, as the Latin terms suggest. The philosopher's primary relationship is to the Truth writ large.

This no doubt oversimplifies Arendt's position, but my point for now is this: were I to sketch the trajectories of Bonhoeffer's and King's lives, Bonhoeffer would come nearer the contemplative side and King, without doubt, the active side. Bonhoeffer was in many ways a theologian's theologian. His work is complex, dense, difficult, and challenging as he situates Christian theology within the context of different strands of theological and philosophical interpretation and as he works through critical assaults on Christianity associated with the work of Nietzsche.

Bonhoeffer tells us that he was a theologian before he became, truly, a Christian. One understands what he is talking about. It is easy enough to see why a brilliant, dedicated, ambitious young man would be drawn like a moth to the flame by theological disputation of the highest order. Coming out of the high Germanic tradition of dedicated learning and lives, Bonhoeffer was, by all accounts, a demanding and impressive student, scholar, and teacher.[2] His precocious entry into the "guild" made him a force to be reckoned with at a very young age. Had he lived in quieter times, it is easy enough to imagine him living out that life in the world of scholarship, mentoring generations of students, attending international conferences, making his mark.

That, of course, was not to be. The horror of the First World War, during which the Bonhoeffer family suffered the first of what would be a string of devastating losses of children with the death of their son and brother Walter on the Western front, and the catastrophic aftermath as Germany suffered through crippling and humiliating reparations, challenged any and all who hoped to be scholars first and foremost while letting others tend to things of public life. Bonhoeffer could not help but be touched by such events. In the interwar years, he became active in ecumenism, searching for interlocutors outside his own milieu. He journeyed to America to study at Union Theological Seminary where, through a black friend, he encountered the African American Christian experience (and music) for the first time. What had begun for Bonhoeffer as a point of theoretical demarcation—his laying out of an account of human nature that stressed what Clifford Green, in his brilliant study, calls "a theology of sociality"—bore fruit in Bonhoeffer's own life.[3] His openness to others and his keen desire to learn and to understand that which was not within his immediate ken is in striking evidence from his experiences in Harlem to his exploration of the possibility of spending time with Gandhi.

From this point on, Bonhoeffer's *vita contemplativa* was intermingled with his *vita activa*, his appearing before others in a public capacity. In other words, his commitments during the Church Struggle and his ever-more sharp confrontations with the National Socialist regime grew directly from the fruits of his contemplative labors even as, in turn, his experiences in that struggle, in the seminary at Finkenwalde, and, finally, in the conspiracy to assassinate Hitler, all had profound consequences for his theology, for those moments that remained to him for contemplation.

The trajectory of Martin Luther King's life is quite different in many respects, just as the church traditions that created (so to speak) these two extraordinary figures are quite far apart. Black Christian churches in America, especially in the South, were sites of both enthusiasm and freedom: here African Americans could gather, could bring to bear an oral biblicism in a community that helped them to live in trying circumstances, to hope for an end to their troubles, and to seek a kingdom of justice on this earth. The enthusiasm of black preaching and singing and the entire responsorial tradition were utterly alien to Bonhoeffer's experience in high German Lutheranism. For German Lutherans, too much enthusiasm is a suspect thing!

Coming out of the southern black Baptist church, with "Daddy" King, his intrepid father, as his mentor, King, an unusually thoughtful and intelligent young man, sought to expand beyond his immediate milieu by journeying "north" to college. His studies at Boston University acquainted him with many important figures, including Reinhold Niebuhr, and later he found a way to weave this learning into his immediate concerns for direct action to end the pernicious rule of Jim Crow in the *de jure* segregated South. King's concerns were always tinged with political ramifications of a sort that took him away from systematic theology and into a world in which thought serves as a goad to action in the world. Here the influence of Niebuhr shows.

One senses a certain impatience in King with the often impossibly difficult and "inward" nature of deep theological disputation. (Inward in the sense that systematic theology involves many hours of intellectual struggle. One is not "alone" as in isolated, for one's theology is always situated within, and for, a community of belief.) For Bonhoeffer, theological explorations aimed at the truth, the truth of Christ as the man for others. How this truth could be "operationalized," if one may put it so simply, was never an easy matter. King was of a more pragmatic nature and he consciously called upon the tradition of American pragmatism. The proof was in the pudding, so to speak, was carved out in action: What happened to these truths if you put them to the test? Bonhoeffer, by contrast, rarely looked for a direct one-to-one correlation between a theological argument and a public activity or course of action. The Sermon on the Mount, for Bonhoeffer, is not a political program as such.

Nor would one call King an original theologian in the way that Bonhoeffer surely was. This is not to suggest that King made no theoretical or conceptual advances. It is to suggest that the intensity of hours spent alone in a study, grappling with complex texts, trying out difficult and intricate ideas with a theologian friend (here Bonhoeffer with Eberhard Bethge) was not the world for King. A rather impatient man who described himself as a "troubled soul," King drew from the tradition of pragmatism the conclusion that the test of an idea lies in experience. He was inclined that direction anyway and he found justification, if you will, in certain modalities of thought.

One of King's contributions had to do with forms of action, namely, his repudiation of the apotheosis of violence found in such thinkers as Frantz Fanon and his homegrown American aficionados in the Black Power movement. As a consequence of the direction his political life took him, King also offered up a potent challenge to the idea that politics is reducible to self-interest, an idea regnant from the 1950s in American political science. Instead, as Richard H. King points out, Martin Luther King touched all the "registers of freedom."[4] Rejecting reductionistic and violent accounts of politics, King embraced and practiced "keeping the faith" as a way of being in the world. Freedom, then, involves a new sense of self, but this self does not stand apart from a community. There is a therapeutic dimension to this struggle. Recall, if you will, King's last speech in Memphis: "And I've seen the promised land. I may not get there with you. But I want you to know tonight, that we, as a people will get to the promised land."[5] For King, we are not alone. We can be healed only if we are together as a people.

For Martin Luther King, political participation was a good, a way to appear in public before others and with others, a pathway toward self-respect for African Americans as they enacted projects consistent with their God-given moral equality. As Richard King observes, public action became a way to confirm one's new sense of self-worth within the civil rights struggle. And freedom is not just "freedom from" a previously unjust status but freedom "for" creating a new self within a transformed participatory community.[6]

King is defined by his activism. His public role absorbed him. He is unthinkable—indeed, we would not know him at all—absent his political role. His public life absorbed nearly all of him and the consequences for his private life were often disturbing and saddening. By contrast, it is far easier to imagine Bonhoeffer living another kind of life, that of Herr Doktor Professor, had he lived in another time and place. Bonhoeffer was so defined by, and absorbed within, family—and the Bonhoeffer family was distinguished, strong, and extraordinary—that familial and collegial relations taken together would have added up to a rich life.

King defined himself through his public struggle for freedom. He held that human essence is freedom, and one must fight and fight unceasingly to realize the fullness of that freedom, a freedom authentically realizable only when one accepts the moral equality of all persons, including one's foes. Richard King argues that Martin Luther King's choice of nonviolent direct action is both a philosophy and a tactic, a brilliant, creative response to a specific historical double bind. King grounds this philosophy of nonviolence theologically—it derives from traces of God's presence in history. It follows that whatever original contribution King made is so tied to his public ministry that you could not disentangle the ideas from the action if you tried. Absent that public ministry, we would not read King—or few would. It is the extraordinary intertwining of action and ideas we seek, and find, in King.

King's "theological justification," if it may be called that, for his public activities resides in the claim that God's natural and moral laws run through creation. Only a corporate experience of deliverance—of ascent from the depths of unfreedom—could give birth to authentic freedom.[7] In his political action, King had a course open to him that was denied Bonhoeffer, namely, he could call America back to her founding principles. Bonhoeffer, by contrast, had to set himself in opposition to the Germany of his time in toto. Asking the National Socialists to live up to their principles was the problem: that is precisely what they were doing. For Bonhoeffer those ideas were in direct opposition to the truths of the Christian-inspired culture of Germany; hence, he was a patriot who upheld those truths. King insisted that Americans, however, were denying their fundamental principles when they embraced the practices of the Jim Crow South. King's movement is not away from American principles but, instead, directed toward their full realization. That is why we find King speaking so frequently in this way:

> We are here this evening for serious business. We are here in a general sense because first and foremost we are American citizens and we are determined to apply that citizenship to the fullness of its meaning. We are here also because of our love for democracy, because of our deep-seated belief that democracy transformed from thin paper to thick action is the greatest form of government on earth.[8]

King speaks repeatedly of "the glory of America, with all of its faults. . . . If we were incarcerated behind the iron curtains of a Communistic nation we couldn't do this. If we were dropped in the dungeon of a totalitarian regime we couldn't do this. But the great glory of American democracy is the right to protest for right."[9] King called for a worldwide fellowship, for a love of all humanity as a necessity, and so on. He often posed the alternatives harshly: "We still have a choice today: nonviolent coexistence or violent coannihilation."[10] This is not the way Bonhoeffer wrote or thought, for King's words are those of the committed activist hoping to bring others into the fold. Bonhoeffer committed himself to activism in a far darker and more desperate situation where the focus was not so much on worthy and good possibilities but on stopping the damage, halting the bleeding, blocking mass death. And all of this was done clandestinely because large-scale open political revolt was impossible.

What about Bonhoeffer's dialectic of thought and action? I have already noted that he was a theologian of depth and audacity, working through challenges to Christian belief found in both Nietzsche and Heidegger, for example. The reference to Nietzsche I found in King is one of straightforward condemnation, a stance that is surely intelligible and defensible. But for Bonhoeffer, as a systematic theologian, Christianity had to take account of the challenge Nietzsche and others represented: Were any of them decisive?[11] Bonhoeffer took leave of "religion" in an older, foundationalist sense in favor of God's revelation grounded in a theology of the cross, although this does not fully capture the complexity of what he is up to.

You cannot understand Bonhoeffer and his contributions to thought absent consideration of his anthropology—a point Clifford Green makes persuasively. The heart of the matter lies in Bonhoeffer's understanding of who we are as creatures; of what we can reasonably expect from ourselves and others; and what power as domination does to violate our interpersonal relations, to undermine and destroy that which is most central to us, our sociality. It is love that liberates us from dominating and exploitative power, not in order to place us in a world utterly beyond power—in some sort of utopia—but in order to locate us in a world in which power as a form of integral human strength takes precedence over the shattering effects of dominating power. Green argues that by "thinking in social rather than epistemological categories, he is able to present a dialectical integration of act and being in the interpretation of revelation."[12] Here is ground on which Bonhoeffer and King share terrain: the ground of mutuality of love and service.

What is striking by way of contrast is the manner in which Bonhoeffer systematically takes up barriers to action, a feature of his resolute anti-utopianism. For him the Nazis were nothing if not utopians who proposed to remake the human race from the genetic ground up and to build a "thousand-year Reich."

He, therefore, contributes to a systematic exploration of politics and limits in a way King does not. Bonhoeffer also concentrates on human finitude and the problem of contempt for persons, which culminates in nihilism; here, again, the theme of limits is cast. On this particular point, I think some shared ground between the two can be found. Certainly on Bonhoeffer's insistence that the problem of truth and telling the truth must take account of human frailty and of the delicate skeins of human relationality, one can relate Bonhoeffer and King, for each emphasizes our sociality, the fact that we are never "selves" standing alone in isolation but only selves in relation and through dialogue.

It is unsurprising that Bonhoeffer confronts Western nihilism, a force he finds unleashed with the horrors of the French Revolution and its "just terror." Modern nationalism arose out of the French Revolution based on the principle of the absolute sovereign will of the people. The upshot was a version of "the liberation of man as an absolute ideal [that] leads only to man's self destruction. At the end of the path which was first trodden in the French Revolution there is nihilism."[13] What is now brought into stark relief is "Western nihilism" of which "the deification of man" is the sign.[14] Hence, Bonhoeffer's criticism of the revolutionary who sees himself justified in his own idea. The architects of the French Revolution and revolutionaries ever since in the West embraced a radical view of human self-sovereignty and self-creation; disdained the God of creation who reminds human beings of their dependence and creatureliness; and embarked on a course of destruction as a perverse mimesis of God's generativity under the presumption that the categories of good and evil no longer applied. Here, too, Bonhoeffer and King link arms for neither believed one could abandon moral deliberation on good and evil. To do such is to abandon a Christian cosmology, to desert Augustinian theology, and to encourage and sustain human hubris.

Freedom

What about freedom, King's central category, the area within which his most important contribution to political thought and practice lies? For Bonhoeffer human freedom is necessarily limited. Freedom as an absolute is perverted and transforms into self-involved willfulness that recognizes no limit.[15] Acts of freedom, undertaken from faith and in love, are acts that recognize a limit. But what is that limit? What is the horizon within which human freedom is realized? The tendency in modernity is for that boundary to be set by collectivities like states as human beings are sacrificed to ends determined by others or, alternatively, to be defined by the putatively sovereign self as I transform my choices into absolutes.[16] In this way, human beings transmogrify into destroyers and misuse freedom. This is tragic, as freedom is a constitutive part of our natures—a claim King would heartily agree to—but it must be freedom that recognizes a limit; that is always situated and concrete; and that necessarily puts us in a world with others.

Analyzing where Bonhoeffer finds resources to articulate limits to freedom is beyond my ken at this point, but it is worth noting that in order to do so, he resurrects nature and "the natural" as central themes for Protestant ethics. Because King's notions of law, including natural law, are so heavily indebted to St. Thomas Aquinas, one might be able to draw parallels between Bonhoeffer's nature and King's natural law. But King does not explore the issue of natural law in any detail—he assumes such exists—and Bonhoeffer's explorations of "the natural" are truncated given the dire circumstances under which he penned *Ethics*, which was left unfinished at his death.[17] Suffice to say that, were Bonhoeffer and King still living, each would be a powerful critic of the distorted notions of human freedom being enacted among us today—understandings of freedom that breach all barriers of shame, that negate the notion of a private world not fully absorbed within some public project, that posit our choices as either abjection or self-sovereignty.

Here we bump up against a potentially interesting line of inquiry, namely, Bonhoeffer and King on what we owe our countries: Do we have a moral obligation to our particular nations, to a life lived as members of a community and of a polity? Both men were patriots who loved their respective countries. King makes no bones about it in sermon after sermon, speech after speech. America must live up to her ideals. Our country must rise above cruelty and pettiness. Indeed, King's vision was of a country as a "beloved community." This is not the way Bonhoeffer would describe a polity and its authoritative tasks. Yes, Bonhoeffer was a patriot but he located his patriotism in relation to the "Christian people of Germany," those who remained Christian, who had not fallen in with the *Deutsche Christen* and perverted their faith in order to earn the good opinion of the Nazi leadership. Germany at her best is the Germany he sought. And that German state, given its central restraining role—stopping the worst things from happening—made possible other forms of human action and realization. For Bonhoeffer, Luther's doctrine of the two kingdoms became distorted in part through a notion that implied the "emancipation and sanctification of the world . . . as Government, reason, economics and culture arrogate to themselves a right of autonomy, but do not in any way understand this autonomy as bringing them into opposition to Christianity."[18] This helped to pave the way for the triumph of a cult of reason and, with it, came an idolatrous faith in progress.

What, then, was the state's legitimate authority and role? The concept of deputyship, presupposing the mandates of church, culture, marriage and family, and government is central to Bonhoeffer's concerns. For example: parents act on behalf of children. What they can and should do is enacted within appropriate boundaries. Responsible action flowing from legitimate authority is always thus limited. How do we determine what can rightfully be exercised by a deputy in the political realm? Bonhoeffer begins by reminding us that the concept of the state "is foreign to the New Testament. It has its origin in pagan antiquity. Its place is taken in the New Testament by the concept of government ('power'). The term 'state' means an ordered community; government is the power which creates and maintains order. . . . Government is deputyship for God on earth."[19] Legitimate government originates in the very nature of human beings and, because our natures are limited, so must be the state. The state can never be its own ground of being. The state does not bring a people into being. It does not complete and fulfill our natures.

An ethical failure on the part of government does not automatically deprive it of its divine mandate. Government's tasks are legitimate, limited, some might say "austere" in Bonhoeffer's characterization. We owe obedience, under normal circumstances. But we do not owe government our very selves. It does not create us. It may curb, compel, and chastise us. Indeed, the individual's "duty of obedience is binding . . . until government directly compels him to offend against the divine commandment, that is to say, until government openly denies its divine commission and thereby forfeits its claims. In cases of doubt obedience is required. . . . But if government violates or exceeds its commission at any point, for example by making itself master over the belief of the congregation, then at this point, indeed, obedience is to be refused, for conscience's sake, for the Lord's sake."[20]

We must not, however, generalize from this dire circumstance to articulate a strong claim or duty to disobey. Disobedience, Bonhoeffer tells us, is always concrete and particular—in this singular case. "Generalizations lead to an apocalyptic diabolization of government. Even an anti-Christian government is still in a certain sense government. . . . An apocalyptic view of a particular concrete government would necessarily have total disobedience as its consequence; for in that case every single act of obedience obviously involves denial of Christ."[21]

King might argue that Bonhoeffer's determination to work the "in between"—in this instance in between state idolatry and state diabolization—makes it difficult for him to see positive possibilities. But again, in context, one can see what Bonhoeffer is trying to do. This government now must be disobeyed; still, one must not draw an abstract, general conclusion from disobedience. That explains why he refused to write up a kind of tick-list for the moment when disobedience kicks in. He did not write about civil disobedience. He did not develop a theory or account of it—this by contrast to King who derives his understanding very much from the thoughts and deeds of Mahatma Gandhi, a figure who intrigued Bonhoeffer and with whom Bonhoeffer would have, perhaps, spent time had events not overtaken him.

While much more could be explored, this must be remembered: neither Bonhoeffer nor King could ever have made his peace with any regime that promoted rabid nationalism with all its bitter fruits; that eclipsed the space for the free exercise of human responsibility; that served the ends of cynicism, collusion in evil deeds, human isolation, human desolation and terror by contrast to trust, solidarity, and responsible freedom; finally, that worshiped History and Power, for such a regime repudiates the Sovereign God who holds the nations under judgment.

The lives and thoughts of these luminary figures put into relief the complexity of human action and the issue of ethics *in extremis*, an ethics, Bonhoeffer insisted, that did not pertain in all its particulars under ordinary circumstances. Nazi terror was not an ordinary circumstance. And, for King, de jure segregation that had come to seem ordinary was, in fact, an extraordinary and evil system that called for an ethic *in extremis* that resisted the seduction of systematic violence. Bonhoeffer signed on with a conspiracy that aimed to assassinate one man, for none saw an alternative way to slow down or halt the "anti-Christ" and the diabolical regime that was Nazism. Bonhoeffer never wrote out a justification for the "just assassin." He knew he was caught in the besmirching, the "dirtying of hands," that comes with responsible action in the world. At times, by contrast, King seems to locate civil rights disobedients outside a system or situation in which they are inevitably going to engage in an intentional calling forth or calling up of violence—forcing a confrontation that has every probability of turning violent.

For this reason, Reinhold Niebuhr argued that the Gandhian method and system of *satyagraha* was a form of moral coercion. There are times King seems to recognize this and other times when he seems not to, when protestors are represented as virtuous by comparison to the malign enforcers of segregation. This, too, would be another line of inquiry to launch: one can never, in Bonhoeffer's terms, avoid the contamination that comes from action in the world. Seeking moral purity, so many Christians flee into "private virtuousness" and presume they are not, thereby, responsible for the unfolding of events. This final claim would unite Bonhoeffer and King.

Part Two

Shared Humanity

CHAPTER 5
Life Worthy of Life
— The Social Ecologies of Bonhoeffer and King —
Larry L. Rasmussen

M
artin Luther King Jr. and Dietrich Bonhoeffer are, at heart, theologians of sociality and solidarity. Each is a communitarian in which the well-being of the other, including the enemy, is placed in the same moral framework as one's own. This relationship of self and other is a relationship of equal regard, nicely captured by Josiah Young as "no difference in the fare."[1] It is also profoundly ecological in a social sense, perfectly captured by King in his conviction that "injustice anywhere is a threat to justice everywhere."[2] The next sentences from "Letter from Birmingham City Jail" are these: "We are caught in an inescapable network of mutuality, tied in a single garment of destiny. Whatever affects one directly affects all indirectly."[3]

Bonhoeffer says much the same in *Life Together*. The subject is specifically Christian community, not all society and all humanity. But since for Bonhoeffer the reality of the world and the reality of God participate ontologically in one another and both have their center in Jesus Christ as the collective person, this description of Christian community pertains more broadly. He writes,

> In a Christian community, everything depends on whether each individual is an indispensable link in a chain. The chain is unbreakable only when even the smallest link holds tightly with the others. . . . Every Christian community must know that not only do the weak need the strong,

but also that the strong cannot exist without the weak. The elimination
of the weak is the death of the community.[4]

"The elimination of the weak is the death of the community" is not a
general truth only but specific and contextual. In Nazi Germany, the remaining Jews have been rendered "weak" as Bonhoeffer is writing. They have been
disenfranchised of rights held under the Weimar constitution, much of their
property has been confiscated, their businesses boycotted, and their persons
maligned. "The weak" also refers to an additional class of persons who have
been labeled *lebensunwertes Leben*—"life unworthy of life." Persons with
genetic and other disabilities were subjected to race-based medical experiments of all kinds. Some were euthanized. For Bonhoeffer, just as the chain
would have been *un*breakable had solidarity with them been maintained, so
also their deaths and the breaking of the chain constitute the fracture and
death of the whole community. It is his version of King's "injustice anywhere
is a threat to justice everywhere" and "any man's death diminishes me."[5]

This communitarian theology is also an utterly this-worldly Protestant
faith that yields motive and energy for faith-based national transformation
together with ecumenical peace and international justice. One of the forms of
this faith is nonviolent resistance, and one of its ends is the firm establishment
of rights for the sake of present justice, a different social and political order,
and the well-being of future generations.

This, then, is the thread of these pages, a thread that belongs to the warp
and woof of their relational theologies and a thread that weaves the fabric of
rights and resistance.

If a theology of relationality, rights, and resistance strikes us as passé on
this side of black, womanist, feminist, and other liberation theologies and the
institutionalization of civil and human rights, then we need to recollect this
history from the front end rather than in the rearview mirror. We ought to
view it as though we were joining it, with the outcome uncertain. From that
perspective, which is Bonhoeffer's and King's, it might look like this. King's
communalism, while in line with one of the languages of U.S. culture, namely,
biblical and republican communitarianism, runs counter to the dominant language of American capitalistic and therapeutic individualism, or what *Habits
of the Heart*, by Robert Bellah and his colleagues, called "Sheilaism" after the
person who decided that, in the end, her religion was herself and her life, and
she was Sheila.[6] The black churches that nurtured King and the prophetic
social gospel ministry were both countercultural and minority traditions in
this nation and its churches. As we discovered anew in the flap around the

Rev. Jeremiah Wright and Trinity United Church of Christ, there still is little understanding of the communitarian prophetic social gospel ministry of racial-ethnic minority communities.

Bonhoeffer's case is different, yet oddly parallel. Unlike most of his fellow church members, Bonhoeffer knows at the very outset of Hitler's accession to power that the churches' form and spirituality are not up to the challenge of the new Nazi Germany and must be radically different. The church must be formed anew in a disciplined life together via a new monasticism initially strange to mainline German Protestants, even if this life together is Scripture based, Christ centered, and confessional in a classic Protestant way. Despite these Protestant marks and Reformation roots, this community of dissent was a path alien to a church accustomed to privilege and well settled into its roles as court chaplain, keeper of bourgeois culture, and agent of social cohesion. Bonhoeffer's communalism was not counter to a dominant culture of economic and solipsistic individualism, as was King's. Germans had a strong sense of corporate identity that nurtured a strong sense of sacrifice for *das Volk*. Bonhoeffer's communalism was counter to a Christianity that gave no offense. The following is from 1934:

> Christianity stands or falls with its revolutionary protest against violence, arbitrariness and pride of power and with its apologia for the weak.—I feel that Christianity is rather doing too little in showing these points than doing too much. Christianity has adjusted itself much too easily to the worship of power. It should give more offence, more shock to the world, than it is doing. Christianity should [. . .] take a much more definite stand for the weak than to consider the potential moral right of the strong."[7]

In neither King's case nor Bonhoeffer's, then, is "that's passé" a historically informed response to their theologies of sociality and solidarity. Nor is it an informed response to the resistance and the struggle for rights that issue from their ecological sense of society. So accustomed are we to the strides in human rights since World War II that we may be startled to learn that Bonhoeffer was about the first Protestant theologian even to broach the theme, much less put it somewhere near the center of his own resistance and his work on rights inhering in bodiliness itself. (More on this soon.) King, of course, personifies the struggle for civil rights. And while that struggle has deep roots in the black churches' centennial struggles for dignity and equality, King, the Southern Christian Leadership Conference (SCLC), and other civil rights organizations took this to the streets and the courts on a scale not seen before. Resistance as a mass-based, nonviolent civic initiative of the churches is a post-King phe-nomenon. Of course, there are antecedents—think of labor history and the suffragette movement. But a threshold in the history of rights and resistance was crossed by King and his lieutenants, following Rosa Parks's initiative and with the adoption of Gandhian methods of citizen-based nonviolence. It was certainly a threshold for citizens in this nation, and it led to the passage of the Civil Rights Act and the Voting Rights Act, without which we would not have elected our first African American president. Citizen-based mass resistance was a threshold crossed in other nations as well, thanks to King. Even in his own abbreviated lifetime, he belonged to the *world* as the effective cham-pion of an international movement for justice, as the 1964 Nobel Peace Prize acknowledged.

In short, if we now assume Christian communitarianism with real back-bone is *good* theology and polity, if we assume the establishment of civil and human rights is a *common* good, and if we assume civil disobedience and other forms of resistance are *legitimate means* in the pursuit of peace and justice, we do so as plain debtors. We are indebted to thousands and tens of thousands, I am sure. I am also sure that among them are Bonhoeffer and King. And I am sure their imprint is deep and clear, with King's the deeper and more evident. Christian ethics is not the same after the ripples their work and witness set in motion.

But to the details.

We understand neither of these figures if we fail to treat them as theolo-gians. Their powerful social ethic is the expression of their powerful theological ethic. King can say that his campaign and place in history are the work of the *Zeitgeist*, the driving spirit of a critical historical moment, but he understands the demands of that *Zeitgeist* theologically. As indicated, his theological center is in the African American prophetic social gospel. It is thoroughly saturated with the scripture that funds it, the Hebrew Bible above all. It is black Baptist in mood and emotional energy and delivery, though King moves far away from the other-worldliness and biblical literalism of his own tradition. This is the result of liberal theology at Crozer Seminary and Boston University, where he came to appreciate reason's role in making the case of faith. He did find liberalism's optimism about human nature a stretch for any who had suffered the sting of endemic racism, so it is not surprising that he found Reinhold Niebuhr more convincing on human sinfulness and the play of power. Still, the beating heart of his theology is the prophetic social gospel of the African American religious experience. And while King was instructed in the idea of personality in his Ph.D. studies, the personal idea of God so crucial to his piety and theology isn't from Boston; it's from Atlanta and it bears the deep imprint of his parents and grandparents. This personal God who is his living source of support, challenge, and consolation is at the center of his faith and thought in a way that parallels the intensely personal relationship with Jesus Christ at the center of Bonhoeffer's life and thought. In both cases (and this is my point) we err badly if we try to explain the animation of King's campaign apart from his theology, just as we err badly if we try to explain Bonhoeffer's search for an effective resisting church and his move into the military-political conspiracy apart from his ecclesiology and Christology. These two were both theologians of relationality and mutuality who thought *as* theologians and whose piety and agency were in accord with their theology and its ethic.

A matter raised in the theology of both men is the issue of power. Both knew that nothing evil happens apart from power. They also knew that nothing good happens apart from power. And for the same reason: nothing whatsoever *can* happen apart from power. Power is the energy inherent in being itself, the animation of every creature and their relationships with other life, and the means of construction as well as destruction. Power forms, reforms, and deforms. If we focus on personal and social forms of power, we watch both Bonhoeffer and King trying to shape and mobilize a collective spirituality that will help move mountains. In Bonhoeffer's case, a good Lutheran one, power in society must address the propensity of the ego to pursue dominating power, a power that isolates oneself from others and fractures the only kind of relationality that achieves the common good, namely, mutuality. Or, to use a different word, the power of the dominating ego isolates the other from love, love as the way all are bound together in Christ and in the interdependence inherent in creation itself. The powerful ego's disruption of mutuality is expressed socially in the destructive forces of corporate life. For Bonhoeffer that was brutally evident in antisemitism and racism generally, in the dehumanizing uses of modern technology, in ruthless forms of capitalism, in militarism and the kind of security based upon aggressive collective assertion, in the power of ideology, and in the way all these came together in goose-stepping fascism.

King could easily identify with Bonhoeffer's list of socially destructive uses of power. But for him the parallel realities were American, not German. They were the violence of systemic racism, the lack of democratic means of representation and reform extended to black citizens, poverty and the gap between rich and poor in a nation with enough for all, and the criminality and waste of war. "We have committed more war crimes almost than any nation in the world, and I'm going to continue to say it," he preached in his famous sermon on the "Drum Major Instinct." "And we won't stop it because of our pride, and our arrogance as a nation."[8] In the equally famous Riverside Church address, "A Time to Break Silence," he cited his own government as "the greatest purveyor of violence in the world today."[9]

But, unlike Bonhoeffer, King's analysis of personal power does not, at least for African Americans, focus on the dominating ego and its abuse of power. Further on in "The Drum Major Instinct" King compares Gibbons's *Decline and Fall of the Roman Empire* to America and finds the parallels frightening. Yet he immediately says that, while this arrogance and imperial domination is the perversion of the drum-major instinct, and while you would expect Jesus to have said,

> "You are out of your place. You are selfish." . . . Jesus says something quite different. In substance it is this: "Oh, I see, you want to be first. You want to be great. You want to be important. You want to be significant. Well you ought to be. If you're going to be my disciple, you must be." But he reordered priorities. And he said, "Yes, don't give up this instinct. It's a good instinct if you use it right. It's a good instinct if you don't distort it and pervert it. Don't give it up. Keep feeling the need for being important. Keep feeling the need for being first. But I want you to be first in love. I want you to be first in moral excellence. I want you to be first in generosity. That is what I want you to do."[10]

In sum, for both King and Bonhoeffer, power is essential to achieving any peace and any justice. Bonhoeffer is wary of the powerful ego and its desire to dominate in intimate relationships and in collectivist forms that exhibit what C. Wright Mills once called a "higher order of immorality." King knows the way of domination well enough and he recognizes powerful egos at work at every turn, but his attention is to empowering those who do not yet think sufficiently well of themselves and their considerable latent powers. I will soon turn to the figure both men look to for lessons in power—Gandhi. But first I want us to listen carefully to King's report on his visit to India in 1959. Note especially that the first of the three lessons he learned from the Mahatma wholly accords with the message of Malcolm X. Namely, "the way of acquiescence leads to moral and spiritual suicide." The other lessons are that while "the way of violence leads to bitterness in the survivors and brutality in the destroyers," "the way of nonviolence leads to redemption and the creation of the beloved community."[11]

King's central theological idea, that of a personal God, bolsters his discussion of personal power. For King human personality bears an infinite value. He never wavered from this conviction of the dignity and worth of all human beings, including that of his enemies. Like Bonhoeffer, he could not, for theological reasons, demonize his opponents even when they acted demonically.[12]

Differently said, both men are inoculated by their core theological and anthropological convictions against the very perspectives that issue in virulent racism, genocide, and the Holocaust. For them, no people is so loathsome, so offensive, so alien that we are obliged to set them outside the circle of normal human compassion and belonging. None are such that we don't have to hear their cries, honor their tears, or respect their dignity, even when they violate it together with the dignity of others. None can be removed from the list of God's children. Nor can any people carry the full burden of all that frightens or threatens us. None can be the scapegoat for all that unsettles and upsets us.[13] All belong inside the circle of life worthy of life.

This said, we turn to their common attraction to Gandhi.

For Bonhoeffer, the crisis of 1933—Hitler's appointment of Reich Chancellor on January 30 and the subsequent one hundred days of laws that cleared the way for Nazi dictatorship—makes starkly clear that German Protestants are not spiritually formed in a way that resists state-sponsored fascism, nationalist appeals draped in Christian rhetoric, and Aryan racism. Deference to the state and its powers in a time of chaos is too ingrained. Bonhoeffer writes Erwin Sutz:

> The next generation of pastors, these days, ought to be trained entirely in church-monastic schools, where the pure doctrine, the Sermon on the Mount, and worship are taken seriously—which for all three of these things is simply not the case at the university and under the present circumstances is impossible. It is also time for a final break with our theologically grounded reserve about whatever is being done by the state—which really only comes down to fear. "Speak out for those who cannot speak" [Prov. 31:8]—who in the church today still remembers that this is the very least the Bible asks of us in such times as these?[14]

Bonhoeffer recognizes these deficits at once and begins his effort to gather students for a different kind of life together as close Christian community. He does so on multiple fronts, some well beyond the university. Among others he turns to Mohandas Gandhi.

His motives are several. The exhaustion of an adequate German Protestant formation in discipleship is one of them. An adequate polity and ministry to resist the enthusiasm for German national rebirth on fascist and racist terms is another. These needs direct his interest to Gandhi's ashram. The ashram may be the kind of school for discipleship and life together that the small confessing movement in Germany needs in order to give its dissent form and skills. Gandhi, please recall, is also an ardent disciple of Jesus and the Sermon on the Mount, and Bonhoeffer wonders aloud whether the gospel itself may not now be found in other words and other deeds in the East. So he seeks an invitation to live in the ashram and learn the arts of nonviolent discipleship and community.

But there is more. Not only is Bonhoeffer in quest of a new monasticism for the Confessing Church. He wants, for the same church, to learn the arts of nonviolence. At this time he is serving German-language congregations in London and visiting intentional Christian communities. One of these is the Bruderhof and we have the letters of Hardy Arnold, the son of the community's founder, letters that are revealing of Bonhoeffer's attraction to Gandhi.

After writing of Bonhoeffer's interest in a community formed around the Sermon on the Mount, Arnold says that "Bonhoeffer's opposition to Hitler was very strong, both as a German citizen and a Christian. At that time he considered the Nazi government to be so fundamentally evil that it had to be eliminated by any means short of violence," and that he planned "to visit Gandhi in India for advice on how to overthrow a hostile government nonviolently."[15]

Putting an end to the fateful theological deference to the state and speaking up for those who cannot speak requires, then, both a new Christian communitarianism and a new mode of active nonviolent resistance in the churches and well beyond.

If we turn from resistance to rights, we discover the following context. In three months, from February through April, 1933, most everything legally required for the organization of barbarism and brutality had been put in place by the Nazi party. It would not be long before most every moral act would be illegal and every legal act a crime. Still, it would take some time before the military, education, religion, judiciary, and administration sectors could all be brought into full conformity with the party platform. Even as late as 1935 Hitler was voicing ultimatums in a protracted struggle of the party with sectors of the state, some of it violent: "What can be resolved by the state will be resolved by the state. What, because of its essence, the state is incapable of resolving will be resolved through the movement"[16] (in other words, through the party). We will visit this on the so-called Jewish Question. For now simply note that the fluidity and chaos in society and the battle between the Nazi party and sectors of the failing constitutional state in the early to mid-1930s is, paradoxically, the source of Bonhoeffer's hope. Uncertainty meant malleability and opportunity.

The immediate circumstance generating both resistance and attention to rights is the treatment of Jews inside and outside the church—that is, both Jewish-Christians and secular and observant Jews. Two matters are especially noteworthy because they are virtually unique in German circles and because Bonhoeffer brings them to the fore very early, in an essay written in April, 1933. This means he is writing "The Church and the Jewish Question" just as the Law for the Reconstitution of the Civil Service is passed (April 7). This legislation banned non-Aryans from the civil service and wrote racial/ethnic discrimination into the law of the land.

The two salient matters are these: the place of race, and not only religion, as the Nazi basis for its virulent antisemitism; and Bonhoeffer's attention to rights. For him these are joined.

The Jewish question is, for Bonhoeffer, the circumstance that demands *status confessionis*—a state of confession in which central truths of faith are at stake.[17] Here is the litmus test of the church's very nature *as* church, he argues. Conceptually, his ecclesiology had turned on the treatment of "the other" since *Sanctorum Communio*'s theology of sociality and mutuality. But now, in the case of the Jews, the test is existential and the response urgent. "The Church and the Jewish Question" ends with this: "The question here is not at all about whether our church members of German descent can be asked to support fellowship in the church with Jews. In reality it is the duty of Christian proclamation to say: Here, where Jew and German together stand under God's Word, is Church; here it will be proven whether or not the church is still church."[18]

What actions are required, if the church is to be church? His essay outlines three possible responses to state injustice:

- In the *first* the church is a critic that, using the criterion of a just order, publicly asks whether the state's actions are legitimate. The state's proper role, as state, is to keep order and mete out justice.
- The *second* task for the church is to help the victims of any illegitimate, in other words, unjust, state action. While again the treatment of the Jews was the precipitating and pressing case, Bonhoeffer's argument pertains to any persons deprived of their rights in a state bearing either "too much" or "too little" law and order. His argument from rights—specifically their deprivation—found no resonance, however. Despite this, or perhaps because of it, Bonhoeffer carried his attention to rights into his later work in *Ethics* when the subject was still largely absent among German theologians. There he writes of natural life and of

bodily integrity as "the foundation of all natural rights without exception." And why? "The living human body is always the human person himself or herself." "The most primordial right of natural life," he says, "is the protection of the body from intentional injury, violation, and killing." "Rape, exploitation, torture and the arbitrary deprivation of physical freedom are all serious invasions of the right conferred on human beings at creation." The rights of natural life are "the reflection of the glory of God the Creator in the midst of the fallen world."[19]

- The *third* church responsibility—to seize the wheel itself and bring crimes to a halt by disabling the state—also followed from the state unscrupulously wielding "too little" or "too much" law and order. Here Bonhoeffer made a plea for an ecclesiastical council to make a collective decision and take action. Regime change was not a step an individual Christian such as himself could or should take on his or her own. When eventually he did conclude that he must be part of the military-political conspiracy to overthrow the regime, he did so aware that he was surrendering his reputation in the church.[20]

It is important to recall that these first months of the Nazi juggernaut were a time when the party sought to synchronize state and society with the party platform but that this was not everywhere successful, even if a path for dictatorship had been legally cleared in a remarkably short time. So please note: Bonhoeffer's essay is *not* about the church's response to the *party*. His appeal, rather, was to the *state* and its responsibilities, specifically in the matter of the Aryan legislation. It was clear what the party wanted. But was it also clear that a legitimate German state was nothing but a shell already in 1933? In this contested space, and in the shared hope that a legitimate constitutional state could still be rescued, Bonhoeffer made his appeal to the church and its responsibilities: let the state be a proper state; if it is not, restore it to its rightful roles of order and justice.

Bonhoeffer's was a conservative argument. Maltreatment of the Jews and further threat of that in the Aryan legislation had pushed him to address the state's very foundation and legitimacy. His answer was a law-and-order answer about the duties of a limited state, limited in its reach by rights it cannot abrogate. As a limited constitutional state, responsibility for a just order means that it, the state, is the proper agent for opposing the programs and pogroms of Nazi organizations. Here was a conservative argument for bold resistance under circumstances of manifest injustice and the failure to be a proper constitutional state.

Readers might easily overlook that Bonhoeffer's argument is not distant from his later reflections on the state in *Ethics*. Nor it is far from his reasons for the conspiracy to seize the wheel ten years later. Bonhoeffer in fact carried out all three of the courses of action he outlined in 1933, and paid with his life.[21] Early in 1933, then, we already have the outlines of the resistance Bonhoeffer called for and came to embody.

Readers might also overlook that Bonhoeffer's argument about treatment of the Jews is on grounds that theologians and the churches ignored; namely, that the state's anti-Jewish legislation was based in *race* identification, not religion. We forget that this was a Nazi innovation for Germany and it meant that all the church discussion about Jewish and Jewish-Christian religious identity was largely beside the point. Bonhoeffer made this critical point at the very outset of "The Church and the Jewish Question":

> The fact, unique in history, that the Jew is subjected to special laws by the state, *solely on the basis of his race and regardless of the religion to which he adheres*, presents theologians with two new problems, which must be dealt with separately. How does the church judge this action by the state, and what is the church called upon to do about it? What are the consequences for the church's position toward the baptized Jews in its congregations? Both these questions can only be answered on the basis of a right concept of the church.[22]

While, as is clear, Bonhoeffer's ethic at this time is strictly a church ethic and his focus is the church's very identity, racism as effectively the law of the land is his reason for decisive church response.

We must not lose our thread. The thread is this: both Bonhoeffer's efforts at creating a community of Christian discipleship and life together, which he will carry out at the Finkenwalde seminary, and Bonhoeffer's efforts at resistance and his case for rights, have vital ties to Gandhi.

King did get to India, although only after Indian independence and Gandhi's death. The visit was "one of the most concentrated and eye-opening experiences of our lives" [his and Coretta's].[23] His interest in Gandhi is theological in that his theology of love and the beloved community finds in Gandhi its practitioner. But the theology of love and its source is not Gandhi, in the first instance. When King told the story of the Montgomery bus boycott, he spoke of "a basic philosophy" that "guided the movement" and said it has been referred to variously "as nonviolent resistance, noncooperation, and passive resistance." But, he goes on, "in the first days of the protest, none of these expressions was mentioned. The phrase most often heard was Christian love.

It was the Sermon on the Mount, rather than a doctrine of passive resistance, that initially inspired the Negroes of Montgomery to dignified social action. It was Jesus of Nazareth that stirred the Negroes to protest with the creative weapon of love." When he did speak of method, King put it this way: "Nonviolent resistance had emerged as the technique of the movement, while love stood as the regulating idea. Christ furnished the spirit and motivation, while Gandhi furnished the method." Yet King also saw in the Gandhian campaigns the same love he saw in Jesus and the Sermon on the Mount. He articulated this kind of love in many places, one of them in the bus boycott account itself. Singling out *agape* love for extended comment, King says the following:

> *Agape* is love seeking to preserve and create community. It is insistence on community even when one seeks to break it. *Agape* is a willingness to go to any length to restore community. It doesn't stop at the first mile, but goes the second mile to restore community. It is a willingness to forgive, not seven times, but seventy times seven to restore community. . . . The resurrection is a symbol of God's triumph over all the forces that seek to block community. The Holy Spirit is the continuing community-creating reality that moves through history. . . .
>
> In the final analysis, *agape* means a recognition of the fact that all life is interrelated. . . . Whether we call it an unconscious process, an impersonal Brahman, or a Personal Being of matchless power and infinite love, there is a creative force in the universe that works to bring the disconnected aspects of reality into a harmonious whole.[24]

Another account comes in the 1961 address on "Love, Law, and Civil Disobedience." Nonviolent love is not aesthetic love, the *eros* that is the soul's longing for the divine, or the romantic version of *eros* to which we are accustomed. It is not friendship, either, the reciprocal love of *philia* exchanged by friends. It is *agape*, what we earlier called "equal regard" no matter what. It is, he says, the love of God operating in the human heart in such a way that it does not require, for its own action, love offered or love returned. It is the love Jesus meant when he commanded us to love our enemies.[25] To which King adds:

> I'm very happy that he didn't say like your enemies, because it is pretty difficult to like some people. Like is sentimental, and it is pretty difficult to like someone bombing your home; it is pretty difficult to like somebody threatening your children; it is difficult to like congressmen who spend all of their time trying to defeat civil rights. But Jesus said love them, and love is greater than like.[26]

Theologically framed with this kind of love, and understanding that following Jesus would mean hardship and suffering, King is interested above all in nonviolence as a way of life that developed effective means for the relatively powerless. "I left India more convinced than ever before that nonviolent resistance is the most potent weapon available to oppressed people in their struggle for freedom."[27] Yes, King *is* aware that practical nonviolence requires the purging of violence within and new habits of heart, soul, and mind. "Our goal," he said in an *Ebony* interview, "is to create a beloved community and this will require a qualitative change in our souls as well as a quantitative change in our lives."[28] Nonviolence will not work apart from a nonviolent spirituality. He fully subscribed to Gandhi's conviction that "nonviolence is not a garment to be put on and off at will. Its seat is in the heart, and it must be an inseparable part of our very being."[29] Yet King already has, in the black churches, a couple centuries of spiritual formation for this struggle. King had a community, and a movement, that could tap the redemptive energy of nonviolent power and it was his genius to rally the piety of black churches and others for this-worldly reform via mass nonviolent action. King thus achieved with Gandhian means what Bonhoeffer could not even begin, since Bonhoeffer did not have the community or movement for it. Furthermore, that movement and community could not, and cannot, be created in the midst of the crisis, or the opportunity, itself. It takes generations. It takes the long, slow conversion of morals one prayer and spiritual at a time, one hymn and offer of hospitality at a time, the molding of one conviction at a time, with one child at a time. It is soulcraft, individual and collective, and it is as indispensable to achieving peace and justice as is statecraft.

Before we draw the final conclusion, allow this review. It can be said either way: the communitarian ethic of both King and Bonhoeffer is inherently a love ethic; or, their love ethic is inherently communitarian. All—self and other—belong in the same framework of moral reference and concern, and bear the same dignity and stamp as a child of God. Sharing vulnerability and sharing power for life worthy of life keeps the circle of love intact. Double standards, and using power to privilege "us" over "them" and sacrifice "them" for our sins as well as theirs, breaks the circle and destroys community. Resistance for the sake of community restoration and structural justice is thus a requirement of peace itself. Or, to say it differently: both King and Bonhoeffer understand goodness as a power. And for both, moral agency based in empathy for the other issues in resistance to violence with means that express the power of goodness.[30] But this resistance is, as indicated, a means, not an end. For Bonhoeffer, resistance is a means to bring an end to war and Germany's crimes against humanity through nothing less than regime change and the establishment of "the other Germany."[31] For King, resistance is also means, not end. It is the means to enact and enforce laws that end discrimination and realize the constitutional promise of a genuine democracy organized around the common good. Resistance is also the means to challenge economic inequity and generate jobs and wealth sufficient to realize the American dream of a decent life for all. Here King and the movement, when it went north, came up against the full force of U.S. American socioeconomic and cultural values that the movement was not prepared to counter. It was not prepared for the degree to which, in the United States, individual success, ownership, the market, and economic power override human sociability and the well-being of society's most vulnerable members. Privatizing property, maximally deregulating markets, and individualizing freedom and choice converged to trump the classic democratic task of carefully balancing freedom, equality, and community. The theology of the ownership society, from Ronald Reagan through George W. Bush, subverts the theology of sociality and solidarity of both King and Bonhoeffer. And King and the movement discovered the pre-Reagan, pre-Bush force of that culture when the movement went north. How to muster a viable social ecology now, as members of what King called "the world house,"[32] when we must add that other threatened ecology, the physical ecology of earth (soil), air, fire (energy), and water, is the task before us, this side of King and Bonhoeffer.

The conclusion is abrupt—a single, long sentence. Whatever else King and Bonhoeffer bequeathed Christian ethics after their deaths in April at thirty-nine years and four months, they handed us, in word and deed, ecological theologies of sociality and solidarity focused so laser sharp on peace and justice that resistance and rights in the interest of a comprehensive common good now belong to Christian theological ethics at its core, and not as an afterthought, an add-on, or the concern of a few marginalized Christians.

CHAPTER 6

Theology and the Problem of Racism

Josiah U. Young III

D ietrich Bonhoeffer and Martin Luther King Jr. courageously opposed racism. In doing so, they asserted that the church must be independent of the state and challenge the state if necessary to counter racism. Bonhoeffer and King differed theologically, but both held that Christ was inseparable from the one Creator. Both also believed that Christ represents the oneness of the human race. For King, this oneness has to do with what Christ taught and his nonviolent praxis. For Bonhoeffer, this oneness has to do with who Christ was as God and as a human being as well as what he taught and did. Both theologians nonetheless held that racism does violence to the one God and the human race. Bonhoeffer and King held that racism constitutes a mortal sin Christians must purge from their churches and undermine where it appears in society.

Martin Luther King Jr.'s maternal great-grandfather, Willis Williams, was "an old time slavery preacher."[1] While enslaved, Willis Williams belonged to a Baptist church in which blacks outnumbered whites, who constituted the church authority and state authority in Georgia. After the Civil War, the blacks founded their own church.[2] Willis Williams's son, Adam Daniel Williams, was also a Baptist preacher as was King's father. Drawing on his black Baptist heritage, King believed the God of his fathers called him to give his life if necessary to end what he called the "doctrine of white supremacy." He believed, in addition, that the poverty in this nation and the war fought in Vietnam were related to white privilege. Wealthy whites controlled the economic system and dictated foreign policies. Only they, for the most part, were comfortable in a society where white supremacy was a dominant ideology and poverty was a fact for millions. Who but this privileged caste, moreover, was largely complicit in sending economically disadvantaged soldiers, a disproportionate number of them blacks, to Vietnam? Race, class, and militarism were inseparable for King. He therefore worked relentlessly to desegregate the South and the urban North; he opposed the war, and he hoped to sustain a national grassroots campaign against poverty out of his conviction that what the gospel proclaims and what nations uphold are not identical. This difference between the church and the state is one of the ways one knows—at least in faith and hope—that God is good, all the time. From this point of view, God's benevolence and righteousness, and the Christian's *freedom* to defy the reigning principalities and powers have everything to do with Jesus of Nazareth, who counted himself as one of the oppressed.

Bonhoeffer believed his God called him to resist the Nazis as early as 1933, five years before the *Kristallnacht* ("crystal night"). He had no use for the Aryan clause and fought it doggedly because he believed that the gospel would only prevail in a church free from racism. His belief began to take shape in the United States when he frequented the Abyssinian Baptist Church in Harlem during the time he studied at Union Theological Seminary (1930–1931). His Abyssinian experiences intensified his consciousness of the historic injustices African Americans faced and underlined some of the points he makes in his Berlin University dissertation, *Sanctorum Communio: A Theological Study of the Sociology of the Church*. He argued that every saint is also a sinner who is no better as such than anyone else. He also argued that God is concerned with the disposition of one's heart rather than one's "outward appearance."[3] He attended Abyssinian because the people exemplified the truth of his arguments and received the gospel in a way that moved him. As Bonhoeffer scholar Clifford Green reports, Bonhoeffer returned to Union Theological Seminary one Sunday after attending the church and "did not try to hide his feelings, which was extremely rare for him."[4]

In his essay "Protestantism without Reformation," Bonhoeffer argues that "racial peculiarities" should not define *churches*. "God's word, God's will, and God's action" explain the existence of the churches.[5] He also argues that if North American white Protestant churches had been true to the gospel, whites would not have forced African Americans to sit in the balcony and receive the Lord's Supper last of all. If the gospel had edified the American churches right from the start, they would have realized that the "freedom of the church is not where it has possibilities, but only where the Gospel really and in its own power makes room for itself on earth, even and precisely when no such possibilities are offered to it."[6] Abyssinian exemplified what he meant by that statement. There he experienced "Christ existing as church-community,"[7] a Spirit-filled communion where society's mores had no true place among the people who were "un-free" by society's standards and those of their founding denomination.

As was the case with King, Bonhoeffer felt that much of the race problem in North America had to do with the white churches' failure to distinguish secular authority from the reign of God. To quote Bonhoeffer's "Protestantism without Reformation": "Nowhere has the principle of the separation of church and state become a matter of such general, almost dogmatic, significance as in American Christianity, and nowhere, on the other hand, is the participation of the churches in the political, social, economic and cultural events of public life so active and so influential as in the country where there is no state church."[8] For Bonhoeffer, the *participation* of the white American churches in *public life* has meant, in effect, that "the state" has been "the executive of the church."[9] If Bonhoeffer is correct, one can only conclude that the state has been racist because the church has sanctioned racism. In his *Where Do We Go from Here? Chaos or Community,* King discusses the church's sanctioning of racism in asserting that "the doctrine of white supremacy was imbedded in every textbook and preached in practically every pulpit. . . . The greatest blasphemy of the whole ugly process was that the white man ended up making God his partner in the exploitation of the Negro." King goes on to ask, rhetorically, "What greater heresy has religion known? Ethical Christianity vanished and the moral nerve of religion was atrophied. This terrible distortion sullied the essential nature of Christianity."[10] Bonhoeffer would have likely problematized King's perspective on ethical Christianity and religion since Bonhoeffer thought Christians were sinners whose ethics never measured up to God's righteousness. He also asserted that religion differed from God-given faith. Both theologians held nonetheless that Christians should have not allowed racism to thrive within their churches.

Bonhoeffer's take on ethics and religion indicates what I have pointed out: that his and King's theological perspectives differed yet they were also similar in their aversion to racism. Although labels such as "liberal" or "postliberal" are often too general, I nonetheless think of Bonhoeffer as a postliberal theologian insofar as he aligned himself with Karl Barth, albeit critically. I think of King as a liberal theologian insofar as he aligned himself with the Boston Personalists: Borden Parker Bowne, Alfred Knudson, Edgar S. Brightman, and Harold

Dewolf. Given Bonhoeffer's "Protestantism without Reformation," I imagine Bonhoeffer would have been critical of the Boston Personalists because he thought "American theology and the American church as a whole" have "misunderstood" Christ's "person and work."[11] Bonhoeffer held that most American theologians thought Jesus Christ was a great ethical teacher who had not come down from heaven, been raised bodily from the dead, nor ascended to heaven. For these theologians, the incarnation, resurrection, and ascension were myths modernity has discredited. "Right to the last," Bonhoeffer writes, "they do not understand that . . . God has founded his church beyond religion and beyond ethics. A symptom of this is the general [American] adherence to natural theology."[12] Given what King argues in his book *Stride Toward Freedom*, I imagine that King would have thought of Bonhoeffer as an antirationalist and a semi-fundamentalist theologian, which is how King thought of Karl Barth—the exemplary postliberal theologian. Still, Bonhoeffer took modernity, *qua* the "world come of age," as seriously as did the liberal King. In addition, the Hebrew Bible and Jesus' crucifixion edified both King and Bonhoeffer. In light of both Testaments, the theologians held, moreover, that the Creator is a *personal* God.

Most important for me is the fact that both held that humankind is in truth a single race by virtue of the fact that all people, regardless of their physical characteristics, bear and obscure the image of the God who created them. King and Bonhoeffer held that racism rips apart sinfully what God has decreed to be one. In their distinctive ways, they believed that Christ by virtue of his true humanity was the archetypical human being rather than an offspring of a particular people. While they acknowledged Jesus' Jewishness, his religion—his culture, the particularity of his ancestors, what some would call his "race"—was not the essential factor for them. The essential factor was his unprecedented God-endowed humanity. Christ's humanity was thus *the* form of the ethnic, cultural, and somatic distinctions one often misconstrues as race. For both theologians, Christ—the Son of man—represents all humankind as the one race of God. During the time he studied in New York City, Bonhoeffer expressed that view in a sermon he delivered on 1 John 4:16. He preached that Christ's cross has drawn all human beings together, making them one, without respect, one may add, to the color of their skins; for no single skin color symbolized justification by grace alone more than did another. No people, then, are in themselves more or less sinful than are other people.[13]

For King, the cross is the most compelling revelation of the *imago Dei*, for the crucifixion mirrors both God's goodness and nonviolent presence in the ethics of the historical Jesus.[14] The problem of sin was also central to King's preaching thanks to Reinhold Niebuhr's disdain for the claim that modernity had brought humankind closer to the attainment of the golden rule than ever before. Racism in the Southland and up north proved to King that human beings were often too wicked for one to be sanguine about achieving the beloved community King was committed to bringing about.

King did not hold that God the Son became flesh in any literal sense. The ancient theologians Bonhoeffer upheld were thus to King archaic in their worldview. When, therefore, King asserted in one of his sermons that "the ultimate meaning of [the doctrine of] the Trinity" is its affirmation that "God and Christ are one in substance," and that to experience "one is to experience the other,"[15] he was not upholding Nicaea (325) and Constantinople (381), but demythologizing them. Bearing more of an affinity to Schleiermacher than to Barth, King held that Christ's consciousness of God rather than his preexistence was the redemptive factor. For King, in addition, Christ's *personality*, wisdom, and ethical correctness, which King understood à la Alfred Knudson as self-consciousness and self-direction, is the image of God. By contrast, Bonhoeffer's interpretations of the *imago Dei* entailed his conviction that Christ mirrors the Creator because he was truly God and truly human.

For Bonhoeffer, Christ reveals that God created persons "to communicate with each other" on the model of the Trinity itself. As images of the Trinity, the community and the individual "have the same structure in God's eyes." According to Bonhoeffer, the one and the many thus "exist in the same moment and rest in one another," both in God and in God's image.[16] King made a similar point in his Boston University dissertation on Paul Tillich and Henry Nelson Weidman. The oneness of the human community and the diversity of its individuals go together as the image of God. "In this way," King writes, "both oneness and manyness are preserved."[17] King's assessment of Tillich is particularly interesting as he held that Tillich's God—the ground and the abyss of being—negates manyness and thus human personality in providing "no place for finite freedom."[18] I take King's critique to mean that Tillich's deity undermines Christ, whose mission, after all, is to glorify God's Personhood and that of human beings rather than to nullify them. I find that Bonhoeffer makes a similar point at the conclusion of his dissertation, *Sanctorum Communio*: "the primordial ground of being"—a phrase that surely alludes to Tillich's position—signifies "the death of all *actual* being."[19] From this perspective, which I am ascribing to Tillich, dead individuals, having actualized their form, would have no hope of resurrection (no potentiality, no future). Tillich's "ground of being" would reabsorb them, as it were, into the void. By contrast, Bonhoeffer's eschatological view is that the Triune Lord is "the God of living persons." The church, "the realm of Christ," is in faith bound to "become the Realm of God. The ministerium Christi [ministry of Christ], of the Holy Spirit," will have attained its purpose when "Christ himself hands over his church-community to the Father (1 Cor. 15:24), in order that God may be all in all."[20] For Bonhoeffer, our *time* here has no real meaning if our personhoods have no eternal significance. If Jesus' death were not the prelude to the deification of created personhood, Good Friday would be a contradiction in terms and Easter a meaningless celebration. One could not believe in a living Christ or an eternal God. Bonhoeffer, however, believed that God in Christ had defeated death, a belief that accounted for his stand against the Nazis and the death they spread around the world, especially in the death camps.

Bonhoeffer would have agreed with King's assertion in 1965 in Montreat, North Carolina, "The ultimate logic of racism is genocide and every Christian must take a stand against it." King made that claim after the members of the 105th General Assembly of the Southern Presbyterian Church had overturned a move to disinvite King to speak to them about the crises of that year.[21] African Americans had rioted in Watts (Los Angeles, California) because of police brutality; an angry white man shot Episcopal seminarian Jonathan Daniels to death in Lowndes County (Alabama) shortly after his release from jail because of Daniel's work in the African American community. The repercussions of the burgeoning antiblack sentiment were dire—certainly in Watts—and a number of Americans did not want to discuss the problem, especially in their churches, despite the fact that they bore huge responsibility for the violence.

King would have greatly respected Bonhoeffer's realization back in the 1930s that "the race question" (as Bonhoeffer called it) had reached crisis proportions and that religious and ethical attempts to resolve it would "turn in a violent political objection."[22] In part, Bonhoeffer inferred that from his reading of James Weldon Johnson's *The Autobiography of an Ex-Colored Man*, a novel about a so-called Negro who was born shortly after the Civil War. Since his father was white and his mother very fair skinned, the ex-colored man looks white.[23] As an adult, he watches angry whites burn a black man alive. The murder sickened and shamed the protagonist into passing for white, which he deeply regrets at the novel's end. Although Americans have come a long way since the 1930s, nothing can obliterate the fact that this country did precious little to protect its black citizens from such an infringement on their human rights. On the final page of his confession, the ex-colored man makes that point. He describes himself as a well-off American, white, who has settled for moral mediocrity rather than the noble cause of his compatriots, many of whom were active in the antilynching crusades. The message of Johnson's novel—namely that the ex-colored man passed for white to protect himself from being lynched—was not lost on Bonhoeffer. He remarked in light of it that blacks would not stand for such mistreatment indefinitely. As he put it in a letter to his brother, Karl Friedrich: "It really does seem to me that there is a great movement forming, and I do believe that the Negroes will still give the whites here considerably more than merely their folksongs."[24]

Bonhoeffer would have found that King's later writings exemplified his observation that African Americans would take radical measures to address their historic abuse. King was a peacemaker, a nonviolent reconciler; but we should never forget that King intended to bring about nothing short of a revolution. Much like elements of Reinhold Niebuhr's *Moral Man and Immoral Society*, King asserts that African Americans (and all other Americans hungry for justice) could not bring about radical change by depending upon the largesse of those in power. They must force the privileged to treat them fairly.[25] His nonviolent militancy posed a serious threat to the status quo. Public records show that J. Edgar Hoover invaded King's privacy through wiretaps and infiltration of the Southern Christian Leadership Conference (SCLC) that King headed. King's militancy does not indicate the *violent* political objection Bonhoeffer found brewing in Harlem in the 1930s. Still, a people who have been abused for centuries are bound to get so fed up with their abuse that some of them will take up arms to advance their human-rights agenda.

Bonhoeffer's prediction of this "violent political objection" was not only influenced by Johnson's novel but also by Countee Cullen's long poem, "The black Christ."[26] The poem's narrator is a lynched black man's brother, who is enraged over his brother's murder and rebukes their mother for what he perceives to be her impotent faith in the white Jesus. Why didn't her Lord deliver Jim? Jim's brother tells his mother (Feuerbach-like): "Better my God should be/This moving, breathing frame of me,/Strong hands and feet, live heart and eyes;/And when these cease, say then God dies."[27] When the murdered and risen Jim appears to his brother, transformed and whole, however, the narrator discovers the "black Christ"—the antidote to both his mother's self-deprecating religion and his atheistic rage. Cullen helped Bonhoeffer see that many young blacks thought their inherited Christianity blocked their self-esteem and their human rights. Bonhoeffer thought their militant rejection of their elders' strong eschatological faith was an "ominous" consequence of the history of the Protestant church in the United States. "If," Bonhoeffer writes in "Protestantism without Reformation," "it has come about that today the 'black

Christ' has to be led into the field against the 'white Christ' by a young Negro poet, then a deep cleft in the church of Jesus Christ is indicated."[28]

King would have agreed that a black Christ who squares off against a white Christ stems from the history of a Protestant church unable to separate the church's role from that of the state. Not unlike Bonhoeffer, King surely understood that many blacks have rejected the white Christ because he has justified a double standard in both the churches and the republic. King himself wondered "what kind of nation" both approves of "nonviolence whenever Negroes face white people in the streets" *and* makes "violence and burning and death" a nationalistic imperative "when these same Negroes are sent to the fields of Vietnam." King was fed up with "white legislators who pass[ed] laws" that were barely implemented for blacks. He was fed up with both "the Christian church that appear[ed] to be more white than Christian and . . . many white clergymen who prefer[red] to remain silent behind the security of stained-glass windows."[29] Even so, King reasoned, there was no good reason to think that the antidote to the equating of God with whites was to make God black. He was not at all opposed to a theological method that deduces the Personhood of the Creator from human beings' attempts to be virtuous; and there was certainly justice in blacks' disdain for the white Jesus. I doubt, though, that King held that virtuousness itself had to do with race, for virtue, for him, originated in God rather than in humankind. For King, the order of being itself indicates that justice is a *theological* attribute primarily and thus a virtue that human beings can only strive for as the *image* of God. No particular racial type, contingent as it is, so totalizes that image as to become God. No racial type can thus claim divine priority over any other. For King, then, both the apotheosis of skin color and the violence it appears to condone on both sides of the color line stem from racist logic.

King wrote in *Where Do We Go from Here?* that "leaders in Germany who sincerely opposed what Hitler was doing to the Jews" nonetheless caved in to him when they "discovered that anti-Semitism was the prevailing trend." They thus "yielded to one of the most ignominious evils that history had ever known."[30] One thing is for sure, Bonhoeffer was not among those leaders.

Hindsight reveals that theologians such as King and Bonhoeffer, who refused to cave in and capitulate to racist logic, no matter how popular at the time, were exceedingly rare. It is precisely their refusals—and the theologies behind them—that edify many today. Their deeply held convictions that racism was a form of apostasy within the churches and their courageous actions against the wickedness of racism are great theological legacies. We could talk for days about whether our governments *can* ever eradicate the problem and whether the churches will make good on the courageous examples of two of their greatest theologians: Dietrich Bonhoeffer and Martin Luther King Jr. Their legacies are nonetheless pearls of great price for those who still believe that human beings are more alike than they are different because the Creator has decreed it to be so in the Christ.

CHAPTER 7

Bonhoeffer, King, and Themes in Catholic Social Thought

M. Shawn Copeland

Relating Dietrich Bonhoeffer and Martin Luther King Jr. with Catholic social thought (hereafter CST) surely occasions pause. On the one hand, with only two published social encyclicals, *Rerum Novarum* (1891) and *Quadragesimo Anno* (1931), few critical interpretations of CST were available to Bonhoeffer during the most crucial years of his theological development, discernment, rethinking of discipleship, and action.[1] While these papal interventions insisted on the dignity of the human person and the primacy of the individual in relation to the nation-state, neither called for thoroughgoing political and economic change. These encyclicals aimed at amelioration of the most egregious injustices and reformation of the social order through the practical exercise of charity, rather than leveling, scouring, and building anew from the ground up.

On the other hand, at the time of the reemergence of the modern civil rights movement, Martin Luther King Jr. would have had access to a small canon of social wisdom that was rooted in insights from biblical prophecy, early Christian writing, scholastic philosophy, and reflection on contemporary human experience and lived faith. Taking inspiration from Pope John XXIII and the Second Vatican Council, Catholic social thought underwent serious development and formulation. In *Mater et Magistra* (1961), Pope John introduced a method of social discernment and action pioneered by Belgian priest Joseph Cardijn, familiarly summarized as "see-judge-act." Two years later in

Pacem in Terris, the pope demonstrated the fruits of this method in the affirmation of the common good, the exercise of rights and duties in society, international relations, and nuclear disarmament. *Gaudium et Spes* (1965) is the most representative elaboration of this method and its theological, ministerial, and social implications. Thus, as King pushed desegregation forward in grappling toward a vision of American society as "the beloved community,"[2] CST might have offered a substantive partnership. But despite episcopal statements repudiating racism, despite the participation of vowed religious women and men and clergy in protest marches, despite the loan of church buildings for civil rights workshops and meetings, historian John Deedy concluded, as an institution, the Catholic Church in the United States left no mark on the civil rights movement.[3]

The task of reading Bonhoeffer and King in relation to CST presents certain difficulties. If pastoral letters from various regional churches are considered, the corpus of CST swells and becomes quite unwieldy; it is reasonable, then, to limit this discussion to papal teaching. Yet, this limitation requires the exclusion of significant material, such as the Medellin documents in which the bishops of Latin America offered a scathing critique of multinational capitalism, massive poverty, and government and ecclesial collusion in social oppression. At the same time, papal social encyclicals must be grasped in relation to particular historical, social, and cultural contexts; still, their application may transcend time and place and circumstance. Then, despite the variety of issues and problems treated in encyclicals and pastoral letters, some urgent social problems remain unaddressed or lack detailed attention. Finally, a feature crucial to the vibrancy of CST is that "cluster of social movements," which contributes to its ongoing development through a remarkable diversity of thought, organization, collaboration, and action.[4]

Even a cursory review of the work of Bonhoeffer and King uncovers several themes common to CST including life and dignity of the human person, love, solidarity, justice, option for the poor and vulnerable, rights and responsibilities as well as participation in the creation of the common good. But Bonhoeffer and King thought and wrote and spoke about and acted on these issues well before the burgeoning of CST in the run-up to and aftermath of the Second Vatican Council. To quote a rueful remark once made by Jesuit theologian and philosopher Bernard Lonergan, CST like "the church always arrives on the scene a little breathless and a little late." Still, a consideration of the thought of Dietrich Bonhoeffer and Martin Luther King Jr. in relation to CST may prove fruitful. To that end, this essay considers two themes foundational to theological reflection on social injustice and to Christian social praxis that responds to injustice: life and dignity of the human person and solidarity. But before taking up this discussion, it is worth noting a few similarities and differences between Bonhoeffer and King.

Some Similarities and Differences between Bonhoeffer and King

Bonhoeffer and King were each the prophetic conscience of his generation. Both died at the relatively young age of thirty-nine, each man cut down by political brutality, disguised as the state in the case of Bonhoeffer and as white supremacist vigilantism in the case of King. Both men were pastors, pacifists, and activists, but the demands of such advocacy spurred rather than prohibited their impressive literary theological output. Even decades later, their lectures and sermons, essays and books, letters and meditations remain intellectually profound and provocative, moving and movingly relevant. With his Berlin degree, Bonhoeffer aimed at and won a coveted university appointment as well as a Sloane Fellowship to New York's Union Theological Seminary. And, on more than one occasion, Harold De Wolfe, who directed King's Boston University doctoral dissertation, tried to interest him in a seminary or university appointment to no avail.

Peter Paris maintains that Martin Luther King Jr. was one of the two major American theologians of the twentieth century, the other being James H. Cone.[5] Arguably, Karl Barth has no equal among European theologians of that century, yet Dietrich Bonhoeffer is a more than worthy contender. Like Barth, Bonhoeffer centered his theology on the Christ-reality, but he contextualized that theology historically and concretely, relating it to sociological theory as well as classical and modern philosophy. King, on the other hand, did not pursue formally dogmatic or systematic theology beyond his dissertation; however, in exhortations at training sessions for marches or demonstrations, in public addresses, and in sermons, he synthesized theological ideas that welled up from his deep Baptist grounding, personal prayer, ongoing study and reflection, conversations, and intellectual and moral orientation to the philosophy of personalism.

As activist theologians, Bonhoeffer and King held a high doctrine of love that emphasized love of enemies and the rejection of violence and the use of coercive power. And they acknowledged the "strangeness" that such love might evoke. In a political situation characterized by growing "disastrous idolatry," Bonhoeffer recognized "humanity's enemy as God's enemy."[6] In a sermon preached at the secret seminary, Gross-Schlonwitz, he urged: "When evil befalls you, it is not you who are in danger, but the others who do you evil; and if you don't help them, they will perish in it. Therefore, for the others' sake, and because of your responsibility to them—repay no one evil for evil. For has God ever repaid you in such a way?"[7] And in *Discipleship* he wrote: "To overcome enemies by loving them—that is God's will which is contained in the law."[8] Similarly, King argued: "To meet hate with retaliatory hate would do nothing but intensify the existence of evil in the universe. Hate begets hate; violence begets violence; toughness begets a greater toughness. We must meet the forces of hate with the power of love; we must meet physical force with soul free."[9] Such a notion of love is neither sentimental nor emotional, but other-directed, exacting, self-transcending, and accepting of responsibility and suffering and sacrifice. "We are called to advocate vicariously for the other in every-day matters," Bonhoeffer insisted, "to give up possessions, honor, even our whole lives. . . . Love demands that we give up our own advantage."[10] King used the term *agape* to refer to this love and described it as "an overflowing love which is purely spontaneous, unmotivated, groundless, and creative. It is not set in motion by any quality or function of its object. It is the love of God operating in the human heart." And, he concluded, "the best way to assure oneself that love is disinterested is to have love for the enemy-neighbor from whom you can expect no good in return, but only hostility and persecution."[11]

Bonhoeffer and King maintained that the church cannot turn away from the world and that any attempt to cordon off the religious from the social order not only endangers faith with privatization, but is likely to result in grave moral confusion, even error. Each man reiterated this in word and in deed and would have welcomed the explicit teaching of the 1971 Synod of Bishops that "Action on behalf of justice and participation in the transformation of the world fully appear to us as a constitutive dimension of the preaching of the Gospel, or, in other words, of the mission of the Church's mission for the redemption of the human race and its liberation from every oppressive situation."[12] Bonhoeffer and King understood that the amelioration of injustice was limited and would never upend social oppression and injustice. King reckoned that thoroughgoing social change necessarily would involve confrontation with political and economic power brokers or their representatives; he opted for nonviolence and passive resistance. In the thick of the devastating human destruction of the Holocaust and the Second World War, Bonhoeffer was driven to support forcible regime change in Germany. But nonviolence remained the preferred response of these activists.

Each theologian sought to release the power of religion for healing and creating in society, for justice and good. King once stated, "any religion which professes to be concerned about the souls of men [*sic*] and is not concerned about the social and economic conditions that scar the soul is a spiritually moribund religion only waiting for the day to be buried."[13] And Bonhoeffer claimed, "A Christianity that withdraws from the world falls prey to unnaturalness, irrationality, triumphalism, and arbitrariness. . . . For the Christian there is no retreat from the world, neither externally nor into the inner life."[14] Thus, in their fearless commitment to live Christian faith as a concrete social witness of solidarity with oppressed humanity, these two Christian thinkers anticipate Johann Baptist Metz's notion of the practical-political theologian. For Bonhoeffer and King sought to grasp and relate, in word and deed, the story and meaning of Jesus directly and clearly, contrasting it to those distorted renditions that truncated the searing demand of the gospel; to counter the silence, the equivocation, the accommodation, the stifling moral atmosphere generated by the malice of state and society and by the reticence of the churches; to preach, speak, and act on behalf of the *sanctorum communio*, the beloved community.

Two Principal Themes

The themes treated here—life and dignity of the human person and solidarity—are stated in the semantics of CST; however, these themes were anticipated and stand out quite clearly and concretely in the thought and Christian social praxis of Dietrich Bonhoeffer and Martin Luther King Jr.

Life and Dignity of the Human Person: In their theology and activism, Bonhoeffer and King emphasized the inestimable, sacred value of the life and dignity of the human person, who, imprinted with the divine image and social by nature, may never be subject to the state exhaustively or absolutely. Christian tradition holds that human beings are made in the image and likeness of God, the doctrine of the *imago Dei*. Each theologian articulated this doctrine in language that penetrated and exposed contempt for Jews, blacks, and others of good will and the idolization of Aryans and whites.

Bonhoeffer interpreted the doctrine of the *imago Dei* through a christological lens, thus affirming God's gratuitous love, expressed ever so concretely in God's

> entering as a human being into human life, by taking on and bearing bodily the nature . . . of human beings. God becomes human out of love for humanity . . . tak[ing] on human nature as it is. . . . Jesus is not *a* human being but *the* human being. What happens to him happens to

human beings. It happens to all and therefore to us. The name of Jesus embraces in itself the whole of humanity and the whole of God.[15]

In response to the mass deportation of Jewish citizens as well as the decree ordering Jews to wear visibly a yellow star of David on their clothing, Bonhoeffer linked Christianity's heritage with the Jews and the Jews with Jesus. "Driving out the Jew(s) from the West," he wrote, "must result in driving out Christ with them, for Jesus Christ was a Jew."[16] He situated the historical and cultural unity of the West in Christ, set the very humanity of God against Hitler's simultaneous contempt for and idolization of humanity.

King's interpretation of the same doctrine insisted that each and every human being "is an heir to a legacy of dignity and worth." He wrote:

> This innate worth referred to in the phrase the image of God is universally shared in equal portions by all men [sic]. There is no graded scale of essential worth; there is no divine right of one race which differs from the divine right of another. Every human being has etched in his personality the indelible stamp of the Creator.[17]

Segregation betrays the sacredness of the human person; it treats human beings as means rather than ends, thus reducing them to objects, to things. Moreover, because human beings are made for relationship, for communion with one another, segregation violates the conditions for the possibility of relationship, of communion. Further, King deemed segregation to be an insult to God and God's creation. Segregation and its twin, discrimination, not only insult God who is the Creator and Giver of human dignity and human rights, but also insult God's image and glory enfleshed in human creation.

Protection of the life and dignity of the human person stands as the basic evocation for the church's social wisdom; but in far too many historical situations the church has been complicit in individual and social attitudes, policies, and acts of racism, ethnocentricity, and xenophobia. The primitive Christian community bowed to anti-Judaism on doctrinal grounds; as that community matured, it formulated a missiology, which was hostile not only to theological and religious divergence, but also to human physiological difference, even heretically admitting a rank ordering of human beings.

During the long period of segregation and discrimination (including more than seven decades of open lynching) that followed Reconstruction in the United States, the silence of the social wisdom of the Catholic Church was conspicuous. As African Americans galvanized in demand for constitutionally guaranteed civil rights, a handful of bishops ordered the desegregation of diocesan parochial schools. However, the general Catholic approach to the racial question coincided with gradualism, an indefensible attitude of "wait and see." Writing from his Trappist abbey in Gethsemani, Kentucky, Thomas Merton called this posture "a onesided and arbitrary attempt to reduce others to a condition of identity with ourselves, one of the most disastrous of misconceptions."[18] The U.S. bishops' signature pastoral letter on racism, "Brothers and Sisters to Us," appeared eleven years after King was assassinated and twenty-five years after the Supreme Court ruled on behalf of desegregation legislation in *Brown v. Board of Education of Topeka*.

By the time Pius XI wrote the encyclical *Mit Brennender Sorge* (1937), Hitler had acquired both the chancellorship and presidency of Germany (1934) and the Nuremberg Laws (1935) had abrogated citizenship for German Jews and banned marriage between Jews and Aryans. The encyclical criticizes individual and group attempts to "exalt" or "divinize" a race or a particular people or the state (#8) and defends the connection of the Old Testament to Christianity as integral and indisputable (#15, 16), but neglects to mention the Jewish people and their religious and social suppression. (It is startling to note that the word *Jew* does not appear at all in the English-language translation.) The horrific events of *Kristallnacht* eighteen months later seem to suggest that the encyclical had little, if any, influence. More than twenty-five years later, *Nostrae Aetate* (the Declaration on the Relation of the Church to Non-Christian Religions, 1965) repudiated the teaching of contempt, which had held the Jews directly, individually, corporately, and historically responsible for the death of Christ. And in 1997 Pope John Paul II in an opening address to a symposium on the roots of anti-Judaism acknowledged the moral collapse of worldwide Christian conscience during the Holocaust, but avoided associating "the church as such" with this failure.

Solidarity: Love of neighbor is a longstanding characteristic of Christianity and furnishes part of the substratum of its social wisdom. Bonhoeffer and King likewise presume the primacy of the neighbor, of the "other," of the solidarity of humanity with regard to racial, cultural-ethnic, national, and ideological differences. But the concrete historical conditions of African Americans under legalized segregation and Jews under Nazi rule put pressure on CST to move beyond toothless moralizing. Again, Bonhoeffer and King outpaced the church. They recognized the social impact of sin on individuals and groups, proposing solidarity as a counter to social sin.

Bonhoeffer came to realize that solidarity with the Jews was "theologically commanded and that the church [was] bound up with their fate."[19] In the 1933 address, "The Church and the Jewish Question," he advocates church resistance to any legal or social compromise with the state that would "endanger the Christian proclamation. . . . The church has an unconditional obligation to the victims of any [lawless or arbitrary] ordering of society, even if they do not belong to the Christian community." Bonhoeffer presents three avenues of solidarity: to dispute the legitimacy of state action, to directly aid the victims of state brutality, and to take "direct political action." In explanation of this third course, he writes: "The third possibility is not just to bandage the victims under the wheel, but to jam a spoke in the wheel itself."[20]

Andreas Pangritz points out that when the Confessing Church proclaimed cooperation in Hitler's war to be a patriotic duty, Bonhoeffer reacted by calling the church to confess its guilt in failing solidarity.[21] "There is only one way to turn back," Bonhoeffer writes in *Ethics*, "and that is acknowledgment of guilt toward Christ." He outlines a confession of guilt that begins with an acknowledgment of individual sin as "a source of poison for the community . . . [which] soils and destroys the body of Christ."[22] He continues:

> The church confesses that it has not professed openly and clearly enough its message of the one God, revealed for all times in Jesus Christ and tolerating no other gods besides. The church confesses its timidity, its deviations, its dangerous concessions. It has often disavowed its duties [Ämter] as sentinel and comforter. Through this it has often withheld the compassion that it owes to the despised and rejected. . . .
>
> The church confesses that it has witnessed the arbitrary use of brutal force, the suffering in body and soul of countless innocent people, that it has witnessed oppression, hatred, and murder without raising its voice for the victims and without finding ways of rushing to help them. It has become guilty of the lives of the weakest and most defenseless brothers and sisters of Jesus Christ.[23]

These passages show Bonhoeffer grappling with solidarity in light of the church's intimate union with Christ; that union requires acceptance of Jews as brothers and sisters of Jesus Christ and as brothers and sisters of those who want to be Christian. Whatever is to be done is to be done in the name of Jesus Christ and in free fidelity to him. "What matters," Bonhoeffer concludes, "is *participating in the reality of God and the world in Jesus Christ today*, and doing so in such a way that I never experience the reality of God without the reality of the world, nor the reality of the world without the reality of God."[24] Further on, he observes:

> Human beings are placed in a position of concrete and thus limited, i.e., created, responsibility that recognizes the world as loved, judged, and

reconciled by God, and act accordingly within it. The "world" is thus the domain of concrete responsibility that is given to us in and through Jesus Christ. . . . We do not create the conditions for our action but find ourselves already placed within them. . . .

All of this must be so because God in Christ became *human* because God said Yes to humanity, and because we as human beings are permitted and called to live and act before God and the neighbor within the confines of our limited human judgment and knowledge.[25]

By the time of the essay "After Ten Years," presented as a gift to his immediate family and co-conspirators in the German Resistance Movement in 1942, he had begun to incarnate the tensions and desires about which he wrote. He knew intimately that to be Christian meant to respond to the here and now in compassion and action, not in "mere waiting and looking." To be Christian, he wrote, is to "have some share in Christ's largeheartedness by acting with responsibility and in freedom when the hour of danger comes, and by showing a real compassion that springs, not from fear, but from the liberating and redeeming love of Christ for all who suffer."[26] For Bonhoeffer, the life and cross of Jesus Christ set the standard and the parameter for his notions of solidarity and compassion in the here and now.

Following the successful conclusion of the Montgomery bus boycott, King addressed the First Annual Institute on Nonviolence and Social Change. He titled his remarks "Facing the Challenge of a New Age." The centerpiece of this presentation was the notion of a new world intimated in the new self-respect and sense of dignity on the part of African Americans and in the demise of worldwide colonialism and imperialism. The most challenging responsibility that King identified for the achievement of this new world, which already has grown geographically close, is spiritual unity. He writes: "Through our scientific genius we have made of the world a neighborhood; now through our moral and spiritual genius we must make of it a brotherhood."[27] This will require, he continues, setting "the Christian virtues of love, mercy and forgiveness . . . at the center of our lives." Only love and justice will prevent the new age from duplicating the old age of violence and fear and hatred. Further, King says, "If we are to speed up the coming of the new age we must have the moral courage to stand up and protest against injustice wherever we find it."[28] Such commitment might lead, he concludes, to suffering, sacrifice, and, perhaps, martyrdom, but this is the price of freedom, of justice.

When confronted with the reticence of black clergy to become engaged in the civil rights struggle, King reminded them that "a minister cannot preach the glories of heaven while ignoring social conditions in his [*sic*] own community that cause men [*sic*] an earthly hell."[29] He did not hesitate to criticize the black church's excessive and unseemly preoccupation with the otherworldly:

> There is something wrong with any church that limits the gospel to talkin' about heaven over yonder. There is something wrong with any minister . . . who becomes so otherworldly in his [*sic*] orientation that he [*sic*] forgets about what is happening now . . . forgets [about] the here. *Here* where men [*sic*] are trampled over by the iron feet of oppression. *Here* where thousands of God's children are caught in an air-tight cage [of poverty]. *Here* where thousands of men and women are depressed and in agony because of their earthly fight . . . where the darkness of life surrounds so many of God's children.[30]

The Christian church, King maintained, had a social mission rooted in its prophetic task and fidelity to the preaching of Jesus. For King, living a social gospel is the only authentic witness of a Christian life in a segregated and oppressive America.

In "A Christmas Sermon on Peace," King again raised his voice against segregation, but also spoke out against war, violence, militarism, economic exploitation, and the proliferation of nuclear weapons. "Our loyalties must transcend our race, our tribe, our class, our nation; and this means we must develop a world perspective. . . . [W]e must either learn to live together as brothers [*sic*] or we are all going to perish together as fools."[31] He challenged all people of good will to find food, clothing, and shelter for "the millions of God's children in Asia, Africa, Latin America and [the United States]." He said: "It really boils down to this: that all life is interrelated. We are all caught in an inescapable network of mutuality, tied into a single garment of destiny. Whatever affects one directly, affects all indirectly. We are made to live together because of the interrelated structure of reality."[32] King never restricted his social concern and compassion to the plight of blacks or even to that of the poor and unemployed in the United States. He believed, "We are all one in Christ Jesus. And when we truly believe in the sacredness of human personality, we won't exploit people, we won't trample over people with the iron feet of oppression, we won't kill anybody."[33]

Conclusion

The world has changed since the deaths of Dietrich Bonhoeffer and Martin Luther King Jr. Their legacies of Christian discipleship, love in action, prophetic self-transcendence, and interruptive speech continue to challenge decisively

Catholic social thought, particularly in its more institutional presentations. The ongoing wars in Iraq and Afghanistan, racism and xenophobia directed at migrants around the globe, ethnic conflicts in Africa, Asia, Europe, and Oceania, threats of genocide, the new global slavery, and organized sex trafficking of children and women: these evils incriminate the whole of humanity and despoil the body of Christ. Bonhoeffer and King were the conscience of their generation; may their example be a goad to those of us who stand by idle, wringing our hands, always arriving a little breathless and a little late.

CHAPTER 8

Church, World, and Christian Charity

Timothy P. Jackson

D ietrich Bonhoeffer and Martin Luther King Jr. lived out, unto death, a drama that began with early Christianity and abides to this day: the complex and tense relation between the church and the world. Their lives and writings followed very different trajectories, but they converged, from opposite directions, on a similar final position. Both were inspired by biblical faith; both attempted to say a prophetic word in the context of grave social injustice; and both were martyred. In the mid-to-late 1930s, Bonhoeffer entertained a view of the church that approached a troubling sectarianism, however, and he progressed to affirm a much more politically engaged and morally implicated community of (German) believers. King, on the other hand, began with a rather comfortable sense of the symbiosis between Christianity and liberal democracy, only to move to a much more radical religious critique of (American) secular society. In the early 1930s, Bonhoeffer had insisted on "the secularity of the church," its being "a reality in the world,"[1] but under the pressures of Nazism his early vision gave way to that of a uniquely inspired church, set apart from the world and sin. By 1937, this ecclesiology threatened to become a self-congratulatory dichotomy between "us Christians" and "them pagans." Even when the target was the Nazified church, the gulf between true Christian community and the corrupt world was overdrawn. King, in turn, never ceased to offer bilingual moral appeals to both Scripture and the founding documents of the American

republic, but he became increasingly clear that his primary identity was as a
Baptist preacher, with his antiwar protests and even his civil rights activism
being secondary. King moved in a very different political environment from
Bonhoeffer's, but the primacy of faith allowed the later King both to criticize
America and to put that critique in a broader, nonsecular frame. In both men's
cases, I shall argue, the development just described was a function of two main
factors: (1) a deepening understanding of the meaning of Christian love and
holiness, and (2) a more mature sense of the urgency, yet ambiguity, of shared
human history.

Bonhoeffer

Dietrich Bonhoeffer's majestic work *Discipleship*, published in 1937, is occasionally marred by a tone of sectarian triumphalism:

> Just as God, the holy one, is separated from anything common, and from
> sin, so too is the community of God's holy realm. God has chosen it. God
> has made it the community of the divine covenant. In this realm of holi-
> ness God has reconciled and purified it. Now this place of holiness is the
> temple, which is the body of Christ. . . . Set apart from world and sin to
> be God's own possession, the body of Christ is God's realm of holiness in
> the world. It is the dwelling place of God and God's Holy Spirit.[2]

As one of the courageous founders of the Confessing Church in Germany and
an architect of its opposition to Nazism, it is understandable that Bonhoeffer in
the mid-1930s would characterize the body of Christ as ideally pure and separate, the world as actually sinful and engulfing. Threatened by fascist tyranny
and its totalizing idolatry, it is only natural that he would equate sanctification
with "our separation from the world in expectation of Christ's coming again."
He even went so far as to aver that "The church-community moves through
the world like a sealed train passing through foreign territory."[3] Attention to
his totalitarian context makes Bonhoeffer's call for a kind of separatist purity
understandable, but the call was nevertheless problematic. His definition of
discipleship as "action which lifts [Christians] out of the world"[4] was bound to
invite spiritual hubris. Such a sublime attitude could not survive the trials of
history and the grace of God in Christ. Any temptation to equate "the world"
with "the sinful" (including genocidal Nazis) and "the church" with "the pris-
tine" (including confessing Christians) proved to be just that, a temptation.

    In 1937, the Confessing seminary at Finkenwalde (a kind of "Protestant
monastery") was shut down by the Gestapo; shortly thereafter, Bonhoeffer

was forbidden to speak in public or to publish; yet through much of 1939 he conducted clandestine classes at various sites in eastern Germany. In 1940, Bonhoeffer met Colonel Oster of the *Abwehr;* he began more actively to plot against Hitler; and he continued to put behind him the *Weltschmertz* ("world weariness and wariness") and hint of *ressentiment* evident in his writings from the Finkenwalde period. Christ's body *on the cross* is anything but a sanctuary from the profane, so how can his body, the church, be unsullied and isolated? To be sure, from his earliest dissertation through his later prison writings Bonhoeffer consistently emphasized that Christians act vicariously for Christ in bearing with and helping to redeem others—the theological principle of *Stellvertretung* ("substitution"). Yet only with *Ethics* (composed 1940–1943) and *Letters and Papers from Prison* (composed 1943–1945) did Bonhoeffer decisively abandon his inclination to limit the Holy Spirit to the church and begin to formulate his "religionless Christianity." Such Christianity rejects the claim of moral purity and the quest for institutional aloofness in favor of contrite service to all others in the messy here and now. Bonhoeffer writes in *Letters and Papers*:

> [Religionless Christians are] those who are called forth, not regarding ourselves from a religious point of view as specially favored, but rather as belonging wholly to the world. . . .
>
> The church is the church only when it exists for others. . . . The church must share in the secular problems of ordinary human life, not dominating but helping and serving. It must tell men of every calling what it means to live in Christ, to exist for others. . . .
>
> May God give [faith] to us daily. And I do not mean the faith which flees the world, but the one that endures the world and which loves and remains true to the world in spite of all the suffering which it contains for us. . . . I fear that Christians who stand with only one leg upon earth also stand with only one leg in heaven.[5]

Far from triumphalist, the later Bonhoeffer offers a striking "Confession of Guilt" for the Protestant churches and defines the Christian church itself as "the place where this acknowledgement of guilt becomes real." He explicitly rejects as unfaithful to Christ *both* a "radicalism" that sees only "the ultimate" and hates time *and* a "compromise" that sees only "the penultimate" and hates eternity. Any opposing of two "realities," the sacred and the profane, as though they are static and independent, is a denial of the reality of the Son. "There are not two realities, but *only one reality*, and that is God's reality revealed in Christ in the reality of the world."[6]

It would be far too simple to suggest that the later Bonhoeffer represents a complete break with the Bonhoeffer of *Discipleship*, but there is no denying that there was real tension and growth here. Undeniably, the resources for a more Christ-like interpretation of church and world were always present in his thought. In 1932 Bonhoeffer asserted that

> It is a denial of the real humanity of Jesus and also heretical to take the concrete church as only a phantom church or an illusion. It is entirely world. This means that it is subjected to all the weakness and suffering of the world. The church can at times, like Christ himself, be without a roof over its head. This must be so. For the sake of real people, the church must be thoroughly worldly.[7]

In "Thy Kingdom Come," also written in 1932, Bonhoeffer again disallows "otherworldliness" and emphasizes that "the kingdom of God is not to be found in some other world beyond, but in the midst of this world."[8] Nonetheless, by 1937 Bonhoeffer had recoiled at the abuses of Nazism and lapsed into the language of reactive separatism. He had subsequently to *overcome* this separatism in and through the fires of history. *Life Together* (1939), published two years after *Discipleship* and written after the Finkenwalde seminary was closed, represents the transition to the far less sectarian perspective of *Ethics*. In *Life Together*, Bonhoeffer reminds us (and himself) that "the Christian . . . belongs not in the seclusion of a cloistered life but in the thick of foes. There is his commission, his work."[9] This deeper perspective, I have argued, was urged on Bonhoeffer by his own conscience and the worsening social conditions in Europe. One must commend him mightily for this growth, an escape from a snare that has captured many to this day.[10]

Bonhoeffer was a brilliant and faithful man, who eventually achieved martyrdom, but he was (like many of us) capable of pride in the church, disdain for the world, and double-mindedness about both. We do Bonhoeffer more honor by acknowledging the ways in which he grew through war and suffering than by imagining that he had a perfectly clear and consistent moral vision all along. Rather than a simple break with *Discipleship*, one sees in the later works a maturation of views, a deepening empathy with "the world" and a more realistic take on "the church" in line with his 1932 lectures and addresses. Still, it is not too much to say that Bonhoeffer reconceived *Discipleship*'s idea of sanctification. It continued to mean Christian growth in holiness, but now it became an engaged leavening of the world rather than a proud escape from it—an open book (a.k.a. the gospel) rather than a sealed train. For the later Bonhoeffer, the point is neither to oppose nor to equate the natural and the supernatural, the secular and the ecclesial, but, instead, to witness to their being reconciled in Christ. Christian witness eschews ideological principles cut off from life in God, and it takes special care not to reduce agapic love to a "vague idea."[11] Such witness is also decisively universal: "in the body of Christ all humanity is accepted, included, and borne," and the church's "concern is the eternal salvation of the whole world."[12]

More recently, John Howard Yoder has employed the "church/world" distinction to bracing effect, but he strikes the proper cautionary note:

> Frequently the faithfulness of the church has been put to the test the moment believers were asked to follow the path of costly conscientious objection in the face of the world's opposition. Yet *we should not over-dramatize the normal expression of our mission in and through society.* The church's calling is to be the conscience and the servant within human society. The church must be sufficiently experienced to be able to discern when and where and how God is using the Powers, whether this be thanks to the faithful testimony of the church or in spite of its infidelity. Either way, *we are called to contribute to the creation of structures more worthy of human society.* But the church will also need to be sufficiently familiar with the manifest ways in which God has acted to reconcile and call together a people for himself, so as not to fall prey to the Sadducean or "German Christian" temptation to read off the surface of history a simple declaration of God's will. *God is working in the world and it is the task of the church to know how he is working.*[13]

The phrases "in and through society" and "in the world" help mitigate any worrisome dualism, even as the call "to contribute to the creation of structures more worthy of human society" guards against sectarian withdrawal. As Yoder observes, the church "is itself a structure and a power in society"; moreover, "the saving work of Christ . . . reaches even beyond the realm of the church."[14] These observations are very much in the spirit of the later Bonhoeffer. Augustine and much of the Christian tradition notwithstanding, Bonhoeffer ultimately tolerates no appeal to two fixed classes of persons, the elect and the damned, for "In the body of Jesus Christ, God took on the sin of all the world and bore it."[15]

"All the world"—not merely the Confessing Church, any more than merely the "German Christians." Such universalism and its attendant behavior is challenging and dangerous. Bonhoeffer himself initially fled from that danger and escaped to safety in England and then New York. Of course, in spite of his pacifist leanings, Bonhoeffer quickly returned to Germany and participated in the plan to assassinate Hitler. Bonhoeffer certainly protested vigorously against

Nazism in the 1930s, and the Gestapo exiled him from Berlin in 1938 as a result. But immediately afterward he (quite naturally) went abroad, only later deciding to return to Germany and participate in truly radical resistance. This geographic movement, a truly heroic refusal of detachment and security, mirrored his moral and theological evolution on church/world relations.

Unlike Martin Luther King Jr., who endorsed nonviolence throughout his mature career, Bonhoeffer came to accept the practical necessity of armed resistance to political murderousness. If King was an in-principle pacifist, however, Bonhoeffer was not a straightforward defender of just war. Whereas classical just war theory finds taking up the sword against tyranny to be fully permissible under certain conditions, Bonhoeffer was too Lutheran and too impressed by the paradoxes of life for such a sanguine view. He considered his own moves against Hitler and Nazism to be simultaneously obligatory and sinful, a dilemmatic sign of our collective fallenness. He stressed the importance of concrete action and was unwilling to make violent resistance to evil into a general principle. Yet he was also unwilling to see his own intended *act* of homicidal resistance as without essential ambiguity and guilt. I find this hyper-tragic stance moving yet difficult to render coherent,[16] but it has palpable affinities with (the sixteenth century) Martin Luther's judgment that Christ on the cross was not merely punished for human sin but became himself actually sinful.

What motivated Bonhoeffer's extreme final thoughts and deeds? With this question, we come to the promised treatment of Christian love. In *Discipleship*, Bonhoeffer had quoted the Sermon on the Mount (Matt. 5:43-48) and emphasized that "love" is "the word which summarizes everything in it." He then spent several pages explaining that love "is put into the clear-cut context of love for our enemies," that "the enemy is always the one who hates me [since] Jesus did not even consider the possibility that there could be someone whom the disciple hates," that love seeks nothing in return but "seeks those who need it," and that in concrete terms love is to "bless . . . do good . . . [and] pray" for enemies "without condition, without regard for who they are." In this way, the Christian overcomes evil with good, vicariously taking onto him- or herself the "neediness and poverty" of enemies and "their being guilty and lost" and thus bringing them "closer to reconciliation with God." Importantly, the governing factor in all this is Jesus Christ. "The actions of the disciples should not be determined by the human actions they encounter, but by Jesus acting in them. The only source of the disciples' action is the will of Jesus." In addition to helping to reconcile others, "Loving one's enemies leads disciples to the way of the cross and into communion with the crucified one."[17]

The later Bonhoeffer speaks less often and less explicitly of "love"—the term does not appear in the subject index of the older English translation of *Ethics*—and he is extremely wary of the ways the term can mislead or lull to sleep. Early on in *Ethics*, Bonhoeffer quotes 1 Corinthians 13:2-3 and tells us that "love" is "the decisive word that distinguishes the human being in disunion from the human being in the state of origin." This can seem to be an echo of the analysis of Matthew 5:43-48 in *Discipleship*, but Bonhoeffer immediately warns that

> After all we have seen thus far, we must exclude any definitions that seek to understand the essence of love as human behavior, as disposition, dedication, sacrifice, will for community, as feeling, passion, service, or deed. All this without exception can exist without "love." . . . Everything we usually call love, everything that dwells in the farthest depths of the soul and in visible deeds, indeed, even brotherly or sisterly service to the neighbor that springs from the pious heart—all this can lack "love." This is not because any human behavior always still contains a "remnant" of selfishness that completely obscures love. Instead, it is because love is something completely different from what these definitions imply.[18]

I sometimes worry that the later Bonhoeffer is *too* reluctant to give substantive content to Christian charity, but it is crucial to realize that he does not leave us with simple skepticism here. The key to appreciating love aright is to focus on 1 John 4:16: "God is love [*agape*]." According to Bonhoeffer,

> *God* is love: that is, love is not a human behavior, sentiment, or deed, but it is God who is love. What love is can be known only by one who knows God; the reverse is not true, that one would first know what love is—that is, from nature—and therefore also know what God is. But nobody knows God except one to whom God reveals himself. Thus nobody knows what love is except through God's self-revelation. Love is therefore God's revelation. God's revelation, however, is Jesus Christ.[19]

Clearly and rightly, Bonhoeffer wishes to avoid all anthropocentric definitions of love, and the later Bonhoeffer would presumably grant that even "love of enemies," if humanly modeled and motivated, is but a glittering vice. It is also evident, however, that, as in *Discipleship*, his criterion is christocentric: the *imitatio Christi* provides the concrete meaning of charity. One is not left with a pure *via negativa* leading to an inscrutable transcendental virtue. Indeed, to the question, "What is love?" Bonhoeffer replies:

> [Love is] the reconciliation of human beings with God in Jesus Christ.
> The disunion [*Entzweiung*] of human beings from God, from other human
> beings, from the world, and from themselves has ended. Their origin has
> once again been given back to them as a gift. . . . Love means to undergo
> [*Erleiden*] the transformation of one's entire existence by God; it means
> being drawn into the world in the only way in which the world is able to
> live before God and in God alone. Love is thus not a choice [*Wahl*] made
> by human beings but their election [*Erwählung*] by God.[20]

In Bonhoeffer's estimation, only such a theocentric understanding of love
can sustain the true love of enemies mandated by the Suffering Servant and
incumbent on all believers.

What if anything changes, then, between *Discipleship* and *Ethics*? In the
former work, Bonhoeffer cannot avoid the language of prideful separatism
even in the discussion of love of enemies. Bonhoeffer writes there: "The community of Jesus' disciples, the community of better righteousness . . . has left
everything behind to gain the cross of Christ."[21] As I have maintained, such
accents on purity and withdrawal all but disappear by the early 1940s. An
element of Christian elitism remains in the later Bonhoeffer's "New Testament" claim that Jesus Christ is "the sole definition of love"[22]—why should
God be so limited?—but *Ethics* is a remarkable affirmation of "the world" and
the Christian's place in it. "The disunion [*Entzweiung*] of human beings from
God, from other human beings, from the world, and from themselves has
ended."[23] Similarly, the *Letters and Papers from Prison* is vigorously inclusive
and kenotic: "The only profitable relationship to others—and especially to
our weaker brethren—is one of love, and that means the will to hold fellowship with them. God himself did not despise humanity, but became man for
men's sake."[24]

In his concluding days, for all their pain and anxiety, Bonhoeffer was a reconciled and transformed man. He was capable of self-doubt and self-criticism,
as he expressed to Eberhard Bethge:

> I often wonder who I really am—the man who goes on squirming under
> these ghastly experiences in wretchedness that cries to heaven, or the
> man who scourges himself and pretends to others (and even to him-
> self) that he is placid, cheerful, composed, and in control of himself, and
> allows people to admire him for it (i.e., for playing the part—or is it not
> playing a part?).[25]

But Bonhoeffer typically took his own advice in *Ethics* and let go of human
psychology, including introspection, to attend to realities beyond himself. Even

as his erotic love for Maria von Wedemeyer grew across 1943–1945, so, too, did his agapic love of all human beings, especially Jews but including Aryans—even those Aryans called *"Deutsche Christen."* Both of these loves were in and by the grace of God. As Bonhoeffer proclaimed in prison, "God wants us to love him eternally with our whole hearts—not in such a way as to injure or weaken our earthly love, but to provide a kind of *cantus firmus* to which the other melodies of life provide the counterpoint."[26] Ironically, it was his election by God for a deepening sense of the obscenity of war and for a widening solidarity with both victims and victimizers that led Bonhoeffer to resolve to kill *der Führer*—the unspeakable idolater but also the fellow sinner, the domestic monster but also the beloved enemy. Bonhoeffer was first imprisoned and then humiliated and hanged for his trouble, but he thereby bequeathed a lasting legacy to the world as well as the church. Part of this legacy is precisely to blur the world/church distinction in the name of biblical charity.

King

Martin Luther King Jr. was the son, grandson, and great-grandson of a minister, so the Christian tradition was "in his blood," so to speak, but he was also a member of an upper-middle-class black family, born in 1929 and raised on "Sweet Auburn" Street, the (relatively) prosperous African American section of pre–World War II Atlanta. Though certainly victimized by legal and social prejudice as a child and young adult—I have no desire to soft-peddle the effects of Jim Crow—King's economic and educational standing nonetheless initially left him comparatively insulated from the more virulent strands of racism. Having graduated from historically black Morehouse College in Georgia's capital, he went north for the rest of his formal schooling, first to Crozer Theological Seminary in Upland Pennsylvania for his Master of Divinity degree and then to Boston University for his doctorate. No doubt, partially as a result of this privileged background, the young pastor who accepted a call from a church in Montgomery in 1954 was not a political firebrand. He was opposed to racial segregation, but it was Claudette Colvin's and Rosa Parks's refusals to give up their bus seats to white passengers in 1955 that first galvanized his activism. More specifically, it was King's election to head the Montgomery Improvement Association and its call for a bus boycott that originally elevated his Sunday sermons to daily social relevance. Even as, to get where he was going, Bonhoeffer had first to unseal his train, so King had to integrate his bus. Yet neither mode of transport could fully anticipate their final common berth on the cross.

From the time of chattel slavery to the present day, the black church in America has typically resisted any sharp contrast between the sacred and the profane.[27] As a haven from abusive, soul-crushing slave owners and the locus of education, self-help, social networking, and civil protest (however tacit), as well as personal spirituality, the African American church has usually transcended any "Enlightenment" gulf between private faith and public politics. From the outset of his career, King's speeches and homilies reflected this holism. He could worry about the social escapism implied by a clergyman's too-heavy accent on "treasures in heaven," but he was following a recognizable pattern in consistently drawing on the civic language of "human rights" and "constitutional law," as well as the biblical diction of "agapic love" and "the kingdom of God," in making his rhetorical points. He called upon the United States to live up to its unfulfilled promise of freedom and equality for all, perhaps most famously by declaring in his 1963 "I Have a Dream" speech that "America has given the Negro people a bad check, a check which has come back marked 'insufficient funds.'"[28] He did not confine himself to references to American history and its declared values, however; nor did he limit his tactics to legal or popular protests. He characteristically accented, even gave priority to, biblical virtue and doing "God's will"; and he justified a conscientious violating of positive "laws" on the basis of their having no binding status if contrary to eternal and natural law.[29] Still, King showed little sense in the 1950s and early 1960s of a possibly tragic and irremediable collision between democratic capitalism and religious faith, hope, and love.[30] The challenge was straightforwardly to synthesize these two cultural strands. In the mid-to-late 1960s, however—with the escalating war in Vietnam, the rise of the Black Power movement, the lingering effects of colonialism, and the general recalcitrance of poverty and racism in spite of legal reforms—the theoretically congenial coexistence of (Christian) church and (American) world became less tenable for him. Integration of American blacks and whites gave way to a more profound interrogation of all cultural systems, past and present.

In *Stride toward Freedom*, published in 1958, King's central action guide was *agape*, which he defined as "understanding, redeeming good will for all men"[31] and which he equated with four main features:

1. "disinterested love . . . a love in which the individual seeks not his own good, but the good of his neighbor";
2. a focus on "the need of the other person";
3. "a willingness to sacrifice in the interest of mutuality";
4. "a recognition of the fact that all life is interrelated."[32]

After the assassination of John F. Kennedy (1963), the assault by police on peaceful demonstrators crossing the Edmund Pettis Bridge (1965), and the Watts race riot (1965), King retained *agape* as his chief moral criterion, but he became increasingly emphatic that "we as a nation must undergo a radical revolution of values" and that "a broader distribution of wealth" is necessary in the United States.[33] This more strident tone was accompanied by the insistence that a more global approach to economic and social justice was required by biblical ideals and commandments. As King put it, "our loyalties must become ecumenical rather than sectional."[34] He was never seduced by the sectarian temptation, but by 1967, King's critique of American society went far beyond an insistence on practical consistency with the Constitution and Declaration of Independence. He called for "a new kind of power . . . infused with love and justice," and he prescribed "profound structural changes in society," including "a contemporary social and economic Bill of Rights to supplement the Constitution's political Bill of Rights."[35] The later King emphasized the need for a guaranteed "annual minimum . . . income for every American family," and his characterization of "the beloved community" became ever more prophetic and eschatological.[36] King less often associated such a community with Americanism and more often highlighted the inevitable slippage between principles and practices for Christians and non-Christians alike, worldwide.

The adult King had long been committed to love of neighbor and nonviolence, insisting that Christ provided the "spirit and motivation," and Gandhi the practical "method," of the civil rights movement.[37] More specifically, King consistently argued that violence is "impractical," because it leads to "a descending spiral ending in destruction for all," and "immoral," because "it thrives on hatred rather than love" and thus "destroys community and makes brotherhood impossible."[38] These basic convictions are controversial, of course. I myself am not so sure that taking up the sword to defend the innocent must always be moved by or thrive on hatred. Indeed, I have contended that, *in extremis*, taking the life of an aggressor is not necessarily incompatible with loving him as a neighbor. Unlike *eros* and *philia*, *agape* does not always connote a warm feeling of empathy or affection for another. Death is not the greatest evil, and it is better—better *for oneself*, as well as for others—to be lethally constrained than to become a successful mass murderer, in my view. But once the commitment to nonviolence was in place for King, it did not change.

Throughout his life, moreover, King remained basically optimistic in metaphysical outlook, famously averring that "evil has a self-defeating quality," that "the arc of the moral universe is long but it bends towards justice," and even that "unearned suffering is redemptive."[39] These sentiments, especially the last one, are also debatable. King was not writing primarily for an academic audience, hence we should not expect him to qualify his claims with philosophical punctilio. Nevertheless, lest one encourage immorality, it is surely better to say that "unearned suffering *can be* redemptive," *under the right conditions*. Those conditions arguably include: (a) that the suffering be voluntary (no coercion), (b) that the suffering not be a function of self-loathing (no masochism), and (c) that the suffering not be futile (no profligacy).[40] Whatever one might think of King's upbeat metaphysics, however, by the time of the planning of the Poor People's March on Washington (1968), his initial reformation of secular culture sounded more and more urgent and more and more revolutionary. He never abandoned nonviolence as an ideal, but he increasingly feared that violence was the all-too-real and predictable outgrowth of injustice. (The 1968 protest by Memphis sanitation workers was the first march personally led by King to turn violent.)

King's assassination by the bigoted James Earl Ray in April of 1968 left us forever unsure of how he would have implemented his deepening ethical and religious vision. But the more plaintive and indicting chord had been decidedly struck. This new chord, I hasten to emphasize, was not a departure from Christian charity but, rather, a working out of its most profound implications. In 1963's *Why We Can't Wait*, King had written that "we need emulate neither the 'do-nothingism' of the complacent nor the hatred and despair of the black nationalist. For there is the more excellent way of love and nonviolent protest."[41] In 1968's *Where Do We Go from Here?*, he sounds the same basic theme, with a decidedly universalist spin: "This call for a world-wide fellowship that lifts neighborly concern beyond one's tribe, race, class and nation is in reality a call for an all-embracing and unconditional love for all men. This often misunderstood and misinterpreted concept has now become an absolute necessity for the survival of man."[42] "All men"—not merely blacks, any more than merely Americans. This is King at his antisectarian best.

Interestingly, if Bonhoeffer in *Discipleship* was tempted to turn his back on the sinful world and escape into an innocent church, the early King was tempted to withdraw from an activist church and to disappear into the secure world of childhood. In the midst of his leadership of the church-based Montgomery Improvement Association (MIA) and its call for a bus boycott, King was arrested for speeding and spent some time in jail. The following night (January 27, 1956), King received at home yet another in a series of menacing phone calls and was driven to what David Garrow calls a "crisis of confidence." Garrow recounts King's remarkable "kitchen table epiphany," in which King, like Bonhoeffer in prison, found direction and meaning in the presence and holiness of God, rather than in either the church or the world alone and as such.[43] King was not promised political victory or even personal safety—after all, he was murdered some twelve years later—but he was given the fortitude to face and transform reality.

In sum, if Bonhoeffer grew out of a potentially prideful sectarianism, King grew into a more realistic appreciation of the enduring tension between Christ-like norms and all temporal political economies. Both men, over time and through the trials of history, struck a wiser balance between pious separatism and impious accommodation in church/world relations. That balance remained nonviolent for King, while for Bonhoeffer it encompassed willingness to commit homicide (if not murder), but I can see no faithful reason to extol the one and fault the other. We need both models of holiness. Both modern martyrs refused personal security and engaged their sinful surrounds with a passion and compassion that transcended too-easy us/them and sacred/profane bifurcations. A similar *phronesis*, animated by love, will surely be required by individuals and groups as long as time and sin endure.

Conclusion

Christian theologians and even Scriptures equivocate at times on the meaning of "the world." Sometimes, the phrase is normatively neutral and connotes the finite, physical universe of sticks and stones, flesh and blood, in which and for which Christ became incarnate (e.g., John 3:16). At other times, the phrase is much more loaded and refers to the fallen realm of ungodly principles and sinful practices against which Christ stands (e.g., John 7:7). In the wake of World War II and the civil rights movement, it is crucial that the two senses not be conflated and that their ambiguities not be exploited to evade the imitation of Christ and love of the neighbor—that is, to belittle others and/or pump up self. More to the point, Dietrich Bonhoeffer and Martin Luther King Jr. help us see that in neither sense of "the world" is it something that disciples (or anyone else) can simply ignore or avoid. Disciples testify to Christ and resist and condemn evil in themselves and others, but they remain finite and sinful *and a loving presence in the world* even when redeemed. Christ-like love affirms just judgments, and divine grace makes it possible to be "not conformed" to the fallen world but rather "transformed" by spiritual renewal (see Romans 12:2, an injunction often quoted by both King and Bonhoeffer). When Christians are starkly contrasted with "the Jews," "the flesh," or "the world," however, one rightly suspects that the wagons are being circled by a phobic or haughty church. This is not fidelity to the Lord but a snide redaction of his life and work, a regrettable tactic evident in the church early and late. Jesus explicitly warned his followers against such divisive judgmentalism (Matt. 7:1-5).

Many sincere Christians fear that a modern loss of faith and the moral "subjectivism" that often accompanies it will leave one unable to judge right and wrong, but, in fact, faithlessness makes it impossible to *decline* to judge others and to forgive. The turn toward self and away from God does not strip us of the power to draw moral contrasts; it *forces* us to draw invidious contrasts everywhere, to bolster our shaky confidence or to survive "the rat race." Absent the light of the world, we "keep our metaphysics warm" (T. S. Eliot) by freezing others out. Yet true unity with God means *not isolation from the world but communion with it*, both because of and in spite of its/our sin. Seeking to elevate self by denying or denigrating others is very close to the core of fallenness, and such a temper spells the end of a prophetic witness that directs attention to God. (The true prophet does not berate or banish people, any more than she capitulates or panders to their evil; instead, she speaks the truth that we are not alone and thereby inspires people with the love of God.) As Bonhoeffer perceived, "For human beings in a state of disunion [with God,] the good consists in a judging whose final criterion is human beings themselves."[44] "Judging stands in absolute opposition to doing [in Christ]."[45] The Nazis were paragons of "discriminating" evaluation—their contrasts between Aryans and non-Aryans, the true *Volk* and the false *Volk*, mirror earlier Christian distinctions between the elect and the damned—and the American South (and North) lived for centuries ruled by "the color line" (W. E. B. Du Bois), a bias that has only partly been overcome. Indeed, even relativists are inevitably dogmatic about their relativism.

Lest I seem too severe here, I grant that sometimes Christian distinctions—for instance, Augustine's "two cities"—*become* invidious over time, perhaps in spite of their authors' conscious intentions. There is no denying, nevertheless, that at other times the distinctions in question—for example, "the saved" vs. "the reprobate" and "us Christians" vs. "them Jews"—are invidious from the outset. They are *meant* to annul outsiders, even as were race-based slavery, the Nazi Nuremberg Laws, and American Jim Crow codes. The political task of Christians like Bonhoeffer, King, *and us* is to say the prophetic word to the world (and the church) in a way that overcomes these vices, voluntary or otherwise. After millennia of ecclesially endorsed pogroms, inquisitions, forced conversions, racial servitude, and holocausts, we must be more than wary of any language that metaphysically divides neighbor from neighbor, for this divides everyone from God. It is also, need I say, an insult to the cross of Christ. Christ could set brother "against" brother, son "against" mother, and so on, but only in the sense of demanding priority for the God who is Love. When God is given that priority, then true reconciliation becomes possible and worldly divisions can cease. To make the name of Jesus Christ itself a tool for writing off or belittling others and for promoting or parading self is more than grotesque, but ecclesial history is full of this.

Dietrich Bonhoeffer and Martin Luther King are rightly our heroes for helping Christians to atone for this regrettable past, for teaching us to be in the world and for the world but not simply of the world. Together with likenesses of Saint Elizabeth of Russia, Archbishop Oscar Romero, and others, their statues now properly grace the façade of Westminster Abbey in the heart of London. Just above the Great West Door, Bonhoeffer and King symbolically bless those going into, but also those coming out of, the historic church. This loving ability to stand with both insiders and outsiders, both believers and atheists, is a gift to the wide world worthy of the Son of God. We can only try to go and do likewise.

CHAPTER 9

The Cross and Its Victims
— Bonhoeffer, King, and Martyrdom —
Craig J. Slane

The stories of Dietrich Bonhoeffer and Martin Luther King Jr. both reveal and contribute to a new landscape of Christian martyrdom. Their respective continents were separated by an ocean, but Bonhoeffer's Germany and King's America lie embedded in common narratives of racism and oppression, accompanied in turn by movements of liberation and social justice. Bonhoeffer and King were slain not chiefly because they confessed faith—though they did confess brilliantly and in this way remained faithful to the conventional martyr pattern—but because they were compelled by the cross of Christ to act in the interest of others. We hear faint echoes of this theme in an early Christian martyr like Polycarp of Smyrna, whose death could be described as a death "for others" because it brought to a close a regional episode of persecution. But martyrs for justice do not take center stage until late modernity. As I have argued elsewhere, recent martyrs have added a new letter to the alphabet of martyrdom.[1]

In this essay I would like to build on the theme of martyrdom and justice, but from an angle different from that of my earlier work. In an age when victims and violence so occupy our attention in theology, we may pose the question: What can be added to our understanding of Bonhoeffer and King as martyrs if we consider them theologians of the cross working in proximity to *violence and its victims*? My thinking takes place within a terminological field defined by a series of complexly interlocking concepts:

Cross—Victim—Martyr—Violence

Thinking for a moment of Jesus, we might bring these terms together in a sentence like "on the cross hangs a victim of violence whose meaning will include the struggles of the martyr" or "the martyr shares in the violent victimization of Jesus on the cross." What I hope to show is (1) that the logic of the cross brings the concepts of "martyr" and "victim" together in a way that deepens our understanding of martyrdom as such, and (2) that King and Bonhoeffer are martyr-victims who reveal complementary but distinct trajectories emanating from the cross: *identification with victims* and *love for oppressors*.

I write fresh from a reading of René Girard's *I See Satan Fall like Lightning* and Mark Heim's interesting appropriation of Girard's broader work in *Saved from Sacrifice*. I will not attempt a Girardian interpretation of King and Bonhoeffer. That is too much for this brief chapter, and besides, I am finding that, despite their many similarities, King and Bonhoeffer are not easily arranged together in any conceptual constellation. Nevertheless, some Girardian terminology bleeds into this manuscript, and I confess openly my sympathy with Girard's conviction that entrenched mechanisms of violence are personified in the figure of Satan, who wishes by deception to perpetuate the illusion that violence is viable, necessary, and socially beneficial for the human race.[2] To Girard, the public concern for victims, which has now become a defining value of democracy, emerges from the momentum of the biblical narrative, wherein God is shown to side with victims. Like the perceptive Nietzsche, Girard finds Christianity and Judaism to have introduced something novel in this regard. But what Nietzsche found repulsive Girard finds promising. Girard depicts the victimization of Jesus as the means through which God most clearly exposes the so-called victim mechanism and ushers the way into a new community of love and nonviolence. In this essay, then, I will follow Girard's understanding of the term *victim* by investing it with the double meaning of one who receives unjust treatment *and* exposes the truth about violence and God's strategy to overcome it.

The Martyr-Victim Caught in the Cross-Logic of Violence

"He disarmed the rulers and authorities and made a public example of them, triumphing over them in it." This provocative statement taken from Paul's letter to the Colossians (2:15) shines a light on the profound-yet-odd logic of the cross. By means of the cross, God manages to expose, weaken, and subvert the

powers that violate and victimize Jesus. The cross is odd logic because, among other things, it fashions an unimaginable *injustice*—the injustice done against a truly innocent victim—into a foundation for justice. With a justice like that, who needs injustice? To say it another way, the logic of the cross includes the call to end human violence even while the cross itself stands as an epic instance of human violence. And if the cross per chance belongs to God such that God can be said to operate by this odd logic, then God by implication would seem to be complicit with human violence—a distasteful assertion for our (and perhaps any) time. How *is* God connected to violence when it targets "innocent" victims? This is surely one of the excruciating questions for which religion is expected to have an answer. Cheap answers do not suffice. Many of Christianity's detractors find the God of the Bible to exacerbate rather than solve the problem of violence.[3] The cross is as scandalous now as it ever has been.

Bonhoeffer and King are martyrs whose lives cannot be extricated from the realities of violence and victimization. Living amidst dehumanizing and exploitive powers, each took stands *against* them as a way of standing *for* victims. Only infrequently do we openly discuss their victimization by those powers. We seem to prefer our martyrs as heroes, masters of their own destiny, stouthearted messiahs who pull us along the curve of human progress and galvanize our collective hopes for a better tomorrow. Indeed, in popular literature the term *martyr* is suffused with heroism. The martyr exhibits a palpable freedom vis-à-vis death and, fully cognizant of danger, continues to witness boldly to truth. By contrast, the term *victim* is laced with passivity. A victim receives the harmful actions of others, exhibiting a strain of weakness and helplessness in the face of danger. For most of us, the compelling features of Bonhoeffer and King have more to do with their activities as free moral agents acting on deeply held Christian convictions than with their victimization by destructive powers.

Bonhoeffer and King have surely won their place in the church's martyr tradition. Yet martyrdom is a many-sided phenomenon. Since martyrs do not kill themselves but, rather, are killed for reasons grounded in powers inimical to Christ, it is possible to treat them as victims, *martyr-victims*, as we have said. Martyrdom always has two sides: the free activities of martyrs in situations of danger and the broader web of earthly power relations in which it apparently becomes "beneficial" to eliminate them. Obviously Bonhoeffer and King do not qualify as innocent victims in the absolute sense. That belongs to Jesus uniquely and remains a cornerstone of Christian confession. Yet that should not be allowed to obscure the fact that Bonhoeffer and King share meaningfully in the victimization of Jesus.[4] As such, they illumine a feature of his life and death that is distinctly relevant to our contemporary discussion of victims, violence, and religion.

To imagine Bonhoeffer and King as martyr-victims requires some surgery on standard treatments of the *theologia crucis*. To be specific, we must connect our interpretation of the cross more securely to the world. Rather than ask first what God is doing in the cross, the standard question, we must learn to ask what the world is doing in this event. To be sure, God was (and still is) doing something vital in the cross of Jesus, as Paul the apostle concluded at the end of what must have been for him an excruciating period of disequilibrium after his experience on the road to Damascus. Christians profess the cross as the very means of God's forgiveness and reconciliation, but that does not exhaust its meaning. Is it not obvious that, as a public instrument of torture designed to deliver strong messages to onlookers—of impotence in the face of imperial power, of competence on the part of politicians to avert the worst in social crises—the cross belongs to the sociopolitical realm? Do we really imagine God to need an instrument like this? And despite Tertullian's confident assertion that the blood of martyrs is "seed," a dictum often pronounced with a tinge of triumphal glee, do we imagine God needing to keep the instrument working in the cruelties meted out on Jesus' followers? Before Jesus' death and resurrection, a cross most certainly would not have resembled a characteristic work of the divine, to Paul or anyone else, unless it were as an indication of divine assent to human judgments about what is necessary to preserve the social order.

The Christian claim that God was up to something in the cross of Jesus was just the sort of thing that could induce ridicule from educated Roman citizens. As Origen describes the logic of the philosopher Celsus, a renowned second-century opponent of Christianity, if Jesus were really a divine figure as Christians claimed, he would have provided a noble defense of himself and condemned his accusers.[5] Celsus could not imagine God becoming a party to an unjust death. Thus, to him, the cross of Jesus must be yet another in a succession of *just* political executions, not a message from the gods. If Christians today are prone to scoff at Celsus, it is because they no longer see clearly that the cross belongs to the world. It marks a characteristic habit of human society: a transaction of controlled violence deployed as a strategy for dealing with its own problem of violence. In the words of Girard, "when unappeased, violence seeks and always finds a surrogate victim."[6] Unresolved violence finds a scapegoat, which in turn alleviates the pressures of violence within the community and brings, at least for a time, a measure of peace. Violence is not without its social benefits, after all.

But the deaths of Bonhoeffer and King should not have happened. Could we say also that the death of Jesus should not have happened? We are so accustomed to the fact that they did happen—so used to making theological meaning out of them—that we tend to miss the obvious: these are *unjust* deaths despite whatever benefits (in Jesus' case *saving* benefits) that accrue to us through them. If we are to say that God is at work in the cross of Jesus and in the "crosses" of those who follow him, as finally we must, it will be a work of the divine provocateur who narrates within human acts of violence so as to deconstruct and to reconstruct their meaning, not the demanding director who walks actors around the stage and scripts their parts. As we would expect, what God is doing in the life and death of martyrs turns out to be very different from what the world is doing, and subtler, too. In cases of Christian martyrdom, as in the cross itself, we are dealing with two circuits, crosswired, such that sparks fly and polarities are reversed. The actors become the acted upon; the ones acted upon become the actors. Human power is exposed; divine power goes undercover. The victims are taken up into the complex if controversial narrative of God's interaction with human history—complex because divine and human actions are surely intertwined beyond our capacity to disentangle, and controversial because, to us, at least, the God of the Bible *seems* to be connected to violence in ways that turn our stomachs and entice us toward other deities.

A full exploration of the martyr-victim motif is too much for this essay. But since we are trying to imagine legacies we must be prepared to think of Bonhoeffer and King as witnesses to God's kingdom in a century that magnified the human condition as one of entrapment in the destructive pattern of reciprocal violence. True, all human history can be described as an episode of protracted violence and victimization. But the fact that we can describe it so, that our perspective has grown wide enough to give violence a name and incisive enough to sicken many of us when we observe it in our Christian ancestors, is due in part to the witness of Christians like Bonhoeffer and King. Their struggles help us to see more clearly that Jesus was a victim of violence—indeed, an expositor of violence extraordinaire—whose cross provides not a divine sanction for violence but a contravention of its canons. As we shall see, Bonhoeffer and King witness to Jesus in quite different ways, from different perspectives, and in very different contexts. Yet the scandal of the cross is a determining factor in each of their dealings with violence.

Bonhoeffer's Cross-Logic: The Martyr Who Reaches to the Victim

I do not wish to exegete Bonhoeffer so much as stay on his trail as he moves from the nonviolent discourse of *Discipleship* to conspiracy against the Nazi government. Clearly Bonhoeffer does not leave the cross behind even when his life makes an unexpected turn toward violence, as his late prison letters reveal. So we find ourselves facing an interpretive challenge. But I am getting ahead of myself.

In *Discipleship*, as Bonhoeffer dealt with the one sermon we know to have changed him, he tried to grasp the meaning of Jesus' admonition not to resist the evildoer (Matt. 5:38-42). In the Old Testament, he noted, retribution is said to stipulate the will of God. There evil meets with retaliation so that it can be identified and eradicated in the interest of constructing a just community.[7] According to Bonhoeffer, Jesus supports the idea of retribution for his followers, but infuses it with another meaning. The retribution that disciples offer is not the kind that gives "blow for blow" but one "patiently bearing the blow, so that evil is not added to evil." Bonhoeffer then makes a set of claims that, given his eventual involvement in conspiracy, give nearly all his serious readers a case of intellectual vertigo:

> The overcoming of others now occurs by allowing their evil to run its course. The evil does not find what it is seeking, namely, resistance and, therewith, new evil which will inflame it even more. Evil will become powerless when it finds no opposing object, no resistance, but, instead, is willingly borne and suffered. Evil meets an opponent for which it is no match. . . . Our voluntary renunciation of counterviolence confirms and proclaims our unconditional allegiance to Jesus and his followers. . . .[8]

In 1937, Bonhoeffer could not imagine an evil so large and strong that it would sever the Christian from this "unconditional" obligation. As is often repeated, for a German Lutheran theologian to assume such a position was both radical and surprising, with precious few historical precedents. But the important thing here is Bonhoeffer's stalwart opposition to the Reformation thinking about war, which legitimated violence as a means of preventing greater evil. For Jesus lays a totalizing claim upon his disciples.

This was no easy position to maintain. Working somewhat like a contortionist, Bonhoeffer maneuvers between the horns of a dilemma. Jesus calls his disciples to a nonviolent way of life, but those who obey his call will run headlong into the teeth of violence. Jesus' way appears to play into the hands

of evil, multiplying victims by allowing evil to run its course, and thus mock-
ing the way of nonviolence. One conclusion we must never draw (and King,
too, insists upon this) is that Jesus' life in rural Palestine rendered him naïve
on matters of institutionalized evil—indeed, his struggle against evil took him
into a prolonged battle with Satan until finally he won by means of the cross.
Assuming Jesus is fully alert to evil, the only way out of this dilemma is to
follow Jesus himself. "There is no other justification for this commandment
of Jesus than his own cross," says Bonhoeffer, which is to say, if I read him
correctly, that for a Christian the cross *is* a fitting retribution for violence, an
effective strategy against evil precisely because it abstains from the vicious
mimetic exchange that feeds violence and causes it to escalate. We should note
that retribution of this sort could abort at any moment if the one suffering
were to give way to retaliatory impulses and lash out against the perpetrators.
Jesus' cross is a retribution for human violence only because he succeeds in the
struggle to the bitter end. Bonhoeffer then quickly adds that one must never
make an ethical program of the cross, for it is not a "good" that overcomes evil,
but, rather, the *suffering love* of God, a vital point, because the cross can be all
too easily coopted into agendas that appear good to those who pursue them.
Pilate and the Roman soldiers surely thought they were acting in the best
interests of Palestine. The twisted cross (swastika) of the Nazis was ostensibly
appropriated from ancient times as a sign of life, strength, and good fortune.
And even (or should we say *especially?*) theologians can easily substitute an
abstract ethic of the cross for concrete acts of love directed to others.

In the suffering love of God the meaning of the cross emerges. Clearly
the cross does not result in the immediate expulsion of violence. In the face
of evil, God is excruciatingly patient, a fact which makes many of us cringe.
But through the patience of suffering love the inner workings of violence are
exposed, if not defused. Despite all rational explanations one might muster in
favor of retributive violence, and there are many from the Reformation to our
own day, it functions as a mechanism that perpetuates and sustains the world
as it is. In the language of Bonhoeffer's *Ethics*, it might be said to surrender to
the penultimate state of affairs. But that is too abstract. For when that mechanism turns against a truly innocent victim it publishes its opposition to God
and the world.

Suffering love, then, accomplishes the *unmasking* or *revelation* of evil, and
therefore constitutes a proleptic-style victory. The Bible portrays a God who
sometimes brings a rapid end to violence, as in the days of Noah's flood and
the coming day when the white rider of the apocalypse will vanquish God's
enemies. But these are violent ends to violence, deployed in situations when

God's patience is exhausted and repentance is no longer possible. By contrast, the cross establishes the proper conditions for reconciliation, making space for repentance and the overcoming of one's enemies through suffering love. Indeed, the love that the victim of injustice shows for her persecutors holds out the prospect of reconciliation, which is why Bonhoeffer calls love for one's enemies the "extraordinary" mark of Christian existence.[9]

A fine-spirited theology indeed, we might say. As with King, a considerable debt is owed to Gandhi for some of these insights. Yet it is just this fine theology that raises eyebrows when we consider the final phase of Bonhoeffer's life. In the course of its sundry interrogations, the Nazi state formed a case against Bonhoeffer by noting his inclinations toward violence as an important factor in his alleged guilt. After the questioning of Constantin von Dietze, the investigative judge of the People's Court in Berlin filed this report: "These statements by the defendant Dietze bring to light that in any case he and Bonhoeffer reckoned with the possibility of *violent* realization of the domestic changes [the coup d'état], which would establish the precondition for their ecclesial and economic-political plans, and that they also consented to this sort of *violent* solution."[10] The irony that a government which sponsored violence on such a massive scale could seriously accuse Bonhoeffer of violence notwithstanding, there is truth in the charge. Bonhoeffer engaged in activities that supported a political reorganization of the Reich triggered by the violent removal of the *Führer*. His conspiratorial activities can be contextualized, explained, understood, defended, justified, and even praised. The evil unleashed in the Holocaust was itself extraordinary, without precedent, and therefore confounding to those who might under very different circumstances remain true to nonviolence. Most of us do not find it hard to cultivate sympathies for Bonhoeffer. Whatever violence he conspired to was not vengeance, and I am rather certain that he took no pleasure in the thought, for example, that Hitler's plane might go down in flames. His activities were undertaken in a spirit of repentance. Even so, Bonhoeffer's contribution to the tradition of nonviolence is problematic, and that means we must work hard to understand how the cross could possibly maintain traction in Bonhoeffer's theology.

If there is a solution to this interpretive problem, it might be this: Bonhoeffer's unswerving dedication to the cross helped him eventually to locate victims and move progressively closer to them. By almost any earthly measure, he was a man of power and privilege. And for a long while, he advocated tenaciously for victims of violence from a *distance* in his writing and speech, as would be expected of his bourgeois class. But distance became a terrible burden. Is this not in part the reason for his summer 1939 crisis in New York?

The decision to return to Germany was much more than geographical relocation, as we know. It was a decision against distance, a decision for a new hermeneutic, for a theology of the cross that modulates into a new key. In *Discipleship*, the focus fell on God's overcoming evil in the world by means of Jesus' cross. More and more, I submit, Bonhoeffer saw the cross as almost no one born into privilege sees it: namely, as the means by which an innocent victim is murdered and by which all other victims burst disturbingly into our field of vision. By making innocent victims of Jews, the world—in the twin forms of the Nazi state and a secularized church—was repeating the evil of the crucifixion, scapegoating Jews under the aegis of so-called positive Christianity. Such scapegoating violence may not have canceled out the so-called unconditional obligation to nonviolence. Nowhere does Bonhoeffer excuse himself from this obligation. To the contrary, he knows himself more deeply as a sinner, as suggested by the late prison poems "The Death of Moses" and "Jonah." But it raises for him a new question: Who will stand beside God when God becomes a victim? This is the provocative theme of Bonhoeffer's poem "Christians and Pagans," and it punctuates the shift of consciousness I am here trying to identify. From the location of the victim the cross looks very much like something engineered by a godless architect. Perpetrators, bystanders, and victims will each have their interpretations. By moving toward victims, Bonhoeffer has seen God more clearly as a victim of violence. That is the "view from below"[11] which changes everything.

Bonhoeffer's movement toward victims meant that he himself became caught in the machinations of violence and retribution. Although we do not know precisely the location of his remains, they are probably mixed together with those of other victims at Flossenbürg, either in a mound outside its crematory or in the mass grave Allied forces prepared to dispose of rotting corpses. This has become for me a symbolic presentation of Bonhoeffer's deep solidarity with victims. When we name him a martyr, we mean that he is a *witness* to Christ, of course. But since martyrs bring many aspects of Christ before our eyes, we ought to say something more specific. Clearly Bonhoeffer does not bear witness to the Christ who resisted the temptation to use violence in his time of trial. That is left to other martyrs. But, unlike many martyrs, Bonhoeffer bears witness to the Christ who was unjustly victimized, tortured, and murdered as a criminal of the Roman state. As such, he causes us to think more carefully about our suspicions that the God of the Bible conspires in violence. Whatever violence we are prepared to predicate *of* God, we must acknowledge new interpretations which suggest that in Jesus Christ a horrific violence has happened *to* God. The contemporary accusation that God is complicit with violence turns out to be true, but not in the way we might expect. God uses violence opportunistically to expose the victim-making mechanism that defines the human condition and lurks behind the inclination to murder. May we not read the entire sweep of narratives that comprise the Hebrew Scriptures as a relentless exposure of victims as victims? From the Cain and Abel story to the evil plots made against Joseph by his brothers, from liberation in Egypt to Abraham's aborted sacrifice of Isaac, from the patient suffering of Job to the patient suffering of the innocent Jesus as portrayed in the Gospels, wherein the one truly innocent victim finally turns the wheel against the perpetrators of violence and puts them on parade as the enemies of God. That this theme would eventually seep into the notion of martyrdom should not surprise us. Much work needs to be done to reconstruct early Christian martyrdom along these lines, for it is likely that, in ways heretofore unconsidered, early Christian martyrs brought other voiceless victims of Roman society into public view.

King's Cross-Logic: The Martyr Who Reaches to the Oppressor

If Bonhoeffer can be called a martyr-become-victim whose eyes were opened to the plight of victims, King might be called a victim-become-martyr whose vision penetrated the façade of the oppressor's power to unveil the oppressor's spiritual vulnerability. Raised in the racist South, King did not have to learn the view from below. His location in the social power matrix would give rise to a quite different task: how to appeal to and move toward the perpetrators of violence. King determined that those who wield their power against the weak are in fact spiritually ill. He perceived that black victims have moral leverage in the taxonomy of reconciliation and therefore become indispensible to the healing of white America's sickness. To put it bluntly, oppressors and perpetrators need the love and forgiveness of their victims in order to be restored to spiritual health. In Genesis, the victim Joseph is the means by which his brothers can find healing. Indeed, Abel is the victim by which Cain can find forgiveness, which reveals why murder is a self-destructive sin. A dead victim does not forgive. That is why the narrative of Jesus' resurrection is vital to any theology which considers the place of victims. The victim Jesus returns to life to testify vis-à-vis his accusers, except that Jesus seeks no vengeance, no payback. Is it not a stunning feature of the Gospels that they do not have the resurrected Jesus meeting up with his enemies? In place of vengeance, Jesus offers love and forgiveness.

King's faith centers on Jesus' love for his enemies. "Love for enemies" cannot be relegated to a principle taught by Jesus, but must be apprehended, rather, in Jesus' movement to the cross. For King, the cross discloses the dire lengths to which God will go to restore broken community. James Cone calls this the basis of King's strength to love. The cross also became the means by which he sifted through and interpreted other faith claims. Moreover, it separated him from both the liberal theology of his training and the ideology of Malcolm X, who would not be persuaded to love the oppressor.[12] There could be no lasting solution to racism, thought King, until the oppressed learned to love their oppressors.[13] Finally, King's commitment to the way of the cross locates him squarely within the tradition of black religious experience where the meaning of the cross is found in the suffering of those who live in its logic.

The alternative to loving the enemy was retaliatory hatred, which only gives evil a double victory. Because hatred multiplies exponentially to consume both the hated and the hater, and because violence only multiplies violence, King saw in Jesus' command an eminently practical solution to violence, a key that could unlock the most devastating problems of humanity. In this vein he could say that loving our enemies is "an absolute necessity for our survival."[14] The trajectory of love is reconciliation, transforming the enemy into a friend. When that happens, says King, we may stand on the side of God and come to know God. In loving our enemies we have an opportunity to know God. Conversely, in hating our enemies we are impeded in our knowledge of God. If King is right that love and hate carry epistemological implications, then failure to love one's enemies will likely result in serious theological mistakes in our judgments concerning God's will for the world, mistakes which further ensnare us in violence and racism.

King lived his life amid constant threats. In January, 1956, in the tumultuous days of the Montgomery bus boycott, King was receiving thirty to forty threats per day. In such conditions, loving enemies was much more than a theological concept; it was a daily struggle. After hearing from friends that a plot was underway to take his life, he made this statement at one of the mass meetings: "If one day you find me sprawled out dead, I do not want you to retaliate with a single act of violence. I urge you to continue protesting with the same dignity and discipline you have shown so far."[15] Shortly thereafter King had his well-known "kitchen experience" in which, through earnest prayer, he found courage to continue the fight for justice despite the loss of safety for himself and his family. Continuing meant loving. After the bombing of his home on January 30, when the police were trying to clear the streets of the angry crowd, King defused the tense atmosphere with these words: "Don't get your weapons. He who lives by the sword will perish by the sword. Remember that is what God said. We are not advocating violence. We want to love our enemies. I want you to love our enemies. Love them and let them know that you love them."[16] Lying awake later that night, King felt anger rising within him as he thought about how his wife and young baby could have been killed. He ruminated on the allegations city commissioners were making against him—that he had brought the bombing on himself by his public statements. "I was on the verge of corroding hatred," he said. Pressured by close friends and associates, he considered an armed bodyguard and applied for a license to carry a gun in his car. But he could not follow through. Instead, he removed an existing weapon from his home. "When I decided that I couldn't keep a gun, I came face to face with the question of death and I dealt with it. From that point on, I no longer needed a gun nor have I been afraid." In Montgomery—a political context ready to explode with violence—King's convictions were tested. Suffering love emerged as his only conceivable weapon.

Although he miscalculated the depth of racism's roots in America and was increasingly confronted with the realities of growing despair and hatred in the civil rights movement, King never wavered on the question of violence. When the collective opinion seemed to drift toward understandings of "Black Power" that opposed nonviolence, King would not yield. Even if every black American turned to violence, King promised to preach that as the wrong way: "I cannot make myself believe that God wanted me to hate. I'm tired of violence. I've seen too much of it. I've seen such hate on the faces of too many sheriffs in the South. And I'm not going to let my oppressor dictate to me what method I must use."[17] To compromise on the question of violence would mean the victims' loss of moral leverage. Whereas violence would only obscure the historical injustices suffered by black Americans in their struggle, nonviolence could expose injustice and bring it into the light of day, not to shame white America, but to save black and white America together.

So what does it mean to name King a martyr? King is no less identified with victims than Bonhoeffer. His racial identity may have identified him *more* closely with victims. But since we are contemplating their legacies together, it seems appropriate here to underscore his appeal to the oppressor. The funeral sermon for the six martyred Sunday school children of Birmingham gives evidence of his remarkable ability both to stand firmly with fellow victims and to plead with the congregation for discipline in the way of nonviolence and continued "faith in our white brothers."[18]

Conclusion

In the end, King and Bonhoeffer were victims of cold-blooded violence perpe-trated in a time of cultural upheaval. As martyrs their witness to Jesus appears to travel along two paths—Jesus' solidarity with victims and Jesus' reconcil-ing love for his enemies. In the end, these are two sides of the one coin, two primary features of one cross. When placed alongside one another, *their lega-cies testify in due proportion to a God who stands by victims and extends the opportunity of reconciliation to their oppressors.* In both cases we are dealing with human beings who realized Jesus' call to find the neighbor, to locate and embrace the "other" as the embodiment of that inclusivity which marks the kingdom of God.

Alas, we should not lose ourselves in fruitless questions of who was more like Jesus, or worse, whether one was right and the other wrong. As Miroslav Volf reminds us, in a world of violence every perpetrator is also a victim and every victim also a perpetrator.[19] I have argued that the cross is an event mired in the complex mechanism of human violence and victim making. We needed that perspective earlier in order to grasp that God in Jesus Christ can be ren-dered as a victim and, moreover, to recognize in the cross not a self-contained episode of victimization but a bellwether for victims *as victims.* When we think of "the cross" we would do well to train ourselves not to see Jesus' cross *alone,* but Jesus' cross together with the crosses of all victims. But perhaps we must now shift the emphasis back toward Paul. For whatever God is doing in the odd logic of the cross, it cannot be fitted completely into the logic of the world. In the cross the voice of God can be discerned as a weak-but-deter-mined call forward to a state of affairs not yet realized. No matter the language by which we grasp for it—peace, justice, reconciliation, the kingdom of God—the fullness of that future eludes us. While we remember the life-witness and death of Bonhoeffer and King because we aspire to stand with victims and love our enemies, we also remember them in order to cultivate deeper longing for what is to come, when the odd logic of God is all in all, when views from above and below are flattened on the broad plain of God's shalom, and all crosses are emptied of their victims.

Part Three

Spaces for Redemption

CHAPTER 10

Bonhoeffer on the Road to King
— "Turning from the Phraseological to the Real" —
Charles Marsh

I

In the late summer of 1930, Dietrich Bonhoeffer came to Union Theological Seminary in Manhattan as a visiting student and postdoctoral fellow supported by the German Academic Exchange Program. When he arrived he was a twenty-five-year-old lecturer at Berlin University. His doctoral dissertation, completed at the age of twenty-one, had been praised by the great Karl Barth as a "theological miracle."

Bonhoeffer had also recently completed his second book, his habilitation thesis in systematic theology entitled *Act and Being*, which many readers will know as a conceptually dazzling and youthfully ambitious exercise that attempts nothing less than a complete overhaul of the German philosophical tradition in view of the axiom "Christ existing as community." A lack of self-confidence was not then, or ever, a problem for Bonhoeffer.

But when Bonhoeffer left New York ten months later, he departed with a new sense of vocation. The technical terminology that distinguished his writings and teaching until 1930 began to fade and a language more direct and expressive of lived Christian faith emerged in its place.

In Tegel prison in 1944, Bonhoeffer would recall the first American visit as one of the three decisive and transformative influences in his life. "I don't think I've ever changed very much," he wrote, "except perhaps at the time of my first impressions abroad and under the first conscious influence of father's personality. It was then that I turned from 'the phraseological to the real.'"[1]

The late David Nelson Duke, a brilliant young historian and professor, in papers written before his untimely death in 2000, said that Bonhoeffer's school year in America cultivated in him "a new kind of moral passion."[2] It was much more than a period of gathering facts and broadening horizons in a different culture, though it was that, too. It was a season of profound personal and spiritual growth sparked by a sober reckoning with the costs of being a Christian, a newfound sense of the multidimensionality of life in Christ, and a more dynamic understanding of the theological vocation.

After his visit to America, Bonhoeffer began calling himself a Christian—rather than a theologian!—and, to the dismay of many of his colleagues and mentors, he began reading the Bible with practical and pastoral focus. His classes at Berlin University often spilled over from the lecture hall to the Bonhoeffer home in Grunewald where a group of young students met to pray, to read Scripture, to drink strong German coffee, to sing and enjoy music—Bach, romantic lieder, and always Negro spirituals—and to brainstorm about new ways of pursuing the theological life. "The questions that Bonhoeffer now posed to his church, its theology, its ethics, and its attitude to Luther were new, an obvious departure from the purely academic sphere."[3] Bonhoeffer returned to Germany "with eyes wider open than before."[4] No longer was it possible "for the young theologian to separate his academic and pastoral activities from the commitment to his vocation."[5]

"Something had happened," Bonhoeffer's close friend and biographer, Eberhard Bethge, noted.

What happened?

I raise this question not only out of interest in Bonhoeffer's biography, but, for the rich possibilities it holds for thinking about the reconfiguration of theology and practice in our time.

Let's start by taking a brief inventory of Bonhoeffer on the eve of his first visit to America, in the generation of Protestant progressives before the King years.

He came to New York restless and unsettled.

The theologian and scholar Clifford Green notes that while still serving as an assistant pastor in the German congregation in Barcelona in 1929, Bonhoeffer was searching for a pathway from the theological ideas he had embraced in his graduate studies to their social expression in lived experience.[6] On June 19, 1929, Bonhoeffer wrote to his former neighbor and teacher, Hermann Thumm, that "principles are quite good, but only until one is taught something better by the language of reality."[7]

His letters from Berlin in the fall of 1929, after his return from Barcelona to complete his second dissertation, reveal even a slight desperation. "The air is close in Germany, close and musty enough to suffocate you. . . . Everything seems so infinitely banal and dull. I never before noticed what nonsense people speak in the trains, on the streets—shocking."[8]

What did he expect of the year in America?

Green draws our attention to an intriguing passage in Bonhoeffer's second theological examination at Berlin that offers a glimpse into his more intimate hopes for the year. In an essay on "choosing texts for preaching," Bonhoeffer suggests that one promising theme for a sermon series is "God's path through history in the church of Christ."[9] Green writes that "the very first text he mentions for such a series is Hebrews 12:1, the verse that culminates the saga of faith from creation to the first Christian martyrs in chapter 11: 'Therefore, since we are surrounded by so great a cloud of witnesses.'"[10]

The verse had particular importance for Bonhoeffer. He told a friend five months later that as he experienced a new country, an unfamiliar theological culture, the churches of the New World, and a country still divided by race, he was searching for "a cloud of witnesses."

In the twelve courses he took during his year as a Sloan Fellow, Bonhoeffer focused on philosophy of religion, theology, and ethics in an educational context and theological climate quite different from the sort to which he was accustomed in Berlin.[11] Bonhoeffer was not impressed with the theology he encountered. He claimed that progressive Protestant thought was "nothing but religion and ethics" determined by a pragmatic calculus. The American seminarians seemed disinterested in the historic Christian doctrines and evaluated theological ideas on the basis of their social utility.

His frequent complaints of the smorgasbord-like character of American theological education most often accompany accounts of his time in the United States; and his observations at the end of the year are no less critical than on that day in the fall of 1930 when he listened in dismay as his fellow students giggled over Luther's doctrine of the bondage of the will.

With so little at stake theologically, and absent the Barthian rediscovery of the revealing and righteous God of Jesus Christ, the American theological seminars, lectures, and discussions, in Bonhoeffer's view, assumed a completely innocuous character. "It has come to this," he complained "that the seminary has forgotten what Christian theology in its very essence stands for." "The principal doctrines of dogmatics are in utter disarray," he said.[12] In America it would appear that it is possible to enter the ministry without having any idea what one believes.

Yet amidst all the hand wringing, we should not lose sight of the important fact that Bonhoeffer had also complained about theology in Germany. He wrote from Berlin, "I'm supposed to be intellectually creative and grade excruciatingly dumb seminar papers!"[13] More significant, however, than the vexing term papers and the claustrophobic trains, Bonhoeffer felt boxed in by institutional constraints and the lack of a vital connection between the classroom and the community. Indeed, I think the larger context of Bonhoeffer's agitated remarks suggests that Bonhoeffer had grown impatient with the enterprise of academic theology, whether taught in New York or Berlin.

In his two dissertations Bonhoeffer had sought to demonstrate the theological necessity of the self coming to itself in community. He had written in *Sanctorum Communio* that "The structural being-with-each-other [*Miteinder*] of church-community and its members, and the members acting-for-each-other [*Fuereinander*] as vicarious representatives in the power of the church-community, is what constitutes the specific sociological nature of the community of love [*Liebesgemeinschaft*]."[14] But he had not experienced the embodiment of such theological affirmations in a community of hope and discipleship; and, more to the point, *he had no way of thinking of theological education as anything other than the work done inside the academy for specialists.*

In America, the central themes in Bonhoeffer's theological thought came to life in unexpected ways. The transformation can be observed in three overlapping areas: in his critical encounter with American social theology, in his exposure to the American organizing tradition, and in his participation in the African American church, all of which offered him theological friendships that crossed national, cultural, and racial boundaries.

II

American Social Theology

In 1930, Union Theological Seminary in New York City was regarded as the bastion of progressive Protestant social thought in North America. The student body was more diverse than at any time in its hundred-year history and included African Americans, Asian Americans, women, and poor whites from the rural South. Union was the flagship seminary of the Protestant liberal establishment, with a faculty of nearly forty that included numerous influential public theologians—none more so than the indefatigable Reinhold Niebuhr, still only two years away from his pastorate in Detroit.

Bonhoeffer had never met anyone quite like Reinhold Niebuhr, the great "dramatist of theological ideas in the public arena" (in Larry Rasmussen's

words), for whom probing analysis of the contemporary situation and existential engagement in its needs and conflicts were more important for theology
than dogmatics and systematic work.[15]

In the concept of "Christian realism," which Niebuhr was working out
in the fall of 1930 and spring of 1931—and which would appear in its most
developed form in his 1932 landmark book, *Moral Man and Immoral Society*—Niebuhr intended to remind modern believers, and all persons, believer
or not, of their thick entanglement in the sinful structures of the world. No
man or woman, however sincere, well-meaning, or pious, could be afforded
final escape in existence from the contradictions and ambiguities in which
human nature is situated. Christian realism means charting a path between
utopianism and resignation, trusting in the grace and forgiveness of God as we
stumble through this world of ethical quandaries and complex political realities. Niebuhr's honest assessments of power and justice struck a chord with a
generation searching for a way beyond liberal idealism and Victorian quietism
to a more realistic and sober assessment of the contemporary situation.

Bonhoeffer took courses both semesters with Niebuhr—"Religion and Ethics" and "Ethical Viewpoints in Modern Literature"—in which he read deeply
in contemporary African American literature. Though Bonhoeffer enjoyed the
courses, he found Niebuhr's views bewildering. Roger Shinn recalls that one
day after "the usual vigorous question period at the close of the class," Dietrich
approached Reinhold and asked indignantly, "Is this a theological school or a
school for politicians?" Bonhoeffer's notebooks are interesting in this light:
after jotting down a few words from Niebuhr's lectures on religion and ethics—"Religion is the experience of the holy, transcendent experience of Goodness, Beauty, Truth and Holiness"—his pen grew still.[16]

But Niebuhr was equally perplexed by the young German, and he was
bold in his criticisms of Bonhoeffer's theology. In response to a remark in a
term paper that the "God of guidance" could be known only from the "God of
justification," Niebuhr noted sharply that Bonhoeffer's doctrine of grace was
too transcendent. Niebuhr pushed Bonhoeffer to think more honestly about
the ethical content and social significance of this "God of guidance." "In making grace as transcendent as you do," Niebuhr said, "I don't see how you can
ascribe any ethical significance to it. Obedience to the will of God may be a
religious experience, but it is not an ethical one until it issues in actions which
can be socially valued."[17]

Niebuhr challenged Bonhoeffer on the doctrine of justification and its
meaning for Christians in the modern world. Justification must be embodied in responsible action and enacted in socially transformative patterns and

practices. Otherwise, one would conclude, a doctrine of grace vanishes into metaphysical abstraction or "purely formal" doctrine. That kind of grace would be cheap grace.

Bonhoeffer never acknowledged an explicit theological debt to Niebuhr and he remained discontent with American Protestant thought throughout his year in New York. Nevertheless, I think it is correct to say that Bonhoeffer was moved and inspired by *the spirit of Niebuhr's theology*, in particular by the vocation of a theologian who engaged the social order with civil courage and ultimate honesty. He had never met a theologian who encouraged robust engagement in the social order or attention to politics, race, and literature; Niebuhr's example opened up new vocational possibilities. In my view, the spirit of Niebuhr's public theology is present every time we hear Bonhoeffer say after 1931 that grace without ethical obedience is a mockery of the cross and that Christ calls us into the midst of the world's conflicts and crises; and when he says, in "After Ten Years," that "civil courage" and "costly discipleship" depend "on a God who demands responsible action in a bold venture of faith, and who promises forgiveness and consolation to the person who becomes a sinner in that venture."[18]

The American Organizing Tradition

Even more formative than Bonhoeffer's encounter with Niebuhr were his experiences in and outside the classroom with representatives of what we might call the American organizing tradition. I refer here to the tradition of progressive Protestant thought characterized by the commitment to piecemeal social reform and the disciplines of community building and organizing.

Since Niebuhr's arrival at Union in 1928, a cadre of Christian social reformers had turned to him for moral and financial support, and time and again, Niebuhr offered it graciously. In his marvelous book *Against the Grain: Southern Radicals and Prophets, 1929–1959*, Anthony Dunbar writes that "without [Niebuhr's] inspiration and practical assistance these movements might not have existed or succeeded to the extent that they did."[19] Niebuhr's encouraging presence and his organizing and fundraising expertise are pervasive in the letters and exchanges of the intentional communities and congregational initiatives that arose and flourished in a remarkably fertile period of American social theology.

Most of the participants in these communities and initiatives worked steadfastly in the tradition of social gospel idealism; which is to say, in the earnest hopes of building the kingdom of God on earth. Clarence Jordan, one of the founders of the Koinonia Farm in Americus, Georgia (which later launched the organization Habitat for Humanity), described the mission of the inter-racial cooperative farm in southwest Georgia as "a demonstration plot for the Kingdom." Of course, these faith-based social reformers hardly had time to sift through the complex ways in which Niebuhr's emerging Christian realist views called into question their own idealism. It speaks to Niebuhr's sensitivities and wisdom, I think, that even as he was rejecting many of the theological and anthropological presuppositions of the social gospel, he embraces the socially transformative energies of the movement, encourages innovation, and does not discourage utopianism at the ground level. He remained grateful for the work of visionaries, dreamers, and idealists, an admirer of the women and men who made great sacrifices to build hope and justice in places of exclusion and distress, and unfailingly affirmed such initiatives as the Delta Cooperative Farm, the Providence Farm Cooperative, the Highlander Folk School, Koinonia Farm, and the numerous other experiments in Christian community arising in the South and around the nation—an admirer even as his own hopes for this-worldly reform were chastened by the sober appraisals of Christian realism.[20]

Nevertheless, Bonhoeffer's knowledge of the American organizing tradition began in his studies with two great teachers at Union, Harry Ward and Charles Webber, and deepened through first-hand participation in their classes in local church-based organizing—as well as in friendships with such theological visionaries as James Dombrowski and Myles Horton. Unfortunately, in the following narrative I will not be able to include Harry Ward; although I recommend to interested readers the first-rate biography written by David Nelson Duke, *In the Trenches with Jesus and Marx: Harry F. Ward and the Struggle for Social Justice.*[21]

Charles C. Webber was a pastor, organizer, professor of practical theology at Union, and author of the book *A History of the Development of Social Education in the United Neighborhood Houses of New York.* In the 1950s and 1960s he was the National AFL-CIO Representative, and the Industrial Secretary for the Fellowship of Reconciliation. Webber's course, "Church and Community," which Bonhoeffer took in the fall semester, resembled what we would later call in the United States a "service-learning experience," though it was much more than that. Webber used the course to introduce seminarians to the lived theologies of a city in the throes of economic distress and to the impressive variety of Christian social ministries in New York. He arranged site visits for students and accompanied them as they journeyed beyond the campus to observe and take part in organizing initiatives based in the churches. Bonhoeffer wrote,

In connection with a course of Mr. Webber's, I paid a visit almost every week to one of these character-building agencies: settlements, Y.M.C.A., home missions, co-operative houses, playgrounds, children's courts, night schools, socialists schools, asylums, youth organizations, Association for advance of coloured people. . . . It is immensely impressive to see how much personal self-sacrifice is achieved, with how much devotion, energy and sense of responsibility the work is done.[22]

The students visited the National Women's Trade Union League and the Workers Education Bureau of America; discussed "labor problems, restriction of profits, civil rights, juvenile crime, and the activity of the churches in these fields"; and studied the role of churches in selective buying campaigns and public policy, drawing on models and insights gleaned from the British Cooperative Movement, whose work Webber praised.[23]

The class also met with officials from the American Civil Liberties Union (ACLU), the nation's premier defender of civil liberties, which, after its founding in 1920, had focused heavily on the rights of conscientious objectors and the protection of resident aliens from deportation. When Bonhoeffer returned to Berlin in the summer of 1931, he told his brother that Germany would need an ACLU of its own.[24] It is important that we recognize his deep commitment to civil liberties. Through his field work with Charles Webber, this nearly forgotten professor of practical theology, Bonhoeffer found a pathway from the theological classroom to the concrete social situation of the church in the world.

In his personal recollection of his cousin's year in the United States, Hans Christoph von Hase said that Bonhoeffer learned so much in America, "more than he probably realized. . . . He learned something that was missing in German theology—the grounding of theology in reality."[25] Whether or not this is a fair claim, what is true is that Bonhoeffer experienced, for the first time, the teaching of theology "to and from embodied, situated particularity" (in Serene Jones's words).[26] He saw, and he felt, the presence of Christ in these spaces of reconciliation and redemption existing outside the walls of the parish church.[27]

The circle of Christian social reformers that Bonhoeffer joined at Union also included such energetic and colorful characters as John King Gordon, William Klein, and Gaylord White, and, most importantly, James Dombrowski and Myles Horton.

James Dombrowski was a white Methodist minister born in Florida who attended Union and then Columbia University, earning a Ph.D. in 1933, with the dissertation "The Early Days of Christian Socialism in America."[28]

Alongside fellow seminarian Myles Horton, Dombrowski cofounded the High-lander Folk School in Tennessee, and based his work there from 1933 to 1942. Dombrowski also established the Conference of Younger Churchmen of the South in 1934, was executive director of the Southern Conference for Human Welfare (1942–1946), edited the progressive *Southern Patriot* from 1942 until 1966, and—in his role as executive director of the Southern Conference Edu-cational Fund (1946–1966)—worked behind the scenes with many of the key players in the 1956 Montgomery bus boycott, including E. D. Nixon, the presi-dent of the Montgomery branch of the Brotherhood of Sleeping Car Porters and leader in the National Association for the Advancement of Colored People (NAACP). Dombrowski was a vital part of a remarkable (and sadly vanished if not vanquished) generation of white southern progressives whose organiz-ing and educational efforts prepared the ground for the civil rights movement of the 1950s and '60s. Among this company of southern dissidents we should also remember Howard "Buck" Kester, Sherwood Eddy, Lillian Smith, Jessie Daniel Ames, and Lucy Randolph Macon.

Long after Bonhoeffer had laid aside his volumes of William James of Har-vard University—whom he read at Union in a yearlong tutorial with Eugene William Lyman—he inquired of the other James (that is, James Dombrowski) and his new friends and acquaintances from New York who would disperse into various and sundry backwater hamlets and urban centers in pursuit of economic justice and racial equality. Like Myles Horton.

Myles Horton was a country boy born in the riverboat town of Savannah, Tennessee, and surely represents a type of theological student and seminar-ian at Union inconceivable to Bonhoeffer before his year in America. Horton grew up in southern rural poverty of the sort documented by James Agee and Walker Evans in their landmark volume *Let Us Now Praise Famous Men*. He was educated at Cumberland College (a school set up for poor whites in Appalachia) and spent many of his student summers working in vaca-tion Bible schools in the mountains of east Tennessee. He was admitted to Union Theological Seminary—he said later in an interview—only because the seminary was looking for a "token hillbilly." Whereas the aristocratic Berliner regarded Union theological education as sophomoric, Horton felt intimidated by the "extremely high" intellectual level at Union, and remained always mindful of his inferior educational and cultural background.[29] It is important not to lose sight of that alternative perception when we listen to Bonhoeffer's complaints.

In 1932 Niebuhr wrote an initial fundraising letter for an organizing ini-tiative called the Southern Mountain School, a project inspired by his former students Dombrowski and Horton. The vision was to create an "experimental school specializing in education for fundamental social change."[30] This was, as mentioned earlier, a fertile time for experimental communities in the United States, and many of these traced their origins to social gospel convictions and quite often to seminary courses at Union. In the 1930s and 1940s, the Highlander Folk School emerged as one of the most important training centers in these golden years of progressive Protestant social missions, equipping southern workers with skills for labor negotiations and mobilization and helping launch the Congress of Industrial Organizations (CIO). In the 1950s, Highlander turned its attention from labor to the burgeoning civil rights movement and helped train a generation of church-based organizers that included such brilliant theological activists as Rosa Parks, Ella Baker, and Martin Luther King Jr. One of the most disgraceful pieces of white anti–civil rights propaganda was the towering billboard along southern highways that featured a photograph of Dr. King attending a 1957 training session at the Highlander Folk School, with the caption "Martin Luther King at Communist Training School."

These representatives of the American organizing tradition "were probably some of the most radical Christians with whom Bonhoeffer ever associated," Clifford Green notes, "and they were radicals not only in theory. . . . They worked on urban and rural poverty, on racial justice and civil rights, on union organizing, on peacemaking, and at the United Nations." These men and women must surely be counted among the greater "cloud of witnesses" of which Bonhoeffer had gone in pursuit. Though it is unlikely they shared similar theological views, "they were all committed to Christian praxis," to lives and careers that were lived in devotion to Jesus, and to the "public, communal, and political" requirements of the gospel.[31]

African American Christian Tradition

The achievement of the recently published translation of Bonhoeffer's writings from America is not only that of highlighting the interconnections between progressive Christian organizing in America in the 1930s and Bonhoeffer's theological transformations. It is also its delineation of "the thread" that links the New York experiences into a coherent life story. The thread that weaves through Bonhoeffer's development in these years and over the coming decade, the thread that gives these years personal and spiritual coherence, is precisely this journey from the "phraseological to the real."

Nowhere in Bonhoeffer's first American encounters is that journey rendered more vividly than in his intense involvement in African American Christian spirituality and in the churches of Harlem, to which I now turn.

Niebuhr's work was challenging; the American organizing tradition was inspiring; but the black church felt like an awakening. Bonhoeffer's experiences there brought theological and personal unity to his year. If in his mature theology the redeemed person, "the self in Christ," is the new being who exists in the togetherness of Christian community, then, as Willie J. Jennings has written in his intriguing essay, "Harlem on My Mind: Dietrich Bonhoeffer, Racial Reasoning, and Theological Reflection," Bonhoeffer's participation in the black church became "the occasion of a new becoming of the self, a new recognition of himself with and in this community."[32] In the black church, Bonhoeffer experienced a vivid manifestation of the new self in Christ, perhaps his first, the vitality of the christological self in a worshiping community.

In his academic writings of 1927 through 1930, let us recall, Bonhoeffer had sketched a bold and ambitious critique of the German transcendental tradition. He objected to the tradition's conception of the world-constitutive subject and its forgetfulness of the Reformation axiom that only God is God. Bonhoeffer worked his way through a thicket of complex themes in his 1927–1930 writings from Berlin, and they were beautiful in their unfolding and explication, but also they produced a certain loneliness. These concepts and categories, for all their scholarly benefits, were bereft of singing and laughter. They were sharp but stark.

Certainly the Christian theologian must heartily affirm God's "being" and God's "act" in formulating the doctrine of revelation; she must say that the meaning of human existence is found not in her own reflections but from the truth revealed in Jesus Christ; the theologian understands that doctrines aspire in their inner logic for social expression. But unless doctrine bursts into life, in preaching, in singing, in friendship, in acts of mercy and justice, doctrine may lead to despair.

When Bonhoeffer arrived for the 1930–1931 academic year at Union Theological Seminary in New York, he had not encountered black people in twenty-five years. His only remark in writing came during his fortnight in North Africa, when he noted his complete bewilderment at the sight of "Arabs, Bedouins, and Negroes sitting on donkeys in great, picturesque white cloaks," traversing the sun-drenched streets of Tripoli in a "colorful throng of peculiar figures." Race, or racism, had not been of concern.

But early in that fall semester of 1930 at Union, an African American seminarian named Franklin Fisher befriended the young Berliner and led him gently into a new ecclesial world of African American Christianity and, I would add, *into a new way of being a Christian.*

Frank Fisher was the son of a Baptist minister in Alabama and had been assigned to the Abyssinian Baptist Church as a pastoral intern. His invitation to Bonhoeffer to join him one Sunday marked the beginning of an intense six-month immersion in the African American congregation. In time, Bonhoeffer, the straight-arrow Lutheran theologian, would begin teaching a Sunday school class for boys and a Wednesday evening women's Bible study, and also assist in various youth clubs. On at least one occasion, he preached in the pulpit of the esteemed Adam Clayton Powell Sr.

Myles Horton vividly recalled an exchange with Dietrich on a Sunday just after he had returned from a morning at the Gothic and Tudor sanctuary on 138th Street between Lenox and Seventh Avenues:

> [Bonhoeffer] was excited and talkative, and instead of going to his room he described the preaching with excitement and audience participation and especially the singing of black spirituals. He was very emotional and did not try to hide his feelings, which was extremely rare for him. He said it was the only time he had experienced true religion in the United States, and was convinced that it was only among blacks who were oppressed that there could be any real religion in this country.[33]

(By the way, that is Albert Raboteau's point in his astonishing essay, "American Salvation," published in the *Boston Review* in summer, 2005.[34])

"Perhaps that Sunday afternoon," Horton commented, "I witnessed a beginning of his identification with the oppressed which played a role in the decision that led to his death. Certainly I witnessed an insight that too few of my countrymen appreciate."[35]

In his theological friendship with Frank Fisher, Bonhoeffer gained "a detailed and intimate knowledge of the realities of Harlem life."[36] And he also learned quickly of the harsh realities of African American life in pre–civil rights America. When it became clear on one occasion that he and Fisher would not be seated in a Manhattan restaurant, they staged a two-man protest and left the restaurant in an outrage. On Thanksgiving Day in 1930, Bonhoeffer joined Fisher and his relatives for turkey and trimmings in Washington, D.C., and later that same academic year, he drove through the Deep South on an auto tour of the country, observing rural poverty and the reign of Jim Crow the same fateful month nine young black men were accused of raping two white women on a freight train, and convicted in a mob atmosphere in successive trials in Scottsboro, Alabama.

Bonhoeffer's presence at Abyssinian in 1930–1931 coincided with significant transformations in Adam Clayton Powell Sr.'s vocational understanding as a minister in an urban congregation. Powell had been the senior pastor since 1908. He was an eloquent preacher and a skilled administrator. But as the Great Depression swept over the neighborhoods of Harlem, Powell was inspired to new spiritual perceptions as a pastor and citizen. In his memoir *Upon This Rock* he said he began to see a Jesus who wandered the streets of Harlem, standing with the poor and distressed as friend and counselor.[37] "Day and night I heard the voice of [the Savior] say, 'I was naked and ye clothed me. I was hungry and ye fed me.'" Powell spoke of the Christian's mission to "preach the unadulterated gospel of Jesus Christ," to bear witness to the "living reality of God," and to make "Jesus Christ real in America and real in the world."[38] And he invited the young German theologian into the full life of the community.

Rudolf Schade, who later taught at Reinhold Niebuhr's alma mater, Elmhurst College, recalled an encounter with Bonhoeffer on a Monday morning after his first experience of preaching at Abyssinian. Bonhoeffer was still elated, and "beaming and enthusiastic," and he asked Schade to take a walk along Riverside Drive. Speaking excitedly in German, Bonhoeffer shared the previous day's events and impressions and conveyed the thrill and joy of having had members of the congregation respond to his message. "The church people had voiced their agreement with his points by punctuating his sermon with 'Amens' and 'Hallelujahs.'"[39] He had never experienced such joy in worship.

Paul Lehmann, a fellow student and later professor of Christian ethics at Union, wondered, curiously, if Bonhoeffer was not spending too much time in Harlem.[40] As early as October, Bonhoeffer signed up for a "Trip to Negro Centers of Life and Culture in Harlem"; he secured a large bibliography on "The Negro" compiled by the Harlem branch of the New York Public Library, and also various orienting articles about the NAACP, the civil rights struggle, and legal aspects of the race issue. Lehmann was a little perplexed by how relentlessly Bonhoeffer pursued "the understanding of the [Negro] problem to its minutest detail through books and countless visits to Harlem." It was as if Bonhoeffer had forged "a remarkable kind of identity with the Negro community," Lehmann said.[41]

Bonhoeffer experienced personal renewal and theological transformation in his brief but decisive participation in the black church and in friendships with Frank Fisher and the other African Americans who welcomed him into their homes. His cousin Christoph von Hase would say that this renewal "prepared him to summon the Confessing Church after 1933 to defend persecuted Jews, . . . and to become engaged at great risk to himself in rescuing individuals."[42] The young philosophical theologian who had found American social theology an offense to doctrinal correctness became the theologian of concreteness.

He was soon calling into question unexamined assumptions that governed the German church and academy and began to rethink the nature of the theological vocation. Eberhard Bethge tells us that Bonhoeffer began going to church. That may sound surprising, but despite the internship in Barcelona, he had never taken much of an interest in public worship until his time at Abyssinian. He fell in love with the Bible and began a rich devotional life, centered on the Moravian Prayer Book, which his governess had given him as a child. He organized spiritual retreats, which were often held at his hut in the forest near Brenau, and encouraged his students to read Scripture with an openness to God's voice and the illumination of the Holy Spirit. He advocated oral confession of sins and was drawn into an intimate reading of the Sermon on the Mount. Colleagues at the university were at first taken aback by these "monkish" practices and made jokes about the ascetic disciplines appearing in the ranks of the "*evangelische*" faculty.[43] But Bonhoeffer was now moving in response to a new understanding of the Christian life; and, as we know, he would only come to speak more passionately of communities of "obedience and prayer," of conformation with Christ, and of spiritual disciplines that bring "purification, clarification and concentration upon the essential thing," as he wrote in *Life Together*.[44]

Under the influence of this "cloud of witnesses," his understanding of the Lutheran doctrine of justification shifted in dramatic ways. He would never again think of grace as a one-sided affirmation spoken by God to sinful humanity but a partnership between the divine and the human enacted out in costly discipleship and in the Christ-shaped polyphony of life. His interest in the essential present form of grace was transformed into the more urgent matter of how Christians should act "under the constraint of grace" and in obedience to Jesus.[45] The grace that frees is the grace that forms, and conformation to Christ became the key that united doctrinal and practical concerns in the theological vocation.

What became of his friend and mentor Frank Fisher? Reverend Fisher graduated from Union, taught at Morehouse College for a spell, and then in 1948 assumed a pastorate at the West Hunter Street Baptist Church in Atlanta. Fisher's tenure began in 1948 and ended with his death in 1960 at the age of fifty-one, as Atlanta was taking center stage in the civil rights movement in the South. He helped quietly build a vital and nurturing Christian community in a city and region divided by race; and the church flourished in Fisher's years of ministry. In 1957, he was one of numerous ministers arrested with Martin

Luther King Jr. for attempting to integrate Atlanta's buses during the Triple L. Campaign. Ralph Abernathy took over pastoral duties at West Hunter after Fisher's death. Franklin Fisher is the most vital historical link between Dietrich Bonhoeffer and Martin Luther King Jr., though the only record of their camaraderie after New York is the lived faith of the movements they served.

III

As I have learned the story of Bonhoeffer's year in America, I have come to see that it offers helpful lessons for thinking about the future of theological education and life in North America. In my own work at the Project on Lived Theology at the University of Virginia, the story of Bonhoeffer in America inspires a commitment to creating *spaces* that foster the revitalization of academic theology through practice. I think of the enterprise of lived theology in this way: as the work of creating spaces where the turning "from the phraseological to the real" is enabled and nourished. This is surely not to presume that one can script the work of the Spirit, to turn the freedom and adventure of theological growth into a pedagogical formula. Still, I have seen how the imaginative use of resources, coupled with creative organizing and design of programs and events, brings to life spaces that encourage a new way of teaching and writing theology.

Dietrich Bonhoeffer did not become a practical theologian as such, at least in the sense in which that term is sometimes used to describe a theological field separate from systematic or philosophical theology; although I would say that the kind of writing he forged in the crucible of the church struggle points us toward a style of theological writing beyond conventional types, or perhaps one that moves us closer to the truth of things: a theology that confesses, that preaches, that prays, that rejoices, that proclaims the Amen and the Yes, that encourages and sustains the redemptive practices of the church; a theology, which even should the church fall into ruins, cleaves to the mysteries of Christ's presence in the world. The tensions ignited in the theological encounter of lived experience are creative and "productive," as Serene Jones has wisely noted, "and the urge to resolve them should be resisted."[46] The turning from the "phraseological to the real" might best be construed as a dialectical pattern essential to the vitality of Christian theology, and thus must be left "irksomely unresolved."

Bonhoeffer does not stop teaching and writing academic theology after 1931. He would offer a seminar on Hegel's philosophy of religion, lectures on nineteenth-century Protestant thought, and the Christology course, which would be published as *Christ the Center*. But Bonhoeffer situates theological teaching and writing in the flow of particular and particularly intense lived pastoral and political realities; and in time, indeed after 1934, the classroom in Berlin became the London pastorate, where he formed alliances with leaders in the ecumenical movement and made sketches for the book on discipleship, the monastic experiment in Finkenwalde, the church struggle, the retreats at the Benedictine monastery in Ettal, the illegal pastorates, and the years of resistance and imprisonment.

In the America of 1930s, among a lost but venerable generation of radical Christians, social gospel preachers, and African American progressives, among the women and men who plowed the soil for the civil rights movement to come, Bonhoeffer, like Martin Luther King Jr. less than two decades later, learned many of the skills and practices that helped him do theology closer to the ground and that enabled the turning from the phraseological to the real.

CHAPTER 11
Interpreting Pastors as Activists
Richard W. Wills Sr.

D ecember 1, 1995, marked the fortieth anniversary of an event
that sparked a movement and initiated a wave of global reform
for justice and freedom that would resonate in regions from
South Africa to the former Soviet Union. It was then that a local
pastor assumed leadership of the Montgomery Improvement Association, a
bus boycott, and an unanticipated civil rights movement. The pastor of Dexter
Avenue Baptist Church, Martin Luther King Jr., could scarcely imagine the
implications of that historic bus incident involving Rosa Parks in 1955, nor the
ways in which his call to the pastorate would subsequently expand his view
of local ministry. As general chair of the effort to commemorate the original
381 days of that historic boycott, I was privileged to discuss the project with
a number of key contributors to the civil rights movement. The most revealing, perhaps, was a conversation I had with a former member of the Carter
administration. "Pastor Wills," he said, "the religious and political right [wing]
s are fast dominating the national agenda with rhetoric that is deepening the
division along class, cultural, and sociopolitical lines. Whatever happened to
the theological mediation expounded by King during the sixties? If we ever
needed that kind of theological sincerity and sensibility to bring us together as
a nation, we need it now!" His commentary was painfully insightful. I looked
away momentarily to an adjacent wall located in the lower unit of the church,
which bore the twenty-six photographs of Dexter's past and present pastors.

My eyes focused on the photo of King. As I gazed I wondered, "What would King do if . . . ?" That initial question came to an abrupt end as another, perhaps more essential, question emerged: What would we do, if we decided to do something instead of simply wondering what King would have done? What would pastors across the state, nation, and around the world do? In fact, what should we do in light of current social trends that threaten to move us in directions that would reverse many civil rights gained over the past four decades? What should the most appropriate pastoral response to this infringement upon our national civic landscape look like?

Prior to my relocation to Montgomery, Alabama, few Richmond, Virginia, congregations, including the one I was associated with, were inclined to support an activist agenda as a means of addressing their adverse social conditions. That sort of approach to community transformation was rarely discussed in clergy circles as a feasible means toward a greater social end, although the import of social gospel ministries had been introduced during our seminary years. We preached, visited the sick and shut-in, counseled the troubled, taught Bible study, and attended meetings. Most of the social issues were addressed by those grassroots activist groups that occasionally sought the support of local congregations (but rarely received it). Surprisingly, church life in Montgomery forty years removed from the days of the bus boycott was not much different. By and large the city climate was one of business as usual. Pastors, and their Montgomery congregations, were not taking a serious stand on any sociopolitical issue of major significance. Most served contentedly within the context of their respective congregational comfort zones. At best, it was a climate of reactive instead of proactive existence. In thinking about what happened to the mediating voice of the sixties it obviously would have been much more convenient to respond to the question of what King would do or say if he were yet alive. Instead I was forced to struggle with the implications of a much more personal response to my colleague's question. What happened to the message and mission of the sixties? Had the activist leanings of the church become a dated means of critiquing a social system that continued to adversely affect the quality of life for their parishioners and our nation? Had pastoral activism seen its day? If so, how could pastors reconcile their newfound complacency with the models of sacrifice and dedication provided by pastors such as Dietrich Bonhoeffer and Martin Luther King Jr., who struggled so courageously and selflessly for the cause of human decency, dignity, and community? How should we understand our respective calls to pastoral ministry? In answer to these musings one might find it helpful to begin with a consideration of H. Richard Niebuhr's attempt to convey the purpose of the contemporary church and its ministry via the lens of our Christian tradition:

> Since the days described in the New Testament Christian ministers have preached and taught; they have led worship and administered sacraments; they have presided over the church and exercised oversight in its work; they have given pastoral care to individuals in need. Though at times these functions have been distributed among specialized orders of the clergy, still each minister, in his own domain, has needed to exercise them all.[1]

From Niebuhr's description, one might readily surmise that the pastor's primary call is grounded in a tradition of preaching, teaching, leading worship, presiding in matters of administration, and caring for those in need. The concern of this essay contends primarily with the last of these, *caring for those in need*. As a function of the call to ministry, pastors are called to care for the needy. Hence, activism becomes a means by which a specific form of care is administered. In the final analysis, pastoral activism might be viewed as an attempt to address human need in keeping with an ancient tradition that is both theologically grounded and contextually driven. The following, therefore, seeks to explicate the place of theology and social context as fundamental influences in the life of activist pastors.

Activism and Theological Foundation

Authentic Christian activism is rarely inspired void of theological grounding. The work of an activist pastor remains deeply rooted in rich theological thinking that views Scripture as normative for all discourse and social engagement. It was belief in a biblical theology that understood God to be keenly aware of and intimately involved with humanity's struggle for freedom that inspired and informed the activism of Bonhoeffer and King most profoundly. While well versed in classical literature and the arguments of modern philosophical thinking, it was the Bible and its record of the New Testament church that represented their final authority and primary theological resource. This certainly appeared to be the point of Wyatt Tee Walker's response to an interview question posed by John Ansbro for his book entitled *The Making of a Mind*.[2] Which writings, he asked Walker (former aide to Martin Luther King Jr.), most influenced King? Some, Ansbro informed him, have suggested Tillich and Barth, still others referred to Brunner and Kierkegaard, Gandhi and Thoreau, but whom do you credit, he asked? In response to Ansbro's inquiry Walker insightfully cited Matthew, Mark, Luke, and John as the writers that informed and influenced King's life in practice and principle most profoundly. Not the great theological thinkers, but the kerygmatic record of Jesus as portrayed by the first-century Gospel writers. Although well versed in the theological investment of others, the Bible was the primary text, the pastor's guide, if you will, to theological formation and its social practice. In a real sense, it was the weight of biblical conviction that became increasingly foundational to Bonhoeffer's and King's activist tendencies. Though their respective calls to the pastorate claimed their central concern, they each held to a theology that viewed social justice as the natural extension of their pulpit ministry into the world beyond. This is a fact that should not be taken for granted, particularly when one realizes that they arrived at a shared place called "activist pastor" traveling two distinct theological paths. In practice, they shared each other's passion for social justice and community, although their respective approaches were theologically varied. Bonhoeffer offers a christological approach to social justice and community while King provides an anthropological approach. It is, therefore, of no small matter to note that although Bonhoeffer and King may have differed in their theological premise, their practice as pastors affirmed a life of Christian activism. While distinctive in their respective theological approaches, both Bonhoeffer and King held to conceptions of community activism as a witness of God's presence with and for the world's redemption. Both individuals embraced theological conceptions that formed the basis of their activist stance as pastors committed to advocating the notions of social justice and community. Their respective commitments to an activist pastoral model continue to serve as sobering reminders of the degree to which one's theological construct may inform the work of the pastor.

Just how critical, then, is the role of theological formation in the development of activist pastors? Certainly, Bonhoeffer and King were pastors who valued the exercise of theological reflection. The influence and impact of their academic rigor within their spheres of involvement are clearly attested and thoroughly documented. Theology undoubtedly served to inform and influence their activist leanings and can similarly serve to inform and inspire countless pastors in this current era's mix of societal wonder and woe. Given the swift currents of our high-tech society and the sociopolitical complexities of the national and global landscape, rich theological conversation may serve to facilitate "the caring for those in need" in a manner that is both socially relevant and theologically sound. A thoughtful theology reminding us who God is, who we are, and how we relate to others may serve as that springboard to courageous caregiving.

Regrettably, few pastors who labor beyond the context of the academic environment are granted the occasion to frequent conversations that engage theology at the sociopolitical boundaries. In fact, many modern-day pastors find themselves hard pressed in their preparation of a Sunday sermon given the multiple demands of a typical week. As such, the extent of their research and writing essentially revolves around the weekly ritual of sermon writing, thereby reducing opportunities for engaging the meaningful discourses provided by theologians past and present. This accounts, at least in part, for the late C. Eric Lincoln's sobering statistics with respect to pastors and their modest theological investments. Most give little or no thought to the place of modern theology. This can be a troubling reality, if in fact one's *pastoral practice* is significantly prescribed by a given *theological outlook*. If theology is in fact the impetus for practice, what does ministry look like apart from thoughtful theological reflection? The pastor's sense of purpose, in such a case, may rarely expand beyond the horizon of a provincial theological view that sees pastoring as little more than a call to preaching, teaching, leading worship, and presiding in matters of administration, with little or no care for the needs of others, especially those not listed in the active column of their membership rosters. Moreover, it perhaps should be noted that all pastoral approaches to theological appreciation are not created equal. That is simply to say, even for those who have tremendous time management skills so as to overcome the underexposure to, and/or the under-appreciation for theology, theological affirmations are by no means monolithic among pastors.

The disparity noted in King's letter written from the Birmingham jail comes as a reminder of the degree to which theological views may vary. This kind of diversity of response is perhaps not at all surprising given the first-century church's eschatological emphasis. Essentially, its worldview was preoccupied with the world to come. Hence, the ambiguous flow of theology's internal witness may paradoxically produce both activist proponents and opponents. Depending, therefore, upon the direction of one's hermeneutic, theology may serve either to further or to frustrate activist efforts. We must never forget that it was opposition borne of theological conviction that led local pastors in Birmingham and elsewhere in the nation to inquire as to whether or not King's premise for clergy involvement was misplaced. Could one effectively pastor a church and engage in the discipline of social activism at the same time? Would these two ideas be congruent with, or in conflict with each other and/or the Bible? To be sure, one could argue that the "fierce urgency of now" announced by Bonhoeffer and King gave expression to a kind of prophetic proclamation and practice that was somehow unrelated to the New

Testament norm. This opposing outlook was commonly argued on the grounds that the New Testament record, which provides a first-century glimpse of the qualifications of the bishop/overseer, does not seem to speak directly to the question of social activism. Additionally, it does not discuss a specific method or to what degree the local pastor should assume this sort of activist response to sociopolitical injustice. For the newly birthed church, a fellowship driven by the *eschatological urgency* of the day, the primary pastoral function was to ready the first-century ecclesia for the eschaton. This perceived function was translated into vigorous evangelism efforts, the provision of doctrinal and practical teachings that reinterpreted old covenant practice into new covenant terms, and the observance of adapted Christian rites and fellowship. There was neither the perceived need nor the criteria by which first-century church leaders felt compelled to move beyond the immediacy of pulpit, pews, and stained-glass windows, so to speak. Personal piety, doctrinal purity, and the urgency of readying for Christ's return drove their theology and dominated the practice of their day. Private faith notwithstanding, Bonhoeffer and King chose to affirm a kind of public activism that refused to overlook the dire social needs of their day. As noted in the New Testament's book of Acts, they held to distinctive theological approaches that rendered care for the least and last among them with a view toward the ensuing community.

Activism and Contextual Foundation

As long as there is a human species, there will be human suffering of one sort or another. To what degree, then, might this context of human perplexity and pain compel pastors to develop a far greater affinity for activist ministries? Theology, as I understand it, may serve as the catalyst for an internal prompting, while the social context by which our lives are defined may serve as an external impetus to actively engage a specific need at a specific historical moment in time. H. Richard Niebuhr further provides an insightful commentary on the impact of one's social context, and the ways in which the human situation (in the interest of theological application) often establishes the need for new pastoral paradigms. As he explains, "It is a conception which has not been manufactured in the study, though theologians in their studies have contributed to its development. It has grown out of the wrestlings of ministers with their problems, out of the experiences of the times and the needs of men, yet it has its roots in the Bible and in the long tradition of the Church."[3] Occasionally, the raw material of life's social context *compels* a pastor's sense of activism in ways that theology might not always *inspire*.

At times it may be the external mandate not the internal reflection of theological abstractions that compels one to service. Over the long span of their nearly-two-thousand-year existence, both pastor and parish have been invited to think and rethink their core assignment, their *raison d'être*. Through the ages, the church has pondered in earnest, Why are we here? and What should we be doing to facilitate the ushering in of God's kingdom most effectively? More specifically, how exactly do we care for those in need now? In many, if not all, instances, the most relevant response to this recurring concern has been contextually based. The challenge of course lies herein. Though in principle the church has sought to remain true to its instruction in personal piety, in practice it has continually been compelled to reconsider and rework its mission with respect to the social and material needs of its community. The New Testament book of Acts provides the classic case study. The mission of the first-century church was considered effective and sufficient until unanswered needs arose within the faith fellowship. The social circumstances of "certain neglected widows" (Acts 6) were in need of being addressed. As a result, new functions, new definitions, new resources were identified, and new roles were developed in an attempt to answer the demand of that material need. This growing edge of newfound service could very well be considered activist in nature. It is ministry taking the form of solutions in direct response to specific social problems. As with our first-century foreparents in the faith, the understanding of what constitutes activist pastoring may emerge primarily out of the needs, not merely the theology, of the church in a given historical/cultural context.

In the absence of World War II and an egregious regime that compromised the tenets of Christian faith, Bonhoeffer might well have settled into a quiet pastorate or fulfilling professorship. Instead, Bonhoeffer is best remembered for his activist stand against the oppressive reign of the Third Reich and the failures of a complicit Lutheran church that served as its theological arm. The demands of that historical context forced the Confessing Church to rethink its relationship to the world it was called to serve so as to make room for what he referred to as the returning child. For Bonhoeffer, social context was critical. It was not simply theology, but the conditions of crisis and social unrest that initiated the return of former disdainers of the church. It appeared providential that in this hour of social crisis the humanist proponents of culture, art, and free expression would experience an awakening which prompted their migration back to the community of faith. Bonhoeffer interpreted this hitherto unlikely societal shift in unmistakable terms, "[I]t was clear that it was not the church that sought the protection and alliance of these concepts but, on the contrary, these concepts, which had somehow become homeless, now sought refuge in the Christian domain, in the shadow of the church."⁴ This shift in context necessitated the provision of some theological rationale for the church's embrace of those (the prodigal populace) who wandered to their *far country* and yet by their fruit (their good works) demonstrated that they were yet of the household of faith, and therefore viable candidates for reinstatement. For Bonhoeffer, the quest was one of locating language that spoke to the church's welcome of concepts that once served as "battle cries against the church" such as reason, culture, humanity, tolerance, and self-determination. In his estimate, their search for haven, amidst an otherwise hostile social context, was not to be interpreted as an initial coming to but, rather, as a *return* to their origin. As Bonhoeffer explained,

> [T]he decisive point is that a return to the origin [*Ursprung*] occurred—in the hour of danger, the children of the church who had become independent and had run away now returned to their mother. Even though their appearance and language had changed a great deal during the time of their alienation, at the decisive moment mother and children recognized one another. Reason, justice, culture, humanity, and other concepts like these sought and found new meaning and new strength in their origin.⁵

Those who embraced humanist values may have physically and ideologically strayed from the household, but at bottom they were to be viewed as children of the Confessing Church who have rediscovered good standing as evidenced in their essential goodness and their renewed confession of Christ. Ultimately, their return was viewed as confirmation of the fundamental fact that life cannot thrive and flourish apart from its origin in Jesus Christ.

In Bonhoeffer's view, the providential purpose of that troubling historical moment was twofold. While the social crisis may have created the catalyst whereby individuals sought refuge in the church, the Confessing Church also was to reaffirm its responsibility to the war-torn world. Bonhoeffer wrote,

> The relationship between the church and the world appears to us today not as the calm, steady unfolding of the power of Christ's name, as it appears in the Middle Ages, nor as the attempt to justify the name of Jesus Christ before the world by connecting it with human names and values in order to honor and to adorn it, as the Apologists endeavored to do in the first Christian centuries. Instead, the relationship between the church and the world appears to us today as this new recognition of the origin that is awakened and bestowed through suffering, that is a flight to Christ resulting from persecution.⁶

In this regard, God redeemed and reformed aspects of both the world and the church simultaneously. Via that context of crisis, Bonhoeffer appropriated an activist position that viewed the world in need of being saved from isolation and abandonment, and the church saved from fanaticism and insensitivity.

Similarly, had Martin Luther King Jr. been birthed under different circumstances, and in a different era, his pastoral approach may have been relative to his improved social experience. King indicated his awareness of the context from which he emerged in his famous "I Have a Dream" address when he stated, "Lincoln had hoped the slavery issue could be relegated to secondary place, but life thrust it into the center of history. There segregation, the evil heritage of slavery, still remains."[7] It was the lingering remnant of the "evil heritage" that King sought to redress and correct. King's questions and conclusions concerning his relationship to God and others were undeniably diffused through the lens of his personal social experience and the historical attachments that defined it. In a very real way, King understood the relationship between the lingering heritage of slavery and his ancestor's hopes for freedom. His theological formation, therefore, emerged out of a specific worldview that had been shaped by specific social realities.

As such, King's dual interest in theology and civil rights can neither be read nor understood apart from his social context and its dire historical attachments. The vestiges of failed social construction, better known as Reconstruction, remained evident to King in and through the oppressive demands of Jim Crow in the South and the more subtle forms of racial redlining and discriminative practices in the North. Although King returned to the South to address the overt forms of racial discrimination evidenced there, he was not unaware of the extent to which the challenges of his hometown were discovered throughout the nation in a less obvious and more understated fashion. In a 1962 address to the National Press Club, King did not fail to point out that although segregation existed in the South in overt and glaring forms, it also existed in the North in hidden and subtle forms. His was a reminder that housing and employment discrimination were often as prominent in the North as they were in the South and that the racial issue confronted in America was not a sectional but a national problem.[8]

As King, therefore, challenged unjust laws and oppressive social practices, he consciously did so out of that specific historical context. The adverse social climate depicted in King's most notable speech provided him with the raw experiential material from which he fashioned a relevant theology of social reform. As such, the unjust social condition simply provided the context and the catalyst for theological reflection and practice. King embraced a theology about God, himself, his relationship to others and the world within this narrow context of persistent social exclusion premised upon race. In so doing, he placed himself in sync with the host of activist clergy that preceded him. His was an activism that emerged from a struggle to be, in a climate that inferred that he didn't belong. The Declaration of Independence stated that all were created with "certain inalienable rights" but his reality defied that bestowal of rights and certain citizen privileges. If the dignity, therefore, of American politics and its democratic ideals were to be redeemed, such a transformation would commence as a result of a moral critique from without. If the republic was in the process of being perfected, as King also imagined, the ideal source from which the democratic concept was derived and directed had divine, not human, origins. This kind of theological thinking was evidenced in King's response to the legalized forms of systemic injustice and his adverse encounters with Jim Crow in Montgomery. As in much of the South, the Montgomery legal structure refused to extend all of the privileges of "first-class" citizenship to residents of African ancestry. The democratic ideal at the heart of American society, therefore, was in perennial need of a theological critique and moral corrective that were posited external to the unjust policies and their illicit practice. Although a democracy "of the people, by the people, and for the people" undeniably represented the most suitable form of just government, King often contrasted the "isness" of a less than desirable social context with the "oughtness" toward which society should progress.

In the final analysis, both Dietrich Bonhoeffer and Martin Luther King Jr. contribute to our understanding of the pastor as activist. For them, caring for those in need involved their response to an invitation to broaden their sense of ministry to include the needs of their wounded communities. Hence, in them we discover quintessential models of the ways in which theological conception and social context can merge to foster a passion for social justice and reconciled community. They serve to demonstrate the degree to which one's biblical hermeneutic and, moreover, the compelling conditions of one's social context can have tremendous bearing on how the biblical text becomes interpreted and ultimately implemented in the interest of others.

Needless to say, Bonhoeffer and King spoke to the needs of their generations. In what ways are we speaking and effecting change in ours? I suspect the more convenient question is to wonder what Bonhoeffer and King would do if they were here. Obviously, the more pertinent question is, What would today's pastors do if they took seriously the urgency of now? If in fact our God of love and justice remains genuinely interested in the world's larger social concerns, as Dietrich Bonhoeffer and Martin Luther King Jr. assumed, the more compelling question may be to what extent the church shares this concern and is willing to cooperate with God's desired activity in human history. Let us not dismiss the activist models of Bonhoeffer and King too quickly, "Forasmuch as we've done it unto the least of these . . . we've done it unto him" (Matt. 25:31-46, NIV).

CHAPTER 12

Preaching and Prophetic Witness

Raphael Gamaliel Warnock

A s a pastor and preacher of the gospel, what is most instructive for me about Dietrich Bonhoeffer and Martin Luther King Jr. is the sheer integrity of their ministries of preaching and prophetic witness. Seldom has the church produced pastors who have effectively embodied, in their ministry, the twin tasks of preaching and prophetic witness as clearly, consistently, and coherently as did these two over the course of their short lives. But if it is true that their historic ministries represent a coherence of speech and action not easily achieved and not often seen, then one should ask, "How can we account for it?" As sophisticated exegetes of texts and times, how did they come to address complex social issues while *living through* their moments with such clarity of voice and vision that many of us still admire their conclusions, even while *looking back through* the lens of our own? What is it in their transformational preaching and prophetic witness that might inform the authenticity and character of the church's work as a divine instrument of liberation today? I argue that their preaching and prophetic witness were linked by the substance and intentionality of their *theological thinking*, which, more than anything else, provided a working hermeneutic for interpreting texts and times, for evaluating Christian speech and moral action.

It should be stated at the outset that for the purposes of this essay, preaching is concerned with *the content of the church's proclamation* within the church and the public square while prophetic witness signifies *the character of the church's activism and social praxis* in a world that needs to both *hear and see* the truth of the gospel. Although these two twentieth-century figures lived through extraordinary times, their work is instructive for the church's mission in all times. Informed by a core set of convictions about the actual meaning of the gospel, Bonhoeffer and King addressed their ministries to the complicated project of social transformation through a creative coupling of *proclamation* and *praxis* so seamless that it is difficult to see where the former ends and the latter begins.

There can be no gainsaying the fact that central to the self-understanding of each was their identity and vocation as preachers. King remarked of himself: "In the quiet recesses of my heart I am fundamentally a clergyman, a Baptist preacher. This is my being and my heritage for I am also the son of a Baptist preacher, the grandson of a Baptist preacher and the great grandson of a Baptist preacher."[1] Likewise, regarding his close friend, Dietrich Bonhoeffer, Eberhard Bethge observed that "Preaching was the great event for him. His severe theologizing and critical love for his church were all for its sake, for preaching proclaimed the message of Christ, the bringer of peace. For Bonhoeffer nothing in his calling competed in importance with preaching."[2] Indeed, this is why Bonhoeffer would continue to preach long after the Nazis forebade him to do so in 1940. He would preach his last sermon to fellow prisoners on Palm Sunday, 1945, the day before his execution at Flossenbürg.

This fact alone speaks volumes about the character and integrity of Bonhoeffer's preaching and the profound ways in which, for him and King, preaching was inextricably bound to prophetic witness. Each had wrestled deeply with *proclamation's prior question*: "Why preach in the first place?" In other words, what is it that the preacher presupposes about the gospel and its meaning and what is it that is critically and urgently at stake? Most preachers spend entirely too much time asking, "What shall I preach?" Bonhoeffer and King got it right because, contrary to this question that is much too driven by institutionalism, as theologians in the pulpit and the public square they asked, "Why do we preach?" Moreover, their ministries and martyrdom suggest that, for them, this question regarding the nature of the gospel and its demands upon one's life was itself a matter of life and death.

This is why, as subjects of study, it is most appropriate to analyze their preaching and their prophetic witness in tandem and as two parts of a whole. One cannot fully understand what is truly at stake in the preachments of Bonhoeffer and King, at a given moment, without reference to their life work. Moreover, one cannot fully account for their struggles outside of the church and inside of the church or the significant shifts in their social praxis without some sense of their evolving self-understanding as expressed through their transformational preaching.

In their respective contexts, Bonhoeffer and King sought to transform not only the world but also the church, as it was mired in a fundamental and recurring crisis in ecclesial identity and mission. They knew that this was what was at stake in their preaching and in their prophetic witness. As we shall see, they sought to give faithful expression to *the reign of God* imbued with love and justice and *to the way of the cross* as it signifies a tough-minded appreciation for the confrontational nature and cost of God's reign in a loveless and unjust world. The content of their preaching gave voice to their understanding of the former while the character of their prophetic witness underscored their enduring commitment to the latter. In order to analyze the role and relationship of both in their ministries, however, we must first examine their respective contexts. For Bonhoeffer and King, preaching and prophetic witness were about standing by the best in an evil time.

"Standing by the Best in an Evil Time"

Borrowing the title from a sermon preached by Harry Emerson Fosdick of New York's Riverside Church, Martin Luther King Jr. once preached a sermon, at his own Ebenezer Baptist Church, entitled, "Standing by the Best in an Evil Time."[3] Preached near the end of his life, it was a sermon steeped in his concern over America's misguided and escalating war in Vietnam. As he saw it, the continuation of the war was indicative of a sickness in a nation whose misplaced priorities had made it "the greatest actual purveyor of violence in the world today."[4] Moreover, he drew deep moral connections between this war against the poor of Vietnam and the nation's failure of will to wage a valiant war against poverty at home. His sermon suggested that a distorted domestic social policy and a dangerous foreign policy were part and parcel of the same moral problem: the fallacious view that self-preservation rather than other-preservation is "the first law of life."[5]

Amidst America's "evil times . . . with the sickness all around," the true vocation of the church, King argued, was to stand by the best.[6] Making deft use of a Lukan christological moment in which Jesus, who is now headed to Calvary, says to his disciples that "it is you who have stood by me through my trials," King suggests that it is the vocation of the church to stand by the truth, especially when truth is on trial. The preacher intones, "I'm going to stand by my convictions. I'm going to stand by the principle that the spirit is mightier than the sword."[7] In practice, that means ". . . I ain't going to kill nobody in

Mississippi and I don't plan to kill anybody in Vietnam, and I ain't going to study war no more."[8]

Given the political climate, it was bold preaching indeed! In essence, King was asking why many of his "friends," who supported nonviolence as a viable and appropriate method for African Americans seeking their freedom and who also criticized the countervailing position of self-defense taken by Black Power advocates, did not level the same moral critique against American imperialism, in general, and its engagement of the Viet Cong, in particular. Authentic Christian witness required deep social consciousness and broad moral continuity, even if it meant the questioning of his patriotism and the alienating of a civil rights president. In this way, King's ministry of preaching and prophetic witness underscored the complex connections between what he often described as the triplet evils of racism, poverty, and war and the ways in which the church must be vocal and vigilant on all fronts if it would bear faithful witness to the truth of the gospel.

Just as King's preaching was shaped by and addressed to an evil time characterized by ethnic and racial bigotry and war, notwithstanding important differences, the same can be said of Bonhoeffer. For in 1933 and just three months before Bonhoeffer delivered his *Christologie* lectures (which are, in my judgment, the key to much of his theological thought), Hitler had become chancellor. Already, it was an evil time and the church, which the adolescent Bonhoeffer had insisted he would change, proved itself to be as consumed with the project of self-preservation and the easy work of worshiping the God of security as much as any other institution in society.[9] For example, the decision of the infamous Brown Synod to accept an Aryan ecclesiology was a dramatic turning point. The "Aryan clauses" strictly prohibited any Jew from holding ecclesiastical office and *rassenhygiene* (racial purity) became its own form of baptism. Combining the work of God with the work of Hitler, one catechism for school children read: "As Jesus set men free from sin and hell, so Hitler rescued the German people from destruction. . . . Jesus built for heaven; Hitler for the German earth."[10]

However, it should not be forgotten that the American churches have had their own history of complicity and active participation in the development of distinctive doctrines and peculiar practices of *rassenhygiene*.[11] Segregation could not have been so well choreographed and slavery could not have lasted so long were it not for the evil theology of American churches during those evil times.[12] Although King never made a *self-conscious* break from the theology of American Protestantism, as James Cone and other black theologians would later do,[13] he did wonder aloud what kind of God rendered people "silent behind the anesthetizing security of stained-glass windows."[14] He says, "I have looked at the South's beautiful churches with their lofty spires pointing heavenward. I have beheld the impressive outlines of her massive religious-education buildings. Over and over I have found myself asking: 'What kind of people worship here? Who is their God?'"[15] Who, indeed? For if ecclesiology is tied to Christology, mission to identity, then Christian proclamation must continually ask, "Who is Jesus Christ for us today?" Where does Jesus stand in relation to the struggles of the poor? As put earlier, why do we preach and what is truly at stake? In answer to this fundamental question, Bonhoeffer and King sought, through the content of their preaching, to bear faithful witness to the reign of God. Through the integrity of their preaching and by their prophetic witness, they also demonstrated their enduring commitment to the realization of God's reign by embracing the way of the cross.

The Reign of God

In their respective contexts, both Bonhoeffer and King were patriots. Their actions and words make it clear that Bonhoeffer loved Germany and King loved America. In fact, so deep was their love of country that each died endeavoring to prod it toward the realization of its best self. King would express this patriot's dream with reference to the nation's charter documents and cultural self-understanding. Accordingly, he lifted up the Constitution and Jefferson's Declaration of Independence: "We hold these truths to be self-evident, that all men are created equal." Viewing the world as his parish and seeking, through his Southern Christian Leadership Conference, "to redeem the soul of America," he appropriately gave his most famous public sermon not in a church but in the shadow of the Lincoln Memorial.[16] He began that day by recalling the sacred memory of the memorial's namesake, that "great American,"[17] while also underscoring the great gulf between the hope African Americans had once attached to Lincoln's Emancipation Proclamation and the reality of "the lonely island of poverty"[18] they occupied one hundred years later. Yet, even while condemning the deep contradiction, King's melodic, baritone voice rang out that day, "My country 'tis of thee; sweet land of liberty; of thee I sing." King loved America.

Showing a similar concern for the direction of his country, Bonhoeffer's patriotism led him to return to his beloved Germany in 1939 against the pleadings of concerned American friends. Early on he critiqued German acceptance of Hitler in a February 1, 1933, radio address and a little over a decade later he would die for Germany, even while praying for its defeat.[19] In

Bonhoeffer's complex biography of prophetic witness, the ostensibly contra-
dictory paths of his shifting actions are tied together, at least in part, by a deep
love for Germany. Both Bonhoeffer and King were patriots who bore deep
personal sacrifice for country. Yet, in the most profound way, these public
theologians offered their preaching up and poured their lives out for an incarnational reality much larger than country—the reign of God, imbued with
love and justice.

Of course, each had his own way of preaching about it and demonstrating
it. King called it "the beloved community." Politically, the beloved community
was approximated by the integration of public facilities and the larger society
itself, the dismantling of systemic inequality, the empowerment of the poor,
and the ending of war. King's was a worldly eschatology that always emphasized the responsibility of the church to be an instrument for the realization
of God's intentions for humanity on earth. For historic reasons, beyond the
scope of our discussion here, worldly views of the reign of God have been
marginal to American Protestantism, which tends to privilege an interiorized,
individualistic piety that eschews sustained resistance to political and economic oppression.[20]

Of the few exceptions to the sharp individualism of American Protestantism, the black church has played, for good historic reasons, a unique part
among a small chorus of principled, contrarian voices.[21] For the black church
was born as a radical response to racism—America's enduring sin and its most
intractable social problem. Standing within this trajectory, while also critiquing its own theologically conservative and politically passive dimensions, King
spent his entire career preaching a thoroughgoing worldly eschatology, one
that held out for the irruption of God's reign from below and within the
events of history.

This is why, when preaching, for example, "The Impassable Gulf (The
Parable of Dives and Lazarus)," King, who did not believe in hell "as a place
of literal burning fire," warns against a literalistic and otherworldly interpretation of the passage.[22] He argues, "We must not take this story as a theology
of the afterlife. . . . He who seeks to describe the furniture of heaven and the
temperature of hell is taking the mystery out of religion and incarcerating it in
the walls of an illogical logic."[23] Taking the language of the parable as symbolic
"and not literal fact," King speaks in social terms of the poor man Lazarus
and the rich man Dives and the gulf fixed between them. He says, "Dives is
the white man who refuses to cross the gulf of segregation and lift his Negro
brother to the position of first class citizenship. . . . Dives is the India Brahman
who refuses to bridge the gulf between himself and his brother. . . . Dives is

the American capitalist who never seeks to bridge the economic gulf between himself and the laborer." Echoing Abraham's response to the rich man who finds himself in hell, King suggests that those in a relative position of privilege, like Dives, are called upon to "build a bridge of compassion" across historic divides before "the gulf is fixed" and "time has run out."[24]

In his sermonic reflections on texts that have been much too tamed by the church, Bonhoeffer preached with the same sense of prophetic urgency. For example, while preaching about the Christmas story, Bonhoeffer insists that the church take seriously its christological claims in an unjust world. He intimates that the story of the Christ Child is more than "just a figure of speech . . . a beautiful, pious legend."[25] God's coming in a manger is a threat to the powerful and the mighty. "The judgment and redemption of the world—that is what is happening here. . . . It is he [the Christ child] who pushes away the great and mighty of this world, who topples the thrones of the powerful, who humbles the haughty, whose arm exercises power against all who are highly placed and strong, and whose mercy lifts up what was lowly and makes it great and glorious."[26]

Both Bonhoeffer and King understood preaching as a faithful response to the incarnation. Irrespective of the preacher's homiletical skills and gifts, authentic preaching can only happen when one asks, What does the reality of God's incarnation in Christ demand? As Bonhoeffer says, "The Kingdom of God is not to be found in some other world beyond, but in the midst of this world. . . . God wants us to honor God on earth . . . and nowhere else. God sinks the kingdom down into the cursed ground."[27] Because God's kingdom is rooted in this earth, preaching must be matched by prophetic action. The church's communication about the reign of God is only credible when joined with a commitment to struggle for it by embracing the way of the cross.

The Way of the Cross

Bonhoeffer and King understood prophetic witness to be the way of the cross and the authentic mission of the church. No theological theme was more central to their thinking than the cross. This is because the cross functions as the epistemological lens through which they accounted for the depth and intractable character of evil in the world. Moreover, it is the primary ethical measure by which each ascertained an appropriate Christian response.

At Finkenwalde, a seminary community that knew the persecution that comes with bearing the cross, Bonhoeffer preached once about "The Secret of Suffering."[28] The biblical text for the sermon reads: "More than that, we rejoice in our sufferings, knowing that suffering produces perseverance, and perseverance produces character, and character produces hope, and hope does not disappoint us, because God's love has been poured into our hearts through the Holy Spirit" (Rom. 5:3-5b). Using this text as the biblical basis of his argument, Bonhoeffer says to a church community whose commitment to justice brought it into principled conflict with the state, "We have peace with God[!]" Deeply committed to the church's oppositional witness, he insists that such peace is not a "worldly peace." Neither, it should be said, is it an otherworldly peace, for Bonhoeffer found this equally offensive. Rather, it is a peace found "beneath the cross."[29] The church must decide: "Do we have peace with God, or have we lived up to now in an entirely worldly peace?"[30] Will the church embrace the costly grace of principled resistance to abusive power or must it too be counted among those who are "despisers of the cross."[31] Only the peace of God embodied in the cross could inspire the courage to prophesy, suffer, and, if necessary, die.

Despite their differences in culture and context, as preachers and theologians of the church, Bonhoeffer and King are clearly connected on this point. The cross was the center of King's theology and the bedrock of his faith. This is how he gained the courage to face death.[32] And it is why he told his SCLC staff that "the cross is something that you bear and ultimately that you die on."[33] Yet, it should be said that while Bonhoeffer spoke for an oppositional ecclesial community, the Confessing Church, which had before it the option to *choose* to embrace the cross, King emerged from an oppositional ecclesial community, the black church, which was born of the lived experience of a people who carried a cross they were *coerced* to endure. As he immersed himself into the spirituality of the black church, attended Harlem's Abyssinian Baptist Church, and sang the spirituals, Bonhoeffer "learned," as he said, to view the events of history "from below."[34] On the other hand, King represented a larger African American community that lived below. So, if Bonhoeffer preached that the Confessing Church ought to fully embrace the cross as a matter of voluntary vocation, historically the cross of the black church, from which King emerged, was not so much a voluntary vocation as it was an existential experience.

King's singular genius was his appropriation of the cross of black experience for the purposes of a movement of nonviolent struggle. He extended and reinterpreted the radical strands of a religion of resistance. For African American Christian faith has always been a religion of the cross. The image of a suffering Savior abides deeply in the religious imagination of a people who knew the political crucifixion and social death of American chattel slavery.[35] That is why the cross is such a prominent theme in the spirituals. At least one spiritual even conflates the distance of time and space in a dirge of collective memory and the knowledge of suffering, as it asks, "Were you there when they crucified my Lord?" Because the question itself emerges as the melancholic, christological call of a people experiencing crucifixion, the response is palpable and personal. "Sometimes it causes me to tremble, tremble, tremble. . . ." The spirituals were anchored in the experience of slavery and that experience was interpreted, in part, through the lens of the cross.

King, the son, grandson, and great-grandson of preachers, instinctively understood this. Hence, his preaching was appropriately informed by and situated within a black preaching tradition that, like the spirituals, has been rife with the theme of the cross, as it signifies suffering and the hope of liberation from the forces of domination and death. One can hear King drawing deeply upon this tradition in all of his preaching, but particularly when he preached in black churches. In one audio recording of a sermon entitled, "Why Jesus Called a Man a Fool," one can hear a preacher, who is wearied by the struggle, encourage the pew while also encouraging himself with the sober and realistic hope of a religion that has known the cross.

> Sometimes I feel discouraged. And think my work's in vain.
> But then the Holy Spirit revives my soul again.
> There is a balm in Gilead to make the wounded whole.
> There is a balm in Gilead to heal the sin sick soul.[36]

The profound faith that "there is a balm"—or in other words, that God will redeem those who suffer—is a basic assumption of the faith of the black church that King had inherited. That the unmerited suffering is itself inherently redemptive was King's own distinctive, albeit controversial, contribution. This claim is the public theologian's hermeneutical move, a creative *second step* in the canon of black faith, which served well as the theological basis of a mass movement of passive resistance, a struggle that was confrontational yet nonviolent. The preacher effectively persuaded those who knew the randomness of violence, terror, and suffering—which encroached upon the lives of black people daily—to suffer in a creative and organized way in the hope of redemption. This public, political struggle was sourced by a centuries-long faith tradition. Present in the voice of King is the pathos of this tradition as he preached in 1967 "A Christmas Sermon on Peace," at Ebenezer Baptist Church:

> We shall match your capacity to inflict suffering by our capacity to endure suffering. We will meet your physical force with soul force. Do to us what you will and we will still love you. . . . Bomb our homes and threaten our

children, and, as difficult as it is, we will still love you. Send your hooded perpetrators of violence into our communities at the midnight hour and drag us out on some wayside road and leave us half-dead as you beat us, and we will still love you. . . . we'll wear you down by our capacity to suffer, and one day we will win our freedom. We will not only win freedom for ourselves; we will so appeal to your heart and conscience that we will win you in the process, and our victory will be a double victory.[37]

When King makes this startling claim, he is speaking not so much of political struggle as he is of the way of the cross. As he had explained to an assembly of Baptists in Amsterdam, "Jesus Christ gave his life for the redemption of *this* world, and as his followers, we are called to give our lives to continuing the reconciling work of Christ in this world."[38] In fact, "whole churches may be crucified."[39] However challenging and problematic, these are the faith claims of a tough-minded, worldly preacher who sought to connect preaching to prophetic witness, proclamation to praxis. King carried out his ministry from a place that presupposed the cross as "an eternal expression of the length to which God is willing to go to restore broken communities."[40] Likewise for Bonhoeffer, "Whenever Christ calls us, his call leads us to death."[41] In summary, each of them preached powerfully and moved with ministerial integrity because they preached and lived from a place of profound clarity about what truly is at stake.

Authentic Preaching & Prophetic Witness

As a pastor and preacher myself, I know that preachers spend a great deal of time asking themselves, "What shall I preach?" without giving sufficient attention to reflecting on the meaning of the gospel itself. Indeed, the weekly task of standing before an awaiting congregation, while also managing other institutional concerns, encourages this obsession. Meanwhile, the church's public voice can scarce be heard on the issues and in the places where it really does matter. In contrast, the powerful ministries of Bonhoeffer and King suggest that it is the "Why?" and not the "What?" that keeps our preaching honest and our witness prophetic.

Authentic gospel preaching and meaningful prophetic witness emerge from a distinctive theological worldview, a prophetic hermeneutic that begins with the premise of a sovereign God standing on the side of the most marginalized members of the human family. Lectionary texts, institutional maintenance, the changing winds of electoral politics and contemporary happenings are, in a real sense, secondary and must be viewed through this primary lens.

For the gospel is the good news of Jesus Christ for the poor who seek liberation and the poor in spirit who seek transformation in a broken, unjust, and sinful world. The ministries of Bonhoeffer and King suggest that the preacher who wrestles deeply and consistently with this sense of the urgency of the gospel is already well on the way to discerning, in the face of an awaiting public, what to preach *and*, in the face of evil and oppression, what to do.

CHAPTER 13

Embodying Redemption
— King and the Engagement of Social Sin —
Stephen G. Ray Jr.

n this essay I will reflect on how an engagement with Martin Luther King Jr.'s understanding of social sin—in light of the larger conversation in this volume about him and Dietrich Bonhoeffer—might evoke and cast new light on the relationship between the church's engagement with social sin and practical ministry. These two twentieth-century martyrs may be connected through the idea of Christian community, specifically in regard to how they understood communal vocation in the face of social evil and how practical ministry fits into these understandings. This essay contributes to the conversation by focusing on how King's project of forming new "publics" into communities of resistance, which engaged structural and social evil, was deeply rooted in a type of cruciform communitarianism. This communitarianism was enlivened by multiple streams of American evangelicalism and these communities of resistance help give us new frames for thinking about sin, evil, and society—in short, about social sin, which I hope may then be brought into dialogue with Bonhoeffer studies.[1] Attention to these structuring dimensions of King's work sharpens the features of a distinctly American Protestant approach to engaging sin and society, thereby helping to identify the formal points of dialogue between him and Bonhoeffer—who exemplifies a distinctly continental Protestant approach. This type of investigation also contributes to our understanding of how King's sense of "ministry" shaped his theological engagement with a social evil of his day.

The undeniable reality is that the contexts in which King's ministry unfolded was one in which there existed gargantuan instances of social sin. As well, many an observer has commented that King and Bonhoeffer approached the work of resisting social sin by using the forms and practices that might best be thought of as emerging from models we identify with practical ministry (e.g., formation of Christian communities and sacred rhetoric as public theology).[2] While it would be an easy thing to make connections between their works on this level, such as King's ruminations on the "true ecclesia" in the "Letter from a Birmingham Jail" and Bonhoeffer's ideal of community in *Life Together*, I would like to complicate matters a bit, to make this piece worthy of inclusion in this august collection. I will do so by framing the matter thus: perhaps a significant way to interpret King's engagements with social sin is to frame it precisely *as* an enactment of practical ministry. Specifically, I will frame his engagements as faith interventions that contribute to the formation of Christian communities embodying the phenomena of contextual Christian faithfulness. This offers very fertile ground for comparative analyses of King and Bonhoeffer, especially given Bonhoeffer's understanding of the church as "Christ existing as community" and his emphasis on it being conformed to the crucified Christ. To give this work a name I offer an interpretation of what might aptly be described as cruciform communitarianism, by which I mean the formation of communities that materialize contemporary embodiments of Christ in the presence of social evil. This account of King's work will necessarily entail a description of the ways that he conceived of the evil that had materialized in his context and the way that embodied discipleship (the point of practical ministry) became his implicit and explicit approach to engaging that evil.

An analysis of King's engagement of social sin must begin with an adequate account of what we mean by the idea of social sin. This is necessary because it is my sense that what the contemporary reflective Christian assumes when this language is deployed is not the immediate way that King would have described the situation. Many socially conscious Christians define social sin as embedded in and furthered by the functioning of social structures within society with the outcome being the oppression and harming of groups within society. This is not the immediate way that King would have described the situation. However, implicit to the argument of this chapter is the idea that King actually participated in the construction of what we today understand in a commonsense way to be social sin, by recasting the ways that social evil and personal sinfulness collude. This redefinition of the collusions of individuals with particular political and economic systems suggests that the systems themselves produce sin (systemic evil). This redefinition not only contributes substantially to contemporary ideas of social sin but also guides the appropriate engagement of it in a Protestant idiom.

If we are to appreciate fully the significance of King's contribution it will be necessary to trace, in brief, the development of the ideas of social evil and sin, and to then identify the ways that King's engagement of them creates a new synthesis that leads to a greater understanding of each. I propose that tracing the development of this idea proceed along two trajectories. The first trajectory winds through the development of evangelical thought in the United States and the second through the development of what may be termed the modernist-liberal approach to religion and society. Tracing these two trajectories requires a journey through the eighteenth and nineteenth centuries. I will follow this by describing how King responds to the working of social evil that creates the type of thread in the history of Christian communal formation which I termed cruciform communitarianism. It is in his enactment of this cruciform communitarianism that I believe he exposes the ways that personal collusion participates either in the workings of systemic evil in such a way that we classify it as social sin or in resistance to it in ways that we may identify as social redemption.

Before going on it is important to note that one thing that complicates this exploration is that King did not, to my knowledge, use this specific linguistic construction: "social sin." Rather, he used language about evil as social ill, thus his frequent use of bodily metaphors. Notice of this point is important because, as we shall see, the particular social theories and doctrines of sin with which he worked led King to a synthesis that would in many ways facilitate contemporary understandings of the intersection of sin and social reality. King's interpretation of the working of sin in his context and narration thereof created a new way to think about sin in its social dimensions in a specifically Protestant idiom.[3] It is this synthesis and his conclusions about a fitting social response that is the interest of this essay. I now turn to tracing the ideas of sin and social reality that enliven the thought of King.

The Two Trajectories—From Slavery to Sweatshops

The first trajectory that we will explore, which is germane to the development of the idea of social evil as a category of American theological discourse, begins with the antebellum debates about slavery in the United States and then develops through the social gospel movement, which arose in response to the distorted social, economic, and racial relations that were attendant to the industrialization of the American economy and society. The antislavery debates of the eighteenth and nineteenth centuries were undeniably the crucible upon which the evangelical framings of social evil and sin that contributed to King's thinking were formed. In these theological discourses the Christian category of sin is placed on a trajectory within which it would be expanded in the American context from the individual category of concupiscence to the broader category of social sin. The Christian discourse of sin would evolve to account for sin as it works in social systems and implicates individuals and groups within those systems. While space does not permit a full description and analysis of this development there are two points of which we want to take notice.

The first is that the entire debate between the abolitionist and slaveholding religionists unfolds itself within a field of vision constructed by the evangelical discourses of the day,[4] by which I mean the Christian movements that were born of the first and second Great Awakenings. These discourses created a field of vision that had as its two points of symmetry the pole of personal righteousness on the one end and the pole of social righteousness on the other. Sin was interpreted in this field of vision as the antitype of this layout—personal failings of virtue at one end and the public display of fallenness at the other. It is in this account of the type and antitype of sin and righteousness in the personal and social realms that we find the beginnings of a distinctly modern discourse of sin in the social order which would frame discourses in the American context for the next two centuries.

This account begins, as does much of the Christian tradition's account of sin, with the category of the personal. That is to say, it is narrated from the perspective of the sinner. This is due in no small part to what scholars such as Donald G. Matthews have identified as the core commitment of the evangelical movement in the United States, namely, the formation and validation of identity for the believer in the face of rigid legal class and social distinctions.[5] In other words, the movement's valorization of the individual would mean that sin, as the "flip side of the coin" of righteousness, would likewise discursively emphasize those personal dimensions of the Western Christian tradition's expositions of sin.

Here it is important to be clear that the way in which American abolitionists of the eighteenth and nineteenth century spoke of systems of sinfulness was not one that understood them in the ways that we often understand systemic evil today. While today we frequently frame and deploy discourses which point to those structural dimensions of society that further oppression and marginalization within society as being the exemplification of social evil

and only secondarily take notice of the ways these systems distort the personality of sinner and sinned against alike, what the evangelical discourse of sin
had in mind was an account of systemic evil as a system of practices that were
evil *because* they brought about vice and acted as a barrier on the journey to
righteousness for individuals and society.[6] This was the approach that underlay
much of the abolitionist argument about slavery. So, while slavery is still seen
as a social "evil," it is not interpreted primarily on the level of material relations embedded within society that destroy persons; rather, the lifestyles that
place vice on *display* are the primary exemplifications of sin and social evil.
Put plainly, slavery was evil because it opened the door to terrible vice and
obscures public righteousness. Theirs was not an argument that turned primarily on the idea that the system was evil because it physically and materially
destroyed persons and communities.[7] What is important to notice is that while
the focus is still ostensibly on sin as a personal category—evangelical abolitionists exclusively focused on the interior life of the sinner rather than the social
effects of sin—the abolitionist understanding of sin marks the developing turn
to the material consequences of sin on the victims that creates the predicate
for later reflection on systemic sin and then social sin.

Structurally this type of discourse sees the power of sin at work in systems
that lead people astray and once they are led astray to propound the work of
vice within society and thus to hamper not only the personal journey to righteousness of individuals, but also to truncate the display of public righteousness within the whole society. This might be thought of as the early evangelical
social theory of sin. It is a theory of sin whose primary focus is on sin and its
effects as they are propagated and felt by individuals. While this tendency to
construct discourses about sin that are wholly personalistic in character occurs
in a significant portion of the Christian tradition, it takes a particular form in
the American context around the slavery debates. For it is undeniable that a
significant portion of the evangelical movement retreated from more material
readings of sin in society which looked upon slaveholding with great appro-
bation to more spiritual readings of sin which made peace with the "peculiar
institution."[8] This fact is a significant impetus for the evangelical framing of the
workings of sin in society.

The evangelical trajectory further evolves during the progression of the
social gospel movement. In this stage of its evolution this trajectory blends
evangelical sensibilities about personal and public righteousness and emerging
liberal theories of religion and society in its analysis of social sin. Relying on
the emerging social sciences, the social gospel reflected explicitly on economic
and political systems as such and on their capacity to further either sin or

righteousness in society. Whereas, earlier in its development thinkers in this trajectory used the sphere of individual autonomy as their primary trope for engagement (i.e., critiques of slaveholding vs. critiques of the "system" of slavery), the analysis of later thinkers began with the systems themselves (industrial capitalism) and proceeded to reflect on sin from there. What we have then is the idea that social evil is not wholly reducible to the leading astray of one person by the example of another. Rather, there is recognition that social and economic systems in their very existence can in an extrapersonal way transmit and perpetuate sin within society. In my opinion this turn cannot be underestimated because it begins the construction of a matrix of ideas in which sin can have a social life apart from its expression in personal relations.

Walter Rauschenbusch develops perhaps the most extensive reflection on sin in this vein.[9] What is notable about his exposition is not only that it provides an entire template for interpreting the way sin migrates between individuals and systems, but also, perhaps more importantly, it shows how systems in themselves can be evil and sinful apart from their working to put vice on display—which was the locus of reflection for earlier thinkers in this stream. This analysis includes, then, not only an account of personal involvement with sinful systems but also an analysis of the ways that discrete systems manufacture and participate in social evil. This type of analysis is taken up by Reinhold Niebuhr in *Moral Man and Immoral Society* and would be a significant source for King. To this point I have identified significant ways a particular trajectory, evangelical-liberal, evolved and shaped an understanding of the workings of sin in a social structure. It is now necessary to identify an additional strand of social analysis and discursive engagement with social sin that would inform King's synthesis: namely, the evangelical tradition of the Black Baptist church.[10]

As we make this turn we will be taking notice of a dimension of King's thought that should, in my estimation, be fully expected in any analysis of his work, but one that is rarely mentioned. That dimension is the Black Baptist synthesis of the evangelical-liberal theological framework alongside an evangelical-conservative piety. This synthesis emerged as a way to make sense of the signal feature of Black Christian experience during much of the two centuries previous to King's life—the continuing presence of a social evil, racism, that expressed itself in a *de jure* and *de facto* racial dictatorship.[11] A significant dimension of King's approach to engaging social sin was precisely borne of this formation. A part of his genius was the ability to synthesize a fundamentally personalistic and conservative piety with an activist posture informed by the evangelical-liberal tradition of Christianity in America against great social evil in a way that galvanized millions in the Black Church whose religious outlook on life was fundamentally evangelical.

While King was not the only exemplar of this particular type of synthesis—his teacher and mentor Howard Thurman was another, for instance[12]—the amalgamation evidenced in his thought and deeds was unique. His synthesis of these three strands—the trajectory emerging from evangelical movements during the antebellum debates over slavery, the synthesis of this movement with the emerging liberal social sciences coinciding with the social gospel movement, and the theological and ecclesial response to social and economic oppression by the predominantly pietistic and conservative Black Church—provided both a distinctive account of social evil and a posture in the face of it. This synthesis evolved in the discrete historical circumstances of the burgeoning civil rights movement of the 1950s and '60s and the later antiwar movement of the '60s. To this point I have done a cursory recovery of some of the significant sources that informed King's interpretation of social sin. Now it is appropriate to turn my analysis to his response to social evil and to amplify the term earlier mentioned: cruciform communitarianism. By cruciform communitarianism I mean embodiment of the cruciform life by a community with the goal of overcoming the structures of evil that are destroying the spiritual and material well-being of God's children. This was exemplified in King's approach to the civil rights movement, both personally and as a part of the leadership of that movement. A fuller description would be helpful here.

Expanding the Field of Vision

Two hallmarks of King's engagement with social evil were his description of it and his prescription for its engagement. King's approach was to describe social evil (i.e., segregation and militarism) as an organic presence within society, albeit a harmful one. This is seen in his frequent likening of it to a cancer in the body politic. In resorting to such a description, King was moving beyond the early evangelical position that relied on the reduction of social evil to a problem characterized by congeries of relations among sinful people. In his assessment, social evil was an actual power within itself. Here King is utilizing the contemporary liberal social theory of his time found in works such as Niebuhr's *Moral Man and Immoral Society*[13] and Myrdal's *An American Dilemma*.[14] Yet King held on to the idea that the society which this "thing" inhabited was still able to repent corporately, even as members of society were able to individually "repent" from their participation with social evil, and move toward social righteousness on the corporate scale and personal righteousness on the individual scale. This recognition of groups as moral agents moved beyond what commentators such as Reinhold Niebuhr contended was possible in human society.[15] This is a substantial reason why he sought to change the hearts of people at the same time as he worked to change the sinful system of segregation. While late in his career, 1965 and later, King was less optimistic about the speed with which this societal and personal transformation occurred, he still maintained the idea of corporate and individual redemption as the larger framing of his work.[16]

To appreciate fully King's synthesis it is necessary to be clear about the two primary alternatives that were being voiced in his context. There was the evangelical-conservative approach that operated purely on the level of personal involvement with sin and refused to expand the analysis of sin to a systemic and social level. This was the approach seen in both the broad stream of the segregationist position in the midst of the civil rights movement, as well as, ironically, in much of the Black Church's engagements with the struggle. It is unfortunate that this particular approach is what became synonymous with evangelicalism during the time and in succeeding decades and thus occluded the substantial framing of the struggle by King and others in evangelical categories. This approach relied on the central themes of evangelicalism—personal experience and holiness—and thus characteristically refused to contemplate a social dimension of sin. This stream of evangelicalism was widespread in both black and white communities throughout the South, so its power cannot be marginalized.

In addition to this evangelical-conservative approach, the liberal-modernist approach provided a significant alternative to King's synthesis. This approach relied heavily on the sciences for the social theory underlying its account of social evil. The focus was placed more on the behavior of groups and to the extent that there was a focus on individuals it was a more psychotherapeutic model (for example, *Moral Man and Immoral Society*). What was significant about this approach was that it was fully able to give an account of how human "selfishness" and self-interest could morph into group pride, but it was unable to provide a significant account of what dimensions of personal righteousness might look like in the social order.

The field of vision that is created by the evangelical-conservative and liberal-modernist approaches reduced engagement with social evil to either one of contested piety or competing ideologies, thus excluding meaningful ground upon which to interpret sin (a personal category) as being applicable to the social, as such. This can be seen in a more contemporary vein by the tendency, on the one hand, of those in the evangelical-conservative camp to tag any theological engagements that rely on the social sciences as being nothing more than ideology, and, on the other hand, by the liberal-modernist assessment of the piety-centered theology of the evangelical-conservative camp as a being a "selfish" theology whose primary effect on the social realm is parochial and unhelpful. What I am suggesting is that while King was influenced by and drew on all of the streams which run through these two fields of vision, he created a synthesis of these sources that is unique and that creates a new way of "thinking" about sin and the social, one that substantially frames the way that we conceive social sin today versus the way earlier generations thought of social evil.

How these strands come together for King is thus. The evangelical (conservative and liberal) synthesis of personal and social righteousness (or sinfulness) focuses on the conversion of the hearts of individual members of society, which brings about a will to live differently and consequently changes the ways these individuals inhabit the social relations of their society, thereby transforming the institutions based upon these relations. Thus, the sinful structures of society are changed by "converting" enough members of society to change the social fabric of that society. This narrative of conversion then finds its fullest expression in the development of communities of the converted that bring about change within the entire society. This understanding is what, in my opinion, stands behind King's image of the beloved community. His work in creating new communities of the converted, or new publics to follow this image to its logical conclusion, might very much be thought of as a type of evangelization of the social order much in the mode of the evangelical abolitionists and the social gospelers. While I think that it would be an unhelpful reduction to identify this evangelistic activity with the "Christianization" of society—for King's work and appreciation of communities of differing faith resist such a move—it is quite clear that his modus operandi in the creation of these new publics is analogous to the dimension of practical ministry understood through an evangelical lens as saving souls, for King, the soul of a nation and the souls of persons who had been brought under the sway of the sin and evil of segregation. In a contemporary vein we might call this the work of constructing communities of resistance.[17]

The other dominant dimension apparent in King's work is his commitment to a type of social analysis that relied on the best of the social/psychological sciences of his day. This approach, which is characteristic of the liberal-modernist synthesis, was evident in King's analysis of the causes and cures of poverty as well as the wars of the emerging neocolonial era. What this meant for his work practically was that he continually focused on the inner workings of political and economic systems as points of focus around which to "evangelize" those members of newly evolving publics. A compelling example is found when he calls those who resist the civil rights movement "vicious racists, with [their] governor having his lips dripping with the words of interposition and nullification."[18] Here King is specifically focusing on legal and political doctrines that were clashing at that historical moment (the success of the civil rights movement largely hung on the result of that clash) by using terms and images that were clearly drawn from the lexicon and tableau of Dante's *Inferno* and other apocalyptic literature to cast the struggle in religious terms. Thus, the civil rights movement is portrayed as a moment in the great unfolding eschatological drama of history. To distinguish more clearly what is going on here we may note that King, while personalizing the workings of the system of southern resistance in this evocation, is resisting the evangelical-conservative analysis of the system, which was nothing more than an evaluation of how white people were individually "treating" their Negro neighbors. King remains focused laser-like on the systemic issues and on which set of political and social theories would prevail. I would argue that this type of engagement, imagistically preaching through *Inferno* to get to the statehouse, was a dominant way that King evidenced his keen use of social scientific analyses, rendered in tent-meeting rhetoric, as a part of his larger project.

King's synthesis might then be described as one that took seriously the personal sources of sin within society, yet also relied on a social-scientific analysis of the ways that sin operated within the systems of society. I would suggest that this twofold synthesis creates a way of talking about sin in the social which has become the commonsense assumption that underlies contemporary expositions of social sin. This is what I meant earlier when I suggested that King's work helped provide the intellectual currency for our very framing of the idea of social sin. It is now possible to turn to King's prescription for engaging social sin. In doing so, I think it is helpful to return to the idea of his evangelization of the larger society with the goal of the creation of new publics.

Embodying Redemption

With evangelization as a lens through which to view King's work, practices and commitments come into view that characterize his "ministry" and bear striking resemblance to the practical ministry of a Christian minister. These practices include catechizing the "faithful" and providing for and administering a table fellowship at the center of the community's life. This is nowhere more apparent than in the Birmingham campaign of 1963 where, by the estimation of many, the civil rights struggle reached it zenith, being highlighted by King's "I Have a Dream" speech. As King recounts in *Why We Can't Wait*, the protestors were formed in both the liturgical practices of the movement (nonviolent and prayerful responses to social sin), and the confessional formation of the protestors (the Commitment Card).[19] It may well have been this dimension of King's work that led a colleague, Melva Costen, to describe the civil rights marches as the church "taking flesh" in the street, or another colleague, Evelyn Parker, to describe her childhood memories of civil rights workers in Hattiesburg, Mississippi, in this way: "they seemed like *walking faith*."[20]

We see the centrality of the cruciform community in King's seamless understanding of the work of civil rights, the opposition to the war in Vietnam, and the Poor People's Campaign. This practical work of evangelizing "the social" as a way of engaging social sin has an additional dimension—it is only through the cruciform life of redemptive suffering that social evil might be overcome. We see this in King's continuing reference to the idea that "unearned suffering is redemptive."[21] What are being redeemed are at once the individuals who are being oppressed by the evil system, in this case, segregation, and those whose souls are being scarred by their participation in the system and the system itself. Here again we see the basic template at work that the converted heart can create a community which works to create a new world. It is this creation of communities that embody the resistance to the forces of evil that I term cruciform communitarianism.

To this point I have argued that what we find in King's work with the civil rights movement, the antiwar movement, and the Poor People's Campaign was a type of engagement which represented a synthesis of multiple streams within the American evangelical and liberal Christian approaches to sin and the social, which might be interrogated through the framework of practical Christian ministry. Specifically, King enacted that ministry in the face of social sin, with the goal of engaging it and ameliorating the suffering of those harmed by the workings of that sin. He did this, on my account, through the formation of new publics, which, through evangelistic conversion, had become communities of resistance. In their very resistance they exposed the workings of sin in social systems, thus giving meaning to the idea of social sin. At this point let me bring all of these together with a thematic exposition of these communities. That theme is bound up in the idea of cruciform existence, personally and communally.

The galvanizing principle King utilized in the formation of these new publics was a commitment to the idea that through the conscious claiming of unearned suffering on their part, these communities might be the redemption of both the larger society of which they were a part and of the individual members who composed them. Indeed, the cruciform life consists for King in unearned suffering being willfully claimed with the goal of accomplishing a larger act of redemption. It is my contention that a significant goal of King's work was to form such communities, whose purpose was the redemption of American society. He sought to accomplish this through his ministry, which was informed and animated by his distinct synthesis of evangelicalism and the liberal tradition of modernity as means to both describe and engage social sin in his time that the larger society might partake in the eschatological experience of the beloved community.

The beloved community is, within its very being, King's answer to the continuing travail of social sin. As mentioned earlier, for King this community *is* the embodiment of Christ in the face of social evil. The idea of the Christian community as the answer to social evil is crucial for Bonhoeffer as well. This is clear from his early support of the Confessing Church resistance movement on to his participation in the plot to kill Hitler. In all of these cases he evoked a commitment to community not only as the basis but also the goal of his actions. Even at those points of practice where Bonhoeffer and King differ in approach there remains the commitment to community as the means and goal of their actions. Space does not permit a full exploration of the ways that a dialogue between King and Bonhoeffer might illumine new ways of understanding Christian responses to social sin; it is my hope that this essay has evoked a new appreciation for the value of practical ministry, in the service of Christian community, as a powerful tool in the struggle against social sin.

CHAPTER 14

Culture in Bonhoeffer and King

— Deweyan Naturalism in Action —

Andre C. Willis

Nature is the mother and the habitat of man, even if sometimes a step-mother and an unfriendly home.—John Dewey, *Art as Experience*

Dietrich Bonhoeffer and Martin Luther King Jr. fought for justice with great vision. Often reduced to mere religionists who responded to troubled times in heroic ways, King and Bonhoeffer were actually thoughtful Christian activists who not only developed philosophic positions that confirmed the importance of standing against corrupt social and political forces, but also they intellectually and psychologically grasped that the realm of culture was the battlefield on which to create contesting social energies in the struggle for more equality, justice, and the rule of God.

Since academics frequently study them as theologians, Bonhoeffer and King are overwhelmingly assessed for how they interpreted Jesus, salvation, and God in relation to issues of justice and equality. Their crucial use of and engagement with culture remains an understudied aspect of their exemplary Christian witness. However, both were highly attentive to the aesthetic details of their sermons, writings, and use of music/art for cultural change. Their radical work depended on an adept handling of theology *and* culture. Investigating the cultural dimension of their work helps us understand their practical philosophy and, at the same time illuminates Tillich's assertion that "religion is the essence of culture."

Though the German Bonhoeffer and African American King did not formally articulate conceptions of culture, their work heavily depended on an understanding of culture as dynamic, interactional, and grounded in community experience. Through their writings, sermons, and speeches they aimed to assist in guiding culture in a gradual shift toward equality. This sense of cultural change is neither reducible to nor dependent on the pragmatic naturalism of American philosopher John Dewey, but it can be rendered clearer by keeping Dewey's work in mind.

The work of John Dewey, largely critical of organized religion, is rarely mentioned in discussions of Bonhoeffer and King. Yet Dewey's notion of culture helps illuminate their approach to culture. Culture, for Dewey, begins with the idea of the human as "individual-in-community"; it emphasizes the social construction of knowledge-in-community, and asserts the importance of the role of aesthetic perception in experience. These central ideas are all implicitly contained within the framework of the cultural strategies of Bonhoeffer and King. My purpose in this essay is to illuminate aspects of King and Bonhoeffer's conception of culture that might remain camouflaged without the lens of Dewey's pragmatic naturalism. If my purpose is achieved I will have exhibited the usefulness of Dewey's pragmatic naturalism for religious-based cultural change.

While it is unquestionable that the Christian worldviews of Bonhoeffer and King were foundational for their thought, it is impossible for any single ideology to satisfy completely the disparate parts of the complex worldviews of the intellectually curious and socially engaged King and Bonhoeffer. Given their training in philosophy/theology and their documented familiarity with the work of Reinhold Niebuhr and William James, it is clear that their conception of culture was drawn from intellectual waters that were flowing during their formative years. While not a direct influence on either figure, Dewey's thought was a vital part of this stream, and I will show that his idea of culture is a useful filter for the work of Bonhoeffer and King.

Dewey's Project of Pragmatic Naturalism

A fundamental element of the complex and vast philosophic project of John Dewey is his "pragmatic naturalism" or "naturalistic realism." Reducing Dewey's work to its most simple themes (he wrote over forty books and at least six hundred articles spanning sixty-five years!) is practically an act of violence, but suffice it to say that his unique form of naturalism grew out of his desire to de-absolutize and de-idealize Hegel, de-externalize Darwin's theory of adaptation of species, and deepen James's notion of radical experience. Dewey's naturalism started with a close look at the existential predicament of humankind and took seriously the ideas of history and development, contingency and experimentation, and science as well as religion.

Dewey's philosophical starting point allowed him to keep an eye on that part of human experience that is "precarious, uncertain, unpredictable, uncontrollable, and hazardous."[1] Unlike classical naturalism (which personified nature as a primordial force), Aristotle's conception of nature as teleological, Kant's stress on nature as a condition for the possibility of experience, and Hegel's nature as the site for the development of freedom, Dewey's work was concerned with the natural problems of organisms in their environments. His pragmatic philosophical project was goal driven: it aimed at the political, social, religious, and metaphysical unity of nature.

Dewey's conception of culture was derived from his naturalism. Unlike the prevailing nineteenth-century Arnoldian notion of culture, "the best of what has been thought and said in the world," Dewey understood culture as natural and dynamic. He wrote, "Culture is the product not of efforts of men put forth in a void or just upon themselves, but of prolonged and cumulative interaction with the environment."[2] Keeping this notion of culture in mind, the work of Bonhoeffer and King is illumined.

I shall proceed to assess King's and Bonhoeffer's use of culture based on three Deweyan insights about culture: the notion of the individual as dependent on community, the idea of the social construction of knowledge, and the conception of human experience as fundamentally aesthetic in character.

The Concept of Human as Individual-in-Community

While Bonhoeffer and King were primarily instructed by their Christian theological worldview, their overall sense of culture is a complicated web of pieces, some of which are more easily understood *without* the Christian filter. Deweyan naturalism is helpful in assessing King's and Bonhoeffer's sense of culture. The first of three insights of Deweyan naturalism that shapes the idea of culture employed by Bonhoeffer and King is that humans should be understood as ever-changing and constituted by community, history, tradition, mood, and so forth. Dewey, and later Bonhoeffer and then King, did not embrace the view that humans are atomistic, distinct, static individuals. They pointed toward the extreme sociality, history, and provisionality at the core of humanness in their work. An intellectual, Dewey explains this best:

> Just as "individual" is not one thing, but is a blanket term for the immense variety of specific reactions, habits, dispositions and powers of human nature that are evoked, and confirmed under the influences of associated life, so with the term "social". Society is one word, but infinitely many things. It covers all the ways in which by associating together men share their experiences, and build up common interests and aims; street gangs, schools for burglary, clans, social cliques, trades unions, joint stock corporations, villages and international alliances.[3]

Dewey started his philosophical work from the idea that humans are limited biological creatures engaging particular contexts, transacting with particular circumstances, in constant interaction with natural and social environments, always in conversation with traditions and values, and fully immersed in time. For him, the human person is fundamentally relational, and this natural relationality forms the basis of culture. Martin Luther King Jr. and Dietrich Bonhoeffer based their work on a similar notion of humanness, albeit a theological one.

Additionally Dewey contended, "rhythm is a universal scheme of existence, underlying all realization of order in change"[4]; it provides the foundation for natural motion and reveals his Hegelian commitment to a form of progressive history without Hegel's strong telos. For Dewey, "life itself consists of phases in which the organism falls out of step with the march of surrounding things and then recovers unison with it—either through effort or by some happy chance."[5] So, both his conception of the individual-in-community and his notion of rhythm—individual-in-time—combine to shape his idea of culture as broad, ever-changing, and dependent on sociality of individuals in community. That is, culture is affected by history and biology but it is not historically or biologically determined. Culture is created by individuals in organic experience with one another, time, environment, region, tradition, desire, biology, history, nature, and the like. Bonhoeffer and King, as I shall show, held ideas about time and personhood that are similar to Dewey's and that lead to a notion of culture very much like his.

The idea of the individual as fundamentally relational and fully immersed in time, and the notion that culture is ever-emerging were not new ideas in the United States. The "schools of thought" called *pragmatism* (James, Peirce), *process thought* (Whitehead), and *personalism* (Bowne, Brightman) undermined the subject-object distinction inherited from Descartes and overcame the individual-community bifurcation prior to Dewey's insights on these issues. Dewey's genius was, in part, how he uniquely combined his philosophic commitments to nature, science, and history with his notions of individuality, temporality, and culture. It is this unique synthesis where the life and work of King and Bonhoeffer seem to be more reflective of Deweyan pragmatic naturalism than process thought, personalism, and the work of other pragmatists. For the remainder of this section, I will focus on King's and Bonhoeffer's reliance on the notion of individual-in-community and show how it is reminiscent of the Deweyan conception.

The central commitments of Dietrich Bonhoeffer were theological, yet he required a recognizable anthropology to fuel his notions of individual-in-community and culture so his theology would resemble the world as most humans experienced it. When read through a Deweyan lens it appears that Bonhoeffer animates his "theology of sociality" by a turn to naturalism. He writes, "human existence is always both historical and natural" and shows that sociality, historicity, and nature are all interrelated anthropological categories. This does not mean that Bonhoeffer is a naturalist or a natural theologian. He strongly disagrees with Dewey's profound faith in the possibilities of natural inquiry, but he confirms—particularly in his later notion of a "religionless Christianity"—Dewey's point that "a body of beliefs and practices that are apart from the common and natural relations of mankind must . . . weaken and sap the force of the possibilities inherent in that relationship."[6] Thus, the attenuated naturalism at the heart of Bonhoeffer's anthropology has something of a Deweyan flavor.

In Bonhoeffer's *Sanctorum Communio* the church is the natural community for the individual. However, this feature of Bonhoeffer's theological anthropology—his conception of spiritual community as natural—requires little theology. For it is fired by a notion of natural community that is very similar to the notion of natural community held by Dewey. Instead of beginning with God, Bonhoeffer's notion of sociality started with overstepping the subject-object distinction that German thinkers had inherited from Kant. Early in his career, Bonhoeffer concluded that the subject-object distinction offered little help "for understanding relations between human persons."[7] Bonhoeffer—influenced by von Harnack and liberal Protestantism—confirmed the world as a place of positive value against neo-orthodox theologies that seemed to suggest the world is the site of evil that has to be transcended. Bonhoeffer asserted—borrowing from Hegel—that Christ is in the world and that it is in the ethical encounter between persons where Christ is to be revealed. Though there is theological action here, this notion of community pushes past Hegel's dependence on the Absolute and is based on natural experience between organisms, their environment, and time.

Bonhoeffer's early writings show his conception of community quite clearly. In his 1930 *Act and Being,* he contends that revelation is not an individual experience, but that it only happens in the "community of faith." He writes, "in reality human beings are never individuals only . . . always part of a community in 'Adam' or in 'Christ.' "[8] That same year he stated,

> Under the cross of Christ we know that we all belong to one another, that we all are brethren and sisters in the same need and in the same hope, that we are bound together by the same destiny, human beings with all our suffering and all our joy, with sorrows and with desires, with disappointments and fulfillments—and most important, human beings with our sin and guilt, with our faith and hope.[9]

Additionally, Bonhoeffer seems to reflect Dewey's obsession with temporality by situating time as essential to his conception of community. For him it is the "temporal actualization" of the centrality of Christ that is most significant for the church. He wrote, "and this community, which in history is never more than incipiently realized and is constantly breaking up, is real and eternal here."[10]

Bonhoeffer's writings surge with the sense of our being time-bound. His awareness that we must presuppose the temporal for all experience of the individual-in-community develops his sense of culture as the site where time-drenched persons moving toward death collectively create and comprehend the variety of dramas that are always unfolding and concluding. Thus, his notion of time, as well as his sense of individual-in-community and his idea of culture, is reminiscent of Dewey's.

Martin Luther King Jr.'s work depended on an understanding of culture as social, interactive, and contingent. Like Dewey, King's conception was based on the idea that there is no such thing as an individual without community. In the historic "I Have a Dream" speech he claims:

> All this is simply to say that all life is interrelated. We are caught in an inescapable network of mutuality; tied together in a single garment of destiny. Whatever affects one directly affects all indirectly. . . . Strangely enough, I can never be what I ought to be until you are what you ought to be. You can never be what you ought to be until I am what I ought to be. This is the way the world is made. I didn't make it that way, but this is the interrelated structure of reality.[11]

Some contend that King's notion of the individual was primarily derived from the personalism he was introduced to in his graduate studies at Crozer by George Davis and at Boston University under the direction of L. Harold DeWolfe in the early fifties.[12] King's personalism—evident in his dissertation and some of his speeches/sermons—asserts that human life is sacred in the view of a Creator and Sustainer God, and that there is no higher principle than the human person.[13] Yet King's strategies in the fight for civil rights and his speeches and books for a popular audience reflect his great esteem for the human personality *and* maintain the necessity of the human community in the formation of the individual personality. King recognized that human personality is by nature social. Finally, and most importantly, King never thought that the spark for change takes place solely in the person; he knew that change takes place in the cultural sphere and that it is always a gradual social force that is generated partially by the natural ebb and flow of the environment, narratives, persons, culture, history, tradition, and energy.

Thus, King's notion of the individual reflects the Deweyan naturalistic conception of individual-in-community. And culture, he accepted (like Dewey), is created by a "social-self" always predicated on relationality within community (and with God). Thus, the human person is important but not more important than the community. For King, "the self cannot be self without other selves."[14] This is an acknowledgment of the importance humans have in the formation of community and the significance community has in the formation of individuals. Thus, King, a serious Christian and a thoughtful theologian—when viewed through the lens of Deweyan naturalism—is better understood as holding a pragmatic naturalist notion of individual-in-community at the core of his worldview.[15]

The upshot of King's and Bonhoeffer's conception of individual-in-community is that it leads to a sense of culture as derived from the ever-shifting cumulative experience of community. Both men realized that to affect a shift in culture one had to affect people's aesthetic experience by addressing their understanding, changing images, shifting metaphors they use, undermining conceptual structures, reorienting vision, and repositioning historical foci. Therefore, they knew that cultural change was prolonged and gradual.

The Social Construction of Knowledge

The idea that knowledge is socially constructed logically follows from the idea of persons as "individuals-in-community." Dewey's naturalism affirms the idea of knowledge as a social product—an edifice of culture—that happens through community and is partially dependent on biology, region, neighbor-hood, and language. For Dewey, this social/cultural product is not grounded in immutable or even secure foundations but in communal engagement that presupposes teaching and learning to acquire the meaning-making traditions of interpretation that are vital for a community. Similarly, language is also a cultural product, not just a system of abstract signs or merely a set of self-referential representations. Language is the preeminent tool of biohistorical beings in time as they attempt to relate to one another while paying attention to wider cultural forces.

For Dewey, knowing takes place organically in the transaction between individual-in-community and environment; thus, it is constructed in experi-ence. Culture is the cumulative ordering of these natural interactions; it is a collection of knowings as they are represented in habits, stories, song, and works. Dewey asserted that knowledge is always communal, situational, and flexible and both knower and known are slightly changed by it. Yet when the transaction between environment and organism is not fluid or easily able to be integrated into the cultural narrative or collective habit, the process of inquiry is sparked. The ideas or knowledge created by this process are, like all ideas, always instrumental: they aim toward action. In this regard, culture is a social force—it is the natural coming to life of knowledge in community.

King's framework for knowledge—when considered via a Deweyan lens—relies on a natural transaction and is constituted by experience. While King never developed or articulated a detailed epistemology, his work was based on an idea of knowledge that was implied in his numerous discussions of suffer-ing. From these we can conclude that, for King, knowledge is mostly the result of a natural transaction between sufferer (African Americans) and the thing suffered (justice) in light of the existence of a good God. That is, the commu-nity of sufferers is always interacting on two levels: the natural—where they experience that which they suffer from (e.g., injustice in the form of racism); and the supernatural—where they have consciousness of something greater experiencing this suffering. Knowledge is the keen awareness of both sides of this experience, the historic momentum in the environment and the cultural temperament of the times. Additionally, knowledge is instrumental; it aims toward justice. King writes, "anyone sensitive to the present moods, morals, and trends in our nation, must *know* that the time for racial justice has come" (emphasis mine).[16]

For King, culture is the interactive space where ever-shifting, trans-actional knowledge is born and from where it gets its direction. Culture, then, is a social force that can be affected and impacted through the shifting dynamics of experience. Hence, King reformed the cultural self-understanding of America via his public work: bold rhetorical imagery and narrative in his sermons and speeches, nonviolent resistance (televised and dependent on a violent response), inspirational African American music, rereading the history of America as moving toward justice, and emphases on the liberal strand of American civil religion. In essence, King took his Christianity seriously, but like Jesus he was a cultural worker, a figure whose cultural contribution was to expand and enrich individual lives in community.

Dietrich Bonhoeffer's conception of knowledge was strongly influenced by his conception of revelation. For him, the Word lived in community and true knowledge was not possible without revelation. He stated, "knowledge of the self and of God is no 'possession without context' but is one which places the knower in an immediate 'possessing' relation to what is known. . . . knowledge in truth about oneself, as well as about God, is already 'being in . . . ,' whether in 'Adam' or in 'Christ.'"[17] Thus, revelation in community (in this case, of disciples) is the condition for the possibility of knowledge for Bonhoeffer. That is, God knows, Jesus knows, the disciple knows, but the nondisciple does not know. It follows that one cannot even *know* revelation until one *obeys* revelation. Thus, for Bonhoeffer, knowledge emanates solely from the realm of discipleship where a few highly disciplined people give themselves completely to Jesus.

On the surface this theological viewpoint seems completely incompatible with the conception of knowledge as socially constructed that I emphasized in Dewey and uncovered in King; for how could an epistemology based on revelation reflect naturalist tendencies?

The answer is that while Bonhoeffer's conception *starts* theologically, once the revelation is in place, knowledge performs identically to natural knowledge: it is transactional (just between God and disciple), constructed in community (of disciples), and is instrumental (it aims toward discipleship). Thus, the spark of knowledge is supernatural for Bonhoeffer, but knowledge itself imitates the "natural" knowledge of Dewey and King.

Bonhoeffer's commitment to revelation as the foundation for knowledge and his idea that this knowledge always leads to action were fundamental to his cultural work. One example of this is his organization of the Pastors' Emergency League in 1933. Bonhoeffer and Martin Niemoller first understood themselves as being divinely inspired. This inspiration led them to the knowledge to respond to the harsh and restrictive rules of the Aryan clause of the Brown Synod, which stipulated that non-Aryan pastors should be removed from their churches. The Pastors' Emergency League called for "a new allegiance to the scriptures and to the confession, resistance to any infringement of these in the church, financial help for those victimized by the new civil laws, and the rejection of the Aryan clause."[18] In essence, Bonhoeffer used his theory of knowledge as revealed in community to help generate and inspire a culture of active resistance against oppressive forces. Though his work was supernatural in its source, revelation is "transactional" (thus, it has a naturalist aspect), and the knowledge that undergirds his activism reflects the naturalist idea of knowledge as socially constructed and instrumental once it is in motion on the ground.

Bonhoeffer's notion of knowledge as social leads to a conception of culture as dynamic, organic, slow-shifting, and dependent on the forces of individuals-in-community. It shows a strong resemblance to Dewey's notion of culture.

Aesthetics of Experience

One of the most important insights of the work of John Dewey was the idea that every human experience contains aesthetic quality. The fact that we do not often notice the aesthetic character of all experience is because we fail to acknowledge the profundity and complexity of our experience as organisms constantly interacting with environments. For Dewey, life is a process of organisms consistently overcoming struggle, disharmony, and oppression within their natural environments. This marvelous and organic journey of adaptation and readaptation through expansion (not destruction) leads to greater equilibrium and order. The creation of order—though always a temporary order—is an aesthetic and artistic achievement as well as a necessary condition of an unfinished world that cumulatively integrates its past as it progresses toward greater harmony, order, and unity.

For Dewey, *impulsion* (sneezing, tantrums, ranting, some forms of crying, impulse) is uncontrollable discharge while *expression* is organic emotion transformed via conscious commitment to achieving a particular end. Expression is a means toward enhanced collectivity; it is communal art that both indicates and creates collective unity. The proper office of expression is to lead the community to greater harmony and balance.

Bonhoeffer and King each confirm the Deweyan role of the aesthetic. They realized the goal to create a greater balance of justice for the collective is accomplishable through the aesthetic sensibilities. Dewey detailed four elements of aesthetic expression that I find to be consistent with the aesthetic expression of King and Bonhoeffer. He claimed that expression: (1) must be the "building up of experience out of the interaction of organic and environmental conditions and energies"; (2) it must be wrung from the producer by the pressure exercised by objective things upon the natural impulses and tendencies; (3) it must be a construction in time, not an instantaneous emission; and (4) it must rely on "storage of attitudes and meanings derived from prior experience."[19] King and Bonhoeffer had a Deweyan sense of the collective power of aesthetic experience. So, they refined their homiletic practices, used spiritual music, and employed poetry and literature in their public witness to their various communities.

Bonhoeffer considered preaching to be the most important aspect of his witness and the most vital of his efforts to transform culture. An intense teacher, intent listener, and incisive speaker, his deep, biblical sermons aimed at creating a community of disciples who would have the integrity to obey Christ's call to justice. To that end, Bonhoeffer meticulously prepared his sermons, carefully avoiding any rhetorical sleight-of-word or verbal trickery. He aimed for aesthetic experience. One of Bonhoeffer's students wrote, "In his sermons he avoided any rhetorical effect. He never gave us anecdotes in them. He chose the most sober, matter-of-fact form, the homily. In spite of this, or perhaps because of it, they were extraordinarily impressive. There was not a word too many. Only the matter itself came to speech, sometimes in such compressed way, that what he had to say almost seemed forced out."[20]

Bonhoeffer's conception of preaching as immediate, continuous with experience, relational, and synchronic meet Deweyan criteria of expression above. Bonhoeffer recognized that to be successful in inspiring his listeners to the passionate obedience of discipleship, he would have to tell stories, craft metaphors, juxtapose compelling phrases like "cheap grace" and "costly grace," and consciously expose his sincerity and vulnerability. In short, he knew that he would have to engender aesthetic experience for his listeners.

Bonhoeffer's early exposure to the arts and his own musical talents (he was an accomplished pianist and almost chose music as a career) helped him understand from an early age that aesthetic expression is a significant cultural force. His powerful piano playing became an integral part of the community at Finkenwalde Preacher's Seminary—the illegal seminary he directed at the behest of the Confessing Church that was closed down by the Gestapo in 1937—confirming both his joy in music and his sense of its indispensability in any collective project. Knowing the power of art he developed a criticism of church aesthetics early in his life. He wrote: "If I consider the pictures hanging in church hall or meeting places, or the architectural styles of churches of recent decades, or the church music provided by Mendelssohn and others, I cannot help thinking that in none of these things is there the slightest understanding of the church's essential social nature."[21]

Bonhoeffer's awareness of the social power of aesthetic experience also enabled him to recognize the immense value of the Negro songs that he encountered during his time at Union Theological Seminary (1930). A fellow student, Albert Frank Fisher, took Bonhoeffer to Abyssinian Baptist Church every Sunday for at least six months. Bonhoeffer would eventually teach Sunday school there and lead an occasional Bible study. What seems to have made the deepest impact upon Bonhoeffer from this immersion in African American religious life was the sense of unmerited suffering at the heart of the African American Christian worldview. This suffering was best embodied in the aesthetic dimension—the Negro spirituals—and Bonhoeffer collected recordings of these songs that he later played for his theology students in Germany. He "described and interpreted" the songs in ways that affirmed the quality of suffering and joy profoundly communicated by this music.[22] Bonhoeffer used this music as an aesthetic example of God's suffering in the world.

In addition to his sermons and songs, it is also worth mentioning that during his final two years (1943–1945) as a prisoner in concentration camps at Tegel and Buchenwald and finally the extermination camp at Flossenbürg, Bonhoeffer wrote numerous letters, ideas for a book, and sermons, but he began his most expressive writing at this time—poetry. This final turn—he knew his time was running out—to the less constrained poetic form may serve as confirmation of the need for an even more open aesthetic to speak to the deeply suffering artist and the broken community.

Martin Luther King Jr.'s early experience in the black Baptist church tradition convinced him early on of the importance of aesthetic experience in community. He not only held preaching, music, and the literary arts in high regard, but also he intentionally used each expressive form in his cultural work for equality. King's brilliant preaching and oratorical genius has been well studied by the likes of Michael Eric Dyson, Keith Miller, and Richard Lischer.[23] These thinkers, among others, have thoroughly described the mechanics of King's rhetoric in relation to African American oratorical tropes, cultural rhythms, and colloquial speech as well as his methodical use of liberal Protestant ideas of American civil religion and topics in progressive Christian preaching. Their conclusions are varied but confirm at least two consistent facts: first, that Martin Luther King was a rhetorical master and, second, that he implicitly conceived of his preaching as aesthetic expression.

For example, King fought hard against the rhetoric of Black Power because he thought it was merely a reaction or an impulsive response to the conditions of black suffering that would ultimately work against greater harmony and justice for Americans. He strove for a more dignified and graceful aesthetic expression—in the Deweyan sense—than the Black Power rhetoric allowed. Second, his words derived from the natural pressures of organic community. Again, fully consistent with Dewey's notion of expression, King's sermons spoke with aesthetic immediacy to ever-changing contexts; they were neither instinctive nor impulsive in the Deweyan sense. Whether eulogy, sermon, or public address his conscientious rhetoric drove toward justice. Finally, King's words—both written and spoken—were constructed thoughtfully over time and they were continuous with meanings derived from prior experience. For King, the act of preaching did not aim toward merely rational argument or creative use of theological symbols; it aimed for aesthetic experience as a means to collective uplift.

King also realized that expressive music (music with inspirational words) generated aesthetic experience. He discussed Negro spirituals as follows:

> An important part of the mass meetings was the freedom songs. In a sense the freedom songs are the soul of the movement. They are more than just incantations of clever phrases designed to invigorate a campaign; they are as old as the history of the Negro in America. . . . We sing the freedom songs today for the same reason the slaves sang them, because we too are in bondage and the songs add hope to our determination that "We shall overcome, Black and white together, We shall overcome someday."
>
> I have stood in a meeting with hundreds of youngsters and joined in while they sang "Ain't Gonna Let Nobody Turn Me 'Round." It is not just a song; it is a resolve. These songs bind us together, give us courage together, help us march together.[24]

In addition to preaching and music, Martin Luther King Jr. also used literature and poetry to assist his oratory. King had developed a love of the written word from his youth. His sermons were peppered with quotations from the high moments of the best of the English poets and writers (Wordsworth, Keats, Shakespeare, Donne). King used these inspirational writings to develop the aesthetic power of his own words and thereby enhance the aesthetic experience of his listener. He knew that "there didn't have to be strife between *lexis* (style, such as metaphor) and *pisteis* (argument and proof). . . . In the best Black oratory, style is not juxtaposed to argument; in fact, style becomes a vehicle of substance."[25]

King's deep commitment to aesthetic expression manifested mainly in his preaching but also is reflected in his conception of music and his use of literature. Cumulatively, King's work was largely based on the Deweyan notion that culture and aesthetics are inseparable but not identical.

If Dewey were alive to read that his naturalism engendered a notion of culture that was at the core of the grand attempts of Bonhoeffer and King to change the destiny of their homelands, he would be discomfited. The deep Christian commitments of Bonhoeffer and King would give him pause. Still, his pragmatic commitment to improving the conditions of individuals in community would be piqued and he might be proud to be affiliated with both men.

Likewise, while both Christian activists might reject the idea that the foundation of their sense of culture is a Deweyan pragmatic naturalism, the advantages to reading their activism through this lens are twofold: we get a clearer understanding of the sense of culture they employed and we keep in view their sense of individual, community, knowledge, and aesthetic expression. This deeper awareness not only allows us to have a better handle on the foundations of their work but also assists us as we do our own cultural work to improve the conditions of humankind.

Part Four

Practices of Peace

CHAPTER 15

Peacemaking
Glen H. Stassen

Bonhoeffer's Ethic of Peacemaking

Heinz Eduard Tödt's comprehensive and insightful analysis of Bonhoeffer's ethic of peacemaking argues that "Bonhoeffer deserves precedence over others because, in the beginning of the 1930s, he developed an ecumenical ethic of peace that was . . . a central part of his theological thinking and political orientation." Tödt goes on to claim, and I agree, that "the path Bonhoeffer traveled in his life as a Christian and as a theologian, in faith and in deed, is disclosed only when we probe into his turning toward and development of an ecumenical ethic of peace. In this context, Bonhoeffer's close bond to the Sermon on the Mount becomes clear."[1] The path Bonhoeffer traveled did not begin with a theology of peacemaking or the Sermon on the Mount but it leads decisively to both.

In 1929, the twenty-three-year-old new Ph.D. graduate wrote a lecture arguing that the Sermon on the Mount and Jesus' ethic *do not apply* to questions of peace and war; instead, such questions should be governed by a nation's drive for more space (*Lebensraum*), and by its vigor and strength in competition with other nations. Here Bonhoeffer resembles the attitude of Reinhold Seeberg, Paul Althaus, and Emmanuel Hirsch, whose nationalistic ethic led them to support Adolf Hitler.

A year later, in 1930–1931, during his study at Union Theological Seminary and involvement with Abyssinian Baptist Church, a turning occurred that Bonhoeffer described six years later:

> Then something happened, something that has changed and transformed my life to the present day. For the first time I discovered the Bible. . . . I had often preached, I had seen a great deal of the church, spoken and preached about it—but I had not yet become a Christian. . . .
>
> Also I had never prayed, or prayed only very little. . . . For all my loneliness, I was quite pleased with myself. The Bible, *and in particular the Sermon on the Mount*, freed me from that. Since then everything has changed. I have felt this plainly, and so have other people about me. It was a great liberation. It became clear to me that the life of a servant of Jesus Christ must belong to the church, and step by step it became clearer to me how far that must go.
>
> Then came the crisis of 1933. This strengthened me in it. Also I now found others who shared this purpose with me. The revival of the church and of the ministry became my supreme concern. . . .
>
> I suddenly saw the Christian pacifism that I had recently passionately opposed as self-evident. . . . And so it went on, step by step. I no longer saw or thought anything else.[2]

When Bonhoeffer came to New York, he was looking for a community, a "cloud of witnesses," whose life fit their theology, and whose theology fit the gospel. But he found American theology woefully thin, and "was equally distressed by most preaching in white churches."[3]

But Bonhoeffer found what he was looking for in Abyssinian Baptist Church in Harlem, and in other black worship services. Here he found that the gospel of Jesus Christ is received with seriousness as the true basis for life in its reality.[4]

> It is clear that whenever the gospel itself really is mentioned, their participation peaks. Here one really could still hear someone talk in a Christian sense about sin and grace and the love of God and ultimate hope. . . . In contrast to the often lecture-like character of the "white" sermon, the "black Christ" is preached with captivating passion and vividness. Anyone who has heard and understood the Negro spirituals knows about the strange mixture of reserved melancholy and eruptive joy in the soul of the Negro.[5]
>
> Nowhere is the revival sermon so widespread and vivid. . . . Here the gospel of Jesus Christ, the savior of sinners, is genuinely preached and appropriated with great receptivity and noticeable excitement. . . .[6]

Bonhoeffer scholar Ruth Zerner observes: "In writing about *other* American church visits he was more precise, logical, thorough, and critical. But whenever Bonhoeffer wrote of his contacts within the African-American community he used words expressing deep feeling." Bonhoeffer's Lutheran students in Berlin, after he returned to Germany, were moved by his description of the suffering of African Americans in America and by the spirituals he played for them.[7] In fact, the themes of the spirituals and of his own theology are remarkably similar—the centrality of Jesus Christ and solidarity with sufferers. He wrote that African American spirituals were an enormous gift for all Christians. He especially mentioned the moving expression of the suffering and comfort of human hearts in "Nobody Knows the Trouble I've Seen," the affliction and liberation of the people of Israel in "Go Down Moses," and love for the Redeemer and longing for the kingdom of heaven in "Swing Low, Sweet Chariot."

"Deeply moved by experiences he shared with [Frank] Fisher, Bonhoeffer later told German students of his friend's admonition to let the suffering of American blacks be known in Germany." He was revolted by segregation and racist language in the South. He wrote home: "In this matter (of segregation), pastors are no better than the others. Racism . . . will be one of the most critical future problems for the white church." He confessed that his identification with the concerns of black Americans might be disproportionate, *since no parallel group existed in Germany*.[8] But soon he was to be awakened to the sufferings of a parallel group in Germany, the Jews. His experience with blacks in the United States must have sensitized him to identify with the sufferings of Jews under Hitler.

Hans Pfeifer shows that "Bonhoeffer wanted to find Christians in America who put their whole existence under the gospel and by this became trustworthy witnesses."[9] He found these witnesses at Abyssinian Baptist Church. Myles Horton offers an eyewitness account of Bonhoeffer's excitement after worship there one Sunday afternoon:

> He was very emotional and did not try to hide his feelings, which was extremely rare for him. He said it was the only time he had experienced true religion in the United States, and was convinced that it was only among blacks who were oppressed that there could be any real religion in this country. . . . He set out for America hoping to find a "cloud of witnesses." In the black church and in a group of friends who were serious about their Christian commitment and practice, who were serious about the Sermon on the Mount, he found them. It was a transforming experience.[10]

I contend that Bonhoeffer's extensive involvement in African American Baptist community life had a deeper impact on him than some Bonhoeffer scholars have adequately recognized. Many who focus more on white, European influences among his friends that year at Union rightly give credit to the influence of French student Jean Lasserre for paying attention to the Sermon on the Mount and to pacifism. But I urge attention to Bonhoeffer's experience with African American Baptists for following Jesus concretely, *in church community*, and for the core of his ethic of peacemaking as commitment to following Jesus Christ.[11] His own letters in that period spend many more words and passion discussing his experience in community with African Americans than his experience with Lasserre.

Bonhoeffer's Close Bond to the Sermon on the Mount

Bonhoeffer's description indicates that his conversion was not first to pacifism, but to the Sermon on the Mount and servanthood to Jesus Christ in Christian community. Pacifism was a secondary, later result. This fits African American Baptist tradition, which has a strong focus on following the Jesus of the Gospels, but not on pacifism. "Lasserre remembered that Bonhoeffer spoke more fervently on behalf of pacifism than he did himself. In other words, what happened . . . was a result of a breakthrough to personal commitment. . . . Discipleship, as commanded by the Sermon on the Mount, involves a deeper commitment than this one issue."[12] Tödt observes: "It is evident that this peace ethic is connected with the Sermon on the Mount—not in the sense of letter-bound directives, but as illustrating what God's commandment can be when heard concretely today and here."[13]

Bonhoeffer's commentary on the Sermon on the Mount sees Jesus' blessing on the peacemakers as a call "not only to have peace, but . . . to make peace. To do this they renounce violence and strife. . . . Jesus' disciples maintain peace by choosing to suffer instead of causing others to suffer. They preserve community when others destroy it. . . . Their peace will never be greater than when they encounter evil people in peace and are willing to suffer from them."[14] Bonhoeffer himself suffered martyrdom faithfully, by hanging—one of Hitler's last dastardly orders before he died ignominiously, by suicide.

Bonhoeffer devotes the longest commentary on any unit in the Sermon on the Mount to Jesus' command to "love your enemies." This love becomes unconquerable

> by never asking what the enemy is doing . . . , and only asking what
> Jesus has done. Loving one's enemies leads disciples to the way of the

cross and into communion with the crucified one. . . . It is not their own love. It is solely the love of Jesus Christ, who went to the cross for his enemies and prayed on the cross for them. Faced with the way of the cross of Jesus Christ, however, the disciples themselves recognize that they were among the enemies of Jesus who have been conquered by his love. This love makes the disciples able to see, so that they can recognize an enemy as a sister or brother and behave toward that person as they would toward a sister or brother.[15]

Practical Ethic of Peacemaking as Discipleship Grounded in Christology

A major puzzle in Bonhoeffer interpretation has been his statement that "pacifism" was part of his conversion, part of his subsequent advocacy in the ecumenical World Alliance of Churches, part of what he tried to teach his students,[16] and evidenced in his refusal to be drafted into the German army. Yet he participated in an attempt at a coup to change Germany's government from war-making to peacemaking, which would have involved killing Hitler. How does that fit pacifism?

Most English-speakers use the word *pacifist* to mean a person opposed on principle to violence in any form, especially in war. But Bonhoeffer explicitly opposed an ethic of principles; his "pacifism" cannot be a principle of non-violence.[17] The leading pacifist theologian, John Howard Yoder, criticized an interpretation of Bonhoeffer that equated pacifism with moral absolutism. "Bonhoeffer was never committed to a position he would have seen as 'abso-lutist,' despite the fact that he referred to himself as a pacifist." His commit-ment to following Jesus and the Sermon on the Mount, to discipleship, was first; and to the revival of the church in its social reality. This commitment is what "led him to embrace what he referred to as pacifism."[18]

Bonhoeffer's pacifism was not an ethic of principles; it was a commitment to a way of life as following Jesus. It was a theologically grounded ethics of peacemaking. Clifford Green calls our attention to Bonhoeffer's important 1932 address "Christ and Peace,"[19] written immediately after his turning from nationalism to formative discipleship. Here Bonhoeffer speaks of "cheap grace," "discipleship," and "peace" in a way that shows he already has his book *Disciple-ship* in mind, and is presenting his theology of discipleship as a peace ethic. He titles his lecture about following Christ, "Christ and Peace." This demonstrates that "his Christian peace ethic is not a discrete and interchangeable part of his theology, to be replaced by something else in a different historical situation; nor is it simply a principle of nonviolence; rather Bonhoeffer's Christian peace

ethic is an ingredient and an implication of his theology as a whole. . . . Bonhoeffer's Christian peace ethic is grounded in his Christology."[20]

Green adds seven clear pieces of evidence that Bonhoeffer did not abandon his Christian peace ethic to participate in the conspiracy. He rarely used
the term *pacifist* to describe himself, but he continued through his life to have
a strong christologically grounded commitment to a peace ethic.[21]

Before suggesting contents of this "peace ethic," not of principle but of following Jesus Christ, let us examine the parallel in Martin Luther King Jr.

The Path King Followed

When King reached the age of six, his white playmate told him his father said
they could no longer play together. He told his parents, and they explained
white racism to him. "I was greatly shocked, and from that moment on I was
determined to hate every white person. As I grew older and older this feeling
continued to grow. My parents would always tell me that I should not hate
the white [man], but that it was my duty as a Christian to love him."[22] King
could not conquer his antiwhite feeling until his college experience. "Some
whites were working, albeit gradually, to eliminate racism. His resentment
slowly began to disappear as he associated with more whites of goodwill,
especially in an interracial Intercollegiate Council. . . . [This] 'convinced me
that we have many white persons as allies, particularly among the younger
generation.'"[23]

King's Close Bond to the Power of Love

King's own experience as an African American, plus his African American
Baptist tradition, like the tradition at Abyssinian Baptist Church, gave him
embodied identification with the suffering of a people oppressed, firmness
in working for justice, and a strong focus on following Jesus, especially Jesus'
teaching on love that included love for the enemy—for whites.

King's father succeeded A. D. Williams as pastor of Ebenezer Baptist
Church in Atlanta. He said that "A. D. Williams inspired him in many ways.
Both men preached a social-gospel Christianity that combined a belief in
personal salvation with the need to apply the teachings of Jesus to the daily
problems of their black congregations."[24] Notice all four dimensions of this
precisely stated summary: (1) They taught and preached a practical Christianity, meant to be lived in daily life; (2) they focused on the teachings of Jesus;
(3) they emphasized personal salvation, what the young King's papers emphasize as personal response, repentance, commitment, and action—"a personal

relationship with God" and "the inwardness of true religion"; and (4) they preached a social gospel that insisted that the Lordship of Christ applies to all of life, not only private relationships—but they did not preach a reductionistic social gospel; instead they emphasized conversion, personal salvation, and living Jesus' way in daily life.

"During King's childhood and teenage years, he became increasingly aware of his father's vocal opposition to segregation." Martin's father said to him, "I don't care how long I have to live with this system, I will never accept it." He was a leader of the Atlanta Civic and Political League and the NAACP, and he advocated a march to city hall as the dramatic beginning of a massive voter registration—despite reluctance by more cautious black leaders. As a teenager, Martin enormously admired both his father's social commitment and its basis in the gospel.[25]

During his second year of high school, King won a public-speaking contest, and competed in the state oratorical contest. His speech stated:

> We cannot have a nation orderly and sound with one group so ground down and thwarted that it is almost forced into unsocial attitudes and crime. We cannot be truly Christian people so long as we flout the central teachings of Jesus: brotherly love and the Golden Rule.
>
> The spirit of Lincoln still lives, that spirit born of the teachings of the Nazarene, who promised mercy to the merciful, who lifted the lowly, strengthened the weak, ate with the publicans, and made the captives free. My heart throbs anew in the hope that inspired by the example of Lincoln, imbued with the spirit of Christ, they will cast down the last barrier to perfect freedom.[26]

Midway through a paper during seminary, King departed from the assigned reading to put his own emphasis on Jesus of Nazareth, his life and his death. He wrote that the kingdom of God "will be a society governed by the law of love. . . . Jesus made love the mark of sovereignty."[27]

King first referred to Anders Nygren's definition of Christian love in a 1950 paper at Crozer, and his second reference to Nygren comes in his 1952 paper at Boston University—both on the meaning of the cross.[28] He said God's love is spontaneous and uncaused by human merit; it creates value in its recipients. "For he maketh His sun to rise on the evil and the good and sendeth rain on the just and unjust" (Matt. 5:45, KJV). But he did not follow Nygren in saying love is uncalculating and unmotivated, love excludes proper self-love, and it contrasts with justice. King's developed definition of love, rather, combines dimensions of equal regard, mutual love, and delivering love, in addition to echoes of Nygren's sacrificial love. It supports strategic calculation motivated to achieve justice and community.[29]

At the first mass meeting of the Montgomery bus boycott, as he was praising Rosa Parks, King said,

> We are not here advocating violence. . . . We believe in the Christian religion. We believe in the teachings of Jesus. . . . We're going to work with grim and bold determination to gain justice on the buses in this city. . . . If we are wrong, Jesus of Nazareth was merely a utopian dreamer that never came down to earth. If we are wrong, justice is a lie. Love has no meaning. And we are determined here in Montgomery to work and fight until justice runs down like water and righteousness like a mighty stream. . . .
>
> But I want to tell you this evening that it is not enough for us to talk about love. . . . There is another side called justice. And justice is really love in calculation. Justice is love correcting that which revolts against love. The Almighty God himself is not . . . just standing out saying through Hosea, "I love you, Israel." He's also the God that stands up before the nations and says: "Be still and know that I'm God, that if you don't obey me I will break the backbone of your power and slap you out of the orbits of your international and national relationships." Standing beside love is always justice, and we are only using the tools of justice. Not only are we using the tools of persuasion, but we've come to see that we've got to use the tools of coercion. . . .
>
> Jesus said: "If you do it unto the least of these, my brethren, you do it unto me." . . . And I've come to see now that as we struggle for our rights, maybe some will have to die. But somebody said, if a man doesn't have something that he'll die for, he isn't fit to live.[30]

King's Turning Toward Nonviolent Direct Action as a Way of Life

Three influences came together for King in a bright flash of illumination: Jesus' teaching of love in the Sermon on the Mount, Gandhi's concept of *satyagraha*, and the actual experience of the effectiveness of nonviolent action. In his description of his pilgrimage to nonviolence, he wrote of what he had been taught in his African American Baptist tradition: "the power of love, . . . the Christian doctrine of love," and "the Sermon on the Mount." But he had been skeptical concerning the power of love. His pilgrimage was a process of overcoming the two-kingdoms split that marginalizes Jesus' way only to individual relations. He came to realize that "the Christian doctrine of love, operating through the Gandhian method of nonviolence, is one of the most potent weapons available to an oppressed people in their struggle for freedom." He "was driven back to the Sermon on the Mount. . . . Christ furnished the spirit and motivation and Gandhi furnished the method."[31] It was a Christian commitment, not only expediency; it "became a commitment to a way of life," not only an abstract principle.

King expanded the scope of his witness from civil rights, to economic justice (especially in his *Where Do We Go from Here?*), and then dramatically to his public and national witness against the Vietnam War in his Riverside Church address on April 4, 1967, exactly one year before he was assassinated.[32] Some scholars rightly study King's writings on the philosophy of personalism, but the seven reasons King gave for his courageous move to speak out against the Vietnam War do not mention tenets of personalism. His three climactic reasons are "my commitment to the ministry of Jesus Christ," "obedience to the one who loved his enemies so fully that he died for them," and "because I believe that the Father is deeply concerned especially for his suffering and helpless and outcast children. . . . Here is the true meaning and value of compassion and nonviolence when it helps us to see the enemy's point of view, to hear his questions, to know his assessment of ourselves."

Rufus Burrow shows perceptively that in several student papers and in his dissertation King wrestles theologically with philosophical personalism's question of the limitation of God's power.[33] King moved toward a resolution that he found in Peter Bertocci, writing of God's "matchless power" (not unlimited but without equal), and God's need for human cooperation and participation. King's theological wrestle with God's power—in his student papers, in his dissertation, and in his own spiritual struggle—lies behind his influential affirmation of faith: "the arc of the moral universe is long, but it bends toward justice." I suggest that King's understanding that the God of the universe is truly revealed *in the way of Jesus Christ* nudged him away from making unlimited power the absolute in his doctrine of God, and toward patient persuasion toward justice.

Practical Peace Ethic of Church Practice and Public Witness

King was committed to nonviolence. His Riverside Church address called on youth to refuse the draft, "urging them, and their ministers, to declare themselves conscientious objectors to military service—based on love of God and of neighbor, based on obedience to the Prince of Peace."[34] The next week he told his Ebenezer congregation that although he would have fought against Hitler, "I happen to be a pacifist."[35] But what kind of pacifist? He resembled Bonhoeffer—committed to nonviolence, following the way of Jesus and the Sermon on the Mount, and the revival of the churches in their engagement for justice, with disciplined practices of peacemaking as nonviolent action.

This was not a legalistic ethic, and not simply the opposite of violence, but a way of life.[36] It was remarkably effective: millions demonstrated, but I know of only one case when some demonstrators turned to violence. Enormous legal, cultural, and attitudinal changes resulted. Liberty and justice for all have taken dramatic steps forward, but have many steps still to go.

Bonhoeffer and King Together

Bonhoeffer and King were committed to a peace ethic that is not absolutist or legalist, but is a way of nonviolence, following Jesus, influenced by African American Baptist tradition. In the words of Clifford Green and H. E. Tödt, it might be better named a christologically based, biblical, and ecumenical ethic of peacemaking.

Can we explain that ethic of peacemaking more adequately in terms of the new paradigm of just peacemaking?[37] Just peacemaking does not focus on the debate over whether war is or is not ever justified, but on the practices that are both theologically supported and are effective in overcoming injustice nonviolently and thereby removing causes of war. It is not merely a thin principle, but thick, proactive practices. Just peacemaking is being affirmed by an increasing number of church assemblies, and now is being joined by some Muslim and Jewish scholars as well. In neither Bonhoeffer's nor King's lifetime had the paradigm of just peacemaking been developed, but now we have it in our vocabulary. It is spreading widely. Can it help identify the kind of peacemaking ethic they were striving for, and illuminate the practicality of their peacemaking practices for our time?

Just peacemaking has ten practices, based both christologically and in their empirical effectiveness.

1. *Nonviolent direct action* was the heart of much that King accomplished. For this, King was awarded the Nobel Peace Prize. In his acceptance speech, he said: "This award which I receive on behalf of that movement is profound recognition that nonviolence is the answer to the crucial political and moral question of our time—the need . . . to overcome oppression and violence without resorting to violence and oppression."[38] It is spreading worldwide.

Hardy Arnold recalls Bonhoeffer explaining: "Hitler and National Socialism were such evil elements that they had to be fought with all means apart from violence. He, Bonhoeffer, wanted to travel to India to learn from Gandhi how to fight a government that one is up against, in order to overcome it with non-violent means." Bonhoeffer developed quite "elaborate plans for training for non-violent resistance . . . in 1933 and 1934."[39]

2. *Independent initiatives.* King advocated the independent initiatives of ending all bombing in Vietnam, declaring a unilateral cease-fire, and setting a date when the United States "will remove all foreign troops from Vietnam in accordance with the 1954 Geneva agreement."[40] Precisely these initiatives were finally adopted by the U.S. government to end the war, *after eight more years* of killing, destruction of the land, and economic bleeding there and here. Oh, that the government had followed his wisdom then! What lives would have been saved!

Bonhoeffer urged the British government to signal that they would welcome a coup and look favorably on a new German regime that would end the war, thereby encouraging Germans to act on their plans for a coup.

3. *Cooperative conflict resolution.* Negotiation with those who were maintaining injustice before any demonstration was essential practice for the civil rights movement. As King declared in his Riverside Church address, "Life and history give eloquent testimony that conflicts are never resolved without trustful give and take on both sides."

For Bonhoeffer, negotiation with the Gestapo was impossible. But he sought dialogue with fellow Germans who could be persuaded to be faithful to the way of Christ.

4. *Acknowledge responsibility for conflict and injustice and seek repentance and forgiveness.* This practice of just peacemaking was initiated by Bonhoeffer's confession of his own, the church's, and the nation's guilt.[41] It then spread to German churches, to the public repentance of Chancellor Willy Brandt and President Richard von Weizsäcker, and now has spread to other nations.[42]

King's Riverside address was a courageous confession of deep error in our values and actions, and a call for repentance, for a revolution of values. He was crying out against the Vietnam War's destruction of the lives of the poor in Vietnam and the hopes of the poor at home. And he began that speech by confessing "the betrayal of my own silences." Repentance, and also forgiveness, was a major theme of King's, and was crucial for preventing retaliatory violence, and for achieving reconciliation after struggles were won.[43]

5. *Advance human rights and democracy.* Bonhoeffer was unique among German theologians in advocating human rights and constitutional law over against Hitler's violations, and this gave him strength to be unique in opposing Hitler and standing up for Jews from the start.[44]

King moved the civil rights movement for American rights into becoming a human rights movement for human needs. "We have moved from the era of civil rights to the era of human rights, an era where we are called upon to raise certain basic questions about the whole society."[45]

6. *Foster just and sustainable economic development.* The young Bonhoeffer was a minister to youth in Wedding, the slum area of Berlin. While at Union Seminary, he spoke passionately of hunger, suffering, and economic depression in Germany, and of the injustice of forced reparations payments.[46] These were major causes of the failure of the Weimar Republic's effort to establish democracy, and of Hitler's rise to power. "The general situation in Germany had become so desolate that Bonhoeffer felt that the church was called to step in and use its whole authority and reputation as well as its economic resources to help fight poverty and misery following the economic crisis."[47]

King's Riverside Church address appeals poignantly and prophetically to the Vietnam War's destruction of the War on Poverty: "I watched the [antipoverty] program broken and eviscerated as if it were some idle political plaything of a society gone mad on war, and I knew that America would never invest the necessary funds of energies in rehabilitation of its poor so long as adventures like Vietnam continued to draw men and skills and money like some demonic destructive suction tube." He said, "I speak as a child of God and brother to the suffering poor of Vietnam. I speak for those whose whole land is being laid waste, whose homes are being destroyed, whose culture is being subverted. I speak for the poor of America, who are paying the double price of smashed hopes at home and death and corruption in Vietnam." He told his SCLC staff, "We must recognize that we can't solve our problem now until there is a radical redistribution of economic and political power . . . a radical redistribution of economic and political power."[48]

7 and 8. *Work with emerging cooperative forces in the international system, and strengthen the United Nations and international efforts for cooperation and human rights.* Despite attacks against Germans who participated in the World Alliance of Churches by nationalistic theologians Paul Althaus and Emmanuel Hirsch and much of the church press, Bonhoeffer accepted the position of part-time youth secretary and engaged deeply in the World Alliance of Churches, calling for repentance for nationalism and war, and advocating international law. He said we should not speak of "church and state," but "international church and international order of peace." The church does not belong to one nation, but is itself an expression of Jesus' great commission.[49] King likewise grew to ever increasing international awareness.

9. *Reduce offensive weapons and weapons trade.* In his Riverside Church address, King said,

> As I have walked among the desperate, rejected and angry young men [in the ghettos of the North] I have told them that Molotov cocktails

and rifles would not solve their problems. . . . Social change comes most meaningfully through nonviolent action. But they asked—and rightly so—what about Vietnam? . . . I knew that I could never again raise my voice against the violence of the oppressed in the ghettos without having first spoken clearly to the greatest purveyor of violence in the world today—my own government.[50]

From the beginning of Hitler's *Führership*, Bonhoeffer's and his family's immediate opposition was based on their loyalty to peace and clear perception that Hitler's taking power "means war."[51]

10. *Encourage grassroots peacemaking groups and voluntary associations.* Bonhoeffer worked mightily to persuade German churches to oppose Hitler's injustice and violence. He worked to develop his underground seminary to become a community committed to Christian discipleship and to peace. When the Nazis closed the seminary, he joined in the conspiracy to organize a coup d'état and thus stop the war.

King is a national hero for his and SCLC's organizing and leading millions of people in church groups and civil rights groups. At Riverside Church, he said, "We in the churches and synagogues have a continuing task while we urge our government to disengage itself from a disgraceful commitment. We must continue to raise our voices if our nation persists in its perverse ways in Vietnam. We must be prepared to match actions with words by seeking out every creative means of protest possible."[52]

Participation in Preparation for the Coup d'État

My *Lebensraum* in this essay is too small to explain and qualify as I'd like. But let me make one more proposal. The best Bonhoeffer scholars interpret Bonhoeffer's participating in the plot to overthrow Hitler by pointing to "The Structure of Responsible Life" in *Ethics*, and to Bonhoeffer's theme of Christ taking our guilt upon himself. Thus, Bonhoeffer's participation is "a singular, extreme case not justified by law or principle but only as a free act of Christian responsibility done in the hope of God's mercy." From my perspective, this is surely right, but alone it feels too situational, too lacking clear guidance, too lacking community checks and balances.[53]

I propose that preservation of the human right to life, based theologically, christologically, and eschatologically, is an essential part of Bonhoeffer's peace ethics. In his *Ethics*, Bonhoeffer argues that without the concept of "the natural," Protestant ethics lacks "the ability to give clear guidance on the burning questions . . . without answers or help in vital decisions." I believe he here intends to develop a concept that can give clear guidance on the burning question of the justice of the conspiracy. But he cannot name Hitler and the coup for fear of discovery, so we have to read between the lines. He develops a theological argument for human rights, and the right to bodily life, as God's gift and God's will. He argues that we can recognize the right to bodily life by Christ's becoming human in bodily form. "Since by God's will human life on earth exists only as bodily life, the body has a right to be preserved for the sake of the whole person. Since all rights are extinguished at death, the preservation of bodily life is the very foundation of all natural rights and is therefore endowed with special importance." Therefore, he argues that the euthanasia policy (carried out under Hitler's orders) of killing persons who are not socially useful violates God's will and the basic right to life.

And then he concludes: "A borderline case for all these considerations would occur if a plague broke out on a ship that had no facilities for isolation and, by human reckoning, the healthy could be saved only by the death of the sick person. In this case the decision would have to remain open."[54]

I suggest that the person with the plague is Hitler. The right to life of the healthy can be saved only by throwing the source of infection overboard. There is no way to prevent Nazis killing people except by a coup d'état, with a new, legally just government replacing Hitler's dictatorship. The point is not to kill Hitler, though unfortunately that will happen; the point is to take the only action that can stop the Nazi killing. This is an act of peacemaking, akin to humanitarian intervention or "the responsibility to protect," which the ethic of just peacemaking affirms in carefully limited conditions. In this light, Bonhoeffer retains his peace ethic. Fortunately for King, there was a democratic process for combating racism, economic justice, and the Vietnam War. What was needed was persuasion, and persuasion was King's gift.

Conclusion

Both Bonhoeffer and King were committed to following the way of the incarnate Jesus—and followed him to death. Both were committed to embodying Jesus' way holistically—not only in one narrow part of life, but in ever-expanding dimensions of life. Both continue to lead us to repent for the racism, authoritarianism, domination, and militarism of ideologies that hijack Christian faith for their self-serving schemes. This is what many of us call the way of incarnational discipleship.

Both Bonhoeffer and King were murdered in April of the year when they had reached age thirty-nine, depriving us of the leadership we so badly needed for healing our shame, and for recovery from authoritarianism and domination. Assassinations always seem to come from the authoritarian and reactionary side, not the peace and justice side, and to deprive us of the leadership for justice and peacemaking that we long for. They deprive us of our future, assassinating the leaders of healing and justice: Abraham Lincoln in 1865, Dietrich Bonhoeffer in 1945, Mohandas Gandhi in 1948, John Kennedy in 1963, Robert Kennedy in 1968, Martin Luther King in 1968, Anwar al Sadat in 1981, Yitzhak Rabin in 1995. This means that the Jesus-following believers in justice rather than racism, and peace rather than violence, need to keep raising up more leaders like Dietrich Bonhoeffer and Martin Luther King Jr. to compensate for the violence of injustice, and to persuade yet more people to follow the way of peacemaking and healing rather than domination, exclusion, violence, and injustice. We will do it.

CHAPTER 16

Spiritualities of Justice, Peace, and Freedom for the Oppressed

Geffrey B. Kelly

I n a dramatic phrase from his spiritual classic, *Discipleship*, Dietrich Bonhoeffer offered a stark commentary on the destiny that disciples would
experience should they remain in communion with Jesus Christ, committed to follow him even to the cross. "Whenever Christ calls us, his call
leads us to death," he writes.[1] Bonhoeffer had been challenging his seminarians
to make the choice before them to embrace the cross of Christ by sharing in
his suffering and death. This essay focuses on how Dietrich Bonhoeffer and
Martin Luther King Jr. each saw the decision to embrace Christ's cross as an
essential demand of his own vocation, and it calls the life-energy animating
this decision "spirituality." In examining their spiritualities, this essay focuses
on how the lives of Bonhoeffer and King were touched by God's Spirit to
become God's own prophetic voices for the achievement of justice, peace,
and freedom in their ministry to the victims of widespread oppression in the
troubled world of the twentieth century.

In a related observation to those same seminarians mentioned above, Bonhoeffer revealed the heart of his own spirituality and shared with them the
spiritual outlook that he contended was requisite for every genuine follower
of Jesus Christ. "To be conformed to the image of Jesus Christ," he later wrote,
"is not an ideal of realizing some kind of similarity with Christ which we are
asked to attain." Instead, he insisted that "it is the very image of God, the form
of Christ, which seeks to take shape within us (Gal. 4:19). It is Christ's own

form which seeks to manifest itself in us. Christ does not cease working in us until he has changed us into Christ's own image. Our goal is to be shaped into the entire form of the *incarnate*, the *crucified*, and the *risen* one."[2] Bonhoeffer went on to explain the far-reaching implications of this conformation with Jesus Christ in which Christ's followers are to enter into solidarity with those who have been victimized by those forces of oppression, political domination, and persecution that rob innocent people of their God-given dignity as created in the image and likeness of none other than Jesus Christ himself. "In Christ's incarnation," Bonhoeffer declared, "all of humanity regains the dignity of bearing the image of Christ." Their calling is, like Christ, to make common cause with society's victims. In declaring his solidarity with the victims of Nazi aggression, Bonhoeffer would conclude: "Whoever from now on attacks the least of the people attacks Christ, who took on human form and who in himself has restored the image of God for all who bear a human countenance."[3] This daring claim on behalf of the victims is a point of convergence for the ethical activism of both Dietrich Bonhoeffer and Martin Luther King, who had themselves in their respective ministries defended "the least of their people" in whom they recognized the presence of none other than Jesus Christ. In the cross of Jesus Christ Bonhoeffer and King experienced God's *way* for them, the *truth* they had to proclaim to the evil powers of their societies, and the *life* they were asked to surrender in obedience to God's will in ways that have continued to attract people inspired through their example to live as Jesus Christ intended for his followers.

Spirituality Nurtured in Sacred Scripture and Social Responsibility

Both King and Bonhoeffer had written early on in their respective careers about how their attitudes had undergone changes that dramatically eroded their previous smugness with regard to the nature of the church. They would be energized by their determination to view reality anew from the perspective of Jesus' teachings. Though both had been trained in the scriptural exegesis then in vogue, each recorded a transformation that would dictate their future activism.

For King, schooled in the fundamentalist tradition of biblical interpretation, this would take him on an intellectual journey during his seminary training in which his studies were directed beyond his biblical literalism toward utterly different, liberal interpretations of the Scriptures. This led him, in turn, to see the positive side of liberalism and helped give him greater familiarity with a more liberal doctrine of humanity that exuded an optimism in the midst of the social ills which were otherwise so depressing to him and his fellow blacks in that disturbing period of American history. This new-felt optimism would be modified, however, under the impact of his reading the realistic social ethics of Reinhold Niebuhr. Niebuhr's analyses of the complexity of social sin and the vagaries of human motivation led King more critically to recognize in naïve forms of liberalism little more than superficial, overly optimistic conclusions about human nature. Niebuhr enabled King to see more clearly the rationalizations invoked by political leaders and the nations they governed that justified blatantly sinful actions as they relentlessly pursued their own special interests to the detriment of the poor and powerless. King recovered his philosophical bearings in a balance between the positive aspects of liberalism's optimism and the more realistic, though pessimistic, understanding of human nature as quite capable of the social injustice that he had experienced and had already begun to reprobate. This moved King to focus his ministry more on the social ethics that he began to associate more cogently with the gospel teachings of Jesus Christ. He saw in Jesus' teachings the personal call to identify with those suffering social ills since hunger, thirst, sickness, imprisonment, and poverty were the lived reality of King's own social setting. He saw in Walter Rauschenbusch's *Christianity and the Social Crisis* the practical wisdom that American Protestantism had to embrace social responsibility or it would risk losing its soul in the political haze of the technological and military prowess that had become the boast of American society. King could now connect the spiritual survival of a people with the crippling economic poverty of those he represented. At this stage of his searching, King turned to the life and teachings of Mohandas Gandhi and his advocacy of the life-forces of truth and love. More and more he came to accept the need for nonviolence as the only way to follow Christ down the paths where hatred and social injustice continued to lurk and continued to victimize the unwary and the powerless.[4]

Like King, Bonhoeffer, too, had been schooled in the scientific exegesis of the Bible then in vogue at Berlin University. At the same time he began to incorporate into this thinking the possibility of separating scientific exegesis from a more spiritual, pastoral approach to the Scriptures. He defended his views in a student paper, "Can a Distinction Be Drawn between a Historical and a Pneumatological Interpretation of the Scriptures and How Does Dogmatic Theology Regard This?" The title suggests that the controlling differential between the two modes of interpretation was, in Bonhoeffer's mind, pneumatological or the meaning-for-life implanted by the Holy Spirit both in the text and in the mind of the believer. The opening words of the essay betray his conclusion. One does read the Scriptures, not in a purely scientific mode, but in a spirit of prayer and faith with the mind open to what God, and not the skilled scientific exegetes, may be saying.[5] By the time Bonhoeffer had written this essay he was already captivated by the exciting crisis theology of Karl Barth, leaving him disgruntled with the more liberal interpretation of his exegetical mentors in Berlin who were not all that friendly with the "pastoral bias" of Barth. For Bonhoeffer, the Scriptures were not only a source of truth, they were also intended as testimony offering inspiration for action on behalf of people in need. In describing his renewed way of reading the Scriptures, Bonhoeffer shared his belief that the words of the Bible had become for him a way of discerning how God wanted him to live.[6]

Throughout their lives both Bonhoeffer and King urged their churches to live up to their social responsibilities, to care for the poor, to take risks for the twin causes of justice and peace, to live daily the Sermon on the Mount, to profess solidarity with the outcasts of their oppressive societies, and even to confront malice in government head-on. Theirs was a spirituality immersed in acts of responsibility and sustained by an intense respect for God's word, which has behavioral ramifications for all who call themselves followers of their crucified Lord Jesus. Following Christ in costly discipleship would never be for them an easy path with social advantages of being a respected citizen. Their Christian spirituality and their vocation as moral leaders demanded that they follow Christ in full awareness of the dangerous consequences that Jesus Christ himself had experienced in his passion and death on the cross.

The Sermon on the Mount in the Spirituality of Bonhoeffer and King

While it is difficult to pinpoint with any precision how Bonhoeffer and King were moved to see their life's calling more intensely as communion with the person of Jesus Christ, giving them renewed courage and Christ-centered motivation, there is little doubt that each was confronted at significant turning points in their lives by the uncompromising challenges of Christ's Sermon on the Mount. For Bonhoeffer this shift in his personal attitudes and his determination to be more fully committed to living out the gospel mandates of the Sermon on the Mount is acknowledged in three significant letters that call his encounter with this sermon a liberation. In a letter to Elizabeth Zinn, a person to whom he had been briefly engaged, he wrote that he had plunged himself into his work in a self-serving, un-Christian way. Then, as he recounts

the changeover, "the Bible, and in particular the Sermon on the Mount, freed
me from that. Since then everything has changed. I have felt this plainly, and
so have other people about me. It was a great liberation. It became clear to me
that the life of a servant of Jesus Christ must belong to the church, and step by
step it became plainer to me how far that must go."[7] Earlier he had written in
a similar vein to his brother, Karl-Friedrich Bonhoeffer:

> I do believe that at last I am on the right track, for the first time in my
> life. I often feel quite happy about it. . . . I think I am right in saying that
> I would only achieve true inner clarity and honesty by really starting
> to take the Sermon on the Mount seriously. . . . The restoration of the
> church must surely depend on a new kind of monasticism, which has
> nothing in common with the old but a life of uncompromising disciple-
> ship, following Christ according to the Sermon on the Mount. I believe
> the time has come to gather people together and do this.[8]

In a letter to his brother-in-law, Rüdiger Schleicher, he confessed that he had
learned from the biblical words of Jesus Christ not to fashion a god of his own
selfish choosing but to let God be God and show him where he, a Christian,
and God were to be found together, namely, "the cross of Christ . . . just as the
Sermon on the Mount demands."[9] In these letters there is unmistakable testimony that Bonhoeffer came to identify himself as a Christian in light of and
inspired by the Sermon on the Mount. This "awakening" on his part took on
added significance in the context of the Nazi persecution of the Jews and the
Nazi attempt to silence any putative opposition from the churches. Christ's
words made it even more imperative that Christians stand up without compromise for peace and social justice, in effect, for Christ himself.[10]

It is equally evident that, in like manner, the Sermon on the Mount took
on added importance for King in the context of his commitment to become
the leader and voice of the poor blacks of Montgomery, Alabama, during the
bus boycott of 1955 and 1956. From the very beginning of his leadership of
the boycott, King acknowledged the double inspiration of Gandhi and the Sermon on the Mount. He could see clearly that once the boycott began to take
effect, Gandhi's method of nonviolence elided perfectly with the Christian
doctrine of love and Gandhi's name became well known among the people of
Montgomery, Alabama. In his essay "An Experiment in Love," King mentions
that the "guiding principle" of their movement had been "referred to variously
as nonviolent resistance, noncooperation, and passive resistance." But he insists
that in the beginning of their organized protest movement, none of those
expressions was heralded. Instead, he writes, "the phrase most often heard was

'Christian love.' It was the Sermon on the Mount, rather than a doctrine of passive resistance, that initially inspired the Negroes of Montgomery to digni-fied social action. It was Jesus of Nazareth that stirred the Negroes to protest with the creative weapon of love."[11] Later King would remark that, whereas Jesus Christ provided the inspiration and motivation, Gandhi furnished the organizational tactics.

King was additionally fascinated with the way Gandhi himself had become attracted to the Sermon on the Mount. Gandhi spoke of how this sermon had opened him up to an understanding of the teachings of Christianity with an entirely new perspective. "The teaching of the Sermon on the Mount," Gandhi wrote, " echoed something I had learnt in childhood and something which seemed to be part of my being and which I felt was being acted up to in the daily life around me."[12] Thanks to this sermon attributed to Jesus Christ, Chris-tianity then could be seen resonating directly with the truths that had become part of Gandhi's own commitment to nonviolence. King recognized further in the nonviolence of Gandhi, and in the correlative of loving enemies in the Sermon on the Mount, the need to recommit oneself to the love espoused throughout Jesus' gospel teachings. His conviction was not only to respond to violence with nonviolence, but to attack the evil system without hatred in one's heart for those who are the tools of the system. Hence, he counseled his followers in the civil rights movement not to attempt to humiliate and hurt their opponents but with patience and with time to win their friendship and, in the spirit of Christ, to achieve a reconciliation that would restore the Christian community.

In his reflections on costly discipleship, Bonhoeffer likewise counsels an attitude of forgiveness in the spirit of Paul's advice to the Christians of Rome who were faced with enemies resentful of their presence and eager to blame them for all sorts of civil disturbances. His words are very close to the spirit of forbearance and reconciliation that were central to the nonviolence of both King and Gandhi. Extrapolating from the Sermon on the Mount, Bon-hoeffer declares that "Jesus does not even consider the possibility that there could be someone whom the disciple hates." Instead, Jesus speaks of forgive-ness despite the physical hurt inflicted on a disciple by the enemy and with-out regard for the enemy's hatred of the disciple. Bonhoeffer then asks the astounding question: "But who needs love more than they who live in hate without any love?," adding that "the more animosity the enemy has, the more my love is required. No matter whether it is a political or religious enemy, they can all expect only undivided love from Jesus' followers."[13] Bonhoeffer was, of course, speaking in the context of the Nazi campaign to hate and exterminate all enemies. According to Bonhoeffer, Jesus' counsel to forgive one's enemies sets Christians apart from those who allow themselves to be led into wars and acts of violence by political leaders who urge others to hate those whom they deem enemies. Like Bonhoeffer, King was astute enough to recognize that, in the campaign of blacks for the recognition of their civil rights, those involved in the movement would arouse the bitter enmity and even acts of violence against them. True to his philosophy of love and Jesus' Sermon on the Mount, King permitted no one in the civil rights movement to nurture hatred or engage in violent retaliation for past sins against them. Time and again, he invoked the example of Jesus Christ and the Gandhian rationale that nonviolence would eventually win over the country to their cause and would shame the racists into one day accepting the full dignity of their black brothers and sisters in a renewed Christian community of peace and justice.

In effect, Bonhoeffer and King had accepted the need as Christians to forgive their enemies not only because of Jesus' command that they love even their enemies but also because they recognized that the determination to love and forgive those who hated and persecuted them was the only effective way to overcome hatred and to restore Christian community. The love for and forgiveness of enemies were for Bonhoeffer and King a crucial path toward the liberation to which they aspired for their people and for a world renewed in the peace and justice that reflect the gospel teachings of Jesus Christ in his all-embracing Sermon on the Mount.

This Christ-centered attitude was for Bonhoeffer and King the very center of their spirituality, as they committed themselves to work in communion with Jesus Christ for peace, justice, and the liberation from the oppression of their people. Their lives were a witness to the wisdom articulated in Bonhoeffer's 1932 sermon on truth and freedom, in which he spoke of those who were the true revolutionaries because of the love they brought to the world as they lived and acted in the freedom of God's own truth: "The people who love, because they are freed through the truth of God are the most revolutionary people on earth. They are the ones who upset all values; they are the explosives in human society. Such persons are the most dangerous. The disturbance of peace, which comes to the world through these people, provokes the world's hatred."[14] Bonhoeffer's words from this sermon could become an accurate description of how both Bonhoeffer and King were judged by their critics in fascist Germany and racist America respectively. They would, in fact, be considered disturbers of the peace as well as explosive revolutionaries against the status quo values of political systems infected with the pathologies of hatred, indifference to peoples' sufferings, and militaristic violence against putative enemies. They would, in fact, be labeled a danger to their enemies. King was himself called an "extremist," an intended insult that he seemed to revel in because it placed him in the same historical league with such "extremists" as Jesus Christ, the prophet Amos, Saint Paul, Abraham Lincoln, Thomas Jefferson, and others now admired for their accomplishments against great odds on behalf of freedom, human dignity, and social justice.[15]

Dietrich Bonhoeffer had himself experienced a disturbing encounter with what Martin Luther King had endured in the civil rights movement in America. Bonhoeffer's personal work in Harlem in 1930–1931 had sobered him to the realities of American racism and made him on his return to Germany doubly sensitive to the dangers of Hitler's own racist policies and hate-filled speeches against the Jews. Even before his involvement in the conspiracy, Bonhoeffer had written that God had proclaimed an irresistible oneness with the destitute and fully shared in the sorrows and joys of those trapped in poverty. As early as his Barcelona ministry in 1928, he had attempted to sensitize his affluent parishioners to the plight of the poor in the dingy slums of the city, telling them that Christianity preaches the "unending worth of the apparently worthless and the unending worthlessness of what is apparently so valuable."[16] These words from that conference could also describe what Martin Luther King had absorbed in his own spiritual outlook as he denounced the values of a racist society and spoke up for the "unending worth" of the black people in the United States. In his *Discipleship*, Bonhoeffer continues to focus on the theme that followers of Jesus Christ must find him among the most despised and rejected. In his Christology lectures he had pointed them to the poor worker on the factory floor, the homeless beggar, and the ragged human being, who had so little to offer them in return but who could provide a more intimate encounter with Jesus.[17] In *Discipleship* he declares that those who embrace the beatitudinal way of compassion "share in other people's need, debasement, and guilt." Christians were asked to join the ranks of disenfranchised by making common cause with those reprobated and marginalized by their government. He praises those who, despite their own needs, "have an irresistible love for the lowly, the sick, the suffering, for those who are demeaned and abused, for those who suffer injustice and are rejected, for everyone in pain and anxiety."[18] In this passage we can see both the decision of Bonhoeffer to defend the reprobated Jews of Nazi Germany and the equally costly decision of Martin Luther King to take up the cause and dangers of the poor blacks of the racist southern states of America.

Spirituality That Proclaims Peace Instead of War

Martin Luther King, like Gandhi, his philosophical mentor, will forever be remembered for his preaching of love, forbearance, and nonviolence toward enemies even as violence was done to him and his followers. His success in the civil rights movement has tended, though, to overshadow his antiwar activism despite the fact that King had presented one of the most dramatic condemnations of the war in Vietnam ever recorded. The occasion was his address of April 4, 1967, before a group of Concerned Clergy and Laity gathered in the Riverside Church of New York City, just one year to the day before his assassination. His words on that occasion would cost him much of his popularity even among his fellow blacks, many of whom had relatives serving in Vietnam.

Because Bonhoeffer took part in the conspiracy plotting the assassination of Hitler and the overthrow of the Nazi government, he is rarely spoken of as a peace activist in the mode of Martin Luther King whose entire apostolate would bear out the nonviolent peace legacy of Jesus Christ. Yet, at significant junctures in the Hitler era, Bonhoeffer presented sermons and speeches at an ecumenical conference that today, in retrospect, stand out as the strongest statements on behalf of peace and against war in that chaotic period of European history. One would miss a central feature of his Christian spirituality if his strong peace ethic were ignored.

King, who had not hesitated to denounce the war in Vietnam in his parish ministry, had also run into unexpected voices that questioned his growing presence in the antiwar movement. He was saddened by the thought that the public refused to connect the war in Vietnam with the civil rights movement. This was the background for his electrifying address at the Riverside Church in which, as his title "A Time to Break Silence" indicates, he was breaking his silence and in the strongest possible terms denouncing the war. King devoted the opening moments of his address to connect the war with the civil rights movement and to offer compelling reasons why he considered the war immoral and ultimately destructive of the values that the United States had proclaimed in its own patriotic documents. He began his critique with a series of statements on why the United States was wrong in having invaded Vietnam. For one thing, the war was expensive. It siphoned off funds needed for the poor of America. The war also was being fought disproportionately by the poor and minorities. These soldiers were being asked to die for a nation unwilling to include them in the same schools as whites. Furthermore, the use of violence by America was a bad example for American youth who could be tempted to solve their problems in a similar manner. The other reasons invoked by King are much closer to the inner biblical core of his Christian spirituality. They pertained to King's desire to carry out the gospel mandate to love one's enemies and to affirm the sonship of all peoples under God and the brotherhood of all peoples as children of God. King went on in his address to point out that in the war the United States was contradicting its own Declaration of Independence, and finally he warned the United States against the self-destructiveness of America's own militarism. "A nation that continues year after year to spend more money on military defense than on programs of social uplift is approaching spiritual death."[19]

Bonhoeffer's own dramatic peace teachings reveal him as fully in accord with King's observations against the Vietnam War. Bonhoeffer was not only christocentric but also ecclesiocentric. He was equally critical of his own church's cowardice in the face of Germany's rising militarism and its gearing up for another war as he was of the attitude of churchgoing Christians who allowed themselves to be naïvely drawn into the culture of war and the glorification of the honors won seemingly only in military combat. He challenged his church in what became his most forceful urging of the churches to live up to their avowed calling to represent Jesus Christ before the world. In his speech at the assembly to the ecumenical conference held in Fanø, Denmark, on August 28, 1934, he argued that Jesus Christ identifies with all peoples such that Christians who wage war are, in effect, using their weapons against Jesus Christ himself. In a sarcastic vein he then mocked the various self-serving ways in which nations try to keep peace, treaties, money, and investments, and try to build up powerful armies and weaponry—strategies not unknown in today's world. He argued that none of these strategies would work because they achieve only a façade of national security. "For peace must be dared. It is the great venture," Bonhoeffer declared. At this juncture he turned to the ecumenical delegates and dared them to live up in all honesty to their proclaimed calling, to actually represent the church of Jesus Christ by undertaking the mission of peacemaking. He asked them to fulfill their claim to be the Ecumenical Council of the Church of Jesus Christ. They had the best opportunity and the responsibility to speak out courageously and convincingly "so that the world, though it gnash its teeth, will have to hear, so that the peoples will rejoice because the Church of Christ in the name of Christ has taken the weapons from the hands of their sons, forbidden war, and proclaimed the peace of Christ against the raging world."[20]

Even more striking were the provocative words that Bonhoeffer incorporated into a sermon that he gave on Germany's "Day of National Mourning" (the equivalent of America's "Memorial Day" services). Speaking to a congregation gathered to commemorate those who died in war and with several men bedecked with their military medals, Bonhoeffer spoke the daring exhortation that, in the name of Jesus Christ, Christians should reject war as one of the insidious powers attempting to wipe the spirit of Jesus Christ from Christian consciousness. In the sermon he accused Germany's warmongers of attempting to replace the spirit of Jesus Christ with the language of political expediency. Knowing that soldiers were encouraged by allusions to their being on the side of God and were pepped up to kill the enemy and shed their own blood "for God and country," Bonhoeffer called such tactics a blatant attempt to confuse the unwary troops, urging them to fight "in the name of Christ against the true Christ." In this sermon he also attempted to expose the national and international deceits aimed at seducing Christians away from following Christ's teachings on peace and justice. He wanted to alert his congregation to the deceptions to which they were exposed and goes on to warn them against succumbing to the skillful blandishments of the military and its alliance with the war-making industries that were claiming the irrelevance of Jesus Christ in times of national conflict:

> When the spirits are once confused, the powers of the world are revealed, and burst forth openly. The powers that want to snatch the disciples from him, that want to show them that it is madness to go with him, that Christ has no power, only words; they, the powers of reality, speak the language of facts and this language is more convincing than the language of Christ. The world bands together against the spirit of Christ, the demons are outraged: it is a revolt against Christ. And the great power of the rebellion is called—war! . . . Thus war, sickness and hunger are the powers who want to take Christ's rule, and they are all incited by the archenemy of Christ, who is the living one from death.[21]

Few statements from peace activists of all ages match the passion and ire of this sermon given at a time when the congregation expected to hear words of commendation for their military heroism and Germany's glory.

Conclusion

This essay has been about the spiritual strengths and Christ-centered outlook in the lives of Bonhoeffer and King. Seen together in the similarity of their lives and in their prophetic mission on behalf of peace and justice, they have become fascinating sources of inspiration for Christians encouraged by their exemplary lives to offer their own self-sacrificing witness to Jesus Christ. The spirituality of both Bonhoeffer and King was grounded in Jesus Christ as they themselves were transformed by God's Spirit to become unabashed foes of the systems that had denied freedom, dignity, and life itself to countless victims of cruel dictatorships and perpetrators of racial, religious, and class repression. Their lives and faith were animated by their love for Jesus Christ, their discovery and acceptance of the demands of Jesus' Sermon on the Mount, and their desire to form genuine Christian communities where faith and love for one another could be shared. Bonhoeffer and King were gifted with uncommon courage and brash outspokenness reminiscent of the prophets of old. And, like those prophets, their sense of justice for the oppressed and their outrage at injustice dictated the way they served the church and their respective worlds, often with scathing criticism but always with the unconditional, agapeic love for their peoples that has been the most visible mark of those who have chosen to follow the way, truth, and life of Jesus Christ.

CHAPTER 17

Overhearing Resonances
— Jesus and Ethics in King and Bonhoeffer —
Gary M. Simpson

K ing and Bonhoeffer were both influential preachers and thus accomplished orators. They were also both theologians whose theological writings were highly autobiographical. Our task is to consider how their understandings of Jesus influenced their ethics and moral leadership.

This is not a comparative study of Christologies that one might find in a traditional theological textbook, which often starts deductively with pre-conceived, abstract conceptions of humanity and divinity provided perhaps by Christian tradition(s) and philosophical analyses and then asks how two or more theologians comparatively understand the God-human relationship in Jesus. Rather, I will work more inductively with Bonhoeffer and King by examining some of the primary ways they each depict Jesus and how these images shape their social ethics.[1] An inductive approach does not try to force either theologian into a procrustean bed of concern not their own but, rather, starts from concerns fitting to each of them. With King, for instance, at no time after entering full-time ministry did he ever sit down and compose a comprehensive and systematic account of the meaning and significance of Jesus. He just never perceived the Holy Spirit's calling to such a task. First, therefore, we will explore in King the significance of Jesus for social ethics from the perspective of oratory, following a clue offered by U.S. Representative John Lewis: "The voice held me right from the start."[2] Second, we will explore the relation between Jesus and social ethics for Bonhoeffer from the perspective of theological autobiography, because "he was one of those people who said what he did and did what he said, so that his life is a commentary on his writings, and his writings on his life."[3]

Both King and Bonhoeffer thoroughly integrated Jesus with social ethics. Such thorough integration perennially frustrates the typical textbook approach, which tends to divide the understanding of Jesus and the interpretation of social ethics into different domains and then tries, awkwardly, to reunite them. I, however, will not rend asunder what the two of them have joined together. Again, from this more inductive approach I will listen for possible resonances between King and Bonhoeffer (and ourselves), though pitched in different keys, when overheard in close proximity to one another.

"Changing the Face of the Enemy": Jesus and the Ethics of Love[4]

"Tell 'em about the dream, Martin; tell 'em the dream." Mahalia Jackson, the "Queen of Gospel Music" in the 1950s and 1960s, had become more and more fidgety as King went on talking on the steps of the Lincoln Memorial on that August 28, 1963, Wednesday. She had just readied the hundreds of thousands of marchers with a rousing rendition of "I've Been 'Buked, and I've Been Scorned."[5] Now she fretted that the precious word of the Lord might be constrained, perhaps by an exaggerated concern for the larger nationwide white audience. King had come with a prepared text, but halfway through it he knew that it was not engaging his audience as hoped. It was King himself who had requested that his old friend Mahalia precede him, and as she sat just behind him on the podium, she could contain her soul no longer. She had heard King's set speech of "The Dream" at previous predominantly African American civil rights events. Now, in Washington, D.C., she willed the black spiritual idiom of faith, hope, and liberation to flow freely into the very speech that would come to embody the twentieth-century civil rights movement.[6] King did indeed speak forth the Dream, rooted in the American dream, but now he merged it with "Negro" idioms that gained for the American dream additional roots, more authentic depth, and thereby practical truth.[7]

As an orator par excellence King always carefully and competently attended to his situated audience and then shaped his presentation of Jesus as love accordingly. So, with different audiences and situations he would bring out a different side of Jesus as love. As we will see, in certain situations Jesus' love shows forth as liberation; on other occasions with a different audience as his hearers, Jesus' love comes home to roost as healing balm. King himself does not seem much interested in or too worried about integrating or harmonizing these two presentations. Therefore, I will not look to impose some overarching synthesis. Instead, I will unearth the audience situations and King's depictions accordingly, and finally note how King's understanding of beloved community is the direct consequence of Jesus' love as either liberation or healing balm. Above all, one must remember that for King "Christ is not only God-like, but God is Christ-like."[8] It is for this reason that King remained more christocentric than theocentric when it comes to Jesus' love bringing about beloved community.[9]

Liberation

"Love your enemies." This exhortation by Jesus always unsettled King. "Yes, it is love that will save our world and our civilization, love even for enemies." By the end of the Montgomery bus boycott (1955–1956) he had also come to appreciate the teaching and witness of Mahatma Gandhi. From then on he promoted "the Christian doctrine of love operating through the Gandhian method of nonviolence."[10] Numerous African Americans in the decade following World War II had come to Gandhian convictions prior to King, including some of King's mentors like Benjamin Mays. Now, he, too, became convinced: "Christ furnished the spirit and motivation, while Gandhi furnished the method." Still, King understood Gandhi's nonviolence as more than a method; it is "ultimately a way of life that men live by because of the sheer morality of its claim."[11]

After the spring of 1956 King always indivisibly and inseparably joined together the spirit and motivation of Jesus with the method of Gandhi, love with nonviolence, in an unbreakable union with the strength of conviction perhaps analogous to the classic Christian conviction of the union of Christ's divinity and humanity. It is conceivable that without this joining of Jesus with Gandhi that King himself might over time have renounced his Christian faith, as he notes happened to other Christians.[12] Still, the indivisibility and inseparability of Jesus and Gandhi never exhausted the significance of Jesus for King, especially when he oratorically faced an audience in dire need of Jesus as healing balm. For King, Gandhi's nonviolent way of life becomes the mediating dynamic that links Jesus and liberation.

As a way of life love as nonviolent direct action liberates by changing the face of three enemies: the face of the oppressed, the face of the oppressor, and the face of the oppressive system. King condensed nonviolent direct action into six practices that change the face of the three enemies. The first two practices *liberate the enemy within oppressed peoples*. First, nonviolent direct action is neither passive nor for cowards, but requires courage. Second, nonviolent direct action avoids not only doing external physical violence to the opponent but also shuns doing internal violence to the resister's spirit. Because "privileged groups rarely give up their privileges without strong resistance," nonviolent direct action must, therefore, be dynamically aggressive spiritually even though it is nonaggressive physically.[13]

Oppressed peoples deal with their oppression in various ways, said King. For instance, they may rise up in hatred and violence. But when the oppressed practice hate, the "nobodiness" introduced by oppression gets doubled and further distorts the personality of the oppressed. Or they may acquiesce, resigning themselves to perpetual oppression. Ultimately this is immoral because "non-cooperation with evil is as much a moral obligation as is cooperation with good."[14] (We will return to this second possible response when we explore Jesus as balm.) Or oppressed people may respond by living in the courage of the more excellent way of nonviolent direct action. The love of nonviolent direct action creates "somebodiness" and gives concrete birth to "the new Negro."[15]

The next two nonviolent practices *change the oppressor*, the face of the enemy without. With the third practice, nonviolent resisters willingly accept suffering for a cause, if necessary, but will never inflict suffering on others. Unearned suffering is redemptive. Love bears suffering and thereby is neither idealistic nor sentimental. King recalls Gandhi's insight:

> Rivers of blood may have to flow before we gain our freedom, but it must be our blood. . . . Things of fundamental importance to people are not secured by reason alone, but have to be purchased with their suffering. . . . Suffering is infinitely more powerful than the law of the jungle for converting the opponent and opening his ears which are otherwise shut to the voice of reason.[16]

Unearned does not mean masochistic. Rather, when reasonable and persuasive speech fails, unearned suffering is the moral means of last resort to awaken the conscience of an oppressive adversary and of a wider passive public. "When a police dog buried his fangs in the ankle of a small child in Birmingham, he buried his fangs in the ankle of every American."[17]

Fourth, nonviolent direct action seeks reconciliation, not defeat of an adversary. After all, said King, oppressors are also victims of their own oppressive behavior. Nonviolent resisters seek to win their adversary's understanding and even friendship rather than to humiliate or defeat them. "The end is redemption and reconciliation. The aftermath of nonviolence is the creation of beloved community, while the aftermath of violence is tragic bitterness."[18]

The last two nonviolent practices *change the face of the unjust system.* In the fifth practice, nonviolent direct action aims to remove evil forces, not to destroy persons who perpetrate evil deeds. Sixth, nonviolent direct action is based on the conviction that the universe is on the side of justice. The true conflict is between justice and injustice. "The arc of the moral universe is long, but it bends toward justice," King regularly intoned.[19] When the justice of nonviolent direct action rolls down like waters and the righteousness of loving the enemy pours forth like an ever-flowing stream, then the face of the third enemy is changed. In these moral practices liberation comes, freedom rings, and love reigns supreme.

Most who came to the now iconic 1963 March on Washington had expected to hear a King who was all about integration, and not simply desegregation. No one was disappointed. However, the common assumption of white American integrationists—20 percent of the marchers that day were white—was that integration meant the fuller inclusion of African Americans into American civic life, that is, into a white-defined America. That, too, was the unexamined assumption of the white liberal Christian social gospel movement, which King had studied as a Ph.D. student at Boston University. While King did indeed imagine full inclusion of African Americans in American civic life, note well how he ended the speech!

> And when we allow freedom to ring, when we let it ring from every village and hamlet, from every state and city, we will be able to speed up that day when all God's children—black men and white men, Jews and Gentiles, Catholics and Protestants—will be able to join hands and to sing in the words of the old Negro spiritual, "Free at last, free at last; thank God Almighty, we are free at last."[20]

Here King proclaims the day when all Americans will join hands, sing together, and be integrated into nothing less than an old Negro spiritual. There's the surprise. Not only are African Americans integrated within American civic life, dominated as it had been by an amalgam of European ethnicities; but white Americans—yes, all Americans—get integrated also into the spiritual force field of African American community. Only when integrated in such a way are all citizens and residents mutually free at last. Only when American civic life is thus rebooted is America as a body politic, not merely its citizens and residents, but America itself concretely liberated. Here we can see how thoroughly entwined is King's liberation Christology with his oratorical wealth and beauty.

The profoundly moral key of King's depiction of Jesus as liberation has much in common with the social gospel of white liberal Protestantism, but he also infused the social gospel with four new elements. First, following Howard Thurman, the legendary African American theologian from earlier in the twentieth century, King made racial injustice for the disinherited, for the "'buked and scorned," a more abiding focus of social gospel concern. Second, borrowing from Reinhold Niebuhr's Christian realism, he added a larger dose of realism about the stubbornness of human sin than liberal Protestantism had; this realism ended the fantasy that privileged groups would willingly and smoothly give up their privileges. Third, as we have seen, true integration is a two-way street; in fact, integration as liberation is more like a traffic circle with mutual integration crossing over a variety of previously segregated worlds. Finally, he added a larger dose of practical activism for the racially oppressed by thoroughly binding Jesus as liberation to the realism of nonviolent direct action.

Balm

Still, King's depiction of Jesus always had another side, the redemptive tenderheartedness of healing.[21] In this way especially did the black Christian folk preacher traditions profoundly shape the significance of Jesus for King. Here, he found the personal God revealed in Jesus of Nazareth compelling, satisfying, healing, and encouraging. So did—and does—the black church. When he had the larger national audience of predominantly white America in his oratorical purview, he practiced a restraint about his own inner spiritual struggles. But he frequently abandoned that restraint when in the presence of the black church, "the safest place on earth."[22] There he shared his own discouragement, communing thereby out of the depths with his black Christian brothers and sisters. On such occasions he stood in the company of the "'buked and the scorned."

Here especially the black Jesus steps boldly forth in King's preaching, often in the words of an old Negro spiritual like "Never Alone." Here Jesus himself personally promises his indomitable solidarity with Martin who, it seemed, had merged himself almost indistinguishably with the congregation.

> And I say it to you out of experience this morning, yes, I've seen the lightning flash. (*Yes, sir*) I've heard the thunder roll. (*Yes*) I've felt sin-breakers dashing, trying to conquer my soul. But I heard the voice of Jesus, saying

still to fight on. He promised never to leave me, (*Yes, sir*) never to leave me alone. (*Thank you, Jesus*) No, never alone. No, never alone. He promised never to leave me. Never to leave me alone. (*Glory to God*)[23]

In black congregations King often recalled how an elderly woman from Montgomery, affectionately called Sister Pollard, had "preached" to him. This was the same woman who during the bus boycott had once been mockingly asked by a bus driver if she wasn't exhausted and wouldn't she like to end her boycott and ride the bus. "Yes," she answered politely, "my feets is tired, but my soul is rested." At one point in that boycott King himself had become quite discouraged, fearing that the struggle had been lost. "You didn't talk strong enough tonight," exhorted Sister Pollard. "Now come close to me," she continued, "and let me tell you something one more time, and I want you to hear it this time. Now I done told you we is with you. Now, even if we ain't with you, the Lord is with you. The Lord's going to take care of you."[24]

In the company of the " 'buked and scorned," he regularly brought Jesus the Great Physician into their midst through the Negro spiritual idiom of "There Is a Balm in Gilead." He reminded black believers what he had learned from Thurman. In the biblical book of Jeremiah, the great prophet himself had only posed the question, "Is there a balm in Gilead?" "Centuries later our slave foreparents came along (*Yes, sir*) . . . and they took Jeremiah's question mark and straightened it into an exclamation point."[25] With that exclamation point the black generations are bound together in one democracy of the dead together with the living. With that exclamation point the healing balm of Jesus dare never be reduced to an otherworldly sop. That exclamation point removes complacency and empowers for this-worldly liberating action. Eternal healing capacitates earthly agency. Balm enables liberation in "the fierce urgency of now" and brings the beloved community into being.[26]

Beloved Community

King used the notion of beloved community where Jesus in the New Testament had intoned the notion of the coming kingdom of God. "The aftermath of nonviolence is the creation of the beloved community. . . ."[27] Here we see that just as nonviolence is the mediating reality between Jesus' love and liberation so also it is the mediating reality between Jesus and beloved community. Likewise, personal redemptive healing never leaves one alone as a self-subsisting individual. Jesus as balm just as surely means community—Sister Pollard's "we is with you." Commenting on the christological source and nature of beloved community King concludes:

Finally, . . . [i]t is this deep faith in the future that causes the nonviolent resister to accept suffering without retaliation. He knows that in his
struggle for justice he has cosmic companionship. This belief that God is
on the side of truth and justice comes down to us from the long tradition
of our Christian faith. There is something at the very center of our faith
which reminds us that Good Friday may reign for a day, but ultimately it
must give way to the triumphant beat of the Easter drums.[28]

Because beloved community is the outcome of both Jesus' love as liberation
and Jesus' love as balm, there is a sense in which beloved community joins
together the two oratorical sides of King's presentation of Jesus, the liberation
side of the social gospel and the healing side of black folk Christianity, though
King himself never says this in so many words.

The nonviolent communication that King used in "Letter from Birmingham
Jail" offers a classic instance of enacting already now the coming and hoped-for
beloved community. Eight prominent white liberal clergy had written an editorial in the *Birmingham News* calling the civil rights campaign in Birmingham
both "unwise and untimely." King countered the accusation of untimely with
his argument for "the fierce urgency of now," as he would put it in "I Have a
Dream" and "A Time to Break Silence." But how would he address the charge of
being "unwise," which channeled the oft-heard southern white complaint that
civil rights advocates are merely outside agitators and troublemakers?

King, at the time officially a minister in Atlanta, had come to Birmingham
because he was president of the Southern Christian Leadership Conference,
which operated in every southern state. Furthermore, the local SCLC affili-
ate had asked him as national president to come. He did not, however, rebut
the charge only with such organizational truths. Other, weightier reasons had
impelled him, spanning an arc commencing with God's own call and stretch-
ing across the entire universe. "But more basically, I am in Birmingham because
injustice is here. . . . Like Paul, I must constantly respond to the Macedonian
call for aid," alluding to Acts 16. The arc ends in a famous oratorical flurry of
cosmic sociality.

Moreover, I am cognizant of the interrelatedness of all communities and
states. I cannot sit idly by in Atlanta and not be concerned about what happens in Birmingham. Injustice anywhere is a threat to justice everywhere.
We are caught in an inescapable network of mutuality, tied in a single garment of destiny. Whatever affects one directly, affects all indirectly.[29]

As an eighteen-year-old, I—the son of a Kentucky "hillbilly" and the
grandson of a Klansman—personally experienced this inescapable network of

mutuality when I read "Letter from Birmingham Jail" for the first time. The oratorical beauty of his argument against the accusation of "untimely" first caught me up short and then enraptured me, quite literally, in beloved community. I dwelt, seemingly forever, on the following lengthy paragraph, cited here in an austerely abridged form:

> I guess it is easy for those who have never felt the stinging darts of segregation to say, "Wait." But when you have seen vicious mobs lynch your mothers and fathers at will and drown your sisters and brothers at whim; . . . when you are forever fighting a degenerating sense of "nobodiness"; then you will understand why we find it difficult to wait.[30]

Here King accomplishes a moment of empathetic insight in his opponents, a moment that social psychologists call "social perspective taking." First, he takes the initial step by imaginatively crossing over into the social reality and perspective of his liberal white critics. "I guess it is easy . . . to say, 'Wait.'" Second, through ten brief, carefully constructed vignettes placed side by side—teachers of oratory call this "parataxis"—he gives verse to the testimony of what every African American had continually experienced on a daily basis, "But when you have seen . . ." Read the entire paragraph, oppressive vignette following oppressive vignette. Could any white person with even a flicker of conscience hear this cumulative testimony of weary years and silent tears and remain unmoved, indifferent, and unrepentant? The beauty and miracle of nonviolent oratory arrives in the last clause when the "you" of African American testimony edges under the skin of white Americans, placing them under the influence of Negro realities. "Then *you* will understand why *we* find it difficult to wait." Through nonviolent communication the inescapable network of mutuality initiates beloved community itself. The timeliness of the Birmingham campaign ultimately rests on the universal wisdom and beauty of beloved community, which King found trustworthy because he believed it flowed from Jesus' love as liberation and balm.

Still, mutual understanding, like authentic oratory, must be embodied. Beloved community only exists as incarnated. As one civil rights activist testified, "The only thing we had was our bodies. They [our movement leaders] were welcome to our bodies, and they could use our bodies the best way they saw fit. And so this was the thing. We put our bodies on the line."[31]

The Birmingham campaign was dying on the vine within its first couple of weeks. King's own imprisonment had done little. Not until over two thousand African American youth, organized by the Student Nonviolent Coordinating Committee and without their parents' permission, put their bodies on the line marching two by two, fifty at a time, did the campaign turn redemptive. Day by day newspapers, magazines, and TV broadcasts displayed their young bodies being pummeled by fire hoses, ripped by police dogs, and hauled away in paddy wagons. Those in the white American public who paid attention and cared were brought to their knees.

As long as injustice persists, King's vision of beloved community remains incarnated in the practice of nonviolent direct action and rooted in the healing balm of Sister Pollard's exclamation, "The Lord is with you." A fuller exploration of the implications of beloved community for King's social ethics would pay attention to the moral import within the matrix of nonviolent direct action, civil society organizations, alliance politics, and the interconnections of racism, classism, and militarism. The momentum gained in Birmingham through this moral matrix made possible the 1963 March on Washington, the 1964 Civil Rights Act, the 1965 Voting Rights Act, and eventually the 2009 inauguration of President Barack Hussein Obama. Where will we "put our bodies on the line" today? Ultimately, for King such a question was a matter of his Christian faith in Jesus, who loved his enemies.

"View from Below": Jesus Christ Himself—The Bearing God Who Shares Our Place[32]

Dietrich Bonhoeffer lived his adult years during the period leading up to and then including Hitler's Nazi reign of wickedness. He therefore wrote theological ethics for "times that are out of joint" but also with a hopeful eye toward "the quiet flow of calmer times." "Today," noted Bonhoeffer, "we have villains and saints again, in full public view. . . . The contours are sharply drawn. Reality is laid bare. Shakespeare's characters are among us. The villain and the saint have little or nothing to do with ethical programs."[33] Here I will explore Bonhoeffer's combination of theology and autobiography through three themes that weave together his Christology, ecclesiology, and social ethics: place-sharing, the communion of saints, and the view from below.

"Who Christ really is, for us today" was for years "bothering" Bonhoeffer, though he did not pen that now-famous question until April 30, 1944, while incarcerated in Tegel Prison. Ten weeks later and just four days before the famous failed attempt to assassinate Hitler on July 20, 1944, Bonhoeffer presciently confessed, "only the suffering God can help."[34] By saying "only" he was consciously rejecting the belief that was dominant among the Nazi Christians who had reduced Christian faith to a god revealed preeminently as divine omnipotence and power as control. Ironically, this false god of omnipotence and control led other Germans to abandon Christianity altogether for various forms of deism, pantheism, or atheism. By the 1940s Bonhoeffer was thoroughly confident that only through the theology and proclamation of the cross of Christ would Germany receive the real help that God promises for the world.

Let us pick up Bonhoeffer's journey to a cruciform "God who bears" in the year 1932. At the age of twenty-six he faced a personal spiritual crisis. The overall nature of this crisis can be reconstructed though the details remain shrouded. In a now well-known letter from Tegel Prison on April 22, 1944, to his former student and now best friend Eberhard Bethge, Bonhoeffer recalled a change that was both heartrending and momentous, of which he had not spoken openly before. Prior to 1932 he had exercised an "ambition that many noticed in me [which] made my life difficult." He related to people "in a very unchristian way," and used his considerable intellectual capabilities in a manner that "turned the doctrine of Jesus Christ into something of personal advantage for myself. . . . I was quite pleased with myself . . . but I had not yet become a Christian." In sum, among his friends and family he exercised a powerful, controlling, and "dominating ego" that belied his Christian faith.[35]

Dietrich Bonhoeffer began working on his most widely read book, *Discipleship*, during this time of personal crisis, though the book was not published until 1937. While he wrote it explicitly for the church, he also oriented it theologically to resolve his own personal crisis. How so? In *Discipleship* Bonhoeffer disciplines his own dominating ego by acknowledging the presence of a more authoritative ego who commands submission in obedience. Jesus is that commanding presence; and the Christ of the Sermon on the Mount is the omnipotent God.

On July 21, 1944, the day after the failed assassination of Hitler, Bonhoeffer admitted to "dangers" in his book, *Discipleship*, though overall he also stood by what he had written. At the heart of the danger is the notion that by submitting obediently to the commanding Christ Bonhoeffer "could acquire faith by trying to live a holy life, or something like it."[36] But buried just beneath *Discipleship's* dominant themes of command and obedience is a hidden treasure found in a subordinate christological motif.

Place-Sharing

In *Discipleship's* subordinate motif we meet a different Jesus, a crucified Christ, "the suffering God." Bonhoeffer's rich metaphor is God as bearer: "God is a God who bears. . . . The Son of God bore our flesh. He therefore bore the cross. He bore all our sins and attained reconciliation by his bearing." There is a sociality in Jesus Christ characterized by bearing the realities and burdens of others. Bearing is the defining feature within Jesus' life, which is circumscribed by his incarnation, ministry of forgiveness and healing, cross, resurrection, and ascension. "That kind of Lord," rather than the varieties of lordship rooted in power as control or command, is the real Jesus for us today.[37]

Bonhoeffer had been exploring the sociality of Christ since his two dissertations written in 1927 and 1930 respectively. "God binds God's self to human beings." In Christ God's true freedom is to be free for, not from, the world. Bonhoeffer used a technical German term to summarize this free sociality of Christ for and with the world: *Stellvertretung*, which is translated "vicarious representative action" or, more usably, "place-sharing." Because of Jesus' place-sharing sociality, Bonhoeffer entreated his university students to discover "where" Jesus is whenever they were inquiring "who" Jesus is.[38] With whom is Jesus sharing a place? Despite significant differences from King's Christology, one might still overhear profound resonances echoing between Bonhoeffer's place-sharing sociality of Jesus himself and the personal solidarity that King trusted when Jesus comes as balm in unyielding solidarity with the " 'buked and scorned." That resonance reverberates even more vigorously as Bonhoeffer knits together his Christology with his ecclesiology.

The Communion of Saints: Where Christ Takes Bodily Form

Already in the 1927 dissertation, *Sanctorum Communio*, the twenty-one-year-old Bonhoeffer took a cue from Martin Luther and developed his place-sharing sociality of Christ as the very heart and soul of the Christian church. The church is Christ's bodily bearing of sufferers and sinners. Bonhoeffer then took Luther's place-sharing understanding of the church and connected it also to ethics as formation. " 'Formation' means therefore in the first place Jesus Christ taking form in Christ's church . . . the body of Christ. . . . The church is nothing but that piece of humanity where Christ really has taken form."[39] In this way Jesus' place-sharing is the form of the church both internally among Christians as they face the perils and burdens that come with this-worldly existence and externally as the church relates to the wider world.

Bonhoeffer astutely interpreted Luther's point that Christ is "for you" precisely by being deeply "with you." Christ, therefore, takes form in the church's being "for-one-another" precisely through the church's being "with-one-another." It is almost as if Bonhoeffer had overheard Sister Pollard nearly thirty years into the future whispering to King, "we is with you . . . the Lord is with you." Christ always exists as concrete churchly sociality and communion in solidarity with the world in its suffering and sin, in its joys and hopes.

View from Below: Ethics in the Midst of the Church and World

Bonhoeffer's conviction that Christ exists today as real churchly communion and solidarity came home to him through his pastoral ministry in two very different congregational settings. Immediately after completing his dissertation in 1927, he became a pastoral intern for a year in a German-speaking church in Barcelona, Spain. There, he witnessed the social and economic extremes of the well-off, on the one hand, and of the large numbers of poor, unemployed, and homeless people, on the other. He came to know people "the way they are, far from the masquerade of the 'Christian world' . . . small people with small goals, small drives, and small crimes—all in all . . . real people."[40]

In 1929–30 he spent a little over a year back in Berlin as an assistant university lecturer and wrote his second dissertation (a German requirement) before going off as a postdoctoral fellow to study at Union Theological Seminary in New York City. There he quickly became friends with an African American student named Frank Fisher. Fisher took him to the prominent African American church in Harlem, Abyssinian Baptist, where Bonhoeffer then attended nearly every Sunday, taught Sunday school, and led a women's Bible study. As Bonhoeffer noted in 1942, his year in New York was "of the greatest significance for me up to the present day," and his experience of Abyssinian Baptist and its people was "one of the most important and gratifying events of my stay in America." He heard "the 'black Christ' . . . preached with captivating passion and vividness . . . [and] the Negro spirituals . . . [with their] strange mixture of reserved melancholy and eruptive joy . . . in the face of their incomparably harsh fate. . . ."[41] Can you imagine the learning curve in this budding German intellectual?

Just a few short years after those congregational entrées into churchly place-sharing and communion Bonhoeffer would help initiate both the Pastors' Emergency League and the Confessing Church, both formed to resist the Nazification of the Protestant church. Resistance was at times effective but more often it was not. Time and again, Bonhoeffer was disappointed but at no time more so than on the night of November 9, 1938. This was *Kristallnacht*, "the night of broken glass," that infamous, violent pogrom against Jews perpetrated throughout Germany, when nearly one hundred Jews were murdered and twenty-five to thirty thousand were taken to concentration camps, when two hundred synagogues were burned to the ground and thousands of Jewish businesses and homes were vandalized and torched. On *Kristallnacht* the

Confessing Church was silent! There was no place-sharing, no solidarity. What Bonhoeffer had said just a few years earlier applied now, "Only he who cries out for the Jews may sing Gregorian chants."[42]

Bonhoeffer's place-sharing Christology begins early in his career and continues all the way through to his imprisonment theology of the suffering God and of Christ as "the man for others."[43] A few months before his imprisonment he wrote a Christmas letter to his close-knit family, friends, and fellow assassination conspirators. It includes reflections entitled "The View from Below," which sums up well the tightly woven fabric of Bonhoeffer's Christology, ecclesiology, and ethics: "There remains an experience of incomparable value. We have for once learnt to see the great events of world history from below, from the perspective of the outcast, the suspects, the maltreated, the powerless, the oppressed, the reviled—in short, from the perspective of those who suffer."[44]

Conclusion: Christian Life as Surprise

Jesus always desires to take his churchly body some*where* in close proximity, indeed, in deep solidarity with sufferers and sinners. This will always, no doubt, surprise his churchly body along the way, and perhaps the world as well, because no sector or segment of contemporary life, whether private or public or some combination, can be in principle off-limits for Christian communion, ethical engagement, and moral leadership. King and Bonhoeffer compose the significance of Jesus for social ethics using different keys, as we have seen. Yet the Jesus they heard and followed took them to places that neither had expected. Because their theologies still resonate today in diverse ears, I expect Jesus might again surprise those who hear and follow him.

CHAPTER 18

Reconciliation as Worshiping Community

Michael Battle

For we do not proclaim ourselves; we proclaim Jesus Christ as Lord and ourselves as your slaves for Jesus' sake. For it is the God who said, "Let light shine out of darkness," who has shone in our hearts to give the light of the knowledge of the glory of God in the face of Jesus Christ. (2 Cor. 4:5-6)

How does reconciliation with others deepen, rather than contradict, personal identity in Christ? The problematic I assume in answering this question is the comfort zone of Western Christians—namely, personal spirituality. Communal spirituality beckons Western Christians like me to function at the edge of competency. Yet communal spirituality is at the heart of Christian faith, even if that is rarely realized by the affluent. As a result, until such persons run ashore in their individualistic mind-sets, the benefits of communal spirituality are not appreciated. Through the witness of Dietrich Bonhoeffer and Martin Luther King, I will try to explain how reconciliation deepens our corporate and personal life together in a twofold manner. First, I use the theology primarily of Bonhoeffer (with commentary by the Anglican theologian Austin Farrer) to make an argument. And then (like any good Western person) I tell my personal story that involves imprinting upon King.

Bonhoeffer: Reconciliation as Revelation and Revelation as Worshiping Community

Reconciliation gives us knowledge of God. It used to be said that it was from our worship we learned to do theology, on the assumption that worship always precedes theology.[1] Likewise, I think it can be said that from reconciliation we learn the identity of Christ. This may no longer seem the case for many of us in the Western world; however, I still believe that God, through Jesus Christ, gives us knowledge through relationality. One reason why worship precedes theology is that relationality lies at its heart. Worship works on the analogy of the knowledge of a child: a child only knows her parent as a child, incompletely. Yet, by being in relationship to its parent, the child's incomplete knowledge becomes satisfied. Jesus has defined our relationship to God as a child to a parent, but it would prove difficult to find many Western Christians who are content with the incompleteness and dependency in that view of relationship to God. Herein is the Western discomfort. Western individualism inevitably confuses the reality of God with one's own idea of reality. Now the child, who becomes aware of her incomplete knowledge, asks a question on the authority of her own reality: How do I know that God is real?

European philosophers tried to answer this question by conceptualizing the notion of God as a supreme idea, described from existence as pure action. Doing so they made God the object of our ideas. Even Immanuel Kant, who questioned the possibility of knowing transcendent objects, reaffirmed the Western cosmology by making subjectivity the ground of epistemology.[2] In such a way of knowing, worship cannot precede theology because individuality becomes primary for knowing, while worship is a way of knowing communally. Without communal epistemology, I argue, we remain stuck in a perpetual search for God at our own convenience, and made in our own individual images. There are Western theologians, however, who help us think through a deepened sense of worship and who challenge Western Christians out of their comfort zones of personal piety.

Dietrich Bonhoeffer's theology teaches that God is both being and action in the person of Jesus Christ. For Bonhoeffer, the church worships the Jesus who constantly points away from himself and to others. Jesus' nature is to be for the other. Bonhoeffer's genius is that he constantly reminds us that we have a hard time with Jesus because we are tempted to worship our individual selves instead of the God who is for others. If we end up trapped in our own solipsistic forms of spirituality, however, we can no longer know God in the manner that God is known—namely, through others. We cannot come to know God through our individual autonomy, for God reveals through sociality.

Bonhoeffer wanted to account for the reality of persons within society, and so sought an epistemology of God in which revelation involved both concrete sociality and concrete personhood. *Act and Being*, one of Bonhoeffer's first and most academic works, demonstrates Bonhoeffer's attempt to battle his culture's modern European assumptions that that one could never know God as an object beyond the human. Bonhoeffer took a stand against the prevailing, transcendental category of "object," replacing in its stead the worshiping community of the church. We come to know God not as an object, but in and as a worshiping community.[3]

So, how does this all help us with the question about how reconciliation can deepen rather than divide our personal identity in Christ? In short, by teaching us that worship is essential for knowing God, Bonhoeffer makes corporate relationality essential for personal identity. In fact, he teaches us that the personal identity of Christians is revealed through corporate worship. Such worship does not know God as "buddy" or a rush of manipulated feelings. Most of Bonhoeffer's life dealt with the problem of being thrown back to the invisible God known only in relationships. This search was begun in his first book, *Sanctorum Communio*, where he states, "God is an impenetrable You whose metaphysical personhood . . . implies nothing at all about God being an I as described above."[4] The futility of trying to intellectually capture God as "I"—that is, as knowing God's Person completely—gives way to knowledge of God in worship. To know God, one must adore God with others.

Bonhoeffer's movement toward a community's life together in which the disciplines of worship are key was movement against idealism, toward the concrete. The struggle against idealism, and the abstraction accompanying it, is about gaining real understanding of the other through the experience of the reality of God known only in community. The result is a workable and real concept of God. Bonhoeffer states that every human attempt to discover God by unveiling God's secret reality is hopeless because the personal reality of God for humanity exists in community, not in the sphere of the ideas. "Personality as reality is beyond idea."[5]

When one worships God, one submits to the view that only God can say who God is and how God is present to us. "God alone is the *concretissimum*."[6] For Bonhoeffer, what matters is not God's omnipresence, nor God's eternity; what matters is the God who is God here and today, the God who is the most concrete reality possible. Our thought cannot grasp God except as in the concrete worship of God. We can only seek God if we worship the God of the cross. Bonhoeffer concludes, "If it is I who determine where God is to be I will always find there a God who somehow resembles me, who pleases me, who is akin to my being. But if it is God who determines where he wants to be it will most likely be in a place which is not akin immediately to my being, which does not please me. That place, however, is the cross of Christ."[7]

Bonhoeffer teaches us that God is no object of our ideas that just statically rests out in space for us to think about. We can only know God's being through God's actions. And we can only make sense of God's actions through worship because the worshiping community is the reality of the God of the cross. Bonhoeffer's central thesis in *Sanctorum Communio* is that "the church is Christ existing as community." In worship we are invited into the mystery of knowing God, who is not an object of our ideas, but the subject of our life together. We know God only through the relationality that Christ creates for us.

Such relationality leads to two growing edges for Western Christians. First, learning to pray in common. We need to do better in creating common circumstances of worship. It is essential that we have common habits of worship, whether we feel like it or not, because it is through the mystery of the community's worship that Christ is known. There Christ exists for us. And so, we answer the child that we know God is real because of the church. Our second growing edge is learning to be like Christ—namely, for the other. Identity in the Christ for others means that we are never alone, but we exist only through the community of Christ, who incorporates our uniqueness—making more of it in relationships. There should be no fear of losing our individual identity because in Christ our identity deepens. Anyone in Christ is someone in community; and where such an individual exists there is community. Ultimately, in Christ we learn something extremely difficult for Western ears—that the individual cannot find God alone, and if such a person tries, more often than not, they will complain that there is no God.

The legacy of Bonhoeffer, then, is that reconciliation is revelation. We come to know God by being connected to God, and are connected to God in the reality of the worshiping community. For Bonhoeffer, only God can say who God is and that God is present with us; and God is present with us and for us personally in the worshiping community. For Western views of the self, then, revelation is also reconciliation; through the community of Christ, God heals us of our pretensions to individuality, granting us personhood through others, as knowledge of God's self in Christ. The connection of reconciliation and Christology in community leads to the impact of Martin Luther King Jr.

King: Reconciliation in the Movement and the Movement as Worshiping Community

Like Bonhoeffer, worship for King was a way of knowing reality, which explains what is so appalling about the most segregated hour in America. King states, "First the church must remove the yoke of segregation from its own body. . . . It is appalling that the most segregated hour of Christian America is eleven o'clock on Sunday morning, the same hour when many are standing to sing, 'In Christ there is no East no West.' Equally appalling is the fact that the most segregated school of the week is the Sunday School."[8] A segregated church would know a segregated reality.

For King, the truth of the segregationists against which he and his fellow witnesses marched was this: the white race is genetically and spiritually superior to all others. That "truth" was the beast, and it put its truth into societal effect through the institutionalized system of segregation.[9] King fought back through the worship of the living God. Worship, however, was more than the sociological groupings of people on Sunday morning; it happened in mass meetings, in the prayers of the Southern Christian Leadership Council, in jailhouse hymns. King struggled for that church against a history of divided worship created by the racial divisions in the United States, especially the denominational splits due to differing positions on slavery. King goes on to say that such divisions became part of the fabric of society in the United States.

> The church once changed society. It was then a thermostat of society. But today I feel that too much of the church is merely a thermometer, which measures rather than molds popular opinion. . . . But the laxity of the white church collectively has caused me to weep tears of love. There cannot be deep disappointment without deep love. Time and again in my travels, as I have seen the outward beauty of white churches, I have had to ask myself, "What kind of people worship there? Who is their God? Is their God the God of Abraham, Isaac and Jacob, and is their Savior the Savior who hung on the cross at Golgotha? Where were their voices when a black race took upon itself the cross of protest against man's injustice to man? Where were their voices when defiance and hatred were called for by white men who sat in these very churches?" . . . Yet white churchgoers, who insist that they are Christians, practice segregation as rigidly in the house of God as they do in movie-houses.[10]

King's vision for the church was true worship, which he found through the civil rights movement. Convinced of the ultimate lordship of Christ over the civil rights movement, King came to understand the reality of history's long bend toward God's justice by experiencing the civil rights movement as a worship-ing community. God's justice not only demanded social justice, it was learned through social justice. King pushed for another truth only known through the worship of God revealed in Jesus: that true worship of God calls for a resis-tance that exists as an oppositional, contrary witness to a corrupt age.

Like Bonhoeffer, King also knew that such worship would entail persecu-tion, suffering, and even death. For he knew that the segregationist age would protect its bifurcated worship of self and idol with fierce hostility. Here, King's vision provides the link for Western Christians to see communal spirituality for the sake of knowing God as opposed to knowing sociological idols. Segre-gationists cut themselves off from God's self-revelation because they worship self, or their individuality, through their whiteness. King's worldview of wor-shiping God was based upon the conviction that those hell-bent on racial seg-regation in any form, rooted in the assumption that people of color are inferior to and cannot live on terms of equality with white people, is the very antithesis of the beloved community, where God and reality are truly known.

King's keen worship demonstrated to all of America how bestial the sys-tem of segregation really was, how hideous the evil that lay behind it through those who gathered to worship God with King. The deepening of reconcilia-tion through worship occurred as those now convinced of Jesus' nonviolent identity participated in the ultimate destruction of segregationism and the ultimate transformation of society. Participation involved suffering, but King did not focus on the suffering or the dying, just as Bonhoeffer had not. They were evils that accompanied the witness of reconciliation. This witness—man-ifested through sermons, marches, songs, and demonstrations—effected the positive societal change King and his civil rights compatriots sought. Martin Luther King Jr. exemplifies worship as reconciliation: bold witness and active resistance to powerful, deeply entrenched forces of institutional evil. This courageous witness may issue in suffering and even death, but also, as King's example shows, in the renewal of worship and the transformation of society.

Those who would remember King must keep in mind that King moved beyond conceptions of "a new South" and "the American dream" to articulate a vision of "the world house." King aimed for a concrete fellowship with univer-sal scope. We must also remember the means by which he sought to translate this vision of "the world house" into practical reality; King's worship of God helped him understand the bend of history, and to anticipate the possibility of an African American president of the United States. King could understand and anticipate the concrete possibilities of beloved community because his worldview was constantly pried open by deeper realities of God. King's legacy here still yields relevance and applicability for a global vision of contemporary and future human relations, as seen in the example of South Africa a generation later.[11]

The transformation of society that King's view of reconciliation sought is best characterized in King's metaphor of the "great world house" or the "worldwide neighborhood," which suggests a totally integrated human family, unconcerned with human differences and devoted to the ethical norms of love, justice, and community: "We have inherited a large house, a great 'world house' in which we have to live together—black and white, easterner and Westerner, gentile and Jew, Catholic and Protestant, Moslem and Hindu—a family unduly separated in ideas, culture and interest, who, because we can never again live apart, must learn somehow to live with each other in peace."[12] The ground of the world house metaphor was King's theology of beloved community, which was "the capstone of King's thought"—"the organizing principle of all his thought and activity."[13] Convinced that community is the ultimate goal of human existence, King insisted that it was imperative for all persons of goodwill to struggle nonviolently against sin and the evil forces that work against harmony and wholeness in God's creation.[14] This view of God had powerful implications for the struggle against America's racism, and it is relevant to the continuing efforts to destroy the last vestiges of other apartheid systems around the world that remain. King's theological vision of beloved community found partial fulfillment in South Africa when, after a generation of church struggle and political resistance, Nelson Mandela and political prisoners were freed, and when the first democratic elections took place in April, 1994. King's beloved community was further realized through the Truth and Reconciliation Commission.

South Africa after King and Bonhoeffer

The Christian understanding that King and Bonhoeffer brought to their rejection of apartheid systems of Nazi Germany and a segregationist United States influenced many others, but were especially resonant in South Africa. Despite the different styles and traditions that separated King, a Baptist clergyman, from Desmond Tutu, the Anglican archbishop of Cape Town, their opposition to apartheid emerged out of a basic understanding of the Christian doctrines of love and worship of God. Tutu agreed completely with King's insistence that racial separation in all forms not only degrades human personality and denies the interrelatedness and interdependence of human beings, but also violates the parenthood of God and the essential oneness of God's creation. Tutu echoed King's belief that the love of God is inseparable from the love of neighbor. For Tutu, as for King, this conviction found its strongest support in the life and ministry of Jesus Christ.[15] This became Tutu's most consistent argument as he confronted apartheid laws and customs through nonviolent action.

Tutu also fully embraced Bonhoeffer's and King's insights into the meaning, character, and actualization of human community. In 1978, he reminded fellow South Africans of King's challenge that "together we must learn to live as brothers or together we will be forced to perish as fools."[16] In the legacy of Bonhoeffer, Tutu stressed the christological ideal, Christ for us, as the organizing principle of all his thought and activities. All other important concepts that pervaded Tutu's writings and public speeches—for example, love, nonviolence, forgiveness, human dignity, morality, freedom, justice, reconciliation—were explicitly related to his understanding of community revealed through the act and being of God being for us through Christ. Here the spirit and influence of Bonhoeffer were unmistakable for Tutu.[17] King's and Bonhoeffer's understanding of the deepening of reconciliation through worship of God became quite significant for Tutu as he promoted, with awesome precision, his own view of "a new South Africa that is just, nonracial, and democratic, where black and white can exist amicably side by side in their home country as members of one family."[18]

In a move that may be crucial for interpreting Bonhoeffer and his influence on subsequent struggles, Tutu questioned King's notion that violence is always an immoral and impractical method for the oppressed. While sharing King's view that nonviolence is always the best and most desirable means for actualizing community, Tutu nevertheless insisted that a violent response to oppression can at times be justified and unavoidable. After expressing his own respect for and identification with nonviolence at the South African Missiological Conference in 1977, Tutu explained why it was irrational for the world to expect oppressed South Africans to limit themselves to nonviolence as an absolute principle:

1. The Christian Church is not entirely pacifist;
2. Blacks are left wondering what practical alternatives are available, given the palpable failure of nonviolent forms for protest and opposition;
3. There is a hollow sound to white arguments for the way of nonviolence, given their at least tacit support for state and legal violence.[19]

Tutu concluded with references to the difficulties he faced in recommending nonviolence to blacks who were constantly bombarded with positive images of Europeans who used violence in redemptive ways during World

War II. For Tutu, it was virtually impossible to overcome the moral dilemma involved in advocating absolute nonviolence for blacks on the one hand, while condoning the use of violence by whites on the other.[20]

The assassination of King evoked mixed responses from white South Africans. Glowing tributes came from a few whites in South Africa's Catholic, Anglican, Methodist, and Dutch Reformed churches—whites who had been genuinely challenged by King's push for unified Christian witness against apartheid. Motivated by a different spirit, Prime Minister John Vorster used the assassination to warn clerics who planned "to do the kind of thing here in South Africa that Martin Luther King did in America," to "cut it out, cut it out immediately, for the cloak you carry will not protect you if you try to do this in South Africa."[21] The repressive violence of South Africa was more akin to Bonhoeffer's context, and seems to have warranted Tutu's option for entertaining Bonhoeffer's "spoke in the wheel."

Conclusion

This essay has argued that worship of God deepens understanding of reconciliation. I have argued that demise of beatific vision of God in worship amounts to demise of justice and peace. For both depend on the imagination and love of God. Attention to God is not irrelevant for revolution. Imaging God through Bonhoeffer, King, and Tutu, we see how imagination of God provides integrity for earthly existence. For all three figures, human imagination of heaven as the community of God shows persons the telos of their createdness. The reconciliation of God lies at the end of creation's journey and at its beginning—as the reconciliation of creation itself. God's reconciliation does not threaten human personality but, rather, realizes and perfects it. Therefore, imagination and love of God are divine gifts that enable human vision to see through the individual existence. This "seeing through" enables one to know sacramental realities beyond the simple conclusion that life is inherently violent and finite. It connects the practice of nonviolence and attention to worship, so that devotion creates an attention span for justice and peace, and allows better vision of how to live here, now, on earth.

Christian Social Ethics after Bonhoeffer and King

Willis Jenkins

P erhaps the feature most shared by Dietrich Bonhoeffer and Martin
Luther King is the peril of compelling legacies. Each has become so
iconic for Christian social ethics that his memory often fails to trouble contemporary readers as much as it might. The aura of social
holiness around each figure sometimes prevents critical reception, proving
Dorothy Day's line about how easily saints are ignored. A book receiving the
two legacies together therefore runs the risk of reinforcing the pieties of sainthood, of domesticating their lives even further. Yet mutual interpretation can
also work to restore their respective challenges. Precisely because Bonhoeffer
and King have become such decisive moral lives in such different contexts and
roles, reckoning with them together can force Christian social ethics to receive
anew difficult aspects of their separate legacies. How we receive these two, I
argue, indicates how we think about the context and role of Christian ethics
in our own generation.

Reckoning with their legacies requires us first to question our reasons
for remembering, and especially the portraits we make from unease with our
own histories. Venerating Bonhoeffer lets Christians remember one of the
few in the German church ready to resist Hitler, and a Gentile we can celebrate in our shame over the Holocaust. Celebrating King lets Americans find
nationalist relief from our racial history, and lets Euro-Americans in particular
remember an African American ready to forgive racism and redeem belief in

a shared national identity. In the midst of such unease, remembering either figure involves the hazards of appropriation and hagiography. Those hazards sometimes work together: we may suspend criticism of a life so that we can more easily identify with its myth.

The hazards increase by remembering these two together. This collection of essays, as well as the classes (including my own) that teach the two together, runs the risk of making the hagiographical haze even more dense by fusing their legacies into a single testament. Their memories have become so powerful for Christian ethics that a book or class considering them together can hardly resist the pull to interpret their separate legacies as one heroic witness. Even the most independent minds hesitate to write a word contrary to a project treating King and Bonhoeffer together, and even the most critical students fail to question the pious myths that led them into the class (and may angrily chafe when a teacher does).

The hazards of memory, however, can also be made to reopen the legacy of each figure. Precisely because they are remembered so intensely, even piously, each legacy has the power to let readers question the other. Fully appreciating King's peace commitment should make us pause over Bonhoeffer's interpretation of peacemaking in his suffering context, and then turn back to King with a new way to debate the connection of peace and suffering. If held together, the two legacies can begin to question our reception of each, and so begin to renew the challenge of each. In the influence of their legacy, Christian ethics sometimes fails to appreciate the riskiness in the way each figure bore witness. Each person's testament was perilous not only for himself but for his world and for his church—and for the exercise of Christian ethics. Receiving the two together can help reopen the challenging ambiguity and perilous originality of each man.

Doing so requires first remembering that these two lives often do not bear the same witness. Their testimonies are as different as their contexts. For Christian social thought, therefore, they do not easily serve as mutual champions of some shared theological principle or moral value that can be applied to contemporary problems. Among the many differences in theology, identity, and context, one of the most important is that Bonhoeffer self-consciously offered a theological performance as representative of an oppressing group, while King self-consciously offered a theological performance as representative of an oppressed group. Remembering that difference helps interpret important divergences in their social ethics. Among the most important, Bonhoeffer comes to emphasize ethics as "vicarious representative responsibility," in part because, as a German Protestant with "Aryan" privileges, he knew that on his person fell burdens of national sin and cultural violence. King, by contrast, emphasizes ethics as nonviolent confrontation, in part because he saw a unique opportunity for African Americans to transform the nation's racist violence by publicly letting it fall on their bodies. Because of those different representative roles, King has become significant to the legitimating narrative of a nation in a way that Bonhoeffer never could. King has become iconic figure of the civil rights movement, hero of nonviolent reform and constitutional democracy, such that every American president must now find some way to claim his legacy. Bonhoeffer is an ambiguous footnote to German national history, as well as post-holocaust Jewish history, which witholds official recognition as a "righteous Gentile."

Holding open the difference in representative role while interpreting them together can help us imagine how Christian ethics must be conducted differently across our own various representations within contemporary economies of power. Their lives make us consider how contingency and context may shape vocation and responsibility. They make us wonder if justice is as multiple as the contexts in which it is pursued, and if love requires differently of differently born individuals. Imagining ethics amidst such moral multiplicity then draws us into fresh ways of thinking about God and morality after the fracture of moral theology's synthesizing traditions.

Holding the two figures together while holding open their differences also invites readers to reflect on the moral intuitions we bring to evaluating political and religious struggles. Consider, for example, likely Christian and American receptions of King had he abandoned his nonviolent commitments and plotted guerilla warfare. Then consider likely Christian and American memories of Bonhoeffer had he been executed for pacifist objection to conscription rather than participation in a conspiracy. Would their lives seem as decisive, their testimonies as luminous? What do we fear and what do we approve in contemporary currents of religion and resistance?

The interpretive tensions between these two lives thus help pose basic questions in Christian ethics. Faced with those questions from two different yet decisive lives can make readers in Christian ethics usefully uncomfortable. However, receiving them together can also make teachers of Christians ethics uncomfortable, for their legacies pose basic questions about the very idea of Christian ethics. Specifically, reading and teaching them together make evident three fundamental challenges for doing Christian ethics.

Three Challenges of Interpretation

First, after Bonhoeffer and King Christian ethics cannot function as an "applied" field of systematic theology and maybe not as a distinct academic field of any sort. Bonhoeffer and King are remembered not only because they wrote socially engaged theological texts, but because they enacted brilliant contextual dramas through which they learned and reinvented their faith. Their social projects were theological productions. They confronted the big questions of theology—creaturely suffering and divine justice, the meaning of Jesus, the nature of revelation, the relation of church and world—but they did so through political strategies, creative performances, and practical collaborations. Making sense of King and of Bonhoeffer therefore seems to require a view of Christian ethics that does not so much apply theological teaching to social problems as it does use theology to *make* social problems. Christian ethics does not appear then as absorbing literature on the churches' social teaching but, rather, as formation into an aptitude for interpreting opportunities for moral agency amidst ambivalence and creating possibilities for witness amidst terror. We remember their lives as brilliant dramas of good and evil only because they were so successful in negotiating concrete arenas for agency and witness. Teaching these two figures as models for Christian ethics, then, cannot rest in simple repetition of their great stories, for their success depended on learning the story they were to live through their participation in their contexts. If Christian social ethics stands in their legacies, it faces a pragmatic challenge of seeking similar ways to drive social creativity, learn from contextual confrontations, and invent possibilities of moral agency.

Second, after Bonhoeffer and King defending schools or traditions of theological thought seems less important than developing capacities of social witness. Each man confounds interpretation as product or representative of a particular school, as seen by the wide range that commentators try to make them fit. Ask students to decide whether one figure seems more "liberal" or more "evangelical" and they will likely find him susceptible of both styles and accountable to neither. Both seem typically liberal in the priority they accord ethics, but evangelical in the way their moral witness is christoform. Each seems evangelical in his sense of a personal relationship with God, but liberal in his openness to learning from the experience of non-Christians. Each seems liberal in his concern for structures of justice, yet evangelical in his sense of God's transforming work in the world. Perhaps most confounding, each insists that humans answer to God through concrete social action, and yet each appeals to the passionist pattern of Christ to explain his commitment to an extraecclesial social movement.

The two men confound typological analysis because both drew from a wide range of intellectual and cultural inheritances in order to confront difficult social problems. Interpreting how each figure made his cultural and theological inheritances reinvent possibilities of agency invites Christian social ethics toward a prophetic pragmatism, in which Christian ethics tries to generate analogous capabilities. Some of our contextual challenges are similar— structural racism and warfaring ideologies—but others are unique, such as climate change, species extinctions, and globalized economic relations. Developing creative capacities for collaborative social action before such problems seems more difficult than eulogizing heroes and offering typologies. That is likely one reason for the pieties of reception.

Resisting the temptation to piety requires not overlooking their personal scandals, nor letting those sins overwhelm interpretation of their legacies. King had numerous affairs and plagiarized his dissertation. Bonhoeffer showed shades of antisemitism and more than once let personal ambition keep him from helping others. Each man acknowledged his own sins, confessed them to others, and fought with accompanying feelings of depression as he sought to follow his sense of God's call. In fact, their struggle with personal darknesses can make their struggle to bear witness even more compelling. When the FBI sent King audio evidence of his infidelity in hopes of shaming him to step down or commit suicide, King instead received it as a temptation to let his personal unworthiness distract him from following God's call, and he recommitted himself to bearing Christ's witness. It seems the perfect portrait of a Protestant saint: tortured by self-doubt and sin, yet faithful enough in God's call to follow it beyond even his own sense of unworthiness.

Too much interpretive attention to personal sin can suppress a perhaps more scandalous affront to received ideas of sin and of person. Here is the third challenge to Christian ethics after Bonhoeffer and King: the most important theological drama does not happen "inside" an interior soul, but "outside" in embodied and public relations. Not only is sin social, but so is the soul. Their view of the self that God addresses, transforms, and saves is a social self. Although brilliantly unique individuals, Bonhoeffer and King each lived and died in faith that his own destiny before God was organically linked with that of every other creature, and that the reality of his self was made in the response he would give to the needs of those around him.

Each of those three challenges has been taken up in the Christian social ethics of the late twentieth century. We find them developed in responsibility ethics after H. Richard Niebuhr and in the ecological spiritualities articulated in environmental theologies; in liberationist analyses of structural sin and summons to do theology through political commitment; in the emphases of womanist and feminist ethics on embodied practices and on learning from communities of social solidarity. Certainly the legacies of King and of

Bonhoeffer helped shape these developments; yet they also stand in uncertain relation to these areas of Christian social ethics because their responses to their own contexts were so ambiguous and risky. Each sought to create space for the embodied, political possibility of the gospel in his context, and each pressed the boundaries of Christian social thought in order to do so. If they share a common witness, it is not because they were prophetic in just the same way, but because they responded to their respective contexts with a theological and social creativity that opened new possibilities for prophetic witness. The rest of this chapter shows how their legacies reframe key arenas of Christian social thought by their challenge for prophetic pragmatism.

The Politics of the Passion

Bonhoeffer and King participated in starkly different political actions; one was a public nonviolent performance, the other a clandestine coup conspiracy. That difference in political action tracks with another in theology: Bonhoeffer's cross is politically weak, while King's is strong. Bonhoeffer thinks responsibility for others takes the form of the God who bears the world's guilt in weakness, while King preaches the redemptive power of suffering and expects cruciform action to transform history toward justice. Yet somehow those different political theologies of the cross support a shared cruciform strategy. What should we make of the fact that, in their struggle for more just liberal democracies, both look to the cross as a central *political* image?

Bonhoeffer's strategy combines theological and political priorities in a particularly risky gambit. Bonhoeffer inherited a Lutheran two-kingdoms worldview that allotted the church authority over matters of the soul and the state over matters of society. Human bodies present the dangerous boundary line in this scheme. If a society perceives certain bodies to bear religious significance—as those of Jewish ancestry did in Bonhoeffer's Germany—then state and ecclesial authority intersect in human skin. The pervasive antisemitism of Bonhoeffer's Germany included the view that Jewish bodies signify the curse of humanity's rejection of God. As such, Jewish bodies posed a paradigm test for a Christian view of the state: What to make of the political status of citizens with theological bodies?

Bonhoeffer confronted that "Jewish question" not by delegitimizing the sort of state that asks such an unjust question but, rather, by interpreting the state (and its questions) from within the image of Christ's body. "Christianity must be used polemically against the worldly in the name of a better worldliness," wrote Bonhoeffer; "where the worldly establishes itself as an autonomous sector, this denies the fact of the world's being accepted in Christ."[1] Does that christocentric strategy work good or ill for the plight of persecuted Jewish citizens? At the moment that one might expect Bonhoeffer to vindicate a properly political realm in order to protect citizens from religiously incited violence, he instead opposes dualist thinking with an image of the body of Christ: "we must get beyond this two-realms image . . . we must turn our eye to the image of Jesus Christ's own body." That "places the church-community into a relationship of responsibility for the world . . . calling individuals and nations to faith and obedience toward the revelation of God in Jesus Christ."[2] That also means, however, that the Christian church-community interprets and bears the political fate of Jewish citizens.

I will soon turn to Bonhoeffer's very controversial way of interpreting "the Jewish question"; for now, consider the significance for Christian political action in Bonhoeffer's views on the weakness of the cross. "God lets himself be pushed out of the world onto the cross," wrote Bonhoeffer from prison; "God is weak and powerless in the world and that is precisely the way, the only way, in which God is with us and helps us." The suffering of the cross, Bonhoeffer comes to think, means that God works in the world through weakness. "Christ helps us, not by virtue of his omnipotence, but by virtue of his weakness and suffering."[3] What sort of political action on behalf of the state's victims does such a view warrant? It might weaken responsibility for publicly helping them even while hyperbolizing their suffering as the suffering of God. Bonhoeffer's contextual answer seems different but no less troubling: politically complicit Christians seeking the pattern of Christ may have special responsibilities, such as participating in secret political actions with secret theological meanings.

King's view of the cross is much different and so is his view of responsible political action; yet his legacy faces similar questions about whether his politics works good or ill for victims of state oppression. King, like Bonhoeffer, looks to the image of the crucified God to explain political suffering, but uses that image to interpret a spate of vicious killings as historically redemptive. When four young girls were killed in a Montgomery church bombing, King preached that God works good from evil and that suffering can redeem history, be historically redemptive. He preached almost the same sermon at the funerals of Jimmy Jackson and James Reeb, protesters who were killed by mob violence.[4] Through innocent deaths God calls us to more action, King preaches, more vulnerability to the world's evil. Nonviolence is a Gandhian tactic that reveals the Christian spirit and the meaning of Jesus, he said. However much those resisting the world's destiny in God keep crucifying, God will keep suffering, and keep raising hope from graves made in violence. King looks to the cross and sees the key of historical change, and so invites the movement to enact the christic pattern of God in the streets, to publicly enact the body of Christ.

King's political theology thus shares a discomfiting similarity with Bonhoeffer's: he addresses America as a moral actor in a christological drama in a way that may make political victims more vulnerable. Rather than subverting the idea of America as a nation with a divine mandate, King recalls the nation to its constitutional vision of that mandate, and asks protesters to give their life for the possibility of America as beloved community. Even late in life, when King's "dream" for an integrated America had almost yielded to the "nightmare" of a nation driven by "racism, militarism, and materialism," King did not detach his politics from theological hope. Instead, he intensified the relationship, telling the board of the Southern Christian Leadership Conference that, like Jesus to Nicodemus, they must say to the nation: "America, you must be born again!" It was no mere homiletic flourish; King had in mind concrete social policies, starting with an expansive employment program that would transform the structure of American social life so as to make possible relationships that lead citizens into their reality as children of God.[5]

The two different political Christologies thus push Christian social thought along a similar dangerous trajectory. Both allow that political struggles may become matters of fundamental Christian practice, cruciform in pattern. King and Bonhoeffer both made resistance to political regimes not just a live option for faith, but the only option, apart from which confession of faith and life in Christ was in peril. After the rise of liberation theologies, perhaps this claim strikes us less freshly, but in context both were criticized, from left and right, for confusing "religious" and "political" commitments. Their challenge to received distinctions of faith and politics remains.

After Bonhoeffer's claim that outside the Confessing Church there is no salvation, and after King's narration of the civil rights movement as God's redemptive movement in history, it is just a half step to Jon Sobrino's claim that outside solidarity with the poor, there is no salvation.[6] After King and Bonhoeffer, social and political struggles may present unavoidable summons to the way of Christ. That seems to stand straight against political liberalism, which forms its civic pluralism from the fear of political practices enacted as religious beliefs. The security and fairness of a society made up of citizens of many faiths and none seems to depend on an observed distinction between the political and the religious, and the ability to discern appropriate spheres for their exercise. As John Rawls puts it, properly political practices must be capable of reasonable acceptance by other citizens without reference to any comprehensive doctrine.[7]

King's role as a modern founding father of American democracy is especially interesting here. For the pastor who subverts political and ecclesial separations, contradicting a basic rule of political liberalism, has become figurehead of the nation's twentieth-century recommitment to constitutional freedom. Rawls contorts his account of "public reason" to accommodate King's speech, as must every American political theorist writing on religion in the public square. Because of his iconic national role, King's speech functions as a standard case, a defining instance, of publicly acceptable religious speech.[8]

King and Bonhoeffer complicate distinctions of religious and political action because they both struggled for a humanely secular society in explicitly christoform patterns of action. They were contextual Christologists, seeking to embody the pattern of Jesus anew by participating in the responsibilities of their situation. There are no a priori rules for this kind of action, only an orientation to the image of the body of Christ. Christian political ethics thus functions by showing the pattern of Christic responsibility amid the everyday dramas of empire and gospel. King and Bonhoeffer saw that everyone participates in those dramas—such that the gospel does not hang on the propriety of its relation to the state, but on whether children marching in Birmingham appear as God's vulnerable body or as minors made strategic pawns, on whether a theological confrontation with antisemitism appears as an interruptive word from God or Christian complicity with cultural evil.

Theocentric Pragmatism

Their focus on discernment and responsibility would seem to make ethics primary for theology. In such open ambiguity, what will guide ways of bearing witness? Yet both Bonhoeffer and King refuse to let us see ethics as the social application of faith—Bonhoeffer by direct assault, King in his strategic pragmatism. In place of an ethical system, we find something more like a summons to participation in reality.

For both figures, discernment of responsible participation displaces the role of professional ethics. Luther Ivory writes that as King worked to resolve the tensions of his vocational identities (pastor, activist, ethicist, theologian), he moved toward a fluid understanding of Christian life as "radical involvement." Oriented by his faith that God works decisively in history for just community, and called to the necessity of responding to God's work, King's distinctive engagement with reality, says Ivory, "combined revolutionary consciousness with a radical pragmatism."[9] Does a radical pragmatism allow for a distinctly Christian ethic?

Bonhoeffer's salvo against the very idea of ethics accentuates that question of King. Bonhoeffer's *Ethics* offers this introductory outrage: "The knowledge of good and evil appears to be the goal of all ethical reflection. The first task of Christian ethics is to abrogate [*aufzuheben*] that knowledge." He goes on: "it is questionable whether it even makes sense to speak of Christian ethics at all." If we do, it can "be considered an ethic only as the critique of all ethics."[10]

Bonhoeffer knows that a contextual notion of responsibility will make conscientious people ask: How, then, can I do good? If everyday life participates in the drama of empire and gospel, how shall I avoid evil and do the good? Bonhoeffer thinks that such questions do not seek to find the pattern of Christ in context but, rather, look to safeguard oneself from the world's ambiguity. For Bonhoeffer, "ethics" stands for the attempt to acquit oneself, to safely extricate oneself from ambiguity. That sort of ethics shuts down theological creativity, insulates oneself from reality, from neighbors, and from God. Bonhoeffer confronts that tendency with the irruption of command: Might not God call us beyond conscience, beyond good and evil, beyond our own selves?

That can sound like Nietzschean heroics, an über-egoism, but Bonhoeffer means that God's call to action comes only within social reality and for the sake of God becoming real in the world. The point of human action is not that the agents would be good or accomplish some goal, but that "the reality of God demonstrate itself."[11] If there is any subject matter for something called "Christian ethics," it is "God's reality . . . becoming real among God's creatures." To treat reality and morality apart, says Bonhoeffer, results in "the complete ethical aporia that today goes by the name 'social ethics.'"[12]

Christianity has to do with humans as whole and social persons, surrounded by creation and members of a reality held in God's hands. "In Christ we are invited to participate in the reality of God and the reality of the world at the same time, the one not without the other." Bonhoeffer refuses the agent any safe moral principles under which to take refuge, but he does outline the shape of a responsible answer: we see it in the figure of God's taking shape in the world. The image is always a christic form, suffering on behalf of others, taking on the guilt of the world. In lieu of ethical criteria for good and evil, Bonhoeffer depicts the image of Christian action: it looks like the body of Christ. Ethics has now become almost theurgic, christo-poietic; it demonstrates God's body becoming real within a broken, hostile world. "The reality of God demonstrates itself only as it places me completely in the reality of the world."[13]

Consider now the challenge of King's pragmatism. King's life makes it clear that Christian ethics is not an applied moral grammar but an embodied capacity to join the movement of God in history. King was an extraordinary improviser, drawing together lines of thought from Gandhi's nonviolence, social gospel, personalism, black church theology, Niebuhrean theological realism, American civil religion, African American social thought, and contemporary political theory. When he claimed that redemptive love summarized all that, his aim was not simply to convey a moral message, but to interpret a complex reality in light of its potential for transformation. Cornel West calls King "the greatest organic intellectual in American history," for the way he pragmatically combined multiple traditions of social thought to produce new cultural possibilities for American society.[14]

For Christian ethics, accustomed to finding in its great authorities a theological principle like "justice" or a Christian reality like "church," King's intellectual bricolage may seem a hallmark of strategy rather than gospel. Perhaps that is one reason why King has been often received as movement leader rather than theologian and pastor. But that is just the contrast—between political strategy and gospel confession—that King's legacy challenges. For King, Christianity transforms the world through creative confrontations aimed for a definite measure of political success, achieved through the transforming power of love and confident in history's long-term arc toward justice. King's pragmatism is at once strategic and theological. The gospel must *work*; or, recalling Bonhoeffer, the gospel must demonstrate itself in the world's reality.

King looked to create that demonstration in creative, concrete moments. The Montgomery bus boycott remained paradigmatic for him throughout his life, not only because it exemplified successful nonviolence, but because it was sustained from week to week as much by savvy strategy and spirited community cooperation as it was by great preaching and theological discernment. The boycott offered an image of God's will for beloved community, embodied and walking to work. Later the student sit-in movement and freedom rides taught King to see the christic image of embodied self-offering in suffering resistance. That image helped draw together King's views of human dignity, his commitment to nonviolence, his theology of love, and his vision of beloved community—and all by giving an innovative refusal to American racism, thereby making new possibilities within American society.[15]

Ivory observes in King not a realist pragmatism, shaping itself to the constraints of coercive powers, but a theocentric pragmatism, seeking the roots of social problems and the concrete, political opportunities for changing them. For example, against advice from those who thought it distracted attention from racism, and in the face of rejection from some political allies, King publicly denounced the war in Vietnam. In his view, the violence of American

racism was related to the violence of American militarism and to racist imperialism generally, and there would be no peaceful solution to one without a
peaceful solution to the other. King was also criticized for taking up structural
economic policy. Again moving contrary to those who thought it more politic to treat racism and economic policy as separate issues, King criticized the
materialism of American capitalism for racist distribution, economic opportunity, and exploitation of all the poor.[16]

In retrospect, many contemporary interpreters laud King's courage in taking these positions. Yet his theocentric pragmatism does not offer a definite
social philosophy so much as a challenge to think in social wholes, to see interrelated evils, to address persons within the whole of creation, and to uncover
the festering wounds that debilitate God's reality becoming real within history. The task for Christian ethics, then, is to create specific strategies that
create at least the possibility for moving in God's direction.

Sometimes one must work from perilous cultural ground, perhaps in contexts almost entirely evil. To appreciate the stakes of strategic pragmatism,
consider Bonhoeffer's dangerous rhetorical strategy in his essay "The Church
and the Jewish Question." The essay is remembered for its foreshadowing sentence that at some point the church may have "to put a spoke in the wheel" of
state oppression. But the essay's primary objective was to convince the Confessing Church to grapple with the reality of Jewish oppression in Germany.
Bonhoeffer's clever, risky gambit was to admit "the Jewish question" as a real
political question, but then argue that for the church, "Jew" is a religious, not a
racial, category. "The people of Israel," who are so frustrating for the state, are
not those of a certain ancestry, wrote Bonhoeffer, but those who live by observance of racially determined laws. His critique of the Aryan laws oppressing
ethnic Jews was that they were "Jewish" in character![17]

A dashing rhetorical move, yes, but in retrospect Bonhoeffer's strategy
seems perilous in its appropriation of the same racial and religious categories
used by others for Holocaust. Maybe he should have attacked and decon-
structed those categories instead. Given the thin cultural possibilities for resistance in his time, what strategy should he have pursued? To appreciate the
pragmatic difficulty, consider in our own time what might be an analogous
challenge: offering theological resistance to anthropocentric violence. The pre-
rogative of humanity to do whatever it will to nonhuman creatures remains
so unquestioned, despite repugnant suffering and obvious destruction, that
to even raise the notion of moral value for animals or ecological communities
risks scoffing dismissal. Should a Christian ethic for relations with other-than-
human creatures form its strategy for environmental reform by working from

within culpable cultural categories, or by trying to replace those with new ones? If the former it seems complicit; if the latter it seems irrelevant.

Bonhoeffer chose to work with his antisemitic inheritance—a decision that must continue to trouble his reception. Whatever we think of that decision or our own analogous challenges, Bonhoeffer and King both turn ethics away from assessing guilt or justification, goodness or badness. They ask us instead: How will we invent the possibility of joining Christ's taking form in the world?

The Church and the Membership of God

Answering that question would have been easier for King and Bonhoeffer if they could have pointed to the church as the site of that invention. Yet the official churches for both men were sluggish and complicit at best, and each came to the end of his life finding the social form of Christ's body well beyond the visible church.

Bonhoeffer's development is especially striking here. The theologian who opened his career boldly proclaiming the church as the reality of God's revelation ends it with anticipations of a religionless Christianity. Bonhoeffer's first book, *Sanctorum Communio*, develops the church as social center of reality, describing it as "Christ existing as church-community."[18] But over the next two decades Bonhoeffer saw the mainstream church appropriated by an Aryanization program, the international ecumenical church unwilling to condemn this, and the Confessing Church offering resistance only for the sake of its own survival. At the end, when his closest community is a political coalition more atheist than Christian, Bonhoeffer asks, "in what way are we . . . secular Christians, in what way are we . . . those who are called forth . . . as wholly belonging to the world?"[19]

King's development is less shattering but similar. King opened his theological career in a respected pulpit and after the success of the Montgomery campaign widely admired for its Christian spirit, he expected support from churches and clergy around the county. Instead, King found himself criticized from white pulpits, ignored by the (black) National Baptist Convention, and rebuffed by Billy Graham's (relatively integrated) crusades. He was especially frustrated with the lack of courage from moderate white churches and conservative black churches. From both quarters, in different ways, King would be received politely, but without commitments to walk, to join the movement. King writes that he looks at such white churches and wonders what God they worship. He looks at complacent black churches and wonders at how God's colony has lost its sacrificial spirit.[20] At the end, his closest community was a coalition made up of saints and sinners of all faiths and none.

At the end of his life, each figure discovered that the community in which they found the gospel enacted and on which they staked their hopes for the next generation was not anything like a recognizable church. In each case it was a marginal group—the radical minority even among dissenters—of those willing to risk themselves for the sake of others. Reverend Bonhoeffer was hung as a traitor among a group of political criminals. Reverend King was shot down among a small group of organizers trying to sustain a sanitation workers' strike.

If the contemporary church wants to claim the witness of their deaths, it must wrestle with the fact that both King and Bonhoeffer gave their definitive witness beyond the bounds of the churches of their time, apart from the great majority of Christians in their country. If they found the body of Christ, it was through solidarity with a company of people representing many faiths and no faith. If they bear witness to God's new reality breaking in from the cruciform margins, then their deaths also testify to a certain death of the official churches.

Stanley Hauerwas has written that "the church *is* a social ethic."[21] Receiving King and Bonhoeffer makes that sort of statement difficult because their witness stands for church's social failure inasmuch as it represents the body of Christ in strange new forms. The lived social ethic of the official churches in their times was ambivalent at best and lifeless at worst, and the best possibilities for the gospel often seemed to form in alternative memberships. After King and Bonhoeffer, then, what does church mean for Christian social ethics?

King's answer by the end of his life was clear: look for the body of Christ becoming real in Christ's simple call to serve others, to love others.[22] Whether generated from churches or not, King saw Christ-like love in those who let their bodies absorb a nation's violence and there redeem it, transforming wounds. Bonhoeffer says something similar: "the gospel will demonstrate itself" in the few remaining people who are just, truthful, and humane. For too long, says Bonhoeffer, the church has rested comfortably in its formula that one must know Christ in order to do justice. The church's failure shows that now it must be said that "unless you have become a righteous person, one who struggles for justice, truth, and humanity, you cannot know and find Christ."[23]

In those persons with the strength to love (says King), in those with the courage to bear responsibility for others (says Bonhoeffer), takes form the reality to which the church stands as faded icon. If theology can still talk of the church, it must say that "the church is nothing but that piece of humanity where Christ really has taken form." It is where "the world has been drawn into the form of Christ."[24] Bonhoeffer wrote that just before his final letters, some written as he watched the firebombing of Berlin from his Gestapo prison window (war crime upon war crime). The theologian of the concrete church-community could only speculate how the visible body of Christ might take shape in the era those bombs were making possible. That he could talk of Christianity at all, even religionless and arcane, seems almost unaccountably hopeful. Maybe he anticipates something along the lines of King's movement church, where the gospel seemed to prove itself in the bodies of nonviolent protesters. Somewhere in the shape of Fannie Lou Hamer's sin-scored body forcing President Johnson's shocking "we shall overcome" speech, in the shape of Birmingham's children's march and King's own nation-building dream speech, the shape of the world was, perhaps, being drawn into the form of Christ. King was showing the church what its Easter story means, preaching history as the drama of Christ, as death and redemption along a long arc toward justice. Join it, or miss the story of God.

Conclusion

The legacies of Bonhoeffer and King seem to push Christian ethics toward a paradoxical social hope: toward making the real presence of Christ in the world through faith in a nearly absent church. For each man, the institutional churches, however listless and self-absorbed, still tell the story by which humans know the pattern of Christ's body, given for the world. Sometimes—maybe most of the time—the churches tell a story their own body does not demonstrate and cannot bear. Nevertheless, the gospel proves itself elsewhere, drawing the world into the form of Christ wherever those willing to bear the cost of discipleship give themselves for the sake of others.

There is no way to know this gospel but to join with those who live into this christic pattern. We only know the church from the inside, says Bonhoeffer, and by the end of his life, he knows that this "inside" is found on the margins, on the cross onto which God has been pushed. We only know Easter by bearing the cross, said King, and by the end of his life, he finds the power of the cross in those willing to risk themselves in service for others. After King and after Bonhoeffer, Christian social thought depends on risk and creativity, on inventing anew the possibility of discovering and joining the body of God taking shape in history. Christian ethics has moved away from adjudicating principles or narrating Christian identity, and toward devising strategies that keep making gospel hope from violent cultures and poor inheritances.

Abbreviations

DB-ER   *Dietrich Bonhoeffer: A Biography,* Revised Edition, by Eberhard Bethge. Revised and edited by Victoria J. Barnett. Minneapolis: Fortress Press. 2000.

DBW   Dietrich Bonhoeffer Werke (German). Edited by Eberhard Bethge, et al. 16 vols. (complete). Munich: Christian Kaiser Verlag.

DBWE   Dietrich Bonhoeffer Works (English). 16 vols. (in progress). Minneapolis: Fortress Press.

Listed below are the volumes of DBWE available at the time of publication as they are cited in the notes, with information on the original DBW editions included.

SC   *Sanctorum Communio: A Theological Study of the Sociology of the Church.* DBWE, vol. 1. Translated from the German edition (*Sanctorum Communio: Eine dogmatische Untersuchung zur Soziologie der Kirche,* DBW 1 [1986]) edited by Joachim von Soosten. English edition edited by Clifford J. Green. Translated by Reinhard Krauss and Nancy Lukens. 1998.

AB   *Act and Being: Transcendental Philosophy and Ontology in Systematic Theology.* DBWE, vol. 2. Translated from the German edition (*Akt und Sein: Transzendentalphilosophie und Ontologie in der systematischen Theologie,* DBW 2 [1988]), edited by Hans-Richard Reuter. English edition edited by Wayne Whitson Floyd Jr. Translated by H. Martin Rumscheidt. 1996.

CF   *Creation and Fall.* DBWE, vol. 3. Translated from the German edition (*Schöpfung und Fall,* DBW 3 [1988]), edited by Martin Rütter and Ilse Tödt. English edition edited by John W. de Gruchy. Translated by Douglas Stephen Bax. 1997.

Disc   *Discipleship*. DBWE, vol. 4. Translated from the German edition (*Nachfolge*, DBW 4 [1989]), edited by Martin Kuske and Ilse Tödt. English edition edited by Geffrey B. Kelly and John D. Godsey. Translated by Barbara Green and Reinhard Krauss. 2001.

LT/PB   *Life Together* and *Prayerbook of the Bible*. DBWE, vol. 5. Translated from the German edition (*Gemeinsames Leben* und *Das Gebetbuch der Bibel*, DBW 5 [1987]), edited by Gerhard Ludwig Müller and Albrecht Schönherr. English edition edited by Geffrey B. Kelly. Translated by Daniel W. Bloesch and James H. Burtness. 1996.

Eth   *Ethics*. DBWE, vol. 6. Translated from the German edition (*Ethik*, DBW 6 [1998]), edited by Ilse Tödt, Heinz Eduard Tödt, Ernst Feil, and Clifford Green. English edition edited by Clifford J. Green. Translated by Reinhard Krauss, Charles C. West, and Douglas W. Stott. 2001.

FTP   *Fiction from Tegel Prison*. DBWE, vol. 7. Translated from the German edition (*Fragmente aus Tegel*, DBW 7 [1994]), edited by Renate Bethge and Ilse Tödt. English edition edited by Clifford J. Green. Translated by Nancy Lukens. 1999.

LPP   *Letters and Papers from Prison*. DBWE, vol. 8. Translated from the German edition (*Widerstand und Ergebung*, DBW 8 [2010]), edited by Christian Gremmels, Eberhard Bethge, and Renate Bethge. English edition edited by John W. de Gruchy. Translated by Isabel Best, Lisa E. Dahill, Reinhard Krauss, and Nancy Lukens. 2010. Not available to contributors.

YB   *The Young Bonhoeffer: 1918–1927*. DBWE, vol. 9. Translated from the German edition (*Jugend und Studium: 1918–1927*, DBW 9 [1986]), edited by Hans Pfeifer in cooperation with Clifford J. Green and Carl-Jürgen Kaltenborn. English edition edited by Paul Duane Matheny, Clifford J. Green, and Marshall D. Johnson. Translated by Mary C. Nebelsick with the assistance of Douglas W. Stott. 2003.

BBNY   *Barcelona, Berlin, New York: 1928–1931*. DBWE, vol. 10. Translated from the German edition (*Barcelona, Berlin, Amerika: 1928–1931*, DBW vol. 10 [1992; 2d ed., 2005]), edited by Reinhart Staats and Hans Christoph von Hase with the assistance of Holger Roggelin and Matthias Wünsche. English edition edited by Clifford J. Green. Translated by Douglas W. Stott. 2008.

Ber   *Berlin: 1932–1933*. DBWE, vol. 12. Translated from the German edition (*Berlin: 1932–1933*, DBW 12 [1997]), edited by Carsten Nicolaisen and Ernst-Albert Scharffenorth. English edition edited by Larry

L. Rasmussen. Translated by Isabel Best, David Higgins, and Douglas W. Stott. 2009.

Lon   *London: 1933–1935*. DBWE, vol. 13. Translated from the German edition (*London: 1933–1935*, DBW 13 [1994]), edited by Hans Goedeking, Martin Heimbucher, and Hans-Walter Schleicher. English edition edited by Keith Clements. Translated by Isabel Best. Supplementary material translated by Douglas W. Stott. 2007.

CI   *Conspiracy and Imprisonment: 1940–1945*. DBWE, vol. 16. Translated from the German edition (*Konspiration und Haft: 1940–1945*, DBW 16 [1996]), edited by Jørgen Glenthøj, Ulrich Kabitz, and Wolf Krötke. English edition edited by Mark S. Brocker. Translated by Lisa E. Dahill with the assistance of Douglas W. Stott. 2006.

Notes

Introduction

1. Dietrich Bonhoeffer, *Letters and Papers from Prison*, ed. Eberhard Bethge, trans. Reginald Fuller, et al. (New York: Touchstone, 1997), 11.

2. The privileged-oppressed distinction is not meant to be a dualism explaining all human suffering, but what the Open Door Community challenges us to see is that much of what we deem mere misfortune is actually injustice. See Judith N. Shklar, *The Faces of Injustice* (New Haven: Yale University Press, 1990).

3. Bonhoeffer, *Letter and Papers from Prison*, 17. Along with Ed Loring and Murphy Davis, the Open Door Community's cofounders include Ron and Carolyn Johnson. For further reading see Peter R. Gathje, ed., *The Open Door Reader: A Work of Hospitality, 1982–2000* (Atlanta: The Open Door Community Press, 2002); Peter R. Gathje, *Sharing the Bread of Life: Hospitality and Resistance at the Open Door Community* (Atlanta: The Open Door Community Press, 2006); http://www.opendoorcommunity.org, accessed March 8, 2010.

4. Interview with Ed Loring, Atlanta, Georgia, June 15, 2009.

5. Ibid.

6. Regarding their attempt to carry on the legacies of Bonhoeffer and King, Murphy Davis says, "We hold the teachings and witness of King and Bonhoeffer (as well as the others) with reverence and humility—knowing that our efforts to be true to the teachings are faltering at best. But these, among the great teachers, give us such wonderful resources for the living of these days that we turn to them again and again—especially in the periods that we are slammed in the face with our own inability to be fully loving and deeply courageous." E-mail correspondence with Murphy Davis, June 25, 2009.

7. For Bonhoeffer's discussion of "contempt for humanity" and Jesus Christ as "the real human being" see "Ethics as Formation" in *Ethics*, DBWE 6, esp. p. 94, and *Letters and Papers*, 9–10. In *Ethics* Bonhoeffer counters Nietzsche's idea of the *Übermenschentum*, or superhumanity, with Christ, who becomes and affirms not the superhuman but the real human being.

8. See Murphy Davis, "Woodruff Park and the Search for Common Ground" and "Toilets, Justice and Hospitality: The Case for Public Toilets" in Gathje, ed., *The Open Door Reader*, 113–21. Atlanta continues to jail those who are homeless for public urination and defecation, and controversy surrounds the few public toilets that were installed. Ed Loring says that he has heard that business leaders want the public restroom at the

downtown Woodruff Park closed, and one of the park attendants recently told Loring that some members of the surrounding community had asked the attendant not to clean it. Loring suspects that the intent is to create complaints so that the restroom would be closed down permanently.

9. Interview with Ed Loring, Atlanta, Georgia, June 15, 2009.

10. Interview with Murphy Davis, Atlanta, Georgia, June 12, 2009.

11. Ibid.

12. Martin Luther King Jr., "I Have a Dream" and "A Time to Break Silence" in James M. Washington, ed., *A Testament of Hope: The Essential Writings and Speeches of Martin Luther King, Jr.* (San Francisco: Harper & Row, 1986), 218, 243.

13. See Bonhoeffer, *London, 1933–1935*, DBWE 13:309. Quote from Bonhoeffer's student, Inge Sembritzki, in Martin Doblmeier's documentary, *Bonhoeffer: Pastor, Pacifist, Nazi Resister* (Alexandria, Va.: Journey Films, 2003). Sembritzki says, "My recollection of Bonhoeffer's Fanø speech is so clear. . . . His last sentences were: 'What are we waiting for? The time is late.'"

14. Wayne Whitson Floyd makes a similar point in reference to Bonhoeffer in "Style and the Critique of Metaphysics: The Letter as Form in Bonhoeffer and Adorno," *Union Seminary Quarterly Review* 46, nos. 1–4 (1992): 247.

15. For Bonhoeffer's account of the destructive character of immediacy and his description of Christ as mediator and thus protector of alterity and distance, see "Discipleship and the Individual" in *Discipleship*, DBWE 4, chap. 5, and *Life Together*, DBWE 5:40–47.

16. Martin Luther King Jr., "Letter from Birmingham Jail" (1963) in Washington, ed., *Testament of Hope*, 290; idem, "A Christmas Sermon on Peace," in ibid., 254. Bonhoeffer, *Eth*, DBWE 6:58–59, 62, 74–75.

Chapter 1

1. Thanks to my friend and former colleague at Saint Paul School of Theology in Kansas City, Mo., Tex S. Sample, for this turn of phrase. His piercing analysis and fine southern gift for a well-shaped sentence have been gifts to many.

2. See Josiah U. Young III's essay in this volume for a discussion of the theological differences between Bonhoeffer and King, "Bonhoeffer and King: Their Theologies and the Problem of Racism" (chap. 6, below).

3. See Robert L. Williams, "The Death of White Research in the Black Community" in *Journal of Non-White Concerns in Personnel and Guidance* (April, 1974): 116–30 for an early study detailing this phenomenon. More recently, there has been a marked rise of white scholars who have doctorates in African American history, but whites with doctorates in black studies remain rare. Of course, the social location of the researcher does not guarantee that he or she will do either a more thorough or inadequate job. My point is that early white researchers who focused on black populations often did so through the lens of their cultural assumptions and biases and saw this as neutral or objective, value-free scholarship.

4. For example, see W. E. B. Du Bois, *The Souls of Black Folk: Essays and Sketches* (Chicago: A.C. McClurg & Co., 1903; reprint, New York: Norton, 1999), 3; Paul Gilroy,

The Black Atlantic: Modernity and Double Consciousness (London: Verso, 1993); and Eduardo Bonilla-Silva, "The Double Consciousness of Black, White, and Brown Folks in the 21st Century," paper presented at the annual meeting of the American Sociological Association, Atlanta Hilton Hotel, Atlanta, Ga., Aug. 16, 2003.

5. Katie G. Cannon, Black *Womanist Ethics* (Atlanta: Scholars, 1988) and *Katie's Canon: Womanism and the Soul of the Black Community* (New York: Continuum, 1995); Delores S. Williams, *Sisters in the Wilderness: The Challenge of Womanist God-Talk* (Maryknoll, N.Y.: Orbis, 1993); and Jacquelyn Grant, *White Women's Christ, Black Women's Jesus: Feminist Christology and Womanist Response* (Atlanta: Scholars, 1989). Dianne M. Stewart has authored *The Three-Eyed God: African Dimensions of the Jamaican Religious Experience* (New York: Oxford University Press, 2005).

6. See the representative songs by The Last Poets ("Wake Up, Niggers" and "Rain of Terror"), Gil Scott-Heron ("The Revolution Will Not Be Televised" and "Winter in America"), Marvin Gaye ("What's Going On" and "Mercy Mercy Me [The Ecology]"), Curtis Mayfield ("Pusherman"), and Arrested Development's album *3 Years, 5 Months & 2 Days in the Life Of* . . . (Chrysalis, 1992).

7. Recent examples of this include Nelly's "Tip Drill" and the work of gangsta rappers like Ice T, N.W.A., and Nas.

8. For an extended discussion of the fantastic hegemonic imagination, see Emilie M. Townes, *Womanist Ethics and the Cultural Production of Evil* (New York: Palgrave McMillan, 2006).

9. Representatives include Madhu Dubey, *Signs and Cities: Black Literary Postmodernism* (Chicago: University of Chicago Press, 2003), and Toni Morrison, *Playing in the Dark: Whiteness and the Literary Imagination* (Cambridge: Harvard University Press, 1992). Also see bell hooks, *Yearning: Race, Gender, and Cultural Politics* (Boston: South End, 1990), 23–31, and "Postmodern Blackness" in *Postmodern Culture* 1, no. 1 (September 1990) Project MUSE. <http://muse.jhu.edu/login?uri=/journals/postmodern_culture/V001/1hooks.html>, and Cornel West, *The American Evasion of Philosophy: A Genealogy of Philosophy* (Madison: University of Wisconsin Press, 1989), 235–39.

10. This a reference to the groundbreaking work edited by Gloria T. Hull, Patricia Bell Scott, and Barbara Smith, *All the Women Are White, All the Blacks Are Men, But Some of Us Are Brave: Black Women's Studies* (Old Westbury, N.Y.: Feminist Press, 1982; reprint, New York: The Feminist Press at CUNY, 2003).

Chapter 2

1. Lawrence S. Cunningham, *The Meaning of Saints* (San Francisco: Harper & Row, 1980), 65.

2. See Manuel Valdes, "Wash. County Trashes Garbage Bags with MLK's Face," *USA Today*, September 3, 2008, http://www.usatoday.com/news/nation/2008-09-03-336654994_x.htm, accessed March 8, 2010.

3. Joe Lapointe, "Mets' Success is Built on a Solid Foundation," *The New York Times*, August 31, 2008, http://www.nytimes.com/2008/08/31/sports/baseball/31manuel.html, accessed March 8, 2010.

4. "The King-ing of Nelson Mandela," *thestateofblog*, July 21, 2008, http://thestateofblog.wordpress.com/2008/07/21/the-king-ing-of-nelson-mandela/, accessed March 8, 2010.

5. A blogger recently wrote of Bonhoeffer that he was "the equivalent of a Christian superhero—he stood firm against all odds in the face of clear evil." "Can Women Be Church Planters?" *She Worships*, July 13, 2008, http://sheworships.com/2008/07/, accessed March 8, 2010.

6. Despite the fact that Bonhoeffer was executed for treason, in June, 2008, the United Methodist Church voted to officially recognize him as "a modern day martyr for the cause of Christ."

7. Dietrich Bonhoeffer, *Eth*, DBWE 6:206.

8. See Haynes, *The Bonhoeffer Phenomenon: Portraits of a Protestant Saint* (Minneapolis: Fortress Press, 2004), 170.

9. Amanda Ripley, "Terrorists and Saints," *Washington City Paper*, February 5–11, 1999; and John Yewell, "Straight Shooters," *Independent Online* (January 24, 2001), at http://www.indyweek.com/gyrobase/Content?oid=oid%3A15407, accessed March 8, 2010. The American Coalition of Life Activists (ACLA) was successfully sued in 1999 over their "Nuremberg Files Project," a website identifying abortion doctors. The project's goal, according to ACLA national director David Crane, was "to gather all available information on abortionists and their accomplices for the day when they may be formally charged and tried at Nuremberg-type trials for their crimes." See Skipp Porteous, "Banquet of the White Rose," *Albion Monitor*, http://www.monitor.net/monitor/abortion/whiterose.html, accessed March 8, 2010.

10. See Haynes, *The Bonhoeffer Phenomenon: Portraits of a Protestant Saint*, 170–72.

11. *The Bonhoeffer Phenomenon*, 171–72.

12. Joe Pavone, "Men of Courage: Paul Hill and Dietrich Bonhoeffer," http://www.calvinistcontender.org/abortion/menofcourage.shtml, accessed March 8, 2010.

13. Robert L. Hunter, "Dietrich Bonhoeffer: A Vision and a Voice for Our Times," *Saturday Evening Post* (September/October, 1997): 50–51.

14. Robert Coles, *Dietrich Bonhoeffer*, Modern Spiritual Masters (Maryknoll, N.Y.: Orbis, 1998), 41.

15. The video can be found at http://scienceblogs.com/dispatches/2008/07/mcdonalds_boycotters_misuse_ma.php, accessed March 8, 2010.

16. Jasmyne Cannick, "Rev. Wright Just History Repeating: They Wanted King to Shut Up Too," *gaywired*, May 6, 2008, http://www.gaywired.com; see also http://fashionboyny.wordpress.com/2008/04/29/rev-dr-martin-luther-kings-speech-america-too-is-going-to-hell/, accessed January, 2009.

17. "'Party Crashers'; Randall Terry of Operation Rescue, Announces Civil Disobedience Times and Forums to Disrupt DNC Events," *Reuters* (August 22, 2008), at http://www.reuters.com/article/pressRelease/idUS188068+22-Aug-2008+PRN20080822, accessed March 8, 2010.

18. Ryan Messmore, "Preparing the Way: Evangelicals and the Election," *National Review* (August 15, 2008), http://article.nationalreview.com/?q=MGI5ZDk1ZTMyMDViYTMxZTRiYzQ4N2ExNThmNTY2MjE=, accessed March 8, 2010.

19. "Common Ground Theatre Presents Awaiting Judgment© at the Bayview Baptist Church—Sunday, April 27," http://www.free-press-release.com/news/200804/1207962397.html (January, 2009). "Awaiting Judgment" was written by Art Cribbs, a UCC pastor in San Diego, and was first performed in 2007.

20. Nagarjuna, "Dietrich Bonhoeffer and William Ayers," *Naked Reflections*, November 1, 2008, http://nagarjuna1953.blogspot.com/2008/11/dietrich-bonhoeffer-and-william-ayers.html, accessed March 8, 2010. "The Prophetic Voice of the Orthodox Monk," *Orthodox Monk*, October 13, 2008, at http://orthodoxmonk.blogspot.com/2008_10_01_archive.html, accessed March 8, 2010. The basis for this claim may be *Wikipedia*, where we read that "like other executions associated with the July 20 Plot, the execution was brutal. Bonhoeffer was stripped of his clothing, tortured and ridiculed by the guards, and led naked into the execution yard. A lack of sufficient gallows to hang the plotters caused Hitler and Nazi propagandist Josef Goebbels to use meathooks from slaughterhouses to slowly hoist the victim by a noose formed of piano wire. Asphyxiation is thought to have taken half an hour," http://en.wikipedia.org/wiki/Dietrich_Bonhoeffer, accessed March 8, 2010. I first noticed this claim in an article by James Dobson in the May, 2000, issue of *Focus on the Family Newsletter.*

21. The poem was quoted by Joseph Lowry in "Civil rights figure Rev. Joseph Lowery reflects on a movement," *Chicago Tribune*, January 19, 2009, http://mobile.chicagotribune.com/inf/infomo?view=nationworld_article&feed:a=chi_trib_5min&feed:c=nationworld&feed:i=44588646&nopaging=1, accessed March 8, 2010.

Chapter 3

1. Dietrich Bonhoeffer, *Letters and Papers from Prison*, ed. Eberhard Bethge, trans. Reginald Fuller, et al. (London: SCM, 1972), 43–44.

2. Dietrich Bonhoeffer, *Zettelnotizen für eine Ethik*, DBW 6 *Erganzungsband*, ed. Ilse Tödt (Munich: Kaiser Verlag, 1993), 86–87. My translation.

3. For discussions of which, see, for example, Rufus Burrow Jr., *God and Human Dignity: The Personalism, Theology, and Ethics of Martin Luther King* (Notre Dame, Ind.: University of Notre Dame Press, 2006), chap. 5. See also Coretta Scott King, *My Life with Martin Luther King, Jr.* (London: Hodder and Stoughton, 1974).

4. He wrote with self-deprecating honesty to Eberhard Bethge: "I would very much like my wife to be as much of the same mind as possible [regarding taste in literature]. But I think it's only a matter of time. I don't like it when husbands and wives have different opinions. . . . Or is that another aspect of my 'tyrannical' nature that you know so well? If so, you must tell me" (Bonhoeffer, *Letters and Papers*, 148).

5. Renate Wind, *Dietrich Bonhoeffer: A Spoke in the Wheel*, trans. John Bowden (Grand Rapids: Eerdmans, 1992), 109. Wind's source is a letter from Elisabeth Zinn (later Bornkamm), the theologian and Confessing Church activist to whom Bonhoeffer decided he could not become engaged in the early years of the church struggle—a woman whom, Wind suggests, "in 'normal' times he almost certainly would have married" (108).

6. See Burrow, *God and Human Dignity*, 152.

7. Ibid., 153.

8. See Katie G. Cannon, *Black Womanist Ethics* (New York: Oxford University Press, 1988), 169–75; Noel Leo Erskine, *King Among the Theologians* (Cleveland: Pilgrim, 1994), 157, 159–72.

9. In the *Ethics* marriage is one of the divine "mandates" by which God orders the fallen world. See Dietrich Bonhoeffer, *Eth*, DBWE 6:70. Bonhoeffer does not at this point discuss sexual inequality specifically, but the wedding sermon (quoted above) clearly connects to his broader thinking about the mandates.

10. See ibid., 221, 257.

11. See the essay, "After Ten Years," in Bonhoeffer, *Letters and Papers*, 9–10.

12. See Charles Marsh, *The Beloved Community: How Faith Shapes Social Justice, from the Civil Rights Movement to Today* (New York: Basic Books, 1996).

13. For "Christ existing as church-community," see Dietrich Bonhoeffer, *Sanctorum Communio*, DBWE 1:190.

14. Cannon, *Black Womanist Ethics*, 169–75.

15. See Lisa E. Dahill, "Jesus for You: A Feminist Reading of Bonhoeffer's Christology," *Currents in Theology and Mission* 33, no. 4 (2007): 250–59. Dahill suggests, in the context of her own constructive feminist project, that Bonhoeffer is "helpful as a resource *even against his own blind spots*" (259). I am grateful to Jennifer McBride for drawing my attention to this article. See also the discussion of *Stellvertretung* and its gendered aspects in Rachel Muers, *Living for the Future: Theological Ethics for Coming Generations* (London: T&T Clark, 2008), chap. 6.

16. Martin Luther King Jr., "Recommendations to the Dexter Avenue Baptist Church for the Fiscal Year 1954–55," in Richard Lischer, *The Preacher King: Martin Luther King, Jr. and the Word That Moved America* (New York: Oxford University Press, 1995), 75–76, suggests that one of the aims of this letter was for a new, relatively young pastor to assert his authority within a congregation dominated by the power of the deacons.

17. Bonhoeffer, *Eth*, DBWE 6:396.

18. Ibid., 6:398.

19. I discuss this further in *Keeping God's Silence: Towards a Theological Ethics of Communication* (Oxford: Blackwell, 2004), chap. 6.

20. Lischer, *Preacher King*, 3. See also Aprele Elliott, "Ella Baker: Free Agent in the Civil Rights Movement," *Journal of Black Studies* 26 (May 1996): 593–603, here pages 597–98: "The preacher's primary authority is ecclesiastical. However, political decision making is in his domain."

21. See the discussions of the *Theologinnen* in Theodore N. Thomas, *Women Against Hitler: Christian Resistance in the Third Reich* (Westport, Conn.: Prager, 1995), and at more length in Andrea Bieler, ed., '*Darum wagt es, Schwestern . . .' Zur Geschichte evangelischer Theologinnen in Deutschland*, Historisch-Theologische Studien zum 19. und 20. Jahrhundert, Vol. 7 (Neukirchen-Vluyn: Neukirchener-Verlag, 1994).

22. See Daphne C. Wiggins, *Righteous Content: Black Women's Perspective of Church and Faith* (Albany: State University of New York Press, 2005). On black women's preaching, see Bettye Collier-Thomas, *Daughters of Thunder: Black Women Preachers and Their Sermons, 1850–1979* (San Francisco: Jossey-Bass, 1998).

23. Elliott, "Ella Baker," 599.

24. In Bonhoeffer's case, one such woman who has received considerable scholarly attention is Ruth von Kleist-Retzow (the grandmother of Maria von Wedemeyer). Von Kleist-Retzow's theologically and politically informed support for the Finkenwalde seminary, for the conspiracy against Hitler and for Bonhoeffer personally was of enormous importance from the mid-1930s onwards. She is one of the models for the trenchant lay critic of bad preaching in the novel fragment Bonhoeffer wrote in prison (*Fiction from Tegel Prison*, DBWE 7:71). For an accessible account of her life, see Jane Pejsa, *Matriarch of Conspiracy: Ruth von Kleist, 1867–1945* (New York: Pilgrim, 1992).

25. Bonhoeffer, *Letters and Papers*, 17.

Chapter 4

1. Hannah Arendt, *The Human Condition* (Chicago: University of Chicago Press, 1958).

2. The source for all this, and more, is, of course, Eberhard Bethge's great biography, *Dietrich Bonhoeffer: A Biography*, rev. Victoria Barnett (Minneapolis: Fortress Press, 2000).

3. Clifford Green, *A Theology of Sociality*, rev. ed. (Grand Rapids: Eerdmans, 1999).

4. Richard H. King, *Civil Rights and the Idea of Freedom* (New York: Oxford University Press, 1992).

5. Martin Luther King Jr., "I See the Promised Land," in James M. Washington, ed., *A Testament of Hope: The Essential Writings and Speeches of Martin Luther King, Jr.* (San Francisco: Harper & Row, 1986), 286.

6. Martin Luther King Jr., *Why We Can't Wait* (New York: Penguin, 1964), 75. Let me note in passing here that one challenge for those bringing King's thought to bear on political life is just how much of a claim it can or should have on non-Christians—and this in light of the undeniably Christian origins, structure, and meaning of his thought. This question also comes up in discussions of Bonhoeffer. I have had the experience, many times over now, of students at the University of Chicago arguing that Bonhoeffer's theology has no bearing on those who do not share his Christology. Trying to solve this problem by redescribing the Christology as something else—as if one could absorb Bonhoeffer's Christology without remainder into an entirely secular idiom, is no "solution" at all.

7. Ibid.

8. Martin Luther King Jr., *A Call to Conscience*, eds. Clayborne Carson and Kris Shepard (New York: IPM [Intellectual Properties Management] in association with Warner Books, 2002), 7.

9. Ibid., 9.

10. Ibid., 162.

11. The Bonhoeffer text central here is *Act and Being*.

12. Green, *A Theology of Sociality*, 89. In an extended study, I would bring in material from *Life Together, Sanctorum Communio*, and other sources in which he meditates on the nature of a Christian community, stressing the embodied nature of that

community as the only view consistent with the concrete embodiment of the Son of God.

13. Dietrich Bonhoeffer, *Ethics*, trans. Neville Horton Smith, ed. Eberhard Bethge (New York: Touchstone, 1995), 103.

14. Ibid., 208.

15. Ibid., 149.

16. See Jean Bethke Elshtain, *Sovereignty: God, State and Self* (New York: The Gifford Lectures, 2008).

17. See King, *Why We Can't Wait*, 70–72.

18. Bonhoeffer, *Ethics*, 96.

19. Ibid., 332.

20. Ibid., 337.

21. Ibid., 343.

Chapter 5

1. The title of Young's book on Bonhoeffer (Josiah U. Young III, *No Difference in the Fare: Dietrich Bonhoeffer and the Problem of Racism* [Grand Rapids: Eerdmans, 1998]).

2. Martin Luther King, Jr., "Letter from Birmingham City Jail," in James M. Washington, ed., *A Testament of Hope: The Essential Writings and Speeches of Martin Luther King, Jr.* (San Francisco: Harper & Row, 1986), 290.

3. Ibid.

4. Dietrich Bonhoeffer, *Life Together* and *Prayerbook of the Bible*, DBWE 5:95–96.

5. "Remaining Awake Through a Great Revolution," a Passion Sunday sermon at the National Cathedral (Episcopal) in Washington, D.C., cited in Washington, ed., *A Testament of Hope*, 269–70.

6. Robert Bellah et al, *Habits of the Heart: Individualism and Commitment in American Life* (Berkeley: University of California Press, 185), 221.

7. Sermon for Evening Worship Service on 2 Corinthians 12:9, in *Lon*, DBWE 13:402–3. The ellipsis indicates an illegible insert.

8. King, cited from "The Drum Major Instinct," in Washington, ed., *A Testament of Hope*, 265.

9. King, cited from "A Time to Break Silence," in ibid., 232.

10. King, cited from "The Drum Major Instinct," in ibid., 265.

11. King, cited from "My Trip to the Land of Gandhi," in ibid., 25.

12. Beyond my use of original sources, I draw upon James Cone, *Martin & Malcolm & America: A Dream or a Nightmare* (Maryknoll, N.Y.: Orbis, 1991), and the discussion of King in Gary Dorrien, *The Making of American Liberal Theology: Crisis, Irony, & Modernity, 1950–2005* (Louisville: Westminster John Knox, 2006), 143–61.

13. This paragraph uses, for its commentary on King and Bonhoeffer, a paraphrase of portions of Leonard Pitts Jr., "Bad treatment of gays isn't the holocaust; however . . ." in *The Houston Chronicle*, Opinion, May 2, 2005.

14. From Bonhoeffer, *Lon*, DBWE 13:217 (1/147).

15. Cited from the *Plough* by Clifford Green in his "Editor's Introduction to the English Edition," *Barcelona, Berlin, New York: 1921–1931*, DBWE 10:42.

16. Cited in Heinz Eduard Tödt, *Authentic Faith: Bonhoeffer's Theological Ethics in Context* (Grand Rapids: Eerdmans, 2007), 102. This is from one of Hitler's speeches in September 1935.

17. See also Dietrich Bonhoeffer, Memorandum, "The Jewish-Christian Question as Status Confessionis," in *Berlin, 1932–1933*, DBWE 12:371–73. It should be noted that even if Bonhoeffer acknowledges in this essay that the church is to help all victims, *status confessionis* for him concerns only whether or not the church will institute an Aryan paragraph and exclude "non-Aryan" members. Nowhere does he say that *status confessionis* arises in the state's treatment of non-Christian Jews.

18. Ibid., 12:370.

19. Dietrich Bonhoeffer, *Eth*, DBWE 6:214, 185–86, 214, 180.

20. *DB-ER*, 275.

21. The discussion of Bonhoeffer's essay is informed by Tödt's *Authentic Faith*, 73–111.

22. Bonhoeffer, *Ber*, DBWE 12:362. Emphasis mine.

23. King, "My Trip to the Land of Gandhi," in Washington, ed., *A Testament of Hope*, 24.

24. All the direct quotations in this account of the bus boycott, Gandhi, and love are from King, *Stride Toward Freedom: The Montgomery Story*, as excerpted in "An Experiment in Love," in ibid., 20.

25. King, "Love, Law, and Civil Disobedience," in ibid., 46.

26. Ibid., 47.

27. Ibid., 25.

28. King, "Nonviolence: The Only Road to Freedom," *Ebony* (October, 1966), as cited in *The Catholic Worker* 75, no. 2 (March-April, 2008): 1.

29. From Gandhi's 1948 writings and cited here from John Dear, "The Consistent Ethic of Life," July 15, 2008, http://www.fatherjohndear.org/articles/the_consistent_ethic.html, accessed March 9, 2010.

30. The power of goodness is available not only for resistance. Such power, inherent in creation itself, is available for all sectors of life. For a touching account of this in his family and culture, see Bonhoeffer's poem, "Powers of Good," in *Letters and Papers from Prison*, 400–401.

31. A phrase used to describe the Germany sought by the military-political conspiracy.

32. See the essay with this title in King's *Where Do We Go From Here? Chaos or Community* (Boston: Beacon, 1967).

Chapter 6

1. Clayborne Carson, ed., *Called to Serve, January 1929–June 1951*, The Papers of Martin Luther King, Jr., vol. 1 (Berkeley: University of California Press, 1992), 1.

2. Ibid., 4.

3. Dietrich Bonhoeffer, *SC*, DBWE 1:255, 204.

4. Clifford Green, "Editor's Introduction to the English Edition," *BBNY*, DBWE 10:31.

5. Bonhoeffer, "Protestantism without Reformation," in *No Rusty Swords: Letters, Lectures and Notes from the Collected Works*, vol. 1 (London: Fontana Library/William Collins, 1977), 100.

6. Ibid., 112, 89.

7. Bonhoeffer, *SC*, DBWE 1:191.

8. Bonhoeffer, "Protestantism without Reformation," 101.

9. Ibid., 103.

10. Martin Luther King, Jr., *Where Do We Go from Here? Chaos or Community* (Boston: Beacon, 1968), 75.

11. Bonhoeffer, "Protestantism without Reformation," 113.

12. Ibid.

13. Dietrich Bonhoeffer, *BBNY*, DBWE 10:580–81.

14. Clayborne Carson, ed., *Advocate of the Social Gospel, September 1948–March 1963*, The Papers of Martin Luther King, Jr., vol. 6 (Berkeley: University of California Press, 2007), 598.

15. Ibid.

16. Bonhoeffer, *SC*, DBWE 1:80.

17. Clayborne Carson, ed., *Rediscovering Precious Values, July 1951–November 1955*, The Papers of Martin Luther King, Jr., vol. 2 (Berkeley: University of California Press, 1994), 548.

18. Ibid., 533.

19. Bonhoeffer, *SC*, DBWE 1:288, emphasis added.

20. Ibid., 1:288–89.

21. Taylor Branch, *At Canaan's Edge: America in the King Years 1965–68* (New York: Simon & Schuster, 2006), 319.

22. Bonhoeffer, *BBNY*, DBWE 10:422.

23. James Weldon Johnson, *The Autobiography of an Ex-Colored Man* (New York: Penguin, 1990), 145.

24. Bonhoeffer, *BBNY*, DBWE 10:293.

25. King, *Where Do We Go from Here?* 90.

26. See my essay, "'Is the white Christ, Too, Distraught by These Dark Sins His Father Wrought?': Dietrich Bonhoeffer and the Problem of the white Christ," in *Perspectives in Religious Studies* 26, no. 3 (Fall 1999): 317–30.

27. Countee Cullen, *The Black Christ and Other Poems* (New York: Harper & Brothers, 1929) 84.

28. Bonhoeffer, "Protestantism without Reformation," 108.

29. King, *Where Do We Go from Here?* 36.

30. Ibid., 63.

Chapter 7

1. The scope and depth of institutional ecclesial protest in Europe against the rise of the National Socialist Party in Germany and the destruction of children, women, and men designated as racial and social "others" during the rise of the National Socialist Party in Germany, in particular the genocide against European Jews, remain contested.

Still, the European hierarchy of the Roman Catholic Church was conspicuous in its reserve and hesitation. At the same time, Pope Pius XI hoped to challenge the Nazi persecution of the Catholic Church in Germany in the encyclical *Mit Brennender Sorge,* "With Burning Anxiety." This encyclical was smuggled into Germany and printed and distributed covertly and read in Catholic parishes on Palm Sunday, March 21, 1937. The pope planned a more direct protest against the Third Reich and commissioned *Humani Generis Unitas,* "The Unity of the Human Race." but he died in February 1939 and the letter was never published, coming to light only in the 1970s. However, that Angelo Cardinal Roncalli (later Pope John XXIII) unequivocally used his position as Apostolic Delegate to Turkey and Greece to assist the Jewish underground is known widely, and recent historical scholarship has uncovered instances of both Jewish and Christian active resistance to the Nazi regime. For an excellent discussion of Catholic social teaching in relation to racism and xenophobia, see Dawn M. Nothwehr, *That They May Be One: Catholic Social Teaching on Racism, Tribalism, and Xenophobia* (Maryknoll, N.Y.: Orbis, 2008), esp. 3–109.

It is interesting to note that Bonhoeffer wrote part of *Ethics* at the Benedictine monastery in Ettal. The editors provide a helpful footnote in DBWE 6:172 n.4. The editors point out that Bonhoeffer is influenced by Catholic interpretations of natural law and the relation of nature and grace. And they quote Ernst Feil, who remarks that Bonhoeffer "reclaimed the concept of the natural for Protestant ethics" (*The Theology of Dietrich Bonhoeffer* [Philadelphia: Fortress Press, 1985], 145 n.73).

2. In the United States, in general, institutional ecclesial protest against the protracted discrimination of African American citizens, particularly in the southern states, was ambiguous. For more than one hundred years, in large measure, even in the North, ecclesial conformity to *de jure* and *de facto* segregation, racial gradualism, and reticence obtained. By the start of the second modern civil rights movement, the American Catholic hierarchy had denounced racism as a sin and some, though not all, bishops began to integrate those parochial schools under their direct control or to condemn publicly the worst examples of discrimination. Here, too, recent historical scholarship has begun to relate the contributions of hundreds of Catholic lay women and men, vowed religious sisters and brothers, and clergy to the social change sparked by the movement. See Cecilia A. Moore, "Dealing with Desegregation: Black and White Responses to the Desegregation of the Diocese of Raleigh, North Carolina, 1953," and Katrina M. Sanders, "Black Catholic Clergy and the Struggle for Civil Rights: Winds of Change," in *Uncommon Faithfulness: The Experience of Black Catholics,* ed. M. Shawn Copeland (Maryknoll, N.Y.: Orbis, 2009).

3. John Deedy, *American Catholicism: And Now Where?* (New York, London: Plenum, 1987), 217.

4. Johan Verstraeten, "Catholic Social Thought as Discernment," *Logos* 8, no. 3 (Summer, 2005): 98.

5. Peter Paris, "Comparing the Public Theologies of James H. Cone and Martin Luther King, Jr.," in *Black Faith and Public Talk: Critical Essays on James H. Cone's Black Theology and Black Power,* ed. Dwight N. Hopkins (Maryknoll, N.Y.: Orbis, 1999), 220.

6. Hans Dirk Van Hoogstraten, "The Enemy and Righteous Action: A Hermeneutical Reassessment," in *Bonhoeffer for a New Day: Theology in a Time of Transition,* ed. John W. de Gruchy (Grand Rapids: Eerdmans, 1997), 188.

7. Dietrich Bonhoeffer, "Christ's Love and Our Enemies," in Geffrey Kelly and F. Burton Nelson, eds., *A Testament of Freedom: The Essential Writings of Dietrich Bonhoeffer*, rev. ed. (New York: HarperCollins, 1995), 286.

8. Dietrich Bonhoeffer, *Discipleship*, DBWE 4:138–39.

9. Martin Luther King Jr., "An Experiment in Love," in James M. Washington, ed., *A Testament of Hope: The Essential Writings and Speeches of Martin Luther King, Jr.* (New York: Harper & Row, 1986), 17.

10. Dietrich Bonhoeffer, *Sanctorum Communio*, DBWE 1:184.

11. King, "An Experiment in Love," in Washington, ed., *A Testament of Hope*, 19.

12. Synod of Bishops, "Justice in the World," in *Catholic Social Thought: The Documentary Heritage*, ed. David J. O'Brien and Thomas A. Shannon (Maryknoll, N.Y.: Orbis, 1992), 289.

13. Martin Luther King Jr., *Stride Toward Freedom* (New York: Harper & Row, 1959), 91.

14. Bonhoeffer, *Eth*, DBWE 6:61.

15. Ibid., 6:84–85.

16. Ibid., 6:105.

17. Martin Luther King Jr., "The Ethical Demands for Integration," in Washington, ed., *A Testament of Hope*, 118–19.

18. Thomas Merton, *The Black Revolution* (Atlanta: The Southern Christian Leadership Conference [1963?]); see also the collective pastoral statement of the U.S. hierarchy in the effort to internalize the directives of the Second Vatican Council, *The Church in Our Day* (Washington, D.C.: U.S.C.C., 1968), 23–24, 57–59.

19. Ilse Tödt, et al., "Editors' Afterword to the German Edition," in Bonhoeffer, *Eth*, DBWE 6:423.

20. Bonhoeffer, "The Church and the Jewish Question," in Kelly and Nelson, eds., *A Testament of Freedom*, 132, 133.

21. Andreas Pangritz, "Sharing the Destiny of His People," in de Gruchy, ed., *Bonhoeffer for a New Day*, 270.

22. Bonhoeffer, *Eth*, DBWE 6:136–37.

23. Ibid., 6:138, 139.

24. Ibid., 6:55 (my italics).

25. Ibid., 6:267, 268.

26. Bonhoeffer, "After Ten Years: A Letter to the Family and Conspirators," in Kelly and Nelson, eds., *A Testament of Freedom*, 483–84.

27. King, "Facing the Challenge of a New Age," in Clayborne Carson, ed., *Birth of a New Age: December 1955–December 1956*, The Papers of Martin Luther King, Jr., vol. 3 (Berkeley: University of California Press, 1997), 456.

28. Ibid., 457, 461.

29. Cited in James H. Cone, *Martin and Malcolm and America: A Dream or a Nightmare* (Maryknoll, N.Y.: Orbis, 1991), 147.

30. Ibid., 147–48.

31. King, "A Christmas Sermon on Peace," in Washington, ed., *A Testament of Hope*, 253.

32. Ibid., 254.

33. Ibid., 255.

Chapter 8

1. Dietrich Bonhoeffer, "The Nature of the Church" (1932), in Geffrey B. Kelly and F. Burton Nelson, eds., *A Testament to Freedom: The Essential Writings of Dietrich Bonhoeffer* (New York: HarperCollins, 1995), 86.

2. Dietrich Bonhoeffer, *Discipleship*, DBWE 4:254.

3. Ibid., 4:259–60.

4. Quoted from the 1966 Reginald Fuller translation, published as *The Cost of Discipleship* (New York: Simon & Schuster), 117.

5. Dietrich Bonhoeffer, *Letters and Papers from Prison*, ed. Eberhard Bethge (New York: Macmillan, 1971), 280–81, 382–83, 415.

6. Dietrich Bonhoeffer, *Eth*, DBWE 6:135, 153–57, 58.

7. Bonhoeffer, "The Nature of the Church," in Kelly and Nelson, eds., *A Testament to Freedom*, 86–87.

8. Dietrich Bonhoeffer, "Thy Kingdom Come: The Prayer of the Church for the Kingdom of God on Earth" (1932), in ibid., 92.

9. Dietrich Bonhoeffer, *Life Together* (New York: Harper and Row, 1954), 17. I thank Jennifer McBride for calling this quote to my attention.

10. I am grateful to Jennifer McBride for helping me to clarify this paragraph. In her doctoral dissertation, "The Church for the World: A Theology of Public Witness" (University of Virginia, 2008), McBride argues, powerfully, that putting *Discipleship* into its historical context helps readers avoid misusing Bonhoeffer to defend a separatist position today in a democratic context. The separatist-sounding rhetoric of 1937 was meant, she contends, to distance his seminary students from complicity in Nazism. I am more willing than McBride to say that Bonhoeffer actually succumbed to the sectarian temptation, in the mid-to-late 1930s, but my key point is that he fairly rapidly got over it. (I take the phrase "the sectarian temptation" from James Gustafson, *Moral Discernment in the Christian Life: Essays in Theological Ethics* [Louisville: Westminster John Knox, 2007], chap. 11.)

11. Bonhoeffer, *Eth*, DBWE 6:241; see also 6:335.

12. Ibid., 6:67, 73.

13. John Howard Yoder, *The Politics of Jesus*, 2d ed. (Grand Rapids: Eerdmans, 1994), 154–55; emphases added.

14. Ibid., 158, 195.

15. Bonhoeffer, *Eth*, DBWE 6:67. Augustine's distinction between "vessels of wrath" and "vessels of grace" presupposes that Christ's atonement is forever limited to the latter.

16. See Timothy P. Jackson, *Love Disconsoled: Meditations on Christian Charity* (Cambridge: Cambridge University Press, 1999), chap. 7.

17. Bonhoeffer, *Disc*, DBWE 4:137, 138–39, 140–41, 139, 141.

18. Bonhoeffer, *Eth*, DBWE 6:332–33.

19. Ibid., 6:334.

20. Ibid., 6:335–36.

21. Bonhoeffer, *Disc*, DBWE 4:145.

22. Bonhoeffer, *Eth*, DBWE 6:335.

23. Ibid., 6:335–36. Even as Thomas Merton is best known for his compelling but rather self-righteous *The Seven Storey Mountain* (1948), written when he was a young monk, so Bonhoeffer is best known for *The Cost of Discipleship*, written primarily for young seminarians. Merton's more earnest *Conjectures of a Guilty Bystander* (1966) is comparatively neglected, even as is Bonhoeffer's better effort in *Ethics*.

24. Bonhoeffer, *Letters and Papers from Prison*, 10.

25. Ibid., 162.

26. Ibid., 303.

27. Darryl Roberts drives home this important point in his Emory doctoral dissertation, "Religious Rhetoric and Public Reasoning: Religious Freedom in the Civil Rights Movement and Its Implications for Free Exercise Law." manuscript pending.

28. Martin Luther King Jr., "I Have a Dream" (1963), in James M. Washington, ed., *I Have a Dream: Writings and Speeches That Changed the World* (New York: HarperCollins, 1992), 102.

29. Martin Luther King Jr., "I See the Promised Land" (1968), in ibid., 203; idem, "Letter from a Birmingham Jail" (1963), in ibid., 89.

30. Yet Clayborne Carson has recently argued that King embraced a radical critique, capitalism long before the last three years of his life. See, for example, Carson's Introduction to the King Papers, vol vi, pp. 11-12.

31. Martin Luther King Jr., *Stride Toward Freedom* (New York: Harper & Row, 1958), 104.

32. Ibid., 104–6. As noted above, Bonhoeffer objected to identifying abstract "features" of Christian love independently of the life and death of Jesus Christ, but King's own list is manifestly christocentric and read off of the biblical record.

33. Martin Luther King Jr., *The Trumpet of Conscience* (San Francisco: Harper & Row, 1967), 32; idem, "Where Do We Go from Here?," in *I Have a Dream*, 176.

34. Martin Luther King Jr., *Where Do We Go from Here? Chaos or Community* (Boston: Beacon, 1968), 190.

35. Ibid., 66, 142, 199–200.

36. Ibid., 189.

37. King, *Stride Toward Freedom*, 85.

38. Martin Luther King Jr., *The Words of Martin Luther King, Jr.*, ed. Coretta Scott King (New York: Newmarket, 1983), 73; see also idem, *Stride Toward Freedom*, 213.

39. Martin Luther King Jr., *Strength to Love* (Philadelphia: Fortress Press, 1963), 82; idem, "Where Do We Go from Here? in Washington, ed., *I Have a Dream*, 179; and idem, *Stride Toward Freedom*, 179.

40. I address these issues in *The Priority of Love*, introduction and chap. 1.

41. Martin Luther King Jr., *Why We Can't Wait* (New York: Signet, 1963), 87.

42. King, *Where Do We Go from Here?*, 190. As with Bonhoeffer, King's references to "men" and "man," we understand, of course, to mean "human beings" and "humanity."

43. David Garrow, *Bearing the Cross: Martin Luther King, Jr., and the Southern Christian Leadership Conference* (New York: Vintage, 1986), 56–58.

44. Bonhoeffer, *Eth*, DBWE 6:314.

45. Ibid., 6:327. Bonhoeffer cites here James 4:11.

Chapter 9

1. See Craig J. Slane, *Bonhoeffer as Martyr: Social Responsibility and Modern Christian Commitment* (Grand Rapids: Brazos, 2004).

2. René Girard. *I See Satan Fall like Lightning*, trans. James G. Williams (Maryknoll, N.Y.: Orbis, 2001), 32–46.

3. Resistance is apt to come from within Christianity, too. For example, theologies of liberation are prone to see in the cross a message of passivity which only perpetuates abuse of various kinds. This concern is certainly justified, but one must ask whether at the deepest level such resistance is aimed at the cross or rather at abusive interpretations of it throughout Christian history. Traditional Christian piety has likely underappreciated the cross as the sign of a tenacious albeit complicated struggle *against* injustice.

4. As Bonhoeffer himself would eventually put it, "we share in God's sufferings." See Eberhard Bethge, ed., *Letters and Papers from Prison*, enl. ed. (New York: Macmillan, 1972), 370.

5. Origen's *Against Celsus* 1 (preface). *Ante-Nicene Fathers*, vol. 4, eds. Alexander Roberts and James Donaldson (Peabody, Mass.: Hendrickson, 1994) 395–96.

6. René Girard, *Violence and the Sacred*, trans. Patrick Gregory (Baltimore: Johns Hopkins University Press, 1977), 2.

7. Dietrich Bonhoeffer, *Disc*, DBWE 4:133.

8. Ibid. In this citation Bonhoeffer seems oblivious to the prospect that evil may be seeking victims.

9. Ibid., 4:137.

10. Dietrich Bonhoeffer, *Conspiracy and Imprisonment, 1940–1945*, DBWE 16:467 (emphasis added).

11. This well-known phrase is culled from Bonhoeffer's essay "After Ten Years." See Geffrey B. Kelly and F. Burton Nelson, eds., *A Testament to Freedom: The Essential Writings of Dietrich Bonhoeffer*, rev. ed. (New York: HarperSanFrancisco, 1995), 486.

12. James H. Cone, *Martin & Malcolm & America: A Dream or a Nightmare* (Maryknoll, N.Y.: Orbis, 1991), 126–50.

13. Martin Luther King Jr., *Strength to Love* (Philadelphia: Fortress Press, 1981), 55.

14. Ibid., 49.

15. Clayborne Carson, ed., *The Autobiography of Martin Luther King, Jr.* (New York: Grand Central, 1998), 76.

16. Ibid., 80.

17. Ibid., 331.

18. Martin Luther King Jr., "Eulogy for the Martyred Children," in James M. Washington, ed., *A Testament of Hope: The Essential Writings and Speeches of Martin Luther King Jr.* (New York: Harper & Row, 1986), 222.

19. See Miroslav Volf, *The End of Memory: Remembering Rightly in a Violent World* (Grand Rapids: Eerdmans, 2006).

Chapter 10

1. Dietrich Bonhoeffer, *Letters and Papers from Prison* (New York: Touchstone, 1971), 275.

2. David Nelson Duke, "The Experiment of an Ethic of (Radical) Justice: The Formative Experiences of Bonhoeffer's American Education," The Archives of the Burke Library (Columbia University).

3. Eberhard Bethge, *Dietrich Bonhoeffer: A Biography*, rev. ed. (Minneapolis: Fortress Press, 2000), 174.

4. Ibid., 3.

5. Hans Pfeifer, "Learning Faith and Ethical Commitment in the Context of Spiritual Training Groups. Consequences of Dietrich Bonhoeffer's Postdoctoral Year at New York City, 1930–31," forthcoming in the *Dietrich Bonhoeffer Yearbook 3*, 9.

6. Dietrich Bonhoeffer, *BBNY*, DBWE 10:182–83.

7. Ibid., 10:186

8. Ibid., 10:178.

9. Ibid., 10:385.

10. Ibid.

11. Ibid., 10:21.

12. Ibid., 10:308.

13. Ibid., 10:189.

14. Dietrich Bonhoeffer, *SC*, DBWE 1:191.

15. Larry Rasmussen, ed. *Reinhold Niebuhr: Theologian of Public Life* (Minneapolis, Fortress Press), 1.

16. Richard Fox, *Reinhold Niebuhr: A Biography* (New York: Pantheon, 1985), 125.

17. Niebuhr cited in *BBNY*, DBWE 10: 403, and in Bethge, *Dietrich Bonhoeffer*, 160. Bonhoeffer wrote on August 7, 1928 to his friend Helmut Rössler of the contrast between his former academic life as a student and his current life as the pastor of the German-speaking congregation: in the latter, "work and life genuinely converge, a synthesis that we all probably sought but hardly found in our student days—when one really lives *one* life rather than two, or better: half a life; it lends dignity to the work and objectivity to the worker, and a recognition of one's own limitations of the sort acquired only within concrete life." Later, after returning to Berlin, Bonhoeffer wrote to Detlef Albers, the teacher of history and geography at the German Protestant school in Barcelona: "Perhaps today as never before, 'spirit' [*Geist*] really is to be found in the particular, that is, precisely in the 'material,' in concretely given reality—and precisely not in 'intellectuality' [*Geistigkeit*]" (*BBNY*, DBWE 10: 126, 182).

18. Dietrich Bonhoeffer, "After Ten Years," in *Letters and Papers from Prison*, 6.

19. Anthony Dunbar, *Against the Grain: Southern Radicals and Prophets, 1929–1959* (Charlottesville: University Press of Virginia, 1981), 41.

20. For more on the intentional community movement in the United States, see Tracy Elaine K' Meyer, *Interracialism and Christian Community in the Postwar South: The Story of Koinonia Farm* (Charlottesville: University Press of Virginia, 1997); Marguerite Guzman Bouvard, *The Intentional Community Movement: Building a Moral World* (Port

Washington, N.Y.: Kennikat, 1975); and Martin B. Duberman's excellent study, *Black Mountain: An Exploration in Community* (Garden City, N.Y.: Anchor, 1973).

21. David Nelson Duke, *In the Trenches with Jesus and Marx: Harry F. Ward and the Struggle for Social Justice* (Tuscaloosa: University of Alabama Press, 2003).

22. Bonhoeffer, cited in Macy Bosanquet, *The Life and Death of Dietrich Bonhoeffer* (New York: Harper & Row, 1968), 84.

23. Bethge, *Dietrich Bonhoeffer*, 162. It is not clear whether Bonhoeffer knew of the Fellowship of Reconciliation (FOR) until coming to the United States, even though the peace organization was founded in 1914 at a railroad station in Germany when an English Quaker named Henry Hodgkin and the German Lutheran social reformer Friedrich Sigmund-Schultze pledged to partner in peacemaking even though the two countries were at war. Out of this pledge Christians gathered in Cambridge, England, in December, 1914, to found the Fellowship of Reconciliation. The FOR-USA was founded one year later, in 1915.

24. Bethge, *Dietrich Bonhoeffer*, 162.

25. Bonhoeffer, *BBNY*, DBWE 10:602.

26. Serene Jones, "Practical Theology in Two Modes," in *For Life Abundant: Practical Theology, Theological Education, and Christian Ministry*, ed. Dorothy C. Bass and Craig Dykstra (Grand Rapids: Eerdmans, 2008), 201.

27. Christoph von Hase, "From the Phraseological to the Real," in Bonhoeffer, *BBNY*, DBWE 10:597.

28. See Frank T. Adams, *James A. Dombrowski: An American Heretic, 1897–1983* (Knoxville: University of Tennessee Press, 1992). His dissertation was published as *The Early Days of Christian Socialism in America* (New York: Columbia University Press, 1936).

29. Myles Horton, *The Long Haul* (New York: Doubleday, 1991), 35.

30. Dale Jacobs, in *The Myles Horton Reader: Education for Social Change*, ed. Dale Jacobs (Knoxville: The University of Tennessee Press, 2003), 33.

31. Clifford Green, "Editor's Introduction to the English Edition," in Bonhoeffer, *BBNY*, DBWE 10:34.

32. Willie J. Jennings, "Harlem on My Mind: Dietrich Bonhoeffer, Racial Reasoning and Theological Reflection," unpublished mss. quoted with permission.

33. Letter to Martin Rumscheidt, December 17, 1986; Bonhoeffer Collection, Union Theological Seminary. First published in the *Newsletter*, International Bonhoeffer Society, English Language Section, No. 39 (October 1988): 3–4.

34. Albert Raboteau, "American Salvation: The Place of Christianity in Public Life," *Boston Review* (April/May 2005).

35. Myles Horton, cited in Green, "Editor's Introduction," in Bonhoeffer, *BBNY*, DBWE 10:31.

36. Bethge, *Dietrich Bonhoeffer*, 150.

37. Adam Clayton Powell Sr., *Upon This Rock* (New York: Abyssinian Baptist Church, 1949), 42.

38. Powell, "What Has the Church Done for the Negro and What Will the Negro Do for the Church?" in ibid., 110.

39. Ruth Zerner, "Dietrich Bonhoeffer's American Experiences: People, Letters and Papers from Union Seminary," paper delivered at the International Bonhoeffer Congress, Geneva, Switzerland, February 4–8, 1976, 269.

40. Ibid., 11.

41. Paul Lehmann, cited in von Hase, "From the Phraseological to the Real," in *BBNY*, DBWE 10:597.

42. Von Hase in *BBNY*, DBWE 10:597–98.

43. Bethge, *Dietrich Bonhoeffer*, 203.

44. Ibid.

45. Ibid., 182.

46. Jones, "Practical Theology in Two Modes," 201.

Chapter 11

1. H. Richard Niebuhr, *The Purpose of the Church and its Ministry* (New York: Harper & Row, 1956), 58.

2. John Ansbro, *Martin Luther King Jr.: The Making of a Mind* (Maryknoll: Orbis, 1982).

3. Niebuhr, *The Purpose of the Church*, 35.

4. Dietrich Bonhoeffer, *Eth*, DBWE 6:340–41.

5. Ibid., 6:341.

6. Ibid., 6:345.

7. Martin Luther King Jr., "Bold Design for a New South, 1963," in *A Testament of Hope: The Essential Writings and Speeches of Martin Luther King, Jr.*, ed. James M. Washington (New York: Harper & Row, 1986), 116.

8. King, "An Address Before the National Press Club" (1962), in ibid., 104.

Chapter 12

1. Martin Luther King Jr., "The Un-Christian Christian," *Ebony* 20 (August, 1965): 76.

2. Eberhard Bethge, *Dietrich Bonhoeffer: A Biography*, rev. ed., ed. Victoria Barnett (Minneapolis: Fortress Press, 2000), 234.

3. Martin Luther King Jr., "Standing by the Best in an Evil Time," King Center Archives, August 6, 1967.

4. Ibid., 6.

5. Ibid., 5.

6. Ibid., 1.

7. Ibid., 6.

8. Ibid., 7.

9. See Renate Wind, *Dietrich Bonhoeffer: A Spoke in the Wheel*, trans. John Bowden (Grand Rapids: Eerdmans, 1992), 27.

10. Dietrich Bonhoeffer, *A Testament to Freedom: The Essential Writings of Dietrich Bonhoeffer*, ed. Geffrey B. Kelly and F. Burton Nelson (San Francisco: HarperSanFrancisco, 1990), 117.

11. See Samuel Blanchard How and Reformed Church in America, General Synod, *Slaveholding Not Sinful. Slavery: The Punishment of Man's Sin, Its Remedy, the Gospel of Christ*, The Black Heritage Library Collection (Freeport, N.Y.: Books for Libraries Press, 1971).

12. See H. Shelton Smith, *In His Image, But . . . Racism in Southern Religion, 1780–1910* (Durham: Duke University Press, 1972); and John Patrick Daly, *When Slavery Was Called Freedom: Evangelicalism, Proslavery, and the Causes of the Civil War*, Religion in the South (Lexington: University Press of Kentucky, 2002).

13. See James Cone's work, beginning with his first two books, *Black Theology & Black Power* (Maryknoll, N.Y.: Orbis, 1969) and *A Black Theology of Liberation* (Maryknoll, N.Y.: Orbis, 1970).

14. Martin Luther King Jr., *Why We Can't Wait* (New York: Harper & Row, 1964), 90.

15. Ibid., 91.

16. See Adam Fairclough, *To Redeem the Soul of America: The Southern Christian Leadership Conference & Martin Luther King, Jr.* (Athens: University of Georgia Press, 1987).

17. Martin Luther King Jr., "I Have a Dream," in James M. Washington, ed., *A Testament of Hope: The Essential Writings and Speeches of Martin Luther King, Jr.* (New York: Harper & Row, 1986), 217.

18. Ibid.

19. From the talk "The Younger Generation's Altered View of the Concept of Führer"; see Bethge, *Dietrich Bonhoeffer*, 260.

20. For a historical analysis of these competing strands in American Protestantism, see Gary Dorrien's *Soul in Society: The Making and Renewal of Social Christianity* (Minneapolis: Fortress Press, 1995). Also see Jean Miller Schmidt, *Souls or the Social Order: The Two Party System in American Protestantism*, Chicago Studies in the History of American Religion, vol. 18 (Brooklyn, N.Y.: Carlson, 1991).

21. Among these voices are the Quakers and the short-lived efforts of Methodist abolitionists. See Timothy Lawrence Smith, *Revivalism and Social Reform: American Protestantism on the Eve of the Civil War* (Baltimore: Johns Hopkins University Press, 1980); and James D. Essig, *The Bonds of Wickedness: American Evangelicals against Slavery, 1770–1808* (Philadelphia: Temple University Press, 1982).

22. "What Happened to Hell?," in Clayborne Carson, ed., *Advocate of the Social Gospel, September 1948–March 1963*, The Papers of Martin Luther King, Jr., vol. 6 (Berkeley: University of California Press, 2007), 411. King goes on to say that "Hell, to me, is a condition of being out of fellowship with God. It is man's refusal to accept the Grace of God. It is the state in which the individual continues to experience the frustrations, contradictions and agonies of earthly life. Hell is as real as absolute loneliness and isolation." Also, see King's sermon entitled, "The Man Who Was a Fool," 411–19.

23. Ibid., 235.

24. Ibid.

25. Dietrich Bonhoeffer, *Lon*, DBWE 13:345.

26. Ibid.

27. Dietrich Bonhoeffer, in Kelly and Nelson, eds., *Testament to Freedom*, 97.

28. Dietrich Bonhoeffer, "The Secret of Suffering," in ibid., 305.

29. Ibid.

30. Ibid., 306.

31. Ibid., 305.

32. James Cone, "Martin Luther King, Jr.: The Source for His Courage to Face Death." in *Martyrdom Today*, eds. Johannes Baptist Metz and Edward C. Schillebeeckx (New York: Seabury, 1983): 74–79.

33. SCLC Staff Retreat Speech, May 29–31, 1967, Frogmore, S.C., King Center Archives.

34. Dietrich Bonhoeffer, *Letters and Papers from Prison* (New York: Macmillan, 1971), 17.

35. See Orlando Patterson, *Slavery and Social Death: A Comparative Study* (Cambridge: Harvard University Press, 1982).

36. Clayborne Carson and Peter Holloran, eds., *A Knock at Midnight: Inspiration from the Great Sermons of Reverend Martin Luther King, Jr.* (New York: Warner, 1998), 164.

37. Martin Luther King Jr., "A Christmas Sermon on Peace," in Washington, ed., *A Testament of Hope*, 257.

38. Martin Luther King Jr., "Revolution and Redemption," King Center Archives, Amsterdam, August 16, 1964.

39. Ibid.

40. King, "A Walk through the Holy Land," sermon given Nov. 15, 1964, at Dexter Avenue Baptist Church, in King Center Archives.

41. Dietrich Bonhoeffer, *Discipleship*, DBWE 4:87.

Chapter 13

1. For further reflections on Bonhoeffer's approach to social sin see my book *Do No Harm: Social Sin and Christian Responsibility* (Minneapolis: Fortress Press, 2002), chap. 3. In that chapter I take particular note of how Bonhoeffer's inattention to the rhetoric he used against social sin rendered his arguments ambiguous, and perhaps harmful. Brought into dialogue with King's purposeful use of rhetoric this unfortunate ambiguity might well be lessened and with it the unintended harm it caused.

2. Richard Lischer, *The Preacher King: Martin Luther King Jr. and the Word That Moved America* (New York: Oxford University Press, 1995); Hak Joon Lee, *We Will Get to the Promised Land: Martin Luther King, Jr.'s Communal-Political Spirituality* (Cleveland: Pilgrim, 2006).

3. Here I do not mean any sort of sectarian inflection; I would rather suggest that beyond the works of figures like Reinhold Niebuhr and others, reflection on what it is that we generally understand as "social sin" has had a much more vibrant development in the Roman Catholic tradition. This development is outlined well in Mark O'Keefe's work, *What Are They Saying about Social Sin?* (New York: Paulist Press, 1990).

4. John Patrick Daly, *When Slavery Was Called Freedom: Evangelicalism, Proslavery, and the Causes of the Civil War* (Lexington: University of Kentucky Press, 2004); John R. McKivigan and Mitchell Snay, *Religion and the Antebellum Debate over Slavery* (Athens:

University of Georgia Press, 1998); Jonathan Earle. "The Making of the North's 'Stark Mad Abolitionists': Anti-Slavery Conversion in the United States, 1824–54," *Slavery & Abolition* 25, no. 3 2004: 59–75.

5. Donald G. Mathews, *Religion in the Old South* (Chicago: University of Chicago Press, 1977), chap. 1.

6. James D. Essig, *The Bonds of Wickedness: American Evangelicals Against Slavery, 1770–1808* (Philadelphia: Temple University Press, 1982), 24.

7. When we think about this whole question of public righteousness we do well to remember that many of the early abolitionists would later become intimately involved with the temperance movement and other "crusades" that sought to counter vice. Jesse Macy, *The Anti-Slavery Crusade: A Chronicle of the Gathering Storm* (New Haven: Yale University Press, 1921), 51–53.

8. Mathews, *Religion in the Old South*, 66–80, chap. 4.

9. Walter Rauschenbusch, *A Theology for the Social Gospel* (New York: Macmillan, 1917), chaps. 7, 8.

10. My reasons for using specific case when referring to the words Black and white are based primarily in their usage. While it is a common practice to use lower case for both of these terms when referring to persons as members of racial groups the practice, in my estimation, overlooks the substantial nuance that attends to the term Black which can be used to signify race and/or ethnicity, and as such can refer to a discrete set of cultural and social practices. This nuance is further textured by the multilayered signification that attaches to it when it is used to describe communal institutions and practice as well as instances of self-identification. For instance, in this chapter upper case is used when referring to Black Baptists and the Black Church. In each of these instances the word functions in much the same way that the words Southern or English might. It is descriptive of a particular form of the faith and a particular instantiation of the church. Lower case usage might well be appropriate if reference were simply being made to persons who were black and Baptist. Here, however, reference is being made to a discrete stream of the Baptist faith (and the church more generally), thus the case usage.

11. Save for work like the earlier mentioned work by Lischer, *The Preacher King*, and Lewis J. Baldwin's *There Is a Balm in Gilead: The Cultural Roots of Martin Luther King, Jr.* (Minneapolis: Fortress Press, 1991), it is still the case that interpreters of King, particularly those who are writing a theological idiom, demonstrate an overreliance on Ansbro's framing in *Martin Luther King, Jr.: The Making of a Mind* (Maryknoll, N.Y.: Orbis, 1982) which identifies the sources of much of King's theological outlook and syntheses as the schools at which he matriculated after Morehouse. Needless to say, I think that this is a naïve and misguided framing.

12. Howard Thurman, *Jesus and the Disinherited* (Boston: Beacon, 1996, reprint ed.).

13. Reinhold Niebuhr, *Moral Man and Immoral Society* (New York: Charles Scribners' Sons, 1932).

14. Gunnar Myrdal, *An American Dilemma: The Negro Problem and Modern Democracy, Vols. I & II* (New York: Harper & Bros., 1944).

15. Reinhold Niebuhr, *An Interpretation of Christian Ethics* (New York: Harper & Row, 1963), chap. 4.

16. Martin Luther King Jr., "Why Jesus Called a Man a Fool," in Clayborne Carson and Peter Holloran, eds., *A Knock at Midnight: Inspiration from the Great Sermons of Martin Luther King, Jr.* (New York: Warner, 1998), chap. 9.

17. Sharon D. Welch, *Communities of Resistance and Solidarity: A Feminist Theology of Liberation* (Maryknoll, N.Y.: Orbis, 1986); A. Sivanandan, *Communities of Resistance: Writings on Black Struggles for Socialism* (London: Verso, 1990).

18. Martin Luther King Jr., "I Have a Dream," in Clayborne Carson and Kris Shepard, eds., *A Call to Conscience: The Landmark Speeches of Martin Luther King, Jr.* (New York: Warner, 2001), 85.

19. Martin Luther King Jr., *Why We Can't Wait* (New York: Signet, 1963), chap. 4.

20. Melva Costen, "Socio-Cultural Realities and a Vision of African American Worship into the Future," The Lutheran Theological Seminary at Philadelphia, October 2, 2007.

21. King, "I Have A Dream," 84.

Chapter 14

1. John Dewey, *Experience and Nature* (New York: Penguin, 1934), 42.

2. John Dewey, *Art as Experience* (New York: Penguin, 1934), 28.

3. John Dewey, *Reconstruction in Philosophy* (Boston: Beacon, 1920), 199–200.

4. Dewey, *Art as Experience*, 156.

5. Ibid., 12.

6. Ibid., 27.

7. Clifford Green, "Human Sociality and Christian Community," in *The Cambridge Companion to Dietrich Bonhoeffer*, ed. John W. de Gruchy (Cambridge: Cambridge University Press, 1999), 115.

8. Dietrich Bonhoeffer, *Act and Being*, in Geffrey B. Kelly and F. Burton Nelson, eds., *A Testament to Freedom: The Essential Writings of Dietrich Bonhoeffer* (New York: HarperCollins, 1990), 73.

9. Dietrich Bonhoeffer, "God's Message of Love to Germany and the Community of Nations," in ibid., 187.

10. Dietrich Bonhoeffer, *The Communion of Saints*, in ibid., 62.

11. Martin Luther King Jr., "The American Dream," in James M. Washington, ed., *A Testament of Hope: The Essential Writings and Speeches of Martin Luther King, Jr.* (San Francisco: Harper & Row, 1986), 210.

12. Rufus R. Burrows, *God and Human Dignity: The Personalism, Theology, and Ethics of Martin Luther King, Jr.* (South Bend: University of Notre Dame Press, 2006).

13. Warren I. Steinkraus, "Martin Luther King's Personalism and Non-Violence," *Journal of the History of Ideas* 34, no. 1 1973: 97–111.

14. Ibid.

15. King's oft-repeated statements "all men are interdependent" and "all life is interrelated" illuminate how he attempted gently to push social culture from segregation to integration, political culture from legal subjugation to legal equality, and a racialized culture into a less racialized one. King's witness forced him to speak to multiple communities—sometimes all at once. There was the world community, the American

community, the African American community, and the community of protesters he was often guiding in an effort for social justice. King knew that all of these communities were distinct but not separate and part of his genius was his ability to provide a narrative emphasis that evoked a tradition larger than the separate communities but still allowed them all to interpret future activity similarly. Paying great attention to rhythm (e.g., "the time is now"), King spoke directly to all of the disparate cultures about shifting the overall cultural awareness to create the social force that would naturally evolve into more freedom for all. Martin Luther King, Jr., *Where Do We Go from Here? Chaos or Community* (Boston: Beacon, 1964), 211.

16. Martin Luther King Jr., "An Address before the National Press Club," in Washington, ed., *A Testament of Hope*, 99.

17. Bonhoeffer, *Act and Being*, in Kelly and Nelson, eds., *A Testament to Freedom*, 67–68.

18. "Pastor's Emergency League," glossary entry in ibid., 548.

19. Dewey, *Art as Experience*, 13.

20. Wolf-Dieter Zimmerman and Ronald Gregor Smith, eds., *I Knew Dietrich Bonhoeffer* (New York: Harper & Row, 1966), 128.

21. Bonhoeffer, *The Communion of Saints*, in Kelly and Nelson, eds., *A Testament to Freedom*, 61.

22. Zimmerman and Smith, eds., *I Knew Dietrich Bonhoeffer*, 64.

23. Michael Eric Dyson, *April 4, 1968* (New York: Basic Books, 2008); Keith D. Miller, *Voice of Deliverance* (Athens: University of Georgia Press, 1998); Richard Lischer, *The Preacher King* (New York: Oxford University Press, 1995).

24. Martin Luther King Jr., "Why We Can't Wait," in Washington, ed., *A Testament of Hope*, 535–36.

25. Dyson, *April 4, 1968*, 42.

Chapter 15

1. Heinz Eduard Tödt, *Authentic Faith: Bonhoeffer's Theological Ethics in Context* (Grand Rapids: Eerdmans, 2007), 112–13. I owe gratitude to Tödt for his teaching, and to Matthew Johnson and Clifford Green for their suggestions and encouragement.

2. Eberhard Bethge, *Dietrich Bonhoeffer: A Biography*, rev. ed. (Minneapolis: Fortress Press, 2000); see also Dietrich Bonhoeffer, DBWE 14:112–14.

3. Clifford Green, "Editor's Introduction," in Dietrich Bonhoeffer, *BBNY: 1928–1931*, DBWE 10:23; also 10:313.

4. Hans Pfeifer, "Learning Faith and Ethical Commitment. . . : Consequences of Dietrich Bonhoeffer's Post-Doctoral Year in New York City 1930/31," *Dietrich Bonhoeffer Yearbook 3 2007/2008* (Gütersloh: Gütersloher Verlagshaus, 2008), 254–56, 259.

5. Bonhoeffer, *BBNY*, DBWE 10:315.

6. Ruth Zerner, "Dietrich Bonhoeffer's American Experiences: People, Letters, and Papers from Union Seminary," *Union Seminary Quarterly Review* 31, no. 4 (Summer, 1976): 270, quoting Bonhoeffer.

7. Ibid., 268, 271, 272, citing James Cone, *The Spirituals and the Blues: An Interpretation* (Maryknoll: Orbis, 1992), 47 and 63.

8. Ibid., 273, 267.

9. Pfeifer, "Learning Faith and Ethical Commitment," 262.

10. Green, "Editor's Introduction," in Bonhoeffer, *BBNY*, DBWE 10:31, 39.

11. Clifford Green agrees, and also adds Paul Lehmann, Franz Hildebrandt, Hardy Arnold, and Herbert Jehle. See Green, "Pacifism and Tyrannicide: Bonhoeffer's Christian Peace Ethic," *Studies in Christian Ethics* 18, no. 3 (December, 2005): 35.

12. Pfeifer, "Learning Faith and Ethical Commitment," 262–63.

13. Tödt, *Authentic Faith*, 126–27, 131.

14. Dietrich Bonhoeffer, *Disc*, DBWE 4:108.

15. Ibid., 4:141; cf. 137–45.

16. Mark Thiessen Nation, "Discipleship in a World Full of Nazis: Dietrich Bonhoeffer's Polyphonic Pacifism as Social Ethics," in *The Wisdom of the Cross: Essays in Honor of John Howard Yoder,* Mark Thiessen Nation *et al.*, eds. (Grand Rapids: Eerdmans, 1999), 265, 267.

17. Clifford Green, "Bonhoeffer: Apostle of Peace, Not Violence," Hugh Price Hughes Lecture, London, July 11, 2006, 6. Cf. Green, "Pacifism and Tyrannicide," 33.

18. Nation, "Discipleship in a World Full of Nazis," 252, 274–76.

19. Dietrich Bonhoeffer, *Ber,* DBWE 12:232–35. Cf. Geffrey Kelly and F. Burton Nelson, eds., *A Testament to Freedom: The Essential Writings of Dietrich Bonhoeffer,* rev. ed. (San Francisco: HarperSanFrancisco, 1995), 93–95; and Clifford Green, *Bonhoeffer: A Theology of Sociality* (Grand Rapids: Eerdmans, 1999), 151–52. "Christ and Peace" is incomplete in *Testament to Freedom*, and also in DBW 12. It is complete in DBW 17, and also in *Ber*, DBWE 12, cited above.

20. Green, "Bonhoeffer: Apostle of Peace, Not Violence," 12.

21. Ibid., 18–19. Clifford Green, review of Stanley Hauerwas, *Performing the Faith,* in *Modern Theology* 21, no. 4 (October, 2005): 676.

22. Martin Luther King Jr., in Clayborne Carson, ed., *Called to Serve: January 1929–1951,* The Papers of Martin Luther King Jr., vol. 1 (Berkeley: University of California, 1992). 362.

23. James Cone, *Martin Malcolm America: A Dream or a Nightmare* (Maryknoll, N.Y.: Orbis, 1991), 23, 26.

24. King, *Called to Serve*, 1:26; cf. 49, 185.

25. Ibid., 1:33–34.

26. Ibid., 1:110–11.

27. Ibid., 1:242, 272, 283–84.

28. Ibid., 1:267, and King, in Clayborne Carson, ed., *Rediscovering Precious Values, July 1951–November 1955,* The Papers of Martin Luther King Jr., vol. 2 (Berkeley: University of California Press, 1994), 127–28.

29. John J. Ansbro, *Martin Luther King, Jr., The Making of a Mind* (Maryknoll, N.Y.: Orbis, 1982), chap. 1; Jerry Ogoegbunem Nwonye, "The Role of Agape in the Ethics of Martin Luther King, Jr. and the Pursuit of Justice," Ph.D. dissertation, Fuller Theological Seminary, Pasadena, California, January, 2009.

30. King, *Called to Serve*, 1:72–74, 79.

31. Martin Luther King Jr., "Pilgrimage to Nonviolence" (1963), in *Strength to Love* (Philadelphia: Fortress Press, 1983), 150–52.

32. Martin Luther King Jr., "A Time to Break Silence," in James M. Washington, ed., *A Testament of Hope: The Essential Writings and Speeches of Martin Luther King, Jr.* (San Francisco: Harper & Row, 1986), 231–44.

33. Rufus Burrow, *God and Human Dignity: The Personalism, Theology, and Ethics of Martin Luther King, Jr.* (South Bend: University of Notre Dame Press, 2006). I have used some phrases from my review in *Journal of Religion* 88, no. 3 (July, 2008): 416–18.

34. Vincent Harding, *Martin Luther King: The Inconvenient Hero* (Maryknoll, N.Y.: Orbis, 1996), 16.

35. David J. Garrow, *Bearing the Cross: Martin Luther King, Jr., and the Southern Christian Leadership Conference* (New York: Vintage, 1988), 560.

36. These practices and nonviolence as a way of life are spelled out in Bernard LaFayette Jr. and David C. Jehnsen, *A Structured Guide and Introduction to Kingian Nonviolence: The Philosophy and Methodology* (Galena, Ohio: Institute for Human Rights and Responsibilities, 1996).

37. Glen Stassen, ed., *Just Peacemaking: The New Paradigm for the Ethics of Peace and War* (Cleveland: Pilgrim, 2008).

38. Martin Luther King Jr., "Nobel Prize Acceptance Speech," in Washington, ed., *A Testament of Hope*, 224.

39. Pfeifer, "Learning Faith and Ethical Commitment," 252, 272–73, 275, paraphrasing Hardy Arnold's statement in *The Plough* 6 (1984). Cf. Nation, "Discipleship in a World Full of Nazis," 263; Tödt, *Authentic Faith*, 83, 126; Green, "Pacifism and Tyrannicide," 37; Bethge, *Dietrich Bonhoeffer*, 105, 148, 164–65, 194, 249, 325–27, 407–11.

40. Martin Luther King Jr., "A Time to Break Silence," 239.

41. Dietrich Bonhoeffer, *Eth*, DBWE 6:134–45.

42. Donald Shriver, "Acknowledge Responsibility for Conflict and Injustice and Seek Repentance and Forgiveness," in Stassen, ed., *Just Peacemaking*, 98-113; and idem, *Honest Patriots: Loving a Country Enough to Remember Its Misdeeds* (New York: Oxford University Press, 2005).

43. Martin Luther King Jr., *Stride toward Freedom: The Montgomery Story* (New York: Harper & Row, 1958), 88.

44. Tödt, *Authentic Faith*, 73, 127–28, 131.

45. Garrow, *Bearing the Cross*, 563.

46. Bonhoeffer, *BBNY*, DBWE 10:272, 413, 416.

47. Pfeifer, "Learning Faith and Ethical Commitment," 255.

48. Garrow, *Bearing the Cross*, 563–64 (King repeated this last phrase for emphasis); see also 549.

49. Dietrich Bonhoeffer, *No Rusty Swords*, ed. Edwin H. Robertson (London: Collins: 1965), 167; idem, *Ökumene, Universität, Pfarramt 1931–1932*, DBW 11 (Munich: Chr. Kaiser, 1994), 329, 338.

50. King, "A Time to Break Silence," 233.

51. Bethge, *Dietrich Bonhoeffer*, 257.

52. King, "A Time to Break Silence," 239.

53. Green, review of *Performing the Faith*, 676; and idem, "Pacifism and Tyrannicide," 43, 45; Christine Schliesser, *Everyone Who Acts Responsibly Becomes Guilty: The*

Concept of Accepting Guilt in Dietrich Bonhoeffer (Louisville: Westminster John Knox, 2009); idem, *Guilt by Doing Right? Responsible Conduct According to Dietrich Bonhoeffer* (Louisville: Westminster John Knox, forthcoming); Sabine Dramm, *Dietrich Bonhoeffer and the Resistance* (Minneapolis: Fortress Press, 2009).

54. Quoted from Dietrich Bonhoeffer, *Ethics* (New York: MacMillan 1955), 154, 163; cf. *Eth*, DBWE 6:172-95.

Chapter 16

1. Dietrich Bonhoeffer, *Disc*, DBWE 4:87.

2. Ibid., 4:284–85.

3. Ibid., 4:285.

4. Martin Luther King, "Pilgrimage to Nonviolence," in James M. Washington, ed., *A Testament of Hope: The Essential Writings and Speeches of Martin Luther King, Jr.* (San Francisco: HarperCollins, 1991), 35–39. This essay reprints King's article in the "How I Changed My Mind" series published in *The Christian Century* 77 (April 27, 1960): 510.

5. For the full text of this student essay, see *The Young Bonhoeffer: 1918–1927*, DBWE 9:285–300. See also the commentary on this essay in Geffrey B. Kelly and F. Burton Nelson, *The Cost of Moral Leadership: The Spirituality of Dietrich Bonhoeffer* (Grand Rapids: Eerdmans, 2002), 54–55.

6. Dietrich Bonhoeffer, Letter to Rüdiger Schleicher, April 8, 1936, in *Illegale Theologenausbildung Finkenwalde 1935–1940*, DBW 14:146–48. An English translation of this letter is found in Geffrey B. Kelly and F. Burton Nelson, eds., *A Testament to Freedom: The Essential Writings of Dietrich Bonhoeffer* (San Francisco: HarperSanFrancisco, 1995), 425–26.

7. Dietrich Bonhoeffer, Letter to Elizabeth Zinn, January 27, 1936, in *Illegale Theologenausbildung Finkenwalde 1935–1940*, DBW 14:112–13. The English translation is from Kelly and Nelson, eds., *A Testament to Freedom*, 424–25. The translation mistakenly dates the letter at January 1, 1937.

8. Dietrich Bonhoeffer, Letter to Karl-Friedrich Bonhoeffer, January 14, 1935, in *Lon*, DBWE 13:284–85.

9. Bonhoeffer, Letter to Rüdiger Schleicher, April 8, 1936, in *Illegale Theologenausbildung Finkenwalde 1935–1940*, DBW 14:147. The English translation is from Kelly and Nelson, eds., *A Testament to Freedom*, 426.

10. See Bonhoeffer's letter to Karl-Friedrich Bonhoeffer, January 14, 1935, in *Lon*, DBWE 13:285.

11. See Martin Luther King Jr., "An Experiment in Love," in *Stride Toward Freedom: The Montgomery Story* (New York: Harper & Row, 1958), in a segment that reprints King's article from *Jubilee* (September 1958), 13. The article cited here is from Washington, ed., *A Testament of Hope*, 16–17.

12. Gandhi, "The Message of Jesus," in Robert Ellsberg, ed., *Gandhi on Christianity* (Maryknoll, N.Y.: Orbis, 1993), 21. Gandhi is quoted here by J. Deotis Roberts, in his comprehensive study of the interrelated achievements of Bonhoeffer and Martin

Luther King, *Bonhoeffer & King: Speaking Truth to Power* (Louisville: Westminster John Knox, 2005), 62–63.

13. Bonhoeffer, *Disc,* DBWE 4:139.

14. Sermon on John 8:32 ("The truth shall set you free") delivered by Bonhoeffer at the religious service marking the end of the academic semester, July 24, 1932. The English translation is from Kelly and Nelson, eds., *A Testament to Freedom,* 206. The German text has been published in the volume of Bonhoeffer's collected writings from his ecumenical, academic, and pastoral work during the years 1931–32. See *Ökumene, Universität, Pfarramt 1931–1932,* DBW 11:461–62.

15. The quotations in this section are taken from King's "Letter from Birmingham City Jail," in Washington, ed., *A Testament of Hope,* 297–99.

16. From Bonhoeffer's conference on "Jesus Christ and the Essence of Christianity," December 11, 1928. This translation is from Kelly and Nelson, eds., *A Testament to Freedom,* 52. The original German text is published in the volume of Bonhoeffer's collected writings from Barcelona, Berlin, and New York during the years 1928–1931. See *Barcelona, Berlin, Amerika 1928–1931,* DBW 10:316–17.

17. See Bonhoeffer's *Christ the Center* (San Francisco: HarperSanFrancisco, 1978), 107.

18. Bonhoeffer, *Disc,* DBWE 4:103–04.

19. King, "A Time to Break Silence," in Washington, ed., *A Testament of Hope,* 231–43, at 241. The address was originally published in *Freedomways* 7 (Spring, 1967): 103–17.

20. "The Church and the Peoples of the World," in Bonhoeffer, *Lon,* DBWE 13:309. It is interesting to note that Bonhoeffer appeals to the example of the nonviolent but effective achievement of Gandhi in a related segment of this ecumenical conference.

21. Sermon on Matt. 24:6-14, delivered in Berlin on the "Day of National Mourning," February 21, 1932. The translation here is from Kelly and Nelson, eds., *A Testament to Freedom,* 202. The German original of this text has been published in *Ökumene, Universität, Pfarramt 1931–1932,* DBW 11:404.

Chapter 17

1. For an example of the benefits and limits of using an inductive methodology relative to a classic author see Ian D. Kingston Siggins, *Martin Luther's Doctrine of Christ* (New Haven: Yale University Press, 1970), 1–11. On the basis of an inductive approach some may even question, notes Siggins, "whether Luther 'has a Christology' at all in the sense of an abstract conceptual account of the hypostatic union" of divinity and humanity (p. 1). And this is the case with someone like Luther!

2. John Lewis with Michael D'Orso, *Walking with the Wind: A Memoir of the Movement* (New York: Simon & Schuster, 1998), 45. Among the valuable rhetorical studies of Martin Luther King Jr. are: Hortense J. Spillers, "Martin Luther King and the Style of the Black Sermon," *The Black Scholar* 3 (September, 1971): 14–27; Keith Miller, *Voice of Deliverance: The Language of Martin Luther King, Jr. and Its Sources* (New York: Free Press, 1992); and Jonathan Rieder, *The Word of the Lord Is Upon Me: The Righteous*

Performance of Martin Luther King, Jr. (Cambridge: Belknap/Harvard University Press, 2008).

3. James Burtness, *Shaping the Future: The Ethics of Dietrich Bonhoeffer* (Philadelphia: Fortress Press, 1985), 173.

4. Martin Luther King Jr., *Why We Can't Wait* (New York: New American Library, 1963), 38. As we will see below, King followed Howard Thurman by analyzing the relation of love to three different enemies, even though he revised Thurman's analysis. See Howard Thurman, *Jesus and the Disinherited* (New York: Abingdon-Cokesbury Press, 1949), 89–109.

5. Lerone Bennett Jr., longtime editor of *Ebony* magazine and a Morehouse College classmate of King, noted that Mahalia Jackson, along with King and John Lewis, were the three keys to understanding the March on Washington. Bennett gives us a glimpse of Mahalia's impact at the March: "A spasm ran through the crowd. There is a nerve that lies beneath the smoothes of black exteriors, a nerve four hundred years old and throbbing with hurt and indignation. Mahalia Jackson penetrated the façade and exposed the nerve to public view." See Lerone Bennett Jr., "The Day They Marched," *Ebony* (October, 1999) at: http://findarticles.com/p/articles/mi_m1077/is_12_54/ai_55982859/pg_1, accessed March 17, 2010. To view the Program for the March on Washington go to http://www.footnote.com/viewer.php?image=4346713, accessed March 17, 2010.

6. Taylor Branch, *Parting the Waters: America in the King Years 1954–1963* (New York: Simon & Schuster, 1988), 882. Among the authoritative interpretations of King's theology and ethics, see especially Peter J. Paris, *Black Leaders in Conflict: Joseph H. Jackson, Martin Luther King, Jr., Malcolm X, Adam Clayton Powell, Jr.* (New York: Pilgrim, 1978); and James H. Cone, *Martin & Malcolm & America: A Dream or a Nightmare* (Maryknoll, N.Y.: Orbis, 1991).

7. It is important not to essentialize audiences. As Rieder wisely notes, "There was no single black backstage, and there were diverse black front stages too, and white equivalents of each" (Rieder, *Word of the Lord Is Upon Me*, 8).

8. Martin Luther King Jr., *Strength to Love* (New York: Harper, 1963), 76.

9. Walter Earl Fluker comes to this rightly argued conclusion in his comparative analysis of Howard Thurman's and Martin King's understandings of community in "They Looked for a City: A Comparison of the Ideal of Community in Howard Thurman and Martin Luther King, Jr.," *Journal of Religious Ethics* 18 (Fall 1990): 33–55.

10. Martin Luther King Jr., *Stride toward Freedom* (1958), in James M. Washington, ed., *A Testament of Hope: The Essential Writings and Speeches of Martin Luther King, Jr.* (San Francisco: Harper & Row, 1986), 447; also 10–40, 75–81. Also see Martin Luther King, Jr., "Loving Your Enemies" (1957), The Martin Luther King, Jr. Research and Education Institute, http://mlk-kpp01.stanford.edu/index.php/kingpapers/article/loving_your_enemies/, accessed March 17, 2010. This Stanford University institute has been restructuring its website and will eventually have in the future, as it has in the past, short two- to four-minute audio excerpts of various King sermons and speeches, which give a small taste of the oratorical impact of Jesus as love, especially of Jesus as healing balm.

11. Martin Luther King, Jr., "An Experiment in Love" (1958), in Washington, ed., *A Testament of Hope*, 17.

12. Martin Luther King, Jr., "Letter from Birmingham Jail" (1963), in ibid., 296–97.

13. Martin Luther King, Jr., "Nonviolence and Racial Justice" (1957), in ibid., 7, 8–9; also see "An Experiment in Love," in ibid., 17–20.

14. Martin Luther King, Jr., "Nonviolence: The Only Road to Freedom" (1966), in ibid., 56.

15. Martin Luther King, Jr., "Our Struggle" (1956), in ibid., 76.

16. King, "An Experiment in Love," in ibid., 18.

17. King, *Why We Can't Wait*, 68.

18. King, "Nonviolence and Racial Justice," in Washington, ed., *A Testament of Hope*, 8.

19. Martin Luther King, Jr., "The Current Crisis in Race Relations" (1958), in ibid., 88.

20. Martin Luther King, Jr., "I Have a Dream" (1963), in ibid., 220.

21. Martin Luther King, Jr., "A Tough Mind and a Tender Heart" (1963), in ibid., 491–97.

22. Robert Franklin, "The Safest Place on Earth: The Culture of Black Congregations," in *American Congregations, Volume 2: New Perspectives in the Study of Congregations*, ed. James P. Wind and James W. Lewis (Chicago: University of Chicago Press, 1994), 257–84. Because of the personal character of black Christian folk religion, King also resonated with the "Boston personalism" tradition that he met during his doctoral studies. On the influence of the black religious heritage on King see Thomas J. S. Mikelson, "Cosmic Companionship: The Place of God in the Moral Reasoning of Martin Luther King., Jr.," *Journal of Religious Ethics* 18 (Fall 1990): 1–14.

23. Martin Luther King, Jr., "Unfulfilled Dreams," sermon delivered at Ebenezer Baptist Church, Atlanta, Georgia, on March 3, 1968, http://mlk-kpp01.stanford.edu/index.php/kingpapers/article/unfulfilled_dreams/, accessed March 17, 2010. Also see King, "Why Jesus Called a Man a Fool," sermon delivered at Mount Pisgah Missionary Baptist Church, Chicago, Illinois, on August 27, 1967, http://mlk-kpp01.stanford.edu/index.php/kingpapers/article/why_jesus_called_a_man_a_fool/, accessed March 17, 2010.

24. King, "The Three Dimensions of a Complete Life," sermon delivered at New Covenant Baptist Church, Chicago, Illinois, on April 9, 1967, http://mlk-kpp01.stanford.edu/index.php/kingpapers/article/the_three_dimensions_of_a_complete_life/, accessed March 17, 2010.

25. King, "Why Jesus Called a Man a Fool," http://mlk-kpp01.stanford.edu/index.php/kingpapers/article/why_jesus_called_a_man_a_fool/, accessed March 17, 2010.

26. King, "I Have a Dream," in Washington, ed., *Testament of Hope*, 218; and idem, "A Time to Break Silence" (1967), in ibid., 243.

27. See King, "Nonviolence and Racial Justice," in ibid., 8; "The Power of Nonviolence," in ibid., 12; "An Experiment in Love," in ibid., 18; and "My Trip to the Land of Gandhi" (1959), in ibid., 25.

28. King, "Nonviolence and Racial Justice," in ibid., 9.

29. King, "Letter from Birmingham Jail," in ibid., 290.

30. Ibid., 292–93.

31. Rieder, *The Word of the Lord Is Upon Me*, 183.

32. Dietrich Bonhoeffer, "After Ten Years," in *Letters and Papers from Prison*, enl. ed., ed. Eberhard Bethge (New York: Simon & Schuster, 1997), 17.

33. Dietrich Bonhoeffer, *Eth*, DBWE 6:347, 85, 76–77. The authoritative biography of Bonhoeffer is Eberhard Bethge, *Dietrich Bonhoeffer: A Biography*, rev. ed. (Minneapolis: Fortress Press, 2000).

34. Dietrich Bonhoeffer, "Letter to Eberhard Bethge (30 April 1944)," in *Letters*, 279; idem, "Letter to Eberhard Bethge (16 July 1944)," in *Letters*, 361.

35. I quote this January 27, 1936, letter selectively from Bethge, *Dietrich Bonhoeffer*, 204–5. "Dominating ego" is Clifford Green's justified description (see Clifford Green, *Bonhoeffer: A Theology of Sociality*, rev. ed. [Grand Rapids: Eerdmans, 1999], 111, 140–79). Green probes "an 'autobiographical dimension' which must be recognized in order fully to understand its [*Discipleship's*] text, and that it contains unresolved theological and personal problems which grow out of the 1932 experience and point forward to their resolution in the prison letters" (Green, 107). While attending to this autobiographical dimension, Green also carefully avoids psychological reductionism.

36. Bonhoeffer, "Letter to Eberhard Bethge (July 21, 1944)," in *Letters*, 369.

37. Dietrich Bonhoeffer, *Disc*, DBWE 4:85.

38. Dietrich Bonhoeffer, *AB*, DBWE 2:112. "Vicarious representative action" is the standard translation of *Stellvertretung* throughout the English-language edition of *Dietrich Bonhoeffer Works*. For his 1933 university Christology lectures, see Dietrich Bonhoeffer, *Christ the Center* (San Francisco: Harper & Row, 1978), 43–60. I borrow the translation of "place-sharing" from my colleague Andrew Root (see Andrew Root, "Examining Relational Youth Ministry: Implications from the Theology of Bonhoeffer," *Word & World* 26 (Summer, 2006): 269–76.

39. Bonhoeffer, *Eth*, DBWE 6:96–97. Bonhoeffer was particularly influenced by Luther's "The Blessed Sacrament of the Holy and True Body of Christ, and the Brotherhoods" (1519), in *Word and Sacrament 1*, Luther's Works, vol. 35 (Philadelphia: Fortress Press, 1960), 48–73. "Here, Luther expresses wonderful and profound thoughts . . . of incomparable beauty, " noted Bonhoeffer in *SC*, DBWE 1:179–80. Heinz Tödt's assessment is right: "In consequence of this loyalty to Luther, Bonhoeffer, in all reverence for and solidarity with Karl Barth, never came to be spell-bound by Barth." See Heinz Eduard Tödt, *Authentic Faith: Bonhoeffer's Theological Ethics in Context* (Grand Rapids: Eerdmans, 2007), 4.

40. Dietrich Bonhoeffer, "Letter to Helmut Rößler (August 7, 1928)," in *BBNY 1928–1931*, DBWE 10:127.

41. Dietrich Bonhoeffer, "Letter to Max Diestel (Munich, November 5, 1942)," in *CI 1940–1945*, DBWE 16:367–68; idem, "Report on My Year of Study at Union Theological Seminary in New York, 1930/31," in *BBNY*, DBWE 10:315. For the lasting impact of Abyssinian Baptist Church on Bonhoeffer and his subsequent seminary teaching see *Bonhoeffer: Pastor, Pacifist, Nazi Resister*, documentary film by Martin Doblmeier, produced by Journey Films (2003).

42. Bethge, *Dietrich Bonhoeffer*, 607.

43. Bonhoeffer, *Letters*, 381–82.

44. Ibid., 17.

Chapter 18

1. See Geoffrey Wainwright, *Doxology: The Praise of God in Worship, Doctrine and Life: A Systematic Theology* (New York: Oxford University Press, 1980).

2. See Immanuel Kant, *Religion and Rational Theology* (Cambridge: Cambridge University Press, 1996); and idem, *Critique of Pure Reason*, trans. N. Kemp Smith (London: Macmillan, 1929).

3. Dietrich Bonhoeffer, *AB*, DBWE 2.

4. Dietrich Bonhoeffer, *SC*, DBWE 1:52.

5. Dietrich Bonhoeffer, *Gesammelte Schriften*, 6 vols., ed. Eberhard Bethge (Munich: Chr. Kaiser Verlag, 1958–74), 3:104.

6. Ibid., 4:41.

7. Ibid., 2:7–28.

8. Martin Luther King, Jr., *Stride Toward Freedom* (San Francisco: Harper & Row, 1986), 184.

9. For an interesting appropriation of King's nonviolent resistance in the book of Revelation, see Brian K. Blount, "Reading Revelation Today," *Interpretation* 54 (October, 2000): 398–412.

10. "Interview with Martin Luther King," *Playboy* 12 (January, 1965): 67.

11. Lewis Baldwin, *Toward the Beloved Community: Martin Luther King Jr. and South Africa* (Cleveland: Pilgrim, 1995), 6.

12. Martin Luther King Jr., *Where Do We Go from Here? Chaos or Community* (Boston: Beacon, 1968), 167–68.

13. Kenneth L. Smith and Ira G. Zepp, *Search for the Beloved Community: The Thinking of Martin Luther King, Jr.* (Valley Forge: Judson, 1998), 119; Walter E. Fluker, "They Looked for a City: A Comparison of the Ideal of Community in Howard Thurman and Martin Luther King Jr.," *Journal of Religious Ethics* 18, no. 2 (Fall, 1990): 33–50.

14. King, *Where Do We Go from Here?*, 173–91; idem, *The Trumpet of Conscience* (San Francisco: HarperCollins, 1989), 67–78.

15. Desmond Tutu, *The Words of Desmond Tutu* (New York: New Market, 1989), 26–91.

16. Desmond Tutu, *Hope and Suffering: Sermons and Speeches*, ed. John Webster (Grand Rapids: Eerdmans, 1983), 69.

17. Ibid., 9; idem, *Crying in the Wilderness: The Struggle for Justice in South Africa* (Grand Rapids: Eerdmans, 1982), 113; and idem, *The Words of Desmond Tutu*, 33, 38–39, 72–73, 83–91.

18. Tutu, *The Words of Desmond Tutu*, 29, 32, 41.

19. John de Gruchy, *The Church Struggle in South Africa* (Grand Rapids: Eerdmans, 1986), 232–33.

20. Ibid., 233.

21. "Roundup: Foreign Tributes to Dr. King," *Christian Century* 85, no. 19 (May 8, 1968): 629–30; and quoted in Shirley DuBoulay, *Tutu: Voice of the Voiceless* (Grand Rapids: Eerdmans, 1988), 126; and de Gruchy, *The Church Struggle*, 118.

Conclusion

1. Dietrich Bonhoeffer, *Eth*, DBWE 6:60.

2. Ibid., 6:66, 357, 360.

3. Dietrich Bonhoeffer, *Letters and Papers from Prison*, ed. Eberhard Bethge (New York: Collier, 1971), 360–61.

4. See "Eulogy for Martryed Children," in King, *A Testatment of Hope: The Essential Writings of Martin Luther King Jr.*, ed. James Melvin Washington (San Francisco: Harper, 1992), 221-23. Texts for the "Eulogy for Jimmy Lee Jackson" (March 3, 1965) and "Statement on the Death of James Reeb" (March 11, 1965) are recorded in Martin Luther King Jr. Papers Project (documents 650303-006 and 650311-002, respectively) and will be published in *The Papers of Martin Luther King Jr.* ed. Clayborne Carson (Berkeley: University of California Press). Accounts can be found in Taylor Branch, *At Canaan's Edge: America in the King Years, 1965-68* (New York: Simon & Shuster, 2006), 23–25, 104–8."

5. "Where Do We Go from Here?," in *A Call to Conscience*, ed. Clayborne Carson and Kris Shepard (New York: Warner, 1991).

6. Jon Sobrino, *No Salvation outside the Poor: Prophetic-Utopian Essays* (Maryknoll, N.Y.: Orbis, 2008).

7. John Rawls, *Political Liberalism* (New York: Columbia University Press, 1993).

8. Ibid., 247–54. Jeffrey Stout agrees on King's authority here; see his *Democracy and Tradition* (Princeton: Princeton University Press, 2004), 81.

9. Luther Ivory, *Toward a Theology of Radical Involvement: The Theological Legacy of Martin Luther King, Jr.* (Nashville: Abingdon, 1997), 111.

10. Bonhoeffer, *Eth*, DBWE 6:299. I have translated *aufzuheben* with "abrogate" rather than "supersede." See 6:47–49 for another draft of the same introduction.

11. Ibid., 6:48. Here I have translated *erweisen sich* with "demonstrate itself" in order to match Bonhoeffer's use of the verb in a later quotation, below.

12. Ibid., 6:49, 51.

13. Ibid., 6:53–55. Again, I translate *erweisen sich* with "demonstrate itself."

14. Cornel West, "Prophetic Christian as Organic Intellectual: Martin Luther King, Jr.," in *The Cornel West Reader* (New York: Basic, 1999).

15. See Martin Luther King Jr., "A Christmas Sermon on Peace," in James M. Washington, *A Testament of Hope: The Essential Writings and Speeches of Martin Luther King, Jr.* (San Francisco: Harper & Row, 1986), 253–58.

16. Both themes appear in "A Time to Break Silence," in ibid., 231–44.

17. Some anthologies excise the risky half of the essay; a complete version in English can be found in *Dietrich Bonhoeffer: Witness to Jesus Christ*, ed. John de Gruchy (Minneapolis: Fortress Press, 1991), 124–30.

18. Dietrich Bonhoeffer, *SC*, DBWE 1, 189–91.

19. Bonhoeffer, *Letters and Papers from Prison*, 280–81.

20. See "Letter from a Birmingham Jail" in *Stride toward Freedom* (New York: Harper and Row, 1958), and "Guidelines for a Constructive Church," in *A Knock at Midnight*, ed. Clayborne Carson and Peter Holloran (New York: Warner, 1998).

21. Stanley Hauerwas, "The Servant Community: Christian Social Ethics," in *The Hauerwas Reader*, ed. John Berkman and Michael Cartwright (Durham: Duke University Press, 2001), 374.

22. See the "The Drum Major Instinct," in *Knock at Midnight*, 165–85.

23. Bonhoeffer, *Eth*, 6:347.

24. Ibid., 6:97, 93.

Bibliography

Major Works (in English) of Dietrich Bonhoeffer

Sanctorum Communio: A Theological Study of the Sociology of the Church. Dietrich Bonhoeffer Works, Volume 1. Translated from the German edition edited by Joachim von Soosten. English edition edited by Clifford J. Green. Translated by Reinhard Krauss and Nancy Lukens. Minneapolis: Fortress Press, 1998.

Act and Being. Dietrich Bonhoeffer Works, Volume 2. Translated from the German edition edited by Hans-Richard Reuter. English edition edited by Wayne Whitson Floyd Jr. Translated by H. Martin Rumscheidt. Minneapolis: Fortress Press, 1996.

Discipleship. Dietrich Bonhoeffer Works, Volume 4. Translated from the German edition edited by Martin Kuske and Ilse Tödt. English edition edited by Geffrey B. Kelly and John D. Godsey. Translated by Barbara Green and Reinhard Krauss. Minneapolis: Fortress Press, 2001.

Life Together and Prayerbook of the Bible. Dietrich Bonhoeffer Works, Volume 5. Translated from the German edition edited by Gerhard Ludwig Müller and Albrecht Schönherr. English edition edited by Geffrey B. Kelly. Translated by Daniel W. Bloesch and James H Burtness. Minneapolis: Fortress Press, 1996.

Ethics. Dietrich Bonhoeffer Works, Volume 6. Translated from the German edition edited by Ilse Tödt, Heinz Eduard Tödt, Ernst Feil, and Clifford Green. English edition edited by Clifford J. Green. Translated by Reinhard Krauss, Charles C. West, and Douglas W. Stott. Minneapolis: Fortress Press, 2001.

Letters and Papers from Prison. Dietrich Bonhoeffer. Edited by Eberhard Bethge. Translated by Reginald Fuller, et al. New York: Touchstone, 1997.

A Testament to Freedom: The Essential Writings of Dietrich Bonhoeffer. Edited by Geffrey Kelly and F. Burton Nelson. Revised edition. San Francisco:

HarperSanFrancisco, 1995. [First edition: San Francisco: Harper & Row, 1990.]

Major Works of Martin Luther King Jr.

The Papers of Martin Luther King, Jr. series. Clayborne Carson, Senior Editor. Berkeley: University of California Press.

Strength to Love. Philadelphia: Fortress Press, 1981. [Original edition: New York: Harper & Row, 1963.]

Stride Toward Freedom: The Montgomery Story. New York: Harper & Row, 1958.

Where Do We Go from Here: Chaos or Community? New York: Harper & Row, 1967.

Why We Can't Wait. New York: Harper & Row, 1963.

I Have a Dream: Writings and Speeches That Changed the World. Foreword by Coretta Scott King. Edited by James Melvin Washington. San Francisco: HarperSanFrancisco, 1992.

A Knock at Midnight: Inspiration from the Great Sermons of Reverend Martin Luther King, Jr. Edited by Clayborne Carson and Peter Holloran. New York: Intellectual Properties Management in association with Warner Books, 1998.

A Testament of Hope: The Essential Writings and Speeches of Martin Luther King, Jr. Edited by James M. Washington. New York: Harper & Row, 1986. [Paperback edition: San Francisco: HarperCollins, 1991.]

Index